MORMON
Beliefs and Doctrines
MADE EASIER

OTHER BOOKS
by David J. Ridges

THE GOSPEL STUDY SERIES

- Isaiah Made Easier
- The New Testament Made Easier, Edition 2, Part 1
- The New Testament Made Easier, Edition 2, Part 2
- The Book of Mormon Made Easier, Part 1
- The Book of Mormon Made Easier, Part 2
- The Book of Mormon Made Easier, Part 3
- The Doctrine and Covenants Made Easier, Part 1
- The Doctrine and Covenants Made Easier, Part 2
- The Doctrine and Covenants Made Easier, Part 3
- The Old Testament Made Easier—Selections from the Old Testament, Part 1
- The Old Testament Made Easier—Selections from the Old Testament, Part 2
- The Old Testament Made Easier—Selections from the Old Testament, Part 3

ADDITIONAL TITLES BY DAVID J. RIDGES

- The Proclamation on the Family: The Word of the Lord on More than 30 Current Issues
- 50 Signs of the Times and the Second Coming
- Doctrinal Details of the Plan of Salvation: From Premortality to Exaltation

Watch for these titles to also become available through
Cedar Fort as e-books and on CD.

MORMON
Beliefs and Doctrines
MADE EASIER

David J. Ridges

CFI

Springville, Utah

ISBN 13: 978-1-4621-3876-0

Published by CFI, an imprint of Cedar Fort, Inc.
2373 W. 700 S., Springville, UT, 84663
Distributed by Cedar Fort, Inc., www.cedarfort.com

Cover design by Nicole Williams
Cover design © 2007 by Lyle Mortimer

Printed in the United States of America

10 9 8 7 6 5 4 3 2 1

Printed on acid-free paper

INTRODUCTION

Mormon Beliefs and Doctrines Made Easier is designed to help members of the Church as well as others quickly gain a basic understanding of over 1,300 topics associated with The Church of Jesus Christ of Latter-day Saints and the restored gospel of Jesus Christ. The entries cover a broad range of subjects and give references for additional study if desired. For the most part, they are brief and to-the-point. Some topics are longer, however, such as BOOK OF MORMON PLATES, GIFTS OF THE SPIRIT, MILLENNIUM, PREMORTAL LIFE, SAME GENDER ATTRACTION, SIGNS OF THE TIMES, THREE DEGREES OF GLORY, WORD OF WISDOM, and others.

This reference book can prove very helpful as a "quick reference" during gospel conversations and study, personal scripture reading, preparation for talks, family home evening lessons, and so forth, as words and topics arise that are not understood. Teachers will find it helpful as they prepare lessons.

Those not of our faith will find this reference book informative and easy to use as they seek a better understanding of what Latter-day Saints (the "Mormons") believe. For example, an entry entitled MORMONS provides a list of forty-four things Mormons believe and do, and thirteen things that Mormons do not believe or do. This entry, with its brief overview of beliefs and practices of The Church of Jesus Christ of Latter-day Saints, can be helpful in light of the many false notions about the Church and portrayals of its members in media and rumor. More information is given under individual topics throughout the book.

This is not an official publication of The Church of Jesus Christ of Latter-day Saints, and the author is solely responsible for its contents.

ABBREVIATIONS

BD	*Bible Dictionary*
CR	*Conference Report of The Church of Jesus Christ of Latter-day Saints*
DS	*Doctrines of Salvation*
EM	*Encyclopedia of Mormonism*
GS	*Guide to the Scriptures*
MD	*Mormon Doctrine*
TF	*True to the Faith*
TPJS	*Teachings of the Prophet Joseph Smith*
JD	*Journal of Discourses*
HC	*History of the Church*
NTSM	*New Testament Student Manual, Life and Teachings of Jesus and His Apostles Rel. 211–212* (used by Institutes of Religion)
MFP	*Messages of the First Presidency*

·A·

AARON, BROTHER OF MOSES

In the Old Testament, the older brother of Moses (Exodus 7:7). He was a spokesman for Moses and assisted him in bringing the Israelites out of Egypt (Exodus 4:10–16, 27–31; 5:1–12:51). While Moses was up on the mountain being taught by the Lord, Aaron made a golden calf for the people to worship (Exodus 32:1–6, 21, 24, 35). What we know as the Aaronic Priesthood was conferred upon Aaron and his descendants (D&C 84:18, 26–27, 30).

AARON, SON OF MOSIAH

One of four sons of King Mosiah in the Book of Mormon. Was rebellious but was converted with his three brothers and Alma the Younger. Became a powerful missionary (Mosiah 27:8–18, 32–37). Taught the gospel to King Lamoni's father (Alma 22:1–26).

AARONIC PRIESTHOOD

See also AARON, BROTHER OF MOSES.

Often referred to as the lesser priesthood to distinguish it from the Melchizedek Priesthood (D&C 107:13–14). Offices within the Aaronic Priesthood are bishop, priest, teacher, and deacon (D&C 84:30; 107:10, 14–15, 87–88). This priesthood was revealed to Moses because the children of Israel rebelled against the higher laws and ordinances of the Melchizedek Priesthood (D&C 84:23–25).

Aaronic Priesthood holders administer in the outward ordinances of the gospel, including the sacrament and baptism. They serve in temporal affairs, including gathering fast offerings (D&C 84:26–27; 107:20). This priesthood holds the keys of the ministering of angels, of the gospel of repentance, and of baptism (D&C 13). It was restored to Joseph Smith and Oliver Cowdery by John the Baptist on May 15, 1829 (D&C 13; JS—H 1:68–73).

ABADDON

Another name for the devil (see Revelation 9:11).

ABBA

In the Garden of Gethsemane, the Savior used this term as He prayed to His Father. It is a special term denoting closeness. "A personal, familial term for *father* as used in Hebrew. It is Aramaic for father, and in Talmudic times was used as a title of honor. It was used in the language of Jesus and the Apostles, and later by Greek-speaking Christians, as an intimate name for the Father in Heaven. See Mark 14:36; Romans 8:15; Galatians 4:6" (BD, under "Abba").

ABEL

A son of Adam and Eve who was born to them after they had already had many children, including Cain (Moses 5:2, 16–17). Was killed by his older brother Cain, who, encouraged by Satan, was jealous of him and who wanted his possessions (Moses 5:18–33).

ABOMINABLE, ABOMINATION

As used in the scriptures, means something which is extremely disgusting and offensive to the righteous and to God. For example, pride is abominable to the Lord (Jacob 2:13–22), and breaking the law of chastity is abominable above all sins except murder and denying the Holy Ghost (Alma 39:3–5).

ABOMINABLE CHURCH

See DEVIL, CHURCH OF THE

ABOMINATION OF DESOLATION

This term comes from Daniel 11:31, 12:11, and Matthew 24:15, in reference to terrible conditions which were prophesied to come upon Jerusalem in the decades following the crucifixion of the Savior, and again in the last days (Matthew 24:15; JS—M 1:12). The first "Abomination of Desolation" was fulfilled when the Roman legions laid siege to Jerusalem in AD 70.

This prophecy will be fulfilled again in the last days when Jerusalem comes under siege again. "And again shall the abomination of desolation, spoken of by Daniel the prophet, be fulfilled" (JS—M 1:31–32).

ABORTION

"Human life is a sacred gift from God. Elective abortion for personal or social convenience is contrary to the will and the commandments of God. Church members who submit to, perform, encourage, pay for, or arrange for such abortions may lose their membership in the Church" (Church website, lds.org, under Gospel Topics, Abortion, 2007).

We will quote from *True to the Faith* for additional counsel on this subject: "Church leaders have said that some exceptional circumstances may justify an abortion, such as when pregnancy is the result of incest or rape, when the life or health of the mother is judged by competent medical authority to be in serious jeopardy, or when the fetus is known by competent medical authority to have severe defects that will not allow the baby to survive beyond birth. But even these circumstances do not automatically justify an abortion. Those who face such circumstances should consider abortion only after consulting with their local Church leaders and receiving a confirmation through earnest prayer" (*TF*, p. 4).

Bishops and stake presidents have materials from the leaders of the Church which suggest that elective abortion for personal or social convenience can be forgiven.

ABRAHAM

The name means "father of a multitude" (see BD, under "Abraham"). Abraham was originally called Abram, which means "exalted father" (ibid.), but his name was changed to Abraham as part of the covenant he made with God (Genesis 17:2–5). Abraham was one of the greatest prophets in the Bible and is revered by Christians, Jews, and Muslims alike. He was born in Ur of the Chaldees (Genesis 11:26–28), which would be near southeastern Iraq today, about 1992 BC, approximately 350 years after the Flood (see chronology chart in the Old Testament Student Manual, Genesis–2 Samuel, used by Institutes of Religion, Religion 301, 1981). He lived to be 175 years old.

He came from a family who had left the true gospel and turned to idol worship (Abraham 1:5–7, 27), but in spite of that he remained true to the Lord, ultimately making covenants with Him (Genesis 12:1–5) and remaining faithful throughout his life.

His faith was tried to the utmost when he was asked to sacrifice his covenant son, Isaac (Genesis 22), which was symbolic of the Father's only begotten Son, our Savior. The Bible tells us that Abraham had faith that if he had to sacrifice Isaac, the Lord would bring him back to life (Hebrews 11:17–19).

The blessings of Abraham are very significant to us today, as members of the Church. They are known as the Abrahamic covenant and are our heritage as covenant Israel today. They are the blessings of exaltation and eventual godhood, if we, too, remain faithful. These blessings can be reviewed in Abraham 2:9–11. Abraham has already become a god (D&C 132:29, 37).

ABRAHAM, BLESSINGS OF

See also ABRAHAMIC COVENANT.

Often referred to as "the blessings of Abraham, Isaac, and Jacob." These are the blessings of exaltation, in other words, the blessings received by the faithful who attain the highest degree of glory in the celestial kingdom and eventually become gods (D&C 76:58; 132:19–20). The Abrahamic covenant along with its accompanying responsibilities is described in Abraham 2:9–11.

ABRAHAM, BOOK OF

The second book in the Pearl of Great Price. It was translated by Joseph Smith from ancient Egyptian papyrus in 1835 and contains writings of Abraham while he was in Egypt. See heading to the book of Abraham. See also *History of the Church*, vol. 2, pp. 235–36, 348–51.

ABRAHAM, BOSOM OF

A term meaning to be with Abraham in the postmortal spirit world paradise (see Luke 15:22).

ABRAHAM, CHILDREN OF

A term often used to mean descendants of Abraham (see JST, Matthew 3:36). It can also mean faithful followers of Abraham with respect to righteousness and faithfulness to the Lord (Galatians 3:7).

ABRAHAM, GOSPEL OF

We will quote from the *Encyclopedia of Mormonism* for a definition of this phrase: "On April 3, 1836, the keys of the 'dispensation of the gospel of Abraham' were committed to the Prophet Joseph Smith and Oliver Cowdery in the Kirtland Temple as part of the restoration of all things in the dispensation of the fulness of times (D&C 110:12). It was promised that through latter-day recipients of the gospel and their seed, all generations who accept it shall be blessed (*HC* 2:434–36). This renewed the promise which was given anciently to Abraham (Genesis 12:1–3; Abraham 2:6, 9–11; cf. Galatians 3:7–9, 29)."

ABRAHAM, SEED OF

A phrase which literally means descendants of Abraham. Symbolically, it means those who live righteously, keeping the commandments and covenants of the gospel, as did Abraham, and who will earn exaltation, thus becoming gods as Abraham did (see D&C 132:37). All who are baptized worthily into the true Church become the "seed of Abraham."

ABRAHAMIC COVENANT

This is perhaps one of the most important and least understood of all gospel concepts and teachings among members of the Church. Those who do understand it have a stronger sense of mission and purpose in this life and a greater capacity to remain loyal to the Savior and His gospel. The Abrahamic covenant becomes the means through which faithful, baptized members of the Church progress toward exaltation and receive "all that my Father hath" (D&C 84:38).

The Lord made this covenant with Abraham (Genesis 12:1–3; 17:1–8), and it became his assurance and guide to obtaining exaltation. It contains all the doctrines and promises of the gospel as well as all the priesthood covenants, from baptism through celestial marriage. It extends to all baptized members of the Church who are faithful and worthy, and thus firmly establishes our identity in mind and heart as children of God. The Abrahamic covenant confirms us as the people of God, just as it did Abraham, Sarah, and their posterity in ancient times.

As baptized members of The Church of Jesus Christ of Latter-day Saints, each of us is a member of the house of Israel (another term for descendants of Abraham) and "of the covenant" (3 Nephi 20:25–26). When we read the promises made to Abraham, we are reading and studying the promises made by the Lord to us, as Abraham's worthy seed. They include:

- His posterity would be numerous (see Genesis 17:5–6; Abraham 2:9; 3:14). This can be fulfilled to some extent in this life but will be fulfilled eternally if we are found worthy to become gods and people our own worlds with countless spirit children of our own.

- His posterity would receive the gospel and bear the priesthood (see Abraham 2:9).

- Through the ministry of his seed, "all the families of the earth [would] be blessed, even with the blessings of the Gospel, which are the blessings of salvation, even of life eternal," which means exaltation (Abraham 2:11). Thus, each of us has the responsibility to share the gospel with others and to serve faithfully in the Church.

ABUSE

Abuse can be defined as the treatment of others or self in ways which cause unnecessary injury, whether physical, mental, emotional, or spiritual. The aftermath of such abuse can be devastating and can include confusion, fear, withdrawal, lowered self-esteem, lack of trusting others, and a host of debilitating thought patterns. Abuse in any form is condemned by the Lord, and those guilty of abuse could face Church discipline.

ACCOUNTABILITY

Being "accountable," in the context of the gospel, means that we must answer to God for what we do and think. In fact, we are taught in the scriptures that we will be asked to answer to the Lord for all we do,

say, and think (Matthew 12:36; Alma 12:12–14).

Those under the age of eight as well as those who are mentally handicapped are not accountable (D&C 29:46–47, 50). Children who die before the age of accountability are saved in the celestial kingdom (D&C 137:10).

ACTING PRESIDENT OF THE TWELVE

The president of the Church is the Apostle who has served the longest as a member of the Quorum of the Twelve Apostles. Usually, the president of the Quorum of the Twelve Apostles is the one who has served next longest. However, when the man who has served second longest as an Apostle is chosen to serve as a counselor to the president of the Church (such as President Thomas S. Monson, under President Hinckley), the Apostle who has been serving third longest (Boyd K. Packer, in this case) is called to "act" in place of the other. Thus, he is called "the acting president of the Twelve" because he is acting or serving in place of the Apostle who would normally be the president of the Twelve.

ADAM

The first of the human race on this earth (Moses 1:34; see also BD, under "Adam"). Also known as Michael (D&C 27:11; 29:26), archangel (D&C 88:112), and Ancient of Days (D&C 138:38). Along with Eve, his wife, he caused the Fall, which was a planned and necessary part of the Father's plan for us (2 Nephi 2:25). He was taught the gospel (Moses 6:51–52) and was baptized and given the gift of the Holy Ghost (Moses 6:64–66). He was given the Melchizedek Priesthood and ordained a high priest (Moses 6:67).

Adam and Eve had a fully developed pure language, kept written records, and taught their children how to read and write (Moses 5:5–6). Adam participated in the creation of the earth and holds a position of authority next to Jesus Christ (*TPJS*, p. 158)

Adam, in other words, Michael, will gather the forces of the righteous and lead them in defeating Satan and his followers in the final battle which will take place after the Millennium and the "little season" that follows it (D&C 88:111–15).

We, as members of The Church of Jesus Christ of Latter-day Saints, hold Adam and Eve in the highest esteem, which is often not the case with other religions. Our advantage is that we have correct doctrine and information about them.

ADAM, DISPENSATION OF

A dispensation is a period of time in the earth's history during which the gospel is revealed or restored. Thus, the dispensation of Adam refers to the "dispensing" of the gospel to Adam and Eve.

ADAM AND EVE

Adam and Eve were chosen by God to be the first humans on this earth. They rank among the most noble and

great of all our spirit brothers and sisters. While many religions look down upon them and teach that their transgression caused untold misery for those of us who followed, we hold them in highest esteem. For more about them and their mission, see information under "Adam" and also under "Eve" in this reference work.

ADAM-GOD THEORY

Some have misinterpreted statements made by Brigham Young in order to teach that Adam was, in reality, Heavenly Father. This has become known as "The Adam-God Theory." It is false doctrine. We will quote from the *Encyclopedia of Mormonism* for clarification: "Adam has been highly esteemed by all the prophets, both ancient and modern. President Brigham Young expressed the idea in 1852 and later years that Adam 'is our Father and our God, and the only God with whom we have to do' (*JD* 1:50). This remark has led some to conjecture that Brigham Young meant that Adam, who was on earth as our progenitor, was in reality God the Father. However, this interpretation has been officially rejected as incorrect (Kimball, p. 77). Later in the same speech Brigham Young clearly stated 'that the earth was organized by three distinct characters, namely Eloheim, Yahovah, and Michael' (*JD* 1:51). Additional information about Brigham Young's feelings on Adam can also be found in a conference speech given October 8, 1854 (*JD* 1:50), clarifying somewhat his earlier statement. It is there implied that through a process known as divine investiture, God delegates his power to his children. Adam was the first on earth to receive this authority, which includes all essential keys, titles, and dominions possessed by the Father (D&C 84:38; cf. 88:107). Thus, he had conferred upon him all things which were necessary for the accomplishment of his manifold responsibilities, and Adam is a name-title signifying that he is the first man and father of all."

ADAMIC LANGUAGE

The language spoken and written by Adam and Eve as well as their children, grandchildren, and so forth. It is referred to in Moses 6:5. Brigham Young informed the Saints that it was spoken from the time of Adam down to the Tower of Babel, at which time the languages were confused by the Lord (see *JD* 3:100). While we do not know for sure, some think that the Adamic language will again be spoken on earth during the Millennium. This thinking is based on Zephaniah 3:9, which reads, "I will turn to the people a pure language, that they may all call upon the name of the Lord." A "pure language" could perhaps eliminate misunderstanding in communicating with each other and thus contribute to peace and the spread of the gospel during the Millennium.

ADAM-ONDI-AHMAN

A beautiful area about seventy miles north northeast of Independence, Missouri. The significance of this site is found in the Doctrine and Covenants and in the Bible. We are taught, for example, that a great conference of Adam and Eve's righteous posterity was held in Adam-ondi-Ahman, three years prior to Adam's death. We read:

D&C 107:53–56

53 Three years previous to the death of Adam, he called Seth, Enos, Cainan, Mahalaleel, Jared, Enoch, and Methuselah, who were all high priests, with the residue of his posterity who were righteous, into the valley of Adam-ondi-Ahman, and there bestowed upon them his last blessing.

54 And the Lord appeared unto them, and they rose up and blessed Adam, and called him Michael, the prince, the archangel.

55 And the Lord administered comfort unto Adam, and said unto him: I have set thee to be at the head; a multitude of nations shall come of thee, and thou art a prince over them forever.

56 And Adam stood up in the midst of the congregation; and, notwithstanding he was bowed down with age, being full of the Holy Ghost, predicted whatsoever should befall his posterity unto the latest generation.

Shortly before the Second Coming of Christ, another great council will be held at Adam-ondi-Ahman. We read of this in Daniel. He had a vision in which he saw that millions of righteous people will attend this great meeting. We will include some explanatory notes within these verses of scripture.

Daniel 7:9–10, 13

9 I beheld till the thrones were cast down [*Daniel saw the future, including the downfall of governments in the last days, as spoken of in D&C 87:6*], and the Ancient of days [*Adam*] did sit [*compare with the last part of this section*], whose garment was white as snow, and the hair of his head like the pure wool: his throne [*symbolizing that Adam is in a position of great power and authority*] was like the fiery flame, and his wheels as burning fire.

10 A fiery stream issued and came forth from before him: thousand thousands [*millions*] ministered unto him, and ten thousand times ten thousand [*a hundred million*] stood before him: the judgment was set, and the books were opened.

13 I [*Daniel*] saw in the night visions, and, behold, one like the Son of man [*a Biblically respectful way of saying Jehovah, in other words, Jesus Christ*] came with the clouds of heaven, and came to the Ancient of days, and they brought him near before him.

Next we see in Daniel's vision that the keys of leadership will be given back to Christ during this grand council, in preparation for His ruling and reigning as "Lord of lords, and King of kings" (Revelation 17:14) during the Millennium.

Daniel 7:14

14 And there was given him [*Christ*] dominion, and glory, and a kingdom, that all people, nations, and languages, should serve him [*during the Millennium*]: his dominion is an everlasting dominion, which shall not pass away, and his kingdom that which shall not be destroyed.

If you have a newer quad or triple combination, you can look at the pictures at the very back, refer to picture number 10, read the information at the bottom, and be taught who will attend the meeting at Adam-ondi-Ahman shortly before the Second Coming. It says: "The Valley of Adam-ondi-Ahman. Here Adam and his righteous posterity met (see D&C 107:53–57). Adam, other prophets, and faithful Saints from all ages will meet the Savior here prior to His Second Coming."

While we do not know the exact meaning of the name "Adam-ondi-Ahman," Bruce R. McConkie explained that we do have some clues. He said:

"Adam was the first man of all men; Ahman is one of the names by which God was known to Adam [D&C 78:20, 95:17]. Adam-ondi-Ahman, a name carried over from the pure Adamic language into English, is one for which we have not been given a revealed, literal translation. As near as we can judge—and this view comes down from the early brethren who associated with the Prophet Joseph Smith, who was the first one to use the name in this dispensation—Adam-ondi-Ahman means the place or land of God where Adam dwelt" (*MD*, p. 19).

ADMINISTERING TO THE SICK

In James 5:14–16, we are taught about administering to the sick. Men in the Church who hold the Melchizedek Priesthood can be called upon to administer to the sick. Normally, the person who is sick is anointed with consecrated olive oil by one of the Melchizedek Priesthood holders, using his priesthood authority and in the name of Jesus Christ. Following this anointing, one or more additional Melchizedek Priesthood holders lay their hands on the sick person's head and, with one of them as voice, they seal the anointing and give a blessing as inspired by the Spirit.

Under rare circumstances when another Melchizedek Priesthood holder is not available, one Melchizedek Priesthood holder may anoint and then seal the anointing himself, pronouncing a blessing as inspired by the Spirit.

ADOPTION OF CHILDREN

We will quote from the booklet *True to the Faith* for the Church's position on this important matter: "Children are entitled to be raised by parents who honor marital vows and who provide love and support. Adoption can be a great blessing for many children who are born without this opportunity.

"When a child is conceived out of wedlock, the best option is for the mother and father of the child to marry and work toward establishing an eternal family relationship. If a successful marriage is unlikely, they should place the child for adoption, preferably through LDS Family Services. Placing the infant for adoption through LDS Family Services helps unwed parents do what is best for the child. It ensures that the child will be sealed to a mother and a father in the temple, and it enhances the prospect for the blessings of the gospel in the lives of all concerned. Adoption is an unselfish, loving decision that blesses the birth parents, the child, and the adoptive family.

"If you are married and you and your spouse want to adopt a child, be sure you know all legal requirements of the countries and governmental agencies that are involved. Counsel with your priesthood leaders and, if possible, with staff members in LDS Family Services. If LDS Family Services is not available in your area, work with your priesthood leaders to locate licensed, authorized agencies that protect both the children and the adoptive parents."

ADULTERY

Sexual intercourse between married individuals who are not married to each other, or between a married person and a single person. It is forbidden by the Lord in the Ten Commandments (Exodus 20:14) and elsewhere in scripture (example: D&C 42:23).

The sin of adultery can be forgiven (D&C 42:25), upon deep and complete repentance, which includes confession to one's bishop or stake president. People who repent completely of adultery can, through continued gospel living, progress to the highest degree in the celestial kingdom, which is called exaltation. Thus, adultery can be forgiven completely, upon proper repentance.

The term "adultery" is often used symbolically in the scriptures to mean apostasy, in effect meaning nations or individuals who "step out on God" through idol worship, breaking covenants, and so forth (example: Jeremiah 3:8).

ADVERSARY, THE
Another name for the devil (1 Peter 5:8).

ADVOCATE WITH THE FATHER
An advocate is one who champions a cause. The Savior is our Advocate with the Father (D&C 45:3). He is doing everything in His power to bring us back into the presence of the Father, without violating our agency, in order for us to live there forever.

AFFLICTION
Troubles, adversity, difficulties.

AFTERLIFE
A term for where we go when we die. It can refer to the postmortal spirit world, which has two main categories, paradise and prison (Alma 40:11–14), or to life after we are resurrected and have been judged and sent to one of the three degrees of glory or to perdition with Satan (D&C 76).

AGE OF ACCOUNTABILITY
Eight years old (D&C 68:25, 27). It is at this age that children begin to be accountable, and it is at this age that Satan can begin tempting them directly (D&C 29:46–47). "All children who die before they arrive at the years of accountability are saved in the celestial kingdom of heaven" (D&C 137:10).

AGENCY
The God-given freedom to choose. The use of agency requires knowledge of options from which to choose. "Ye are free; ye are permitted to act for yourselves; for behold, God hath given unto you a knowledge and he hath made you free" (Helaman 14:30–31). God will not violate our agency. Satan wants to, and he has a goal to take our agency away and gain all power over us (Alma 34:35). This was Lucifer's goal in the beginning (Moses 4:1–4).

We were given agency in our premortal life (D&C 29:36). Agency brings with it ultimate accountability for out eternal destiny ("ye are free to act for yourselves—to choose the way of everlasting death or the way of eternal life" (2 Nephi 10:23).

AGNOSTICISM
A belief held by some that it is impossible to prove that there is a God, and that, likewise, it is impossible to prove that there is not a God.

AHMAN

The name of God in the pure language (see D&C 78:20; 95:17). "There is one revelation that this people are not generally acquainted with. I think it has never been published, but probably it will be in the Church History. It is given in questions and answers. The first question is, 'What is the name of God in the pure language?' The answer says, 'Ahman.' 'What is the name of the Son of God?' Answer, 'Son Ahman" (*JD* 2:342).

AIDS

The following quote regarding AIDS is helpful:

"The First Presidency statement on AIDS (acquired immune deficiency syndrome) released May 27, 1988, admonishes Church members to become informed about AIDS and to avoid all actions which place themselves or others at risk. Members are also encouraged to become informed about AIDS-related laws and policies in the country where they live and to join in wise and constructive efforts to stem the spread of AIDS.

"The statement calls for Church members to extend Christlike sympathy and compassion to all who are infected or ill with AIDS. Particular concern and sympathy are expressed for those having received the virus through blood transfusions, babies infected by their mothers, and marriage partners infected by a spouse. Leaders and members are encouraged to reach out with kindness and comfort to the afflicted, ministering to their needs and assisting them with their problems.

"While hope is expressed that medical discoveries will make it possible both to prevent and cure AIDS, the observance of clearly understandable and divinely given guidance regardless of such potential discoveries will do more than all else to check a potential AIDS epidemic: 'That guidance is chastity before marriage, total fidelity in marriage, abstinence from all homosexual relations, avoidance of illegal drugs, and reverence and care for the body, which is the temple of God.'

"The First Presidency statement includes remarks given about AIDS by Gordon B. Hinckley, First Counselor in the First Presidency, in the April 1987 general priesthood meeting: 'Prophets of God have repeatedly taught through the ages that practices of homosexual relations, fornication, and adultery are grievous sins. Sexual relations outside the bonds of marriage are forbidden by the Lord. We reaffirm those teachings. . . . Each of us has a choice between right and wrong. But with that choice there inevitably will follow consequences. Those who choose to violate the commandments of God put themselves at great spiritual and physical jeopardy.'

"In January 1989 a special bulletin on AIDS was sent to Church leaders throughout the world to provide (1) scientific and medical information about AIDS; (2) counsel reaffirming the blessings and protection which come from living God's commandments; and (3) guidelines and policies dealing with interviewing and assisting those infected with the AIDS virus. Some items treated in the four-page special bulletin are:

• Church teachers and activity leaders who on occasion may be involved in cleaning up blood or rendering first aid should become aware of, and follow, local health department recommendations regarding the prevention of AIDS infection.

• AIDS-infected individuals who may be contemplating marriage are to be encouraged by local Church leaders to be honest with potential marriage partners and to disclose their AIDS infection. For a person to do less would be deceitful, and in violation of one's covenants with God.

• Where transgression of God's laws has resulted in infection, the Church advocates the example of Jesus Christ, who condemned the sin but loved the sinner.

• AIDS victims who seek membership in the Church, temple recommends, or other blessings are treated as all others who express faith in God, repent, request baptism, and are living the teachings of Jesus Christ" (*EM*).

ALCOHOLIC BEVERAGES

Drinks that contain alcohol. They are forbidden by the Word of Wisdom (D&C 89:5, 7).

ALIENS

We do not believe in aliens as they are commonly portrayed, as strange, somewhat human-like life forms from outer space.

However, in the sense that "aliens" can be defined as "people from somewhere else in space," we believe that they exist. In fact, we know that Heavenly Father has "worlds without number" (Moses 1:33), and that some have already finished up but many are out there now (Moses 1:35). The inhabitants of those worlds are His children, just as we are. Thus, they are our brothers and sisters, and would not be strange "alien" life forms. Also, this earth has had and continues to have many "visitors" in the form of heavenly beings who do not currently reside on our earth.

ALLEGORY OF ZENOS

Found in Jacob chapter 5. An allegory is a teaching story or parable which uses things from real life to teach a lesson. This allegory comes from the writings of Zenos (Jacob 5:1), a prophet whose writings are not found in the Bible. It is about olive trees (symbolic of covenant Israel) which the Lord plants in various locations throughout the earth during the history of this world. Some groups of Israel remain faithful (tame olive trees) and produce righteous people (good fruit—example: Jacob 5:17), but some rebel and become wild olive trees (wicked people), producing bad fruit (example: Jacob 5:32). In the allegory, Gentiles are grafted into covenant Israel, symbolizing that all people are invited to become the Lord's people.

In the allegory we see the constant efforts of the Lord and His servants as they do everything possible to nourish and strengthen God's children in order to bring them home to Him.

We will draw on the Institute of Religion Book of Mormon Student Manual, 1996 edition, pages 47 and 48 for help with some of the symbolism in this allegory:

Item	Interpretation
1. The vineyard	1. The world
2. Master of the vineyard	2. Jesus Christ
3. The servant	3. The Lord's prophets
4. Tame olive tree	4. The house of Israel, the Lord's covenant people
5. Wild olive tree	5. Gentiles, or non-Israel (later in the parable, wild branches are apostate Israel)
6. Branches	6. Groups of people
7. The roots of the tame olive tree	7. The gospel covenant and promises made by God that constantly give life and sustenance to the tree
8. Fruit of the tree	8. The lives and works of men
9. Digging, pruning, fertilizing	9. The Lord's work with his children, which seeks to persuade them to be obedient and produce good fruit
10. Transplanting the branches	10. Scattering of groups throughout the world, or restoring them to their original position
11. Grafting	11. The process of spiritual rebirth wherein one is joined to the covenant
12. Decaying branches	12. Wickedness and apostasy
13. Casting the branches into the fire	13. The judgment of God

It is helpful to know that in the cultivation of olive trees, a green slip of an olive tree must be carefully pruned and fertilized, and the soil around it kept loose. Otherwise, the result is a wild olive bush that grows into a tangled mess of limbs and branches and produces small, worthless fruit.

ALLELUIA
Praise ye the Lord (example: Revelation 19:1–6).

ALMA
There are two prophets named Alma in the Book of Mormon.

(1) The priest who was converted (Mosiah 17:1–2) when Abinadi taught before King Noah and his wicked priests (Mosiah 12–17). After his conversion, Alma went on to reestablish the Church and lead his followers into the wilderness, where they remained for over twenty years (Mosiah 23–24). Eventually, he and his group were discovered by the Lamanites and put in bondage. Finally, they were enabled by the Lord to escape and go to the land of Zarahemla where King Mosiah appointed Alma to be the president of the Church (Mosiah 25:19).

(2) Alma the Younger, the son of Alma. He rebelled, along with the four sons of King Mosiah (Mosiah 27:8–10) and caused great trouble for

the Church. He was converted when an angel appeared and called him and the sons of Mosiah to repentance (Mosiah 27:11–19). He went on to become a powerful missionary and eventually became the president of the Church (Mosiah 28:20). The book of Alma is the account of his ministry.

ALMIGHTY

All powerful. A word used to describe God.

ALMS

Donations for the poor (Matthew 6:1–4). Can also include personal righteousness and acts of religious devotion (Matthew 6:1, footnote b).

ALPHA AND OMEGA

The first and last letters of the Greek alphabet. Often used in the scriptures as a descriptive name for Jesus Christ, symbolizing that He is the First and the Last and depicting His all-encompassing role in our salvation, from beginning to end (D&C 19:1; 45:7; Revelation 1:8; 3 Nephi 9:18). In other words, He is wonderfully involved in all our needs, guiding and helping us in everything from "A to Z" toward our salvation, if we choose to follow Him.

ALTAR

A stone structure in ancient times upon on which sacrifices were offered (example: Genesis 8:20). Altars played an important role in the ordinances of the law of Moses (see BD, under "Altar").

In modern times, we have altars in our temples at which people kneel as they participate in sacred ordinances of the gospel, including celestial marriage and sealing families together. Altars symbolize "sacrificing" whatever is necessary to follow Christ and thus gain exaltation in the celestial kingdom.

In a symbolic sense, the Garden of Gethsemane and the cross were altars upon which Christ voluntarily placed Himself as a sacrifice for our sins.

AMEN

"May it be so," "so it is" (*GS*, under "Amen"). Saying "amen" at the end of a prayer, sermon, and so forth, denotes agreement and acceptance of what was said.

Symbolically, Christ is sometimes referred to as "the Amen" (example: Revelation 3:14).

AMERICA

In its broadest use in the scriptures, America means the Western Hemisphere, including North and South America (1 Nephi 2:20; Ether 2:7–8).

More specifically, America is often used to refer to the United States. Elder Ezra Taft Benson used it this way when he said, "Having declared America to be a land of liberty, God undertook to raise up a band of inspired and intelligent leaders who would write a constitution of liberty [D&C 101:77–80] and establish the first free people in modern times" (CR [Oct. 1961]:69–71).

AMMONITES

In the Bible, a group of people who descended from Lot, Abraham's nephew (Genesis 19:38; Deuteronomy 2:19). Historically, they were bitter enemies to the Israelites and the Jews.

AMORITES

We will quote from the Bible Dictionary for this definition: "There is some uncertainty as to the use of this name; it probably denotes a fair-skinned and blue-eyed race (as we learn from Egyptian monuments) who inhabited the south of Palestine before Semitic tribes like the Israelites, Ammonites, Edomites, etc., made their appearance there. Lachish was one of their chief cities. In the Tell el-Amarna tablets Amurri is the common name for Palestine. Among the Amorites were included the Hivites" (BD, under "Amorites").

AMULEK

In the Book of Mormon, a missionary companion to Alma the Younger (Alma 8:18–30). He had resisted the promptings he had been given over many years to become committed to the Lord (Alma 10:5–6), but when Alma came to him and taught him, he became a mighty missionary and teacher (example: his sermon given in Alma 34).

ANARCHY

Lack of strong central government. Lawlessness, with everyone doing their own thing, which usually leads to much misery and suffering among people.

ANATHEMA

Something which causes severe spiritual damage. Paul uses the term in 1 Corinthians 16:22 when he says, "Anathema Maran-atha." Maranatha means "The Lord will come!" (see 1 Corinthians 16:22, footnote a, in your Bible). The two words combined might be translated to mean, in effect, "those who reject Christ will reap the punishment that will come upon the wicked when He comes."

ANCESTORS

Relatives who have gone before us, such as parents, grandparents, great-grandparents, and so on, eventually back to Adam and Eve.

ANCESTRAL FILE

A very large database of genealogical records produced by the Church and available to all who desire to do family history work. One can get help in accessing this vast collection of family history information by going to lds.org on the Internet.

ANCIENT OF DAYS

Another name for Adam (Daniel 7:9; D&C 138:38). The name implies that Adam is the "most ancient" of any of us on this earth and that he has the "most days" or is the oldest of us all, as far as this earth is concerned.

ANGELS

Simply put, there are three main categories of angels, as referred to in the scriptures. Two types are righteous and one type is evil. (1) Righteous, resurrected beings who once lived on this earth (D&C 129:1). Moroni is an example of this type of angel, along with John the Baptist, Peter, James, Moses, Elijah, and Elias, all of whom ministered to the Prophet Joseph Smith. (2) Righteous spirits who have not yet been resurrected (D&C 129:3). (3) Evil spirits or "angels of the devil" (Revelation 12:9; D&C 29:37).

There are also other less frequent uses of the word "angel" in the scriptures. These can include translated beings such as John the Beloved (D&C 7:1–3) and the Three Nephites (3 Nephi 28), and also human messengers as seen in JST, Genesis 19:15.

ANGEL MORONI

Moroni, the son of Mormon, was the last prophet in the Book of Mormon. It was he who buried the gold plates about AD 421 (Moroni 10:1–2). As an angel, a resurrected being, he appeared to young Joseph Smith on September 21, 1823, and began instructing him concerning the gold plates and his mission as the prophet of the Restoration (JS—H 1:29–54). He continued to instruct Joseph for a number of years.

ANGEL OF LIGHT

This phrase is used in D&C 129:8 and refers to the devil when he attempts to deceive someone by impersonating a true angel or messenger sent from God.

ANGEL OF THE BOTTOMLESS PIT

Another term for Satan (Revelation 17:8).

ANGELS OF THE DEVIL

Another term for the evil spirits who were cast out with Satan as a result of the war in heaven. They are now on earth with him, tempting us (Revelation 12:4).

ANGER

We are counseled by the Lord to control our anger (Matthew 5:22; 3 Nephi 12:22). Loss of temper is not in harmony with the teachings of the gospel.

ANIMAL SACRIFICE

Commonly practiced in the Old Testament to symbolize the coming sacrifice of the Son of God (example: Moses 5:4–8). Animal sacrifice was a prominent part of the law of Moses and was designed to point the people's minds toward the future atoning sacrifice of Jesus Christ for our sins. An example of Atonement symbolism embodied in animal sacrifices within the law of Moses is found in Leviticus. We will add some explanatory notes in brackets within these two verses.

Leviticus 14:19–20

19 And the priest [*symbolizing the Savior*] shall offer the sin offer-

ing [*symbolic of Christ's Atonement*], and make an atonement for him [*symbolic of us*] that is to be cleansed from his uncleanness; and afterward he shall kill the burnt offering:

20 And the priest shall offer the burnt offering and the meat offering upon the altar [*symbolic of the Garden of Gethsemane and the cross*]: and the priest shall make an atonement for him, and he shall be clean [*symbolic of the effects of the Atonement upon us*].

ANIMALS, RESURRECTION OF

The scriptures teach that all animals will be resurrected. "All old things shall pass away, and all things shall become new . . . both men and beasts, the fowls of the air, and the fishes of the sea" (D&C 29:24).

ANNIHILATION, FALSE DOCTRINE OF

There are some who have taught that it is possible, through serious sin, to become extinct, in other words, that a person's body, spirit, and intelligence would cease to exist. This is a false doctrine. The scriptures teach: "For as in Adam all die, even so, in Christ shall all be made alive" (1 Corinthians 15:22). Furthermore, we are taught that "it is appointed unto man once to die" (Hebrews 9:27). Even those who are born here on earth and then become sons of perdition will be resurrected (D&C 88:32). They will ultimately be cast out with "the devil and his angels in eternity, where their worm dieth not

[*in other words, where they do not cease to exist*]" (D&C 76:44).

ANNUNCIATION, THE

Refers to the wonderful occasion on which the Angel Gabriel announced to the Virgin Mary that she was to be the mother of the Son of God (Luke 1:26–38). Joseph Smith taught that Gabriel is Noah, the faithful Old Testament prophet who preached the gospel and built the Ark (*HC* 3:386).

ANOINT

The act of placing a drop or two of consecrated olive oil on a person's head. Melchizedek Priesthood holders anoint individuals as part of the ordinance of administering to the sick. In ancient times, the Lord's prophets anointed those who were called to perform special duties for the Lord's people. Examples of this were the anointing of Aaron and his sons (Exodus 28:41; 29:4–9) and the anointing of kings who were to rule over Israel, such as Saul (1 Samuel 10:1; 16:13).

The word "anointed" can be used symbolically to mean "appointed" or "called" to a particular position. For example, we sometimes refer to priesthood leaders, who have been called by the Lord, including the General Authorities, as "the Lord's anointed."

ANOINTED ONE

Jesus Christ. The phrase "Anointed One" means that Jesus Christ was the one spoken of in prophecy to represent the Father in making salvation available to all people. The words "Messiah" and "Christ," in their original languages, mean "anointed."

ANOINTINGS

See WASHINGS AND ANOINTINGS.

ANTHON TRANSCRIPT

A copy of some characters or writings on the gold plates which Joseph Smith copied and gave to Martin Harris (JS—H 1:63). Joseph translated some of the characters on the paper. Martin took the copy of the characters to Professor Charles Anthon in New York City. Professor Anthon was a noted expert in ancient languages. He said that the characters were authentic and gave Martin a certificate stating that the characters were true and that the translation of them was correct. However, Anthon asked Martin how he got the characters. When Brother Harris told him that an angel had showed the gold plates to Joseph Smith and that is where the characters came from, Professor Anthon asked for the certificate back and promptly tore it up, telling Martin to bring the gold plates to him and he would translate them (JS—H 1:64–65).

ANTICHRISTS

People who oppose Christ and His teachings. There are several examples of anti-christs in the Book of Mormon, such as Sherem (Jacob 7:1–4), Nehor (Alma 1:2–15), and Korihor (Alma 30:6–21). John uses the term

in 1 John 2:18 and elsewhere. In a general sense, "antichrist" can mean anything that opposes Christ and His teachings.

APOCALYPSE, THE

Another name for the book of Revelation in the New Testament. "Apocalypse" is a Greek word which means "revealed or uncovered" (BD, under "Revelation of John").

APOCRYPHA, THE

A set of fifteen books found between the Old Testament and the New Testament in some Bibles. The word "Apocrypha" comes from a Greek word meaning "hidden or obscure." The word "apocryphal" means of doubtful origin or authenticity. These fifteen books are not considered to be valid books of the Bible by most scholars.

The Bible which Joseph Smith used for his work on the JST (the Joseph Smith Translation of the Bible) had an Apocrypha. He asked the Lord if he should translate it. The Lord's answer to him was no, and the reasons are given in D&C 91.

APOSTASY

See also APOSTASY, THE GREAT. Falling away from the truth. The word is commonly used to refer to times when the Church has ceased to exist on the earth, such as after the New Testament church fell away. It is also sometimes used to refer to members who fall away from the principles and commandments found in the gospel of Jesus Christ and become inactive or leave the Church (examples: Galatians 1:6, 2 Thessalonians 2:3, 2 Timothy 1:15).

APOSTASY, THE GREAT

The apostasy that took place after the Savior's crucifixion and resurrection. The Church that He established during His mortal mission fell away after the Apostles were killed and John the Apostle was banished to the Isle of Patmos (Revelation 1:9). Without the foundation of Apostles and prophets (Ephesians 2:20) to keep it on course, the true Church finally ceased to exist, resulting in the Dark Ages. It was restored again to earth by the Prophet Joseph Smith (JS—H).

APOSTATE FACTIONS

Groups who have left the true Church and attempted to establish their own churches. Some examples of this are the breakoffs from our Church who claim that polygamy should not have been stopped. Other examples include a number of churches which were established after the death of Joseph Smith.

APOSTATES

People who leave the true Church. The word is often used in referring to those who not only leave the Church but afterward fight against it in public settings, publishing anti-Mormon literature, and giving media interviews in which they attempt to discredit the Church and its leaders.

APOSTLE

Jesus called and trained twelve men, whom He called Apostles (Luke 6:13) to lead the Church after His crucifixion and resurrection. Our Apostles, whom we sustain as "prophets, seers, and revelators," form the foundation of the organization of the true Church (Ephesians 2:20). Apostles are special witnesses of Jesus Christ to all the world (D&C 107:23). The members of the First Presidency and the Quorum of the Twelve are Apostles. The three in the First Presidency form a quorum and the Twelve form a quorum (D&C 107:22–24).

Apostle is an office in the Melchizedek Priesthood. Apostles are given all the priesthood keys when they are ordained to the office of Apostle and set apart as members of the Quorum of the Twelve, but only the president of the Church has the authority to exercise all of these keys. He authorizes the use of the priesthood by the Apostles and all other priesthood holders, as needed in their service in the Church.

APOSTLES, THE TWELVE

Twelve men who are ordained to the office of Apostle in the Melchizedek Priesthood and who have been set apart to serve in the Quorum of the Twelve Apostles. They serve under the direction of the First Presidency (D&C 107:33).

APRIL 6, 1830

The day the Church was organized in our day (the dispensation of the fulness of times). It was organized in Fayette, New York, in the home of Peter Whitmer Sr. (D&C 21), with six members forming the official Church, according to the laws of the state of New York for forming a church.

ARCHANGELS

Chief angels, angels high in authority in heaven. An example is Adam (D&C 29:26; 88:112; Jude 1:9).

AREA

The largest geographical divisions in the Church are called areas. Each area is presided over by an area presidency consisting of three men, usually three Seventies, who serve under the direction of the First Presidency and the Quorum of the Twelve Apostles. Each area can consist of several stakes and/or districts and usually has one or more missions within its boundaries.

AREA SEVENTY

Brethren who are ordained as Seventies but who are not General Authorities (*TF*, p. 35). They generally are still employed in their profession and serve on a part-time basis, usually within a given area, carrying out whatever responsibilities are assigned to them by the General Authorities, including dividing stakes and calling stake presidents. If needed, they can go on assignments anywhere, under the direction of the First Presidency and the Twelve. Their calling is described in D&C 107:98.

ARK OF THE COVENANT

The oblong chest or box, covered with gold, made by Moses (Exodus 25) and used by the children of Israel for storing the stone tablets on which the Ten Commandments were written (1 Kings 8:9). Paul tells us that it also contained a pot of manna and Aaron's rod (Hebrews 9:4). The Ark was 2½ cubits long, 1½ cubits wide, and 1½ cubits high (Exodus 25:10). A cubit is about 15–18 inches.

ARK OF NOAH

A vessel or ship built by Noah as commanded by God in preparation for the Flood. It was 300 cubits long, 50 cubits wide, and 30 cubits high (about 450 feet by 75 feet by 45 feet), 3 stories high, and was divided into various compartments (Genesis 6:13–22).

ARMAGEDDON

A beautiful area about fifty miles north of Jerusalem. The name is a Greek approximation of "Har Megiddon" or "Mountain of Megiddo." Megiddo is a hill which overlooks the general area, and the surrounding areas have also come to be called Armageddon. The Megiddo valley is in the western part of the plain of Esdraelon in northern Israel. Many violent battles were fought in this region during Old Testament times (Judges 5:19; 2 Kings 9:27; 23:29).

ARMAGEDDON, BATTLE OF

A terrible final battle, involving all nations of the earth, which will take place near the Second Coming of Christ (Revelation 16, heading and verse 16; Zechariah 11–14).

"Prior to the second coming of Christ, all nations of the earth shall be gathered together to battle against Jerusalem. This tremendous war, one of the final great events prior to the Savior's second coming, has been fore-seen and described in detail by many of the Lord's ancient prophets. (See, for example, Ezekiel 38, 39; Joel 2, 3; Isaiah 34; Jeremiah 25; Daniel 11, 12; Zechariah 12–14.) Jerusalem will be under siege and great suffering will be the lot of her inhabitants. Evidently, Armageddon, which is north of Jerusa-lem, will be the site of the great decisive battle of this war" (*NTSM*, p. 463).

"During this siege, when the nations are gathered and the Lord comes, there will be great destruction. The armies will become so confused they will fight among themselves. There will be great slaughter. Then the Lord comes to the Jews. He shows Himself. He calls upon them to come and examine His hands and His feet, and they say, 'What are these wounds?' And He answers them, 'These are the wounds with which I was wounded in the house of my friends. I am Jesus Christ.'

"Then they will accept Him as their Redeemer, which they have never been willing to do" (Smith, *Signs of the Times*, p. 171).

ARMIES OF HEAVEN

Generally speaking, the combined forces of the righteous both in heaven and on earth. The Savior is spoken of as leading these armies (Revela-tion 19:14). Michael, or Adam, is also spoken of as having a major role in leading these righteous forces, both in the War in Heaven (Revelation 12:7) and in the final battle after the "little season" at the end of the Millennium (D&C 88:111–15).

ARTICLES OF FAITH

Thirteen brief statements of beliefs of The Church of Jesus Christ of Latter-day Saints, written by Joseph Smith as part of what is known as the Wentworth Letter. It included a brief history of the Church and was written at the request of John Went-worth, editor of the *Chicago Democrat*. Although Wentworth did not publish the letter, it was published later in the Church's newspaper, *Times and Seasons*, in Nauvoo, Tuesday, March 15, 1842. These "articles of our faith" were written for non-Mormons and were not intended by the Prophet to be a comprehensive treatment of beliefs and doctrines of the Church.

The Articles of Faith were included in the first edition of the Pearl of Great Price, which was published in England, in the British Mission, in 1851, and were "canonized" (accepted as official scripture of the Church) in 1880. They can be found at the end of our Pearl of Great Price today. They are as follows:

Articles of Faith

1 We believe in God, the Eter-nal Father, and in His Son, Jesus Christ, and in the Holy Ghost.

2 We believe that men will be punished for their own sins, and not for Adam's transgression.

3 We believe that through the Atonement of Christ, all mankind may be saved, by obedience to the laws and ordinances of the Gospel.

4 We believe that the first principles and ordinances of the Gospel are: first, Faith in the Lord Jesus Christ; second, Repentance; third, Baptism by immersion for the remission of sins; fourth, Laying on of hands for the gift of the Holy Ghost.

5 We believe that a man must be called of God, by prophecy, and by the laying on of hands by those who are in authority, to preach the Gospel and administer in the ordinances thereof.

6 We believe in the same organization that existed in the Primitive Church, namely, apostles, prophets, pastors, teachers, evangelists, and so forth.

7 We believe in the gift of tongues, prophecy, revelation, visions, healing, interpretation of tongues, and so forth.

8 We believe the Bible to be the word of God as far as it is translated correctly; we also believe the Book of Mormon to be the word of God.

9 We believe all that God has revealed, all that He does now reveal, and we believe that He will yet reveal many great and important things pertaining to the Kingdom of God.

10 We believe in the literal gathering of Israel and in the restoration of the Ten Tribes; that Zion (the New Jerusalem) will be built upon the American continent; that Christ will reign personally upon the earth; and, that the earth will be renewed and receive its paradisiacal glory.

11 We claim the privilege of worshipping Almighty God according to the dictates of our own conscience, and allow all men the same privilege, let them worship how, where, or what they may.

12 We believe in being subject to kings, presidents, rulers, and magistrates, in obeying, honoring, and sustaining the law.

13 We believe in being honest, true, chaste, benevolent, virtuous, and in doing good to all men; indeed, we may say that we follow the admonition of Paul—We believe all things, we hope all things, we have endured many things, and hope to be able to endure all things. If there is anything virtuous, lovely, or of good report or praiseworthy, we seek after these things.

—JOSEPH SMITH

ARTIFICIAL INSEMINATION, CHURCH'S POLICY ON

We will quote from the *Encyclopedia of Mormonism* for the policy on this matter: "Artificial insemination is defined as placing semen into the uterus or oviduct by artificial rather than natural means. The Church does not approve of artificial insemination of single women. It also discourages artificial insemination of married women using semen from anyone but the husband. 'However, this is a personal matter that ultimately must be left to the husband and wife, with the responsibility for the decision resting solely upon them' (*General Handbook of Instructions*, 11–4). Children conceived by artificial insemination have the same family ties as children who are conceived naturally. The *General Handbook of Instructions* (1989) states: 'A child conceived by artificial insemination and born after the parents are sealed in the temple is born in the covenant. A child conceived by artificial insemination before the parents are sealed may be sealed to them after they are sealed.' "

ASCENSION OF CHRIST

The Savior's return to heaven after His resurrection. Generally speaking, this refers to His ascension from the Mount of Olives, after He had spent forty days teaching His disciples (Acts 1:3, 9–11).

ASSISTANT PRESIDENT OF THE CHURCH

A position held during the early days of the Church, by Oliver Cowdery and then Hyrum Smith. "December 5, 1834, Oliver Cowdery was ordained by Joseph Smith by the command of the Lord, an Assistant President of the High Priesthood, to hold the keys of presidency with Joseph Smith in this ministry. This was in harmony with the ordinations he received under the hands of John the Baptist and other holy messengers in 1829" (Smith, *Essentials in Church History*, pp. 150–51).

After Oliver Cowdery left the Church, Hyrum Smith was given this position (D&C 124:91–95).

ASSISTANTS TO THE TWELVE

Assistants to the Quorum of the Twelve Apostles. The first Assistants were called in 1941 when five men were sustained as General Authorities in this office due to the rapid growth of the Church and the increasing demands on the Twelve. They had authority to minister throughout the Church as directed by the Twelve. A total of thirty-eight men served as Assistants to the Twelve before the office was discontinued in 1976 and those then serving became members of the First Quorum of Seventy. A number of men who served as Assistants are familiar to members today (2007). They include: Boyd K. Packer, L. Tom Perry, James E. Faust, Joseph B. Wirthlin, and Gordon B. Hinckley.

ASSOCIATE PRESIDENT OF THE CHURCH

See ASSISTANT PRESIDENT OF THE CHURCH

ASTROLOGY

A pseudoscience involving the predicting of events and giving of advice based on the positions of heavenly bodies. Horoscopes are used in conjunction with it. Astrologers have been around for a long time (example: Daniel 1:20). If people fall into the trap of believing in astrology, it can become a false religion and a substitute for true revelation from God.

ATHANASIAN CREED

A statement of belief about the Trinity (the Godhead) not subscribed to by The Church of Jesus Christ of Latter-day Saints. It is generally associated with the Catholic Church but has been effectively dropped from the Catholic liturgy in recent times. Some believe that it originated around AD 500. A portion of the creed follows:

"So the Father is God, the Son is God, and the Holy Ghost is God. And yet they are not Three Gods, but One God. So likewise the Father is Lord, the Son Lord, and the Holy Ghost Lord. And yet not Three Lords but One Lord. For, like as we are compelled by the Christian verity to acknowledge every Person by Himself to be God and Lord, so are we forbidden by the Catholic Religion to say, there be Three Gods or Three Lords. The Father is made of none, neither created, nor begotten. The Son is of the Father alone; not made, nor created, but begotten. The Holy Ghost is of the Father, and of the Son: neither made, nor created, nor begotten, but proceeding.

"So there is One Father, not Three Fathers; one Son not Three Sons; One Holy Ghost, not Three Holy Ghosts. And in this Trinity none is afore or after Other, None is greater or less than Another, but the whole Three Persons are Co-eternal together, and Co-equal. So that in all things, as is aforesaid, the Unity in Trinity, and the Trinity in Unity is to be worshipped. He therefore that will be saved, must thus think of the Trinity."

ATHEISM

Believing or claiming to believe that there is no God.

ATONEMENT OF JESUS CHRIST

See also FALL OF ADAM AND EVE.

The voluntary act and mission of the Savior, in which He overcame physical death for all (2 Nephi 9:22) and spiritual death for those who repent of their sins (2 Nephi 9:21).

Physical death is the separation of the body from the spirit and was introduced by the Fall of Adam and Eve. The Fall was a vital and planned step in our progression to become like our Heavenly Father. It was indeed part of the plan (2 Nephi 2:24; 9:6). The Atonement overcomes physical death for everyone ever born. All will be resurrected, regardless of whether they are righteous or wicked (1 Corinthians 15:22).

One definition of spiritual death, as used in scripture and gospel teaching, is being cut off from the presence of God (Alma 42:9; Helaman 14:16, 18). Those who are assigned on Judgment Day to any category other than the celestial kingdom (whose inhabitants will dwell in the presence of Heavenly Father and Jesus Christ "forever and ever"—D&C 76:62) are said to suffer spiritual death. In other words, they are cut off from living in the literal presence of God. The Atonement makes it possible for us to overcome spiritual death and return to the presence of God forever.

The Atonement goes hand in hand with the Fall of Adam. Both are integral components of the Father's plan for His spirit children (Alma 22:12–14).

The Atonement is the central focus of the Father's plan for us. It influences every aspect of our lives. It allows us to be optimists (2 Nephi 2:25) in spite of mistakes and sins we commit as we earnestly strive to improve and grow toward exaltation.

Jesus volunteered and covenanted with the Father in premortality to perform the Atonement (Moses 4:2; Revelation 13:8; Ether 3:14). His Atonement reaches all of the inhabitants of all of the worlds which have been and will yet be created for the Father's spirit children (D&C 76:24).

The Atonement was carried out by the Savior in the Garden of Gethsemane (Matthew 26:36–44; Luke 22:44; D&C 19:18) as well as on the cross (Matthew 27:26–50). "To this we add, if we interpret the holy word aright, that all of the anguish, all of the sorrow, and all of the suffering of Gethsemane recurred during the final three hours on the cross, the hours when darkness covered the land. Truly there was no sorrow

like unto his sorrow, and no anguish and pain like unto that which bore in with such intensity upon him" (McConkie, *The Mortal Messiah*, 4:232 p. 22).

In order for the Atonement to work for us, we have been given our moral agency (D&C 29:36) and have been and are being taught the gospel of Jesus Christ, which brings accountability for our choices (2 Nephi 2:10).

The Atonement works for our shortcomings and inadequacies as well as for our sins (Alma 7:12).

The law of justice requires that a penalty be paid for all sins committed. The law of mercy allows the Savior's payment for our sins to satisfy the law of justice, if we repent (Alma 42:15; D&C 19:16). Thus, we can accept the Savior's payment for our sins by making the "payment" He requires to Him, rather than making the payment required by the law of justice. The payment which the Savior requires from us consists of nothing but things that benefit us and make us happy. For example, He requires repentance and living the gospel, which bring inner peace and joy to us here and exaltation in the hereafter.

Through the Atonement, we can be completely cleansed and healed from sin, if we choose to repent and live the gospel of Jesus Christ (Isaiah 1:16–18). The Savior receives great joy when we accept His marvelous gift to us (Isaiah 53:11).

AUTHOR OF SALVATION

Another name for Jesus Christ, meaning that He is the Savior and Redeemer, who makes salvation available to us (Hebrews 5:9).

AUTHORITIES, GENERAL

The members of the First Presidency, Quorum of the Twelve Apostles, and First and Second Quorums of the Seventy are General Authorities of the Church (*TF*, p. 35). All other quorums of the Seventy, as well as general auxiliary officers in the Church, are not General Authorities. They serve under the direction of the General Authorities.

AUTHORITY

In a general sense, permission from a higher power to perform or function in a specific setting. In terms of the Church, the authorization from God or His servants to carry out a specific calling, function, or mission; perform ordinances; and so forth. Authority to act for God for the salvation of mankind is held only in the true Church of Jesus Christ of Latter-day Saints. Priesthood authority is centered in the living prophet, who holds and is authorized to exercise all the priesthood keys. With his authorization, this authority is conferred upon worthy priesthood holders throughout the Church.

AUTHORIZED VERSION OF THE BIBLE

Another name for the Joseph Smith Translation of the Bible (JST).

AUTOPSY

The examination by medical experts of a person's body after death, to determine the cause of death. The Church does not discourage autopsies.

AUXILIARY ORGANIZATIONS OF THE CHURCH

See also GENERAL AUXILIARIES. Relief Society, Young Women, Primary, Sunday School, and Young Men are auxiliary organizations. Their role is to support the priesthood in bringing souls unto Christ.

·B·

BAAL

A false god used in idol worship often mentioned in the Bible (1 Kings 16:30–33; 2 Kings 3:2). Baal was known by many different spellings or combinations of words, for example, "Baal-peor" (Numbers 25:3), and sexual immorality was often associated with worshipping him (Numbers 25:1–2).

One of the best known Bible incidents involving Baal is the account of Elijah and the 450 prophets of Baal.

Elijah challenged them to set up an altar for sacrifice and have Baal light the fire. When their attempts failed, he did the same, first soaking his sacrifice with water, then calling upon the true God of Israel to provide fire. The Lord did and the sacrifice, the altar, and the water around it were completely consumed by the fire from heaven (1 Kings 18:19–39).

BABEL

Another term for Babylon (see BD, under "Babel").

BABEL, TOWER OF

A huge tower, planned and undertaken some time after the Flood by wicked people in defiance of the Lord (Genesis 11:1–9). They claimed that they would build a tower that reached to heaven (Genesis 11:4), implying that they would find a way to get to heaven other than living in obedience to the laws and commandments of God.

Another aspect of their disobedience was that the Lord had commanded Noah and his family (and consequently, their descendants) to "multiply upon the earth" after the Flood (Genesis 8:17), whereas those who planned to build the Tower of Babel determined not to be "scattered upon the face of the whole earth" (Genesis 11:4).

As a consequence of their disobedient work on the tower, the Lord confounded their language (caused them to speak different languages) with the result that they could not understand each other. The work on the tower stopped, and they were scattered (Genesis 11:7–9).

Genesis 11:4 presents yet another indicator of evil associated with the building of the Tower of Babel. The people had obviously been overcome by pride such that one of their objectives was to become well known for building a tower so massive that they could reach heaven on their own, without God's help.

Jared (in the Book of Mormon) and his brother, along with their families and friends, lived at the time these wicked people decided to build the tower (Ether 1:33). Jared asked his brother to plead with the Lord not to confound their language (indicating that the people had been warned by the Lord of the coming confounding of language, if they did not repent). The Lord answered his prayers and did not confuse their language. He led them away from the tower (Ether 1:34–42). They were eventually led to the "promised land" of America (Ether 6:11–12).

BABYLON

An enormous city in ancient Babylonia, sometimes called "Babel" (BD, under "Babylon"). It became a very wicked city and a center for all types of evil, so evil in fact that the term "Babylon" became a generic term later in the scriptures meaning extreme wickedness (example: 1 Nephi 20:20; D&C 1:16) and also came to mean Satan's kingdom (Revelation 14:8; D&C 86:3).

The actual ancient city of Babylon was huge, with walls that were 56 miles around, 335 feet high, and 85 feet wide (BD, under "Babylon"). It was powerful and seemed invincible. Just as it seemed impossible for Babylon to fall, so also it seems to some to be impossible for Satan's kingdom to fall, because it is so vast and influential today. Babylon, the city, fell easily and quickly to the Persians in 538 BC. (BD, under "Assyria"), and Satan's kingdom will fall for a thousand years at the time of the Second Coming (Revelation 14:8) and forever, after the little season at the end of the Millennium (D&C 88:111–14).

BAPTISM

The Savior was baptized by immersion in the Jordan River by John the Baptist, thus setting the example for us (Matthew 3:13–17; 2 Nephi 31:4–10).

The basic meaning of the word *baptize*, in its Greek form, is "to dip or immerse" (BD, under "Baptism"). It is the ordinance required by the Lord for entrance into His Church (John 3:5). It must be done by complete immersion in water by someone having authority to perform this ordinance. Those who are thus baptized and confirmed become official members of The Church of Jesus Christ of Latter-day Saints.

Little children "cannot sin" (D&C 29:46–47) and, thus, children are not to be baptized "until they begin to become accountable before [the Lord]" (D&C 29:46–47). The Lord has set the age for baptism as eight (D&C 68:27). The seriously intellectually handicapped do not need baptism and come under the same rules as little children (D&C 29:50).

Baptism was practiced anciently. Adam was the first mortal to be baptized on this earth (Moses 6:64–65).

Baptism symbolizes the death and burial of the old self and coming forth of a new person, cleansed from sin with new opportunities for progression (Romans 6:4–6).

Priests in the Aaronic Priesthood (D&C 20:46) as well as Melchizedek Priesthood holders have authority to baptize, when authorized by those who hold the keys to direct the performing of such ordinances. Two Melchizedek Priesthood holders serve as witnesses to assure that the baptismal prayer (D&C 20:73) is said correctly and that the person baptized is completely immersed.

One of the great blessings of being baptized is receiving the gift of the Holy Ghost. If we pay attention to His promptings, the Holy Ghost guides and directs us throughout our lives, thus making our baptism and the Atonement of Christ effective in our lives, and eventually leading us back to the presence of the Father for eternity.

BAPTISM, COVENANT OF

When we are baptized, we covenant to take upon ourselves the name of Jesus Christ (which includes doing our best to act like He would act in our daily lives) and keep His commandments. We also covenant to serve Him throughout the rest of our lives

(2 Nephi 31:19–20), which includes church attendance (D&C 59:9) and service to others, which is the main way we serve Him (Mosiah 18:8–10).

We renew our covenant of baptism each time we worthily partake of the sacrament.

BAPTISM, EARLIEST AGE FOR

See also BAPTISM. Eight years old is the earliest age designated by the Lord for baptism (D&C 68:27).

BAPTISM FOR THE DEAD

See also DEAD, BAPTISM FOR. The ordinance of baptism, performed by mortals who serve as proxies for those who died (after age eight) without being baptized. It was practiced in the New Testament (1 Corinthians 15:29) and was restored in this dispensation through the Prophet Joseph Smith (D&C 127:5–10, 128:18). It is performed in temples (D&C 124:30–33).

The dead, for whom we are baptized, and who now dwell in the postmortal spirit world, do not automatically become members of the Church when someone is baptized as proxy for them. Rather, they are free to accept it or reject it. If they accept the gospel there, when it is preached to them (D&C 138:30–34), and repent from their sins, they can join the Church as soon as someone is baptized on earth for them. Thus, they can continue growing and progressing in the gospel of Jesus Christ and, through their faithfulness, attain exaltation (D&C 138:58–59).

BAPTISM OF FIRE AND THE HOLY GHOST

A phrase describing the effect the Holy Ghost can have upon people. The Holy Ghost bears witness of the Father and the Son as well as of the gospel of Jesus Christ to us. The accompanying feelings of spirituality, joy, and gladness are often described as "fire" burning within us.

Additional imagery is found as the Holy Ghost inspires and directs us, leading us to having our sins and imperfections purged or "burned" out of our souls in order for the Atonement to work for us. This is sometimes compared to the refining of gold, where the imperfections and impurities of gold ore are removed by the refiner's fire.

BAPTISM, PREPARATION FOR

Faith in Jesus Christ and sincere repentance for sins are important parts of preparation for baptism. A person desiring baptism should be living the gospel (D&C 20:68–69). Before a person can be baptized, he or she is interviewed by the appropriate priesthood leader who determines if the candidate for baptism is adequately prepared. This interviewer is usually a designated missionary in the mission field or a bishop or branch president in established wards and branches of the Church.

BAPTISMAL FONTS

Specially constructed basins or fonts in many church buildings and in temples which can contain enough water for both the person being baptized and the person doing the baptizing to enter the water (D&C 20:73). A normal bathtub will not do for baptizing because both persons cannot enter the water appropriately in it. The water in a font must be deep enough for the person being baptized to be completely immersed.

Any body of water, the ocean, rivers, large enough streams, lakes, ponds, and so forth can be used for baptizing.

BAPTISMAL PRAYER

The prayer repeated by the priesthood holder doing the baptizing. It is a set prayer which must be given exactly. The priesthood holder calls the person by his or her full name and says: "Having been commissioned of Jesus Christ, I baptize you in the name of the Father, and of the Son, and of the Holy Ghost. Amen" (D&C 20:73).

Another version of the baptismal prayer is found in 3 Nephi 11:25. However, we have been instructed by the Lord to use the one found in the Doctrine and Covenants, as referenced above.

BAPTIST, JOHN THE

The messenger of God who prepared the way for the Savior to perform His mortal ministry (Matthew 3:1–12). He was the son of Zacharias and Elizabeth (Luke 1:4–13). His birth was a miracle, since Elizabeth was long since beyond the age of child bearing (Luke

1:7). His mission was prophesied by Isaiah and others (Isaiah 40:3; Malachi 3:1; 1 Nephi 10:7–10).

He baptized the Savior (Matthew 3:13–17) and directed his disciples to follow Jesus (John 1:35–37; 3:26–30). Jesus paid John the highest compliment when He said that no one born of woman was greater than John the Baptist (Matthew 11:7–11).

John was eventually put in prison for criticizing Herod's unlawful marriage to his step-niece, Herodias (Matthew 14:3–4; Mark 6:16–29). After nearly a year in prison, he was beheaded at the request of Herodias, after her daughter, Salome, danced for the king (Mark 6:21–28).

John the Baptist spent relatively little time in the postmortal spirit world, since he was resurrected at the time of the Savior's resurrection (D&C 133:55).

BATTALION, THE MORMON

See MORMON BATTALION.

BATTLE OF ARMAGEDDON

See ARMAGEDDON, BATTLE OF.

BATTLE OF GOG AND MAGOG

See also BATTLE OF THE GREAT GOD. Sometimes used to mean the Battle of Armageddon, which will take place in the Holy Land near the time of the Second Coming (BD, under "Gog"). However, the name "Battle of God and Magog" is most commonly used to mean the final battle between Satan and the forces of evil and Michael (Adam) and the forces of righteousness, after the "little season" at the end of the Millennium (BD, under "Gog"; D&C 88:111–15). It is this battle which will conclude the battle for our souls which began with the War in Heaven.

BATTLE OF THE GREAT GOD

See also BATTLE OF GOG AND MAGOG. Another name for the battle which takes place when Satan is turned loose during the "little season" at the end of the Millennium (D&C 88:114). This war is often called the Battle of Gog and Magog. It is the final battle between good and evil on this earth, the end of the war which started in heaven (Revelation 12:7), after which the final judgment takes place.

BEARING FALSE WITNESS

Lying, in one way or another. One of the Ten Commandments commands, "Thou shalt not bear false witness against thy neighbour" (Exodus 20:16).

BEATITUDES

Another name for a portion of the Sermon on the Mount sometimes referred to as "the Blessed Are's" (Matthew 5:3–12) because they contain promised blessings for those who heed them. This sermon was given again by the Savior during His visit to the Nephites in America and included the Beatitudes, with some significant wording changes (3 Nephi 12:3–12).

We learn from 3 Nephi 3:1–2 that the Beatitudes were given to baptized members of the Church and thus are instructions which, when followed, lead to celestial glory. You may have noticed that verses 3, 5, 8, 10, and 12 all refer, one way or another, to the celestial kingdom.

Countless lessons can be learned from the Beatitudes and applied in our lives, as we are taught by the Holy Ghost.

BEEHIVE, SYMBOLISM OF

The beehive was a prominent symbol used by the early pioneers who settled in the Utah Territory. It symbolizes people working together for the common good. The *Deseret News* (11 Oct. 1881) described the symbol of the beehive as follows: "The hive and honey bees form our communal coat of arms. . . . It is a significant representation of the industry, harmony, order and frugality of the people, and of the sweet results of their toil, union and intelligent cooperation."

The beehive is seen in the Book of Mormon where the Jaredites carried swarms of bees (Ether 3:2). We learn from the same verse that "deseret . . . is a honey bee."

BEELZEBUB

The chief of the devils (Matthew 12:24). Another name for Satan (BD, under "Beelzebub"). The Jewish religious leaders accused Christ of being Beelzebub (Matthew 12:22–30).

BEGINNING

In a technical sense, there is no beginning, since we have always existed as intelligence or intelligences—we don't know quite what to call it (D&C 93:29). However, "beginning" often refers to our premortal existence as spirit sons and daughters of our heavenly parents (Job 38:7; D&C 93:21, 23). It also refers to the initial stages of the earth's creation (Genesis 1:1).

BEGINNING AND END, THE

The Savior often introduces Himself in the scriptures as "the beginning and the end" (D&C 35:1; Revelation 1:8). Among other things, the phrase represents the fact that He was the firstborn spirit child of our heavenly parents (Colossians 1:13–15) and thus was there to help us in the beginning as He volunteered to be our Savior and Redeemer in the premortal spirit realm (Moses 1:1–4). He has continued His divine efforts to help us and save our souls through His infinite Atonement and will be there also in the end to be our final judge (John 5:22) and to take us into the Father's realm (D&C 45:3–5). Thus, He will have worked for us and with us from beginning to end, when this world is all finished up and has become our celestial kingdom (D&C 130:9–11).

BELIAL, SONS OF

Wicked people (Deuteronomy 13:13). The term means "wicked" (BD, under "Belial") and is also used on occasions to refer to Satan (2 Corinthians 6:15).

BELIEF

This term is almost always used in the scriptures as a synonym for faith. Faith and belief are interchangeable. However, in our conversations with others we sometimes use belief to be somewhat weaker and less motivating than faith. An example of this might be someone who believes in God and Christ but who does not change lifestyles as a result. Someone who has faith in God the Father and Jesus Christ is constantly striving to improve and do a better job of keeping the commandments.

BELOVED SON, THE

Another name for the Savior (Matthew 3:17).

BENJAMIN, KING

A prophet-king in the Book of Mormon whose farewell address to his people, about 124 BC, is quite well known and often quoted among members of the Church. Among his better-known teachings are "when ye are in the service of your fellow beings ye are only in the service of your God" (Mosiah 2:17), his prophecies about the Savior (Mosiah 3:5–10), his teachings about the "natural man" (Mosiah 3:19), and his teachings about how to treat beggars (Mosiah 4:16–25).

BESTIALITY

The use of animals in committing sexual acts. It is strictly forbidden by the laws of God (Leviticus 18:23).

BETTING

See GAMBLING.

BIBLE

A collection of sacred writings accepted as scripture by The Church of Jesus Christ of Latter-day Saints. It consists of the Old Testament, with thirty-nine books, and the New Testament, with twenty-seven books. Some Bibles also contain what is known as the Apocrypha. You may wish to refer to "Apocrypha" in this reference book for more information.

Because the Church holds so tightly to Bible teachings, including the Ten Commandments, the literal resurrection of Jesus Christ and eventually all mortals, the law of chastity, and so forth, it can well be said that members of the Church believe in and adhere to the Bible much more than many Christians who claim to believe it exclusively but no longer believe that its teachings are binding on society. For example, they excuse sexual relations outside of marriage by saying that the Bible is out of date. They do not actually believe that Jesus was literally the Son of God, nor do they believe that He was literally resurrected. They subscribe to so-called "situational ethics" rather than adhering to the strict standards of honesty and integrity embodied in the golden rule and taught elsewhere in the Bible. They have abandoned any attempt to keep the Sabbath holy, as taught in the Bible (Exodus 20:8–11).

The eighth Article of Faith indicates that some portions of the Bible are not correct because they have not been translated correctly. We quote: "We believe the Bible to be the word of God as far as it is translated correctly; we also believe the Book of Mormon to be the word of God."

BIBLE DICTIONARY

A reference section contained in the back of the English LDS Bible (a special printing of the King James Version of the Bible).

BIBLE, LDS

Where English is spoken as the dominant language, the Church uses a special printing (beginning in 1979) of the King James Version of the Bible, which includes footnotes and help sections in the back that give explanations and cross-references to other LDS scriptures and the JST (the Joseph Smith Translation of the Bible).

In other language settings, a number of different versions of the Bible are used in conducting missionary work and teaching and preaching in the Church.

BIGAMY

Technically, this term means being legally married to more than one living wife or more than one living husband at the same time. In courts of law, "bigamy" is often used in place of "polygamy" in dealing with the legal proceedings concerning plural marriage.

BIRTH

Three births are a vital part of the Father's plan for us: (1) spirit birth in premortality, where our intelligence was clothed with a spirit body; (2) mortal birth that provides us with a physical body; (3) spiritual birth or being "born again" through accepting and living the gospel of Jesus Christ.

The exact timing as to when the spirit enters the mortal body before birth has not been revealed.

BIRTH, SPIRIT

We were each born as a "spirit son or daughter of heavenly parents" in the premortal realm (see "Proclamation," paragraph 1). Our eternal intelligence (D&C 93:29) was thus clothed in a body consisting of spirit, which is a type of matter (D&C 131:7–8). Our spirit bodies had all the parts that our physical bodies have. Apostle Parley P. Pratt taught: "The spirit of man consists of an organization of the elements of spiritual matter in the likeness and after the pattern of the fleshly tabernacle. It possesses, in fact, all the organs and parts exactly corresponding to the outward tabernacle" (Pratt, *Key to the Science of Theology*, p. 79).

BIRTH CONTROL

We will quote from *True to the Faith* (2004 edition) for current counsel on this matter:

"When married couples are physically able, they have the privilege of providing mortal bodies for Heavenly Father's spirit children. They play a part in the great plan of happiness, which permits God's children to receive physical bodies and experience mortality.

"If you are married, you and your spouse should discuss your sacred responsibility to bring children into the world and nurture them in righteousness. As you do so, consider the sanctity and meaning of life. Ponder the joy that comes when children are in the home. Consider the eternal blessings that come from having a good posterity. With a testimony of these principles, you and your spouse will be prepared to prayerfully decide how many children to have and when to have them. Such decisions are between the two of you and the Lord.

"As you discuss this sacred matter, remember that sexual relations within marriage are divinely approved. While one purpose of these relations is to provide physical bodies for God's children, another purpose is to express love for one another—to bind husband and wife together in loyalty, fidelity, consideration, and common purpose" (*TF*, p. 26).

BIRTHRIGHT

In ancient times, the special right or inheritance of the firstborn, usually including extra land and the right to preside over other siblings and descendants (Genesis 43:33) when the father dies.

BISHOP

The presiding officer in a ward or congregation of Latter-day Saints. He serves without pay. He must be a worthy high priest and is ordained and set apart by the stake president, with the direct approval of and under the direction of the First Presidency and the Quorum of the Twelve Apostles.

The office of bishop is an office in the Aaronic Priesthood (D&C 20:67), and the bishop serves as president of the priests quorum (D&C 107:87–88).

BISHOP'S COURT

See DISCIPLINARY COUNCIL.

BISHOPS' STOREHOUSE

The Lord has commanded His people to care for one another (Mosiah 4:26). Surplus goods and commodities including those specifically produced to provide for the poor and needy, are kept in what are called bishop storehouses (D&C 42:33–34), which are located in various places throughout the Church.

BISHOPRIC

The presiding officers in a ward, consisting of a bishop and a first and second counselor. On a general Church level, there is a presiding bishopric, consisting of a presiding bishop and two counselors.

BLACK MAGIC

A type of the occult, found in many forms, by which the devil deceives many and causes much suffering.

BLACKS AND THE PRIESTHOOD

For reasons not yet revealed by the Lord, blacks were not allowed to hold the priesthood until 1978. In the Pearl of Great Price, we see that descendants of Cain were denied the priesthood as far back as the days of Pharaoh, after the Flood (Abraham 1:26).

From time to time in the history of the Church, extreme pressure was brought to bear on Church leaders to change this policy, but their answer was always that this was not a decision to be made by man but that permission would have to come by revelation from God. That revelation came from God through President Spencer W. Kimball and was announced to the Church on June 9, 1978. It is now in the Doctrine and Covenants, as Official Declaration—2, at the end of the book. Because of this revelation, the priesthood is now available to all worthy men in the Church.

BLASPHEMY

Any contemptuous speaking or behavior that subjects God or His sacred teachings and commandments to mocking or extreme ridicule. Taking the name of God in vain; blatant, racy sexual talk; and demeaning the prophet, the temple, or other sacred institutions are all examples of blasphemy. One of the most severe forms of blasphemy against God is human sacrifice, which is Satan's mocking counterfeit of the sacrifice of the Only Begotten Son of God for our sins.

BLASPHEMY AGAINST THE HOLY GHOST

The willful denying of Christ after having received a perfect testimony and knowledge of Him from the Holy Ghost. It is the unforgivable sin (Matthew 12:31–32; Mark 3:28–29; D&C 76:35; 132:27).

BLESSING OF CHILDREN

A priesthood ordinance, performed by Melchizedek Priesthood holders, in which they give a name and a blessing to infants and young children (D&C 20:70). This ordinance is not necessary for salvation. Baptism is the first ordinance required for salvation and is not administered to children until they are eight years old (D&C 68:25, 27).

BLESSING ON THE FOOD

A prayer of thanks and gratitude for the food, preceding a meal, which can include a request that Heavenly Father bless the food to nourish and strengthen those who partake of it. It is closed in the name of Jesus Christ, and "amen" is the final word of the prayer. Such prayers are given in faithful LDS homes as well as in many other Christian homes before each meal and can be given by any person there. There is no set form for this prayer.

BLESSINGS, PRIESTHOOD

Any of several types of blessings given by Melchizedek Priesthood holders. Proper procedure includes

(1) the priesthood holders (or holder) place their hands on the person (usually on his or her head), (2) the speaker states that the blessing is being given by the authority of the Melchizedek Priesthood, (3) blessings are pronounced as inspired by the Spirit of the Lord, (4) the blessing is given in the name of Jesus Christ.

There are many types of priesthood blessings, including administering to the sick, blessing babies and children, being set apart for a particular calling, father's blessings, husband's blessings, blessings of comfort and counsel, and patriarchal blessings.

BLOOD ATONEMENT

Misunderstanding of this topic has often led critics of the Church to make false accusations against the Mormon people. In the *Encyclopedia of Mormonism*, we read: "The doctrines of the Church affirm that the Atonement wrought by the shedding of the blood of Jesus Christ, the Son of God, is efficacious for the sins of all who believe, repent, are baptized by one having authority, and receive the Holy Ghost by the laying on of hands. However, if a person thereafter commits a grievous sin such as the shedding of innocent blood, the Savior's sacrifice alone will not absolve the person of the consequences of the sin. Only by voluntarily submitting to whatever penalty the Lord may require can that person benefit from the Atonement of Christ.

"Several early Church leaders, most notably Brigham Young, taught that in a complete theocracy the Lord could require the voluntary shedding of a murderer's blood—presumably by capital punishment—as part of the process of Atonement for such grievous sin. This was referred to as 'blood Atonement.' Since such a theocracy has not been operative in modern times, the practical effect of the idea was its use as a rhetorical device to heighten the awareness of Latter-day Saints of the seriousness of murder and other major sins. This view is not a doctrine of the Church and has never been practiced by the Church at any time.

"Early anti-Mormon writers charged that under Brigham Young the Church practiced 'blood Atonement,' by which they meant Church-instigated violence directed at dissenters, enemies, and strangers. This claim distorted the whole idea of blood atonement—which was based on voluntary submission by an offender—into a supposed justification of involuntary punishment. Occasional isolated acts of violence that occurred in areas where Latter-day Saints lived were typical of that period in the history of the American West, but they were not instances of Church-sanctioned blood Atonement" (*EM*).

BLOOD OF ISRAEL

A term meaning a person who is a descendant of one of the twelve sons of Jacob (Genesis 29–30), whose name was changed to Israel (Genesis 32:28). Abraham was Jacob's grandfather, and

Abraham was promised by the Lord that great blessings would be available to his descendants (Genesis 12:2–3; Abraham 2:9–11). Thus, the "blood of Israel" is a reference to those who are heirs to the promised blessings of the Lord, through their faithfulness. All people can become "blood of Israel," regardless of genealogy, by being baptized and remaining faithful to the gospel of Jesus Christ.

BLOOD SACRIFICES

A prominent part of religious worship in the Old Testament. These blood sacrifices were symbolic of the sacrifice of the Son of God (Moses 5:4–8), whose Atonement provided resurrection for all (1 Corinthians 15:22) and paid for the sins of all those who repent and keep His commandments (2 Nephi 2:7). They were designed by the Lord to point the people's minds toward the future mission of Jesus Christ.

Blood sacrifices were done away with after the Savior's mortal mission was completed, because His was the "great and last sacrifice" (Alma 34:10).

BLOOD TRANSFUSIONS

The Church does not discourage individuals from giving or receiving blood or blood products. In fact, wards and stakes often promote blood drives. However, it is up to individuals and family members as to whether or not they choose to participate or allow transfusions and other medical uses of donated blood for loved ones who are not able to choose for themselves.

BODIES, PHYSICAL

One of the main reasons for coming to earth is to get a physical body. It is a major step in our Father's plan to become like Him (Matthew 5:48). He, Himself, has a glorified, resurrected body of flesh and bone (D&C 130:22).

BODIES, SPIRIT

Spirit is an actual form of matter (D&C 131:7–8). Thus, our spirit bodies, which we received when we were born to our heavenly parents in premortality ("Proclamation," 1995, paragraph 2), consist of actual matter. They have all the body parts our physical bodies have (Pratt, *Key to the Science of Theology*, p. 79).

BODY PARTS, DONATION OF

The Church approves the practice of donating organs and body parts. However, individuals are free to choose to do so or not. It is not a matter of righteousness or unrighteousness. Many members designate on their driver's licenses that they are organ donors.

BONDAGE, SPIRITUAL

Coming under the influence and control of the devil through sin or ignorance of the gospel (D&C 84:49; 138:57).

BOOK OF ABRAHAM

The translation by Joseph Smith of some ancient writings of Abraham, which were on papyrus and were acquired by the Church in 1835 for $2,400. In 1851, the Book of Abraham was published in England as part of the Pearl of Great Price, by Apostle Franklin D. Richards. It was officially accepted by the Church as scripture in general conference on October 10, 1880, in Salt Lake City, Utah. It is contained in the Pearl of Great Price today, which is one of the four books of scripture or "standard works" of the Church (the Bible, Book of Mormon, Doctrine and Covenants, Pearl of Great Price).

BOOK OF COMMANDMENTS

The predecessor to the Doctrine and Covenants. In a special conference held on November 1, 1831, approval was given to print a compilation of revelations which had been received by Joseph Smith over a period of time. Oliver Cowdery was instructed to take the manuscript for the Book of Commandments to Missouri where it was to be printed (D&C 69, heading). However, mobs in Missouri destroyed the press and the type as well as almost all of the copies of the Book of Commandments. Only a few were saved and are in existence today.

The Book of Commandments was 160 pages long and contained sixty-five revelations (D&C 2–66). By the time the Church was prepared to reprint the Book of Commandments, a number of additional revelations had been received by the Prophet; therefore, in 1835 the first publication of the Doctrine and Covenants was completed, which contained the sixty-five revelations along with more recent revelations.

BOOK OF ENOCH

A book of scripture that we have not yet been given, which will come forth to us sometime in the future (D&C 107:57).

BOOK OF JOSEPH OF EGYPT

Joseph Smith reported that, along with the scroll that contained writings of Abraham, he also had a scroll that contained some writings of Joseph, who was sold into Egypt (*HC* 2:236). However, nothing more is heard about this, and it is assumed by some that this scroll was destroyed or lost by enemies of the Church after the Prophet's martyrdom.

Other writings of Joseph of Egypt are found in 2 Nephi 3:6–17 and JST Genesis 50:24–38 (found in the JST section at the back of your LDS English edition of the Bible).

BOOK OF LIFE

The record kept in heaven of our lives, deeds, thoughts, and so forth, mentioned in Revelation 20:12 and elsewhere in scripture (D&C 128:7), which will be used at our final judgment.

The scriptures also speak of a "book of life" (Alma 5:58) which is also known as "the Lamb's Book of Life" (D&C 132:19) in which the names of those who will receive eternal life (exaltation) are written.

BOOK OF MORMON

A book of sacred scripture, translated from gold plates by Joseph Smith, which contains an account of ancient inhabitants of the Americas and the dealings of the Lord with them. Among other things, it contains a record of the visit of the resurrected Christ to these people (3 Nephi 9–28).

The Book of Mormon is another witness of Jesus Christ. On average, Christ is mentioned every 1.7 verses in its pages. Joseph Smith said that "the Book of Mormon was the most correct of any book on earth, and the keystone of our religion, and a man would get nearer to God by abiding by its precepts, than by any other book" (see Introduction to the Book of Mormon, paragraph 6).

The Book of Mormon consists of 15 books, and covers from 600 BC to AD 421, with one book (Ether) dealing with the Jaredites, whose record covers from the Tower of Babel to sometime after 600 BC (Omni 1:21–22).

The Book of Mormon is one of four books considered to be scripture by members of The Church of Jesus Christ of Latter-day Saints (the "Mormons"), and fulfills the prophecy of Ezekiel in which he foretold that the stick of Judah (the Bible) and the stick of Joseph (the Book of Mormon) would someday be joined together as witnesses for the truth of the gospel (Ezekiel 37:16–20).

BOOK OF MORMON AUTHORSHIP

As one reads the Book of Mormon, it becomes readily apparent from writing styles that it is a compilation of the writings of several different ancient authors. A number of studies have been conducted that verify this by "word prints."

BOOK OF MORMON, BIBLICAL PROPHESIES ABOUT

Prophecies about the Book of Mormon contained in the Bible include Isaiah 29, which gives fascinating detail about the coming forth of the Book of Mormon (see especially verses 11–12, whose fulfillment is recorded in JS—H 1:63–65, in the Pearl of Great Price).

The verses in Isaiah 29:13–14 foretell the role of the Book of Mormon in restoring the truths that are needed so that people can once again worship God in truth and light.

Isaiah 29:18 prophesies the good that will come to the honest of heart when they read the Book of Mormon (compare these verses of Isaiah with 2 Nephi 27:6–24, 29). Ezekiel 37:15–20 prophesies that the Book of Mormon will someday join forces with the Bible in bearing witness of the Lord's work. Yet another biblical prophecy foretells the visit of the resurrected Lord to the Americas (John 10:16), where He taught His "other sheep," as recorded in 3 Nephi in the Book of Mormon.

BOOK OF MORMON MANUSCRIPTS

There are two manuscripts for the Book of Mormon. The original was the manuscript that was handwritten mainly by Oliver Cowdery as Joseph Smith dictated to him as he translated from the gold plates. The second manuscript is referred to as the "printers manuscript," which was a copy of the original made by Oliver and two other scribes and which was used by the printer as the type was set for the first printing of the book.

Today, about 25 percent of the original manuscript pages exist and are in possession of the LDS Church Historical Department in Salt Lake City, Utah. One half of a sheet of the original manuscript is owned by the University of Utah.

BOOK OF MORMON PLATES

The gold plates, which Joseph Smith received from the angel Moroni, consisted of thin metal sheets, bound together by three rings, measuring about six inches wide, eight inches long, and about six inches thick (*HC* 4:537). It was estimated by one of the Eight Witnesses of the Book of Mormon, William Smith, that the stack of plates weighed about sixty pounds (Anderson, *Investigating the Book of Mormon Witnesses*, p. 23).

The set of plates was made up of:

1. The plates of Mormon (on which Mormon and his son, Moroni, made their abridgement of many records spoken of in the Book of Mormon)

2. The small plates of Nephi

3. Moroni's abridgment of the twenty-four gold plates of Ether

4. Some additions by Moroni

5. The sealed portion.

This stack of plates was buried in the earth by Moroni about AD 421. About 1,400 years later, in 1823, he appeared as a resurrected being to the Prophet Joseph Smith and revealed to him the location of the gold plates, which were buried in the Hill Cumorah in New York. Over the next four years, Moroni instructed Joseph and then allowed him to take the plates home on September 22, 1827, in order to begin translating them.

Within the Book of Mormon itself, several sets of metal plates are mentioned. They are:

1. The large plates of Nephi, from which the following books in the Book of Mormon came:

    a. The book of Lehi (the lost 116 pages)

    b. Mosiah

    c. Alma

    d. Helaman

    e. 3 Nephi

    f. 4 Nephi

2. The small plates of Nephi (which Mormon put in his stack of plates), from which the following came:

    a. 1 Nephi

    b. 2 Nephi

    c. Jacob

    d. Enos

    e. Jarom

    f. Omni

3. The plates of Mormon, which contain Mormon's abridgment of the large plates of Nephi along with his commentary and teaching, plus additional history and notes by Mormon and Moroni (the Words of Mormon, Mormon, and Moroni).

4. The plates of Ether (Moroni's abridgment of the twenty-four gold plates of Ether), from which the following came:

    a. Ether

5. The plates of brass (brought from Jerusalem by Lehi and his people). These plates contained the five books of Moses (what we know as Genesis, Exodus, Leviticus, Numbers, and Deuteronomy), the history of the Jews down to King Zedekiah (about 600 BC), and "the prophecies of the holy prophets" (1 Nephi 5:11–13), including Isaiah and others. Many quotes from these prophets appear in the Book of Mormon.

BOOK OF MORMON, TRANSLATION OF

Little is known about the actual process used in translating the gold plates. On one occasion, when asked to give details about how he translated them, Joseph Smith replied, "It was not intended to tell the world all the particulars of the coming forth of the Book of Mormon" (*Church History in the Fulness of Times*, p. 66, footnote 14).

Although Emma Smith, John Whitmer, and Martin Harris served

briefly as scribes during the translation, Oliver Cowdery was the main scribe. None of them ever said much about the translation process.

BOOK OF MORMON WITNESSES

There were two sets of witnesses to the Book of Mormon and the fact that Joseph Smith had the gold plates.

1. The Three Witnesses
2. The Eight Witnesses

The Three Witnesses, Oliver Cowdery, David Whitmer, and Martin Harris, whose testimony is recorded at the front of the Book of Mormon, were shown the gold plates by a heavenly messenger near the end of June 1829. In addition, the voice of God bore witness to them that the book is true. They were invited by the angel to handle the plates themselves. David Whitmer opted not to handle them, but Oliver Cowdery and Martin Harris did (Cook, *Revelations of Joseph Smith*, p. 28).

None of these witnesses ever retracted their testimony of the Book of Mormon, even though all three eventually left the Church. Oliver and Martin came back to the Church, but David did not.

The Eight Witnesses, whose testimony is likewise recorded in the introductory pages at the front of the Book of Mormon, were shown the gold plates by Joseph Smith, shortly after the Three Witnesses were shown them by an angel. The Eight testified that they lifted and handled the plates and paid special attention to the engravings thereon. The eight men were Christian Whitmer, Jacob Whitmer, Peter Whitmer Jr., John Whitmer, Hiram Page, Joseph Smith Sr., Hyrum Smith, and Samuel H. Smith. Three of the eight left the Church and never returned. They were Jacob Whitmer, John Whitmer, and Hiram Page. However, none of the Eight Witnesses ever retracted their testimony.

One additional witness to the Book of Mormon, Mary Whitmer, was shown the gold plates by an angel. This was for her own personal benefit rather than as an official witness. She was the wife of Peter Whitmer Sr., who had invited Joseph Smith and his wife, Emma, along with Oliver Cowdery, to move in with them while completing the translation of the gold plates. They accepted the invitation and moved from Harmony, Pennsylvania, to the Whitmer farm in Fayette, New York. This resulted in much additional work for Mrs. Whitmer, but she never complained. One evening, while going out to milk the cow, the angel appeared to her, complimented her for her uncomplaining acceptance of the additional workload, and showed her the plates so that she would know for herself that what Joseph was doing was the work of the Lord (*Church History in the Fulness of Times*, pp. 57–58).

BOOK OF MOSES

The first book contained in the Pearl of Great Price. It was given to Joseph Smith by direct revelation between June 1830 and February 1831 and is not a translation of ancient records by him. It is an extract of some chapters of Genesis from Joseph Smith's inspired translation of the Bible. It provides much that was left out of the Bible.

BOOK OF REMEMBRANCE

Journals or scrapbooks kept by many members of the Church containing family records, histories and accounts of their personal and family activities. The first book of remembrance was kept by Adam and Eve (Moses 6:5).

BOOK OF REVELATION

The last book in the New Testament, written about AD 95, by John, the Apostle. Revelation, which is also known as the Apocalypse, is not the last book written by John. He wrote the Gospel of John after the book of Revelation. The JST (Joseph Smith Translation of the Bible) makes changes in over eighty verses in Revelation, and thus becomes a significant key for understanding it. D&C 77 is also very helpful.

Chapters 1–3 of Revelation deal mainly with things in John's day, and chapters 4–22 are mainly about the future, including much about the last days before the Second Coming of the Savior. There is much use of symbolism in this book of scripture. You may wish to study the information given in this reference book under "Symbolism."

BOOK OF THE LAW OF GOD

Referred to in D&C 85:5. In this context, it was the official tithing record of the Church, as explained by Joseph F. Smith, October 1899 general conference.

BOOK OF THE NAMES OF THE SANCTIFIED

See BOOK OF LIFE.

BORN AGAIN

The process of being made a new person, a different person spiritually, through baptism and living the gospel as directed by the gift of the Holy Ghost. It can also be defined as the process of being made eligible, by living the gospel of Jesus Christ, to eventually return to the presence of the Father and live with Him forever (John 3:3, 7; Alma 5:49; 7:14; Moses 6:59).

BORN IN SIN

See also CONCEIVED IN SIN. Being born into a world in which there is much of sin and wickedness (Moses 6:55).

BORN IN THE COVENANT

Being born to parents whose marriage has been sealed in the temple for time and eternity (D&C 132:19).

BORN OF GOD

See BORN AGAIN.

BOTTOMLESS PIT

Another term for Satan's domain (Revelation 9:1–2), for the devil's status during the Millennium (Revelation 20:1–3), and ultimately his final destination— perdition, or outer darkness (Isaiah 14:15; D&C 76:36–38, 43–48).

BRANCH PRESIDENTS

Presiding officers in local Church units where there are not sufficient members to have a ward with a bishop presiding.

BRASS PLATES, THE

Records on thin metal plates kept by Laban (1 Nephi 3:1–4). They basically contained the Old Testament, up to and including some writings of Jeremiah (1 Nephi 5:10–16). Nephi and his brothers were commanded by the Lord to go back to Jerusalem and get them and bring them into the wilderness so that they would have access to the scriptures (1 Nephi 3–5). The brass plates are still in existence, in the care of the Lord, and will someday be made available to us (1 Nephi 5:18–19).

BRAZEN SEA

A baptismal font placed on the backs of twelve brass oxen in Solomon's Temple. It was about fifteen feet in diameter and seven and a half feet deep (1 Kings 7:23–25). Baptisms were performed in Old Testament times, but all direct references to this ordinance have been taken out of the Old Testament (*MD*, pp. 103–4). We do have a direct reference to baptism by Isaiah, as given in 1 Nephi 20:1.

We understand that there would have been no baptisms for the dead performed in this font, because there were no baptisms for the dead until after the Savior's resurrection. The gospel was first preached in the post-mortal spirit world after the crucifixion (1 Peter 3:18–20; D&C 138). Baptism for the dead was mentioned by the Apostle Paul (1 Corinthians 15:29).

BRAZEN SERPENT

A figure of a serpent, made of brass by Moses under the direction of the Lord. He placed it on a staff and invited Israelites who had been bitten by poisonous "fiery flying serpents" to look at the brass serpent and be healed (Numbers 21:4–9). We are taught in the Book of Mormon that this is symbolic of looking to Christ and being healed by Him (Alma 33:19–22; Helaman 8:14–15).

BREAD OF LIFE

Another name for the Savior. He gave a sermon, often referred to as "the Bread of Life sermon," in which He compared Himself to bread from heaven (John 6:30–65). Symbolically, He was the "bread of eternal life" by which we are nourished and enabled to grow to the point of obtaining eternal life, meaning exaltation in the celestial kingdom of heaven.

BREATH OF LIFE

Symbolic of mortal life, given to us by God (Genesis 2:7; Moses 3:7; Ezekiel 37:5–10).

BRETHREN, THE

A term commonly used by members to refer to the General Authorities, who form the central leadership of the Church.

BRIDE, SYMBOLISM OF

There are two elements to this symbolism: the Bridegroom or Groom, who is Christ, and the bride, meaning the Church, or faithful, covenant-keeping members. Such faithful followers of Christ will ultimately belong to Him (Revelation 21:2) in the sense of being His "children," in other words, His faithful followers (Mosiah 5:7). At the Second Coming, the "Groom" will come for the "bride" (D&C 109:72–74). More of this symbolism is given in Isaiah 62:5.

BRIDE OF THE LAMB

See BRIDE, SYMBOLISM OF.

BRIDEGROOM, SYMBOLISM OF

See BRIDE, SYMBOLISM OF.

BRIGHAM YOUNG

The second president of the Church. He was sustained as president on Monday, December 27, 1847, at a conference of the Church held in Kanesville, Iowa, after having led the Church for about three years as the president of the Quorum of the Twelve Apostles. Brigham Young led the Saints west to the Salt Lake Valley after the martyrdom of the Prophet Joseph Smith in Carthage, Illinois, on June 27, 1844.

He is considered the greatest colonizer in American history, having directed the settlement of hundreds of communities in the West. He died on August 29, 1877, in Salt Lake City.

BRIGHAM YOUNG UNIVERSITY

A private university, owned and operated by The Church of Jesus Christ of Latter-day Saints, and located in Provo, Utah. It has an enrollment of over 30,000 students.

BRIGHT AND MORNING STAR

Jesus Christ (Revelation 22:16). Symbolically, Jesus "stands out" as the "brightest star" among all the spirit children of the Father.

BRIMSTONE

Molten sulfur, often associated symbolically in the scriptures with fire and the punishments of God upon the wicked (Luke 17:29; Revelation 9:17–21). There is no such thing as a literal "lake of fire and brimstone" (Revelation 20:10; 2 Nephi 9:16).

BROKEN HEART

See CONTRITE SPIRIT.

BROTHER OF JARED, NAME OF

The brother of Jared was an ancient prophet who was led to the Americas by the Lord, along with his brother, Jared, and their families and friends, at the time of the Tower of Babel (Ether 1:33–42).

We learn from modern revelation that his name was Mahonri Moriancumer. "Elder George Reynolds has left us this account of the circumstances under which the full name was revealed to the Prophet: 'While residing in Kirtland, Elder Reynolds Cahoon had a son born to him. One day when President Joseph Smith was passing his door he called the prophet in and asked him to bless and name the baby. Joseph did so and gave the boy the name of Mahonri Moriancumer. When he had finished the blessing, he laid the child on the bed, and turning to Elder Cahoon he said, the name I have given your son is the name of the Brother of Jared; the Lord has just shown (or revealed) it to me. Elder William F. Cahoon, who was standing near, heard the Prophet make this statement to his Father; and this was the first time the name of the Brother of Jared was known in the Church in this dispensation.' (*Juvenile Instructor,* vol. 27, p. 282; *Improvement Era*, vol. 8, pp. 704–705.)" (*MD*, p. 463).

BUFFETINGS OF SATAN

Being turned over to Satan to be tormented and afflicted, without any protection from God. Such punishment is only for those who have an extensive knowledge of the gospel of Jesus Christ, who have made covenants with God, and then turned from Him and violated their covenants (D&C 78:11–12; 82:20–21; 104:9–10; 132:26). For such individuals, this is the only way in which complete forgiveness is available to them.

Apostle Bruce R. McConkie taught: "To be turned over to the buffetings of Satan is to be given into his hands; it is to be turned over to him with all the protective power of the priesthood, of righteousness and of godliness removed, so that Lucifer is free to torment, persecute, and afflict such a person without let or hindrance. When the bars are down, the cuffs and curses of Satan, both in this world and in the world to come, bring indescribable anguish typified by burning fire and brimstone. The damned in hell so suffer" (*MD*, p. 108).

BURIAL

The Church counsels its members to bury their dead in graves, unless the laws of the country in which they live require cremation or the deceased requested cremation. The final decision whether to bury, cremate, place in the ocean, etc., is ultimately left to the family of the deceased. It is not a matter of good or evil.

An endowed member is buried in temple clothing. A deceased sister is dressed in her temple clothing by Relief Society sisters. A brother is so dressed by priesthood brethren. If the body is in such condition of degradation that it cannot be dressed, the temple clothing may be laid over it. If a body is to be cremated, it may be dressed in temple clothing and then cremated.

Normal practice of the Church is to

have a funeral, conducted by or under the direction of the bishop or branch president. Where possible, they are to be about the same length as a sacrament meeting, and the teaching of the plan of salvation should be given a prominent role.

At the burial, after the funeral, a Melchizedek Priesthood holder may be asked to dedicate the grave as the final resting place for the deceased. He does so by the power of the priesthood he holds and in the name of Jesus Christ, saying other things as directed by the Spirit.

BURNINGS, EVERLASTING

A description of the glory that exists in the presence of God (D&C 137:2–3). Joseph Smith taught: "The spirits of the just are exalted to a greater and more glorious work; hence they are blessed in their departure to the world of spirits. Enveloped in flaming fire, they are not far from us, and know and understand our thoughts, feelings, and motions, and are often pained therewith. Flesh and blood cannot go there; but flesh and bones, quickened by the Spirit of God, can" (*TPJS*, p. 326).

· C ·

CAFFEINE DRINKS

Before we address the topic of caffeine drinks, we will note that tea, coffee, alcohol, and tobacco are substances to be avoided by faithful members of the Church, as stated in the Word of Wisdom (D&C 89:5, 7–9). Temple recommends can be withheld for violation of these commandments from God. Drug abuse is also to be avoided.

The Church leaves the matter of caffeine drinks up to individual members, with counsel such as the following: "With reference to cola drinks, the Church has never officially taken a position on this matter, but the leaders of the Church have advised, and we do now specifically advise, against the use of any drink containing harmful habit-forming drugs under circumstances that would result in acquiring the habit. Any beverage that contains ingredients harmful to the body should be avoided." (Priesthood Bulletin, February 1972, p. 4). Drinking colas and other caffeine drinks are not grounds for withholding a temple recommend.

CAIN

The son of Adam and Eve who killed his brother, Abel (Genesis 4:8). Adam and Eve had numerous children before they had Cain (Moses 5:2, 16). Cain had a rebellious attitude (Moses 5:16) and, over time, came to the point where he "loved Satan more than God" (Moses 5:18). He held the priesthood

(*TPJS*, p. 169) and was expected to offer sacrifices as a part of worshipping the Lord. He apparently refused to do so, until Satan commanded him to make an offering (Moses 5:18). He obeyed Satan and brought "fruit of the ground" (Moses 5:19) rather than an animal sacrifice, which was required in order to symbolize the blood of the Lamb of God (*TPJS*, p. 58).

His inappropriate offering was rejected by the Lord, and Cain became bitter and angry (Moses 5:20–21). Cain was given the opportunity to repent (Moses 5:22–25), but he refused (Moses 5:26).

Satan taught him how to murder and, eventually, he killed Abel (Moses 5:28–33). He was cursed by the Lord (Moses 5:36–37), and a mark was placed upon him (Moses 5:40). When faced by the Lord for his terrible sin, he had no remorse or concern for Abel and his family, but only for himself (Moses 5:35–39). Since his time, murder and killing have been a common part of society.

CALAMITIES, LAST DAYS

There are many prophecies in the scriptures foretelling severe troubles and calamities in the last days, leading up to the Second Coming of the Savior (Matthew 24:6–8; JS—M 1:23, 29–30, 32; Revelation 8–9, 16–17). Many of these "signs of the times" are in the process of being fulfilled in our day. The counsel of the Church to its members is to not panic or get caught up in gloom and doom.

Rather, they are counseled to be prepared with sufficient food storage and financial resources to tide them over in case of natural disasters or other emergencies. They are also counseled to listen to the living prophets through whom the Lord speaks, in order to best use their resources and have stability and happiness in spite of last day's conditions.

CALLING AND ELECTION SURE

The basic meaning of the phrase, as used by Peter (2 Peter 1:10) is to faithfully live the gospel such that you ultimately receive exaltation in the highest degree of glory in the celestial kingdom. Peter gives counsel as to how this is accomplished (2 Peter 1:3–10).

In addition to acquiring the character qualities listed by Peter, a faithful member of the Church must receive the ordinances of the gospel, including the temple ordinances (D&C 131:2–3; 132:19–20) in order to make his or her calling and election sure.

In a simple and basic explanation of this phrase, one might think of it as follows: God "calls" or invites all of His children to live so that they can return to live with Him in exaltation. At the time of final judgment, He "elects" or votes for those who have proven worthy to attain exaltation. When He "votes" for such a person, he or she is in, for "sure."

Another way of looking at the wording in this phrase is as follows: If

God "calls" you to Him, on the day of final judgment, and informs you that He has "elected," or chosen, you for exaltation, it is for "sure" that you are in. And the reason He can do this for you is that you lived the gospel and the Atonement of Jesus Christ made you clean and worthy to dwell with Him forever.

There is some speculation and discussion among members of the Church, occasionally, about a ceremony or ordinance which has been performed for some in which their calling and election has already been made sure. However, until the living prophet gives clear instruction about this, it is best not to draw final conclusions about it.

CALVARY

The place outside of Jerusalem where the Savior was crucified (Luke 23:33). It is also called Golgotha, which means "a place of a skull" (Matthew 27:33).

CANCELLATION OF SEALING

The proper term for what some members mistakenly refer to as "a temple divorce." When conditions warrant it, people who were sealed in the temple and later obtain a civil divorce may apply through their bishop and stake president for a cancellation of sealing. Such applications go directly to the First Presidency, who hold the keys to "bind" and "loose" (Matthew 16:19), for inspired consideration. When granted, such a cancellation

allows a worthy member to be sealed to someone else in the temple.

CANON OF SCRIPTURE

The Bible, Book of Mormon, Doctrine and Covenants, and the Pearl of Great Price. "Canon" means a collection of religious literature considered to be scripture. "Canonized" means sacred writings which have been accepted as scripture by a church.

CAPITAL PUNISHMENT

The death penalty. Ancient scriptures endorse capital punishment as an appropriate penalty for murder (Leviticus 24:17; JST, Genesis 9:12). In the days of the Old Testament, civil and religious leaders were the same people, and thus, capital punishment was administered.

In modern times, however, with separation of church and state, capital punishment is the responsibility of the state, after proper and lawful legal proceedings. Modern revelation does not oppose capital punishment but clearly states that it is the domain of the state, not the Church (D&C 42:19, 79).

CARD PLAYING

There are many games which are played using various types of cards which are wholesome, entertaining, and which promote social interaction. Many are educational (see *New Era*, Oct. 1984, pp. 49–50). The use of face cards as a means of gambling is not in harmony with the teachings of the Church.

CARNAL, CARNALITY

Lifestyles which reflect giving in to the desires of the flesh (Moses 5:13). Carnal living can include sexual immorality, robbery, plundering, murder, abusive behavior, and anything which takes the place of Christlike living.

CARTHAGE JAIL

The jail in Carthage, Illinois, in which the Prophet Joseph Smith and his brother, Hyrum, were murdered on June 27, 1844. It is now owned by the Church and has been turned into a beautiful visitors' center.

On the day of the martyrdom, shortly after 5:00 PM, a mob of men with blackened faces, called the Carthage Greys, stormed the jail, went up the stairs, and began shooting through the closed wooden door into the room where Joseph, Hyrum, Willard Richards, and John Taylor were staying.

Hyrum was the first one hit and fell to the floor mortally wounded. John Taylor was critically wounded but survived. Joseph was shot by the mob from inside the jail as well as by members of the mob firing from outside, below the window, and fell from the window landing by a well, thus sealing his testimony with his blood. Willard Richards was miraculously unscathed except for a tiny bullet nick in one ear.

John Taylor later wrote: "Joseph Smith, the Prophet and Seer of the Lord, has done more, save Jesus only, for the salvation of men in this world, than any other man that ever lived in it. In the short space of twenty years, he has brought forth the Book of Mormon, which he translated by the gift and power of God, and has been the means of publishing it on two continents; has sent the fulness of the everlasting gospel, which it contained, to the four quarters of the earth; has brought forth the revelations and commandments which compose this book of Doctrine and Covenants, and many other wise documents and instructions for the benefit of the children of men; gathered many thousands of the Latter-day Saints, founded a great city, and left a fame and name that cannot be slain. He lived great, and he died great in the eyes of God and his people; and like most of the Lord's anointed in ancient times, has sealed his mission and his works with his own blood; and so has his brother Hyrum. In life they were not divided, and in death they were not separated!" (D&C 135:3).

CAVE MAN

We do not have sufficient revelation on this subject to do more than speculate. However, we are told that all things will be revealed when the Savior arrives for the Millennium (D&C 101:32–34). We do know that Adam and Eve were not cavemen. Rather, they were highly intelligent, knew how to read and write, and taught their children to do so (Moses 6:5–6).

CELESTIAL BEINGS

People who are resurrected with celestial bodies (D&C 88:28) and who will live in the celestial kingdom. This earth will become a celestial planet, and celestial beings from it will dwell on it forever (D&C 130:9–11). The bodies of celestial beings differ from the bodies of terrestrial and telestial beings, just as the sun differs from the moon and the stars (1 Corinthians 15:39–42; D&C 88:28–32).

CELESTIAL BODIES

Glorified, resurrected physical bodies of flesh and bone, such as those possessed by the Father and the Son (D&C 76:70; 130:22). Each celestial body is made up of intelligence, spirit, and a physical body of flesh and bone, permanently joined together by the resurrection.

Celestial bodies have all the powers of "natural" bodies (D&C 88:28), including the powers of procreation (D&C 132:19), and will be our "same" body (D&C 88:28) which has been perfected through the resurrection (Alma 40:23).

We suspect that no matter how "perfect" or healthy our mortal bodies have been at some point in our lives, celestial bodies will be vastly better.

CELESTIAL EARTH

This earth will die, be resurrected (D&C 88:26), and will eventually become the celestial kingdom for those from it who prove worthy of celestial glory (D&C 130:9–11). Joseph Smith taught that the earth will eventually be "rolled back into the presence of God, and crowned with celestial glory" (*TPJS*, p. 181).

Other earths will become celestial kingdoms for their worthy inhabitants, and they, too, will be moved back into the presence of God to live in celestial glory (*JD* 17:331–32).

CELESTIAL KINGDOM

The highest of the three degrees of glory spoken of in scripture (1 Corinthians 15:40–42; D&C 76:50–70). Within the celestial kingdom itself, there are three degrees (D&C 131:1). The highest of these degrees is called "exaltation." It is the glory in which marriage and the family unit will exist (D&C 131:1–4). Those who attain exaltation will be gods (Psalm 82:6; John 10:34; 132:19–20).

CELESTIAL LAW

The laws and commandments which must be kept if one is to inherit the celestial kingdom. The basic requirements are listed in D&C 76:50–53.

CELESTIAL MARRIAGE

Often referred to in our day as "temple marriage." Such marriages are performed in temples operated by the Church by authorized priesthood holders who hold the keys to perform these ordinances (D&C 132:19). Worthy couples who are thus married, and who continue to live the gospel faithfully, will be married to each other in the next life and will become gods and continue as a family unit eternally (D&C 132:19–20).

CELESTIAL TIME

Mentioned in Abraham, Facsimile No. 2, Explanation, Fig. 1. God's time system is the same as the time system on the planet Kolob (Abraham 5:13). One day on Kolob is equal to one thousand years on earth (Facsimile No. 2, Fig. 1; 2 Peter 3:8).

CELIBACY

The practice of avoiding marriage because of one's religious beliefs. Celibacy, as a religious teaching, is contrary to the commandments of God (Genesis 1:28; D&C 49:15). "Forbidding to marry" was a sign of apostasy mentioned by the Apostle Paul (1 Timothy 4:3).

CHAINS OF HELL

Being in the captivity of the devil (Alma 12:11).

CHAPLAINS

Military officers who serve as religious advisers and ministers to personnel in the armed forces. The Church has a corps of trained chaplains who conduct religious services and provide counseling, classroom instruction, and other support to soldiers and their families.

CHARITY

There are many definitions of charity, including the giving of assistance to the poor and a general attitude of unselfish service to others. The highest definition of charity is "the pure love of Christ" (Moroni 7:47), which encompasses a number of desirable character traits and Christlike qualities (Moroni 7:44–48; 1 Corinthians 13:1–13). Without possessing the virtue of charity, it would be impossible for an individual to enter celestial glory (Ether 12:34).

CHASTENING

Being scolded for inappropriate behavior by the Lord because of His love for us. It is designed to help us change our ways and eventually return to live with Him (D&C 95:1).

CHASTITY, LAW OF

The Church teaches strict avoidance of sexual involvement before marriage and complete fidelity to one's spouse after marriage. The law of chastity refers to the laws of God forbidding any sexual activity outside of marriage, including adultery (Exodus 20:14), fornication, homosexual relations, incest, bestiality (Exodus 22:16; Leviticus 18:6–23), pornography, necking, petting, masturbation, and so forth (D&C 59:6). The gospel teaches that sexual sin is next to murder in seriousness (Alma 39:5).

One severe penalty for failing to repent of breaking the law of chastity and continuing in such activity is the loss of the Spirit (D&C 42:23), which leaves a person an easy target for Satan.

The Lord does not require that physical desires for sexual activity be done away with and destroyed in us. Rather, He requires that these passions be "bridled" (Alma 38:12) to be used appropriately only within the bonds of marriage.

It is possible to repent sincerely and completely from breaking the law of chastity (D&C 42:25; Isaiah 1:18; D&C 58:42–43), thus qualifying for the highest blessings of the gospel of Jesus Christ, including exaltation.

CHERUBIM
A type of angelic being in heaven (Moses 4:31; Exodus 24:18).

CHILDREN OF ABRAHAM
See ABRAHAM, SEED OF.

CHILDREN OF BELIAL
See BELIAL, SONS OF.

CHILDREN OF CHRIST
Faithful followers of Jesus Christ (Mosiah 5:7).

CHILDREN OF DISOBEDIENCE
The wicked (Ephesians 2:2; D&C 21:17).

CHILDREN OF GOD
All of us are spirit sons and daughters of the Father (Hebrews 12:9). But, in the scriptures, this phrase usually refers to the righteous (Genesis 6:2; Mosiah 5:7) and ultimately to those who are exalted by their faithfulness to the gospel and through the Atonement of Jesus Christ (D&C 76:24).

CHILDREN OF ISRAEL
See also ISRAEL. The descendants of Abraham, through Isaac and Jacob.

Jacob had twelve sons (Gen 29–30). His name was changed by the Lord to "Israel" (Genesis 32:28). Thus, his descendants are called "the children of Israel" (Genesis 45:21; 46:8). Moses led the children of Israel out of Egypt (Exodus 1:13; 12:40; 15:19), and Joshua led them into the promised land (Joshua 3–4).

CHILDREN OF JACOB
See CHILDREN OF ISRAEL.

CHILDREN OF LIGHT
The righteous, who believe in and follow Jesus Christ (John 12:36).

CHILDREN OF THE COVENANT
The faithful followers of Jesus Christ, who make and keep covenants and receive all of the blessings of the gospel (3 Nephi 20:24–27) as promised in the covenant that the Lord made with Abraham (Abraham 2:9–11). All people, regardless of lineage, who join the Church and faithfully continue learning and living the gospel, are "children of the covenant."

CHILDREN, SALVATION OF LITTLE
We read that "all children who die before they arrive at the years of accountability are saved in the celestial kingdom of heaven" (D&C 137:10). We are told that the age of accountability is eight (D&C 68:27). Furthermore, we are taught that such

children will "inherit their exaltation" (Smith, *Gospel Doctrine*, p. 453). Thus, we understand that, as adult spirits in paradise, they will have the opportunity to socialize and choose a mate, to whom they can be sealed during the Millennium, thus eventually entering exaltation with their own family units and becoming gods.

CHOICE

Another term for agency (1 Nephi 7:15). Also means highly favored or blessed (1 Nephi 2:20).

CHOSEN ONE, THE

Jesus Christ (Moses 4:2; 7:39).

CHOSEN PEOPLE

Those who, through their righteousness, are chosen to receive the blessings of the Lord (Helaman 15:3; D&C 121:34). The term is sometimes used to refer to the Lord's covenant people or Israel.

CHRIST, JESUS

See JESUS CHRIST.

CHRIST AS THE FATHER

Through His gospel and Atonement, Jesus Christ is the "father" of our salvation (Mosiah 15:1–3). This imagery is used commonly in other ways, such as George Washington is the "father" of our country, Henry Ford is the "father" of the assembly line and mass production, Thomas Edison is the "father" of the incandescent light bulb, and so forth.

CHRIST, LIGHT OF

Christ is "the true light which lighteth every man that cometh into the world" (John 1:9). It is often referred to as being our conscience, which indeed it is, but it is far more. D&C 88:6–13 gives much more insight as to the powerful influence of the light of Christ.

Ultimately, the purpose of the light of Christ is to guide people to the true gospel, where they can receive baptism and the gift of the Holy Ghost. With the constant companionship of the Holy Ghost, which is a far more powerful "light," we are led forward toward exaltation.

CHRISTIANITY

In a general sense, the term for those who, to one degree or another, believe in Jesus Christ. Some Christians claim that members of The Church of Jesus Christ of Latter-day Saints are not Christians. Their thinking is derived from their belief that, since Mormons do not believe in the same Christ as they do (which, for example, for them involves being saved by grace and not by works), Latter-day Saints can't be considered Christians.

In reality, members of The Church of Jesus Christ of Latter-day Saints believe in Christ much more thoroughly that any others can, because they have the restored gospel. "And we talk of Christ, we rejoice in Christ, we preach of Christ, we prophesy of Christ, and we write according to our prophecies, that our children may know to what source they may look for a remission of their sins" (2 Nephi 25:26).

CHRISTMAS

We believe in celebrating Christmas on December 25, along with other Christians, even though we believe that the Son of God was born in the springtime (D&C 20:1), while shepherds were "keeping watch over their flock by night" (Luke 1:8) in the Holy Land. "Most Latter-day Saints include some of the traditions, games, decorations, music, and food associated with the Christmas customs of their homelands in their family celebrations. Such items as Christmas trees, stockings, gifts, and greeting cards add to the beauty of the holiday and are not discouraged. But the recommended focus is religious. The Church encourages family closeness, concern for neighbors, thoughtfulness for fellow workers, renewal of friendships, and acts of Christlike love, giving, and celebration. Appropriate sermons, lessons, songs, and programs are presented in Sabbath services during the Christmas season. Latter-day Saints are cautioned that holiday shopping, decorating, and festivities should not obscure the remembrance of Christ nor hinder the quest for peace on earth" (*EM*).

CHURCH DISCIPLINE

See DISCIPLINARY COUNCIL.

CHURCH EDUCATIONAL SYSTEM

The Church has established educational programs throughout the United States and in over ninety other countries in order to provide a balance between secular education and religious education. Brigham Young University, BYU–Hawaii, BYU–Idaho, and LDS Business College provide higher education opportunities. Seminaries and Institutes of Religion provide weekday religious education for high school age and college age students.

CHURCH AND STATE

We believe in the separation of church and state and that it should continue until the arrival of the Millennium, when the Savior will become "King of Kings, and Lord of Lords" (Revelation 19:16), resulting in the "full end of all nations" (D&C 87:6).

Some critics get irritated when the Church speaks out on issues that they consider to be political but which the Church considers to be matters of morality. Such issues in the past have included gambling, sale and distribution of alcohol, the Equal Rights Amendment, and the legalization of gay marriages.

CHURCH HISTORIAN

On March 8, 1831, John Whitmer was called to be Church historian (D&C 47:1). Before that time, Oliver Cowdery had served in that capacity (D&C 47, heading). Keeping historical records has always been a part of the Lord's Church and began with

Adam and Eve (Moses 6:5).

The office of Church historian continues today and the Church Historian's Office contains voluminous records pertaining to the history of the Church.

CHURCH OF JESUS CHRIST OF LATTER-DAY SAINTS, THE

The official name of the Church, given by the Lord in a revelation to the Prophet Joseph Smith (D&C 115:3–4). Prior to the time of this revelation, several names for the Church had been used, including "The Church of Christ," "The Church of Jesus Christ," "The Church of God," and "The Church of the Latter-day Saints."

CHURCH OF THE DEVIL

Another name for "Satan's kingdom" (1 Nephi 22:22–23). We are taught that the church of the devil consists of all entities and philosophies that exist in opposition to the "church of the Lamb of God" (1 Nephi 14:10). Thus, anything that leads people away from God can properly be called the church of the devil.

CHURCH OF THE FIRSTBORN

Another name for exaltation (D&C 76:54–56, 58).

CIRCUMCISION

Circumcision was the token of the covenant that Abraham made with God when his name was changed from Abram to Abraham (Genesis 17:9–14; BD, under "Circumcision"). Circumci-

sion was continued throughout the Old Testament and became a strict part of the law of Moses (Exodus 12:48). It became a source of extreme controversy in the New Testament church (Acts 15:1–31), since it was done away with by the gospel which Jesus brought (Moroni 8:8). Some Jewish converts insisted that it be continued in the Church which Jesus established. It is not required in the Church today.

CITY OF ENOCH

The city which Enoch (approximately 3400–3000 BC) established by preaching the gospel to very wicked people (Moses 7:32–36). Those who repented joined Enoch and his people, building the City of Enoch. The city is described by Moses: "And the Lord called his people Zion, because they were of one heart and one mind, and dwelt in righteousness; and there was no poor among them" (Moses 7:18).

The city was eventually taken up into heaven (Moses 7:16–21, 69). The residents of the city were translated and taken up with their houses, land, gardens, cattle, and so forth (*Discourses of Brigham Young*, p. 105). They were resurrected at the time the Savior was resurrected (D&C 133:54–55). The City of Enoch will return to earth with the Savior in conjunction with His Second Coming (Moses 7:62–65).

CITY OF ZION

There are several different definitions for this term, including the City of

Enoch (Moses 7:19, 69), New Jerusalem (D&C 84:1–4, Moses 7:62), and the early settlement of the Saints in Jackson County, Missouri (D&C 104:48).

Joseph Smith provided an inspired plan or layout for the City of Zion in a document known as the City of Zion plan, in 1833. This plan included "a regular grid pattern with square blocks, wide streets (132 feet), alternating half-acre lots so that houses face alternate streets on each block, uniform brick or stone construction, homes set back twenty-five feet from the street, front yard landscaping, gardens in the backyard, the location of farms outside of town, and the designation of central blocks as a site for temples, schools, and other public buildings" (*EM*, under "City Planning").

Elements of this plan for a City of Zion are seen in many early Latter-day Saint settlements, including the original layout of Kirtland, Ohio; Salt Lake City, Utah; and numerous cities and towns settled by the Saints in Utah and surrounding states.

CIVIL GOVERNMENTS, THE CHURCH'S STAND ON

The Church teaches its members to honor and respect the law of the land in which they live. This includes saluting the country flag and showing appropriate respect to government leaders. "We believe in being subject to kings, presidents, rulers, and magistrates, in obeying, honoring, and sustaining the law" (Articles of Faith 1:12).

The following verses from the Doctrine and Covenants state the Church's position on several aspects of civil government:

D&C 134:1–9

1 We believe that governments were instituted of God for the benefit of man; and that he holds men accountable for their acts in relation to them, both in making laws and administering them, for the good and safety of society.

2 We believe that no government can exist in peace, except such laws are framed and held inviolate as will secure to each individual the free exercise of conscience, the right and control of property, and the protection of life.

3 We believe that all governments necessarily require civil officers and magistrates to enforce the laws of the same; and that such as will administer the law in equity and justice should be sought for and upheld by the voice of the people if a republic, or the will of the sovereign.

4 We believe that religion is instituted of God; and that men are amenable to him, and to him only, for the exercise of it, unless their religious opinions prompt them to infringe upon the rights and liberties of others; but we do not believe that human law has a right to interfere in prescribing rules of worship to bind the consciences of men, nor dictate forms for public or private devotion; that the civil magistrate

should restrain crime, but never control conscience; should punish guilt, but never suppress the freedom of the soul.

5 We believe that all men are bound to sustain and uphold the respective governments in which they reside, while protected in their inherent and inalienable rights by the laws of such governments; and that sedition and rebellion are unbecoming every citizen thus protected, and should be punished accordingly; and that all governments have a right to enact such laws as in their own judgments are best calculated to secure the public interest; at the same time, however, holding sacred the freedom of conscience.

6 We believe that every man should be honored in his station, rulers and magistrates as such, being placed for the protection of the innocent and the punishment of the guilty; and that to the laws all men show respect and deference, as without them peace and harmony would be supplanted by anarchy and terror; human laws being instituted for the express purpose of regulating our interests as individuals and nations, between man and man; and divine laws given of heaven, prescribing rules on spiritual concerns, for faith and worship, both to be answered by man to his Maker.

7 We believe that rulers, states, and governments have a right, and are bound to enact laws for the protection of all citizens in the free exercise of their religious belief; but we do not believe that they have a right in justice to deprive citizens of this privilege, or proscribe them in their opinions, so long as a regard and reverence are shown to the laws and such religious opinions do not justify sedition nor conspiracy.

8 We believe that the commission of crime should be punished according to the nature of the offense; that murder, treason, robbery, theft, and the breach of the general peace, in all respects, should be punished according to their criminality and their tendency to evil among men, by the laws of that government in which the offense is committed; and for the public peace and tranquility all men should step forward and use their ability in bringing offenders against good laws to punishment.

9 We do not believe it just to mingle religious influence with civil government, whereby one religious society is fostered and another proscribed in its spiritual privileges, and the individual rights of its members, as citizens, denied.

CIVIL MARRIAGE

The Church teaches that civil marriages are legal and binding and that the covenants made by the husband and wife are to be honored and respected.

In many countries and municipalities, civil law requires that even a Latter-day Saint couple who plans to marry in the temple must first be married in a civil ceremony. In cases where the couple is married only in the temple, the priesthood holder performing the ceremony has been given authority by the civil government to perform marriages in that jurisdiction.

CIVIL RIGHTS

A statement made on August 17, 1835, summarizes the Church's stand regarding civil rights: "We believe that no government can exist in peace, except such laws are framed and held inviolate as will secure to each individual the free exercise of conscience, the right and control of property, and the protection of life. We believe that religion is instituted of God; and that men are amenable to him, and to him only, for the exercise of it, unless their religious opinions prompt them to infringe upon the rights and liberties of others; but we do not believe that human law has a right to interfere in prescribing rules of worship to bind the consciences of men, nor dictate forms for public or private devotion; that the civil magistrate should restrain crime, but never control conscience; should punish guilt, but never suppress the freedom of the soul" (D&C 134:2, 4).

CIVIL WAR PROPHECY

Joseph Smith prophesied the Civil War twenty-eight years before it started. On December 25, 1832 he said:

"Verily, thus saith the Lord concerning the wars that will shortly come to pass, beginning at the rebellion of South Carolina, which will eventually terminate in the death and misery of many souls; and the time will come that war will be poured out upon all nations, beginning at this place. For behold, the Southern States shall be divided against the Northern States, and the Southern States will call on other nations, even the nation of Great Britain, as it is called, and they shall also call upon other nations, in order to defend themselves against other nations; and then war shall be poured out upon all nations" (D&C 87:1–3).

Later, on April 2, 1843, Joseph Smith stated, "I prophesy, in the name of the Lord God, that the commencement of the difficulties which will cause much bloodshed previous to the coming of the Son of Man will be in South Carolina. It may probably arise through the slave question. This a voice declared to me, while I was praying earnestly on the subject, December 25th, 1832" (D&C 130:12–13).

COFFEE

In the law of health and spiritual well-being known to the Church as the "Word of Wisdom," the Lord said: "Hot drinks are not for the body or belly" (D&C 89:9). "Hyrum Smith, Assistant President of the Church, later defined 'hot drinks' as coffee and tea (*Times & Seasons* 3 [June 1, 1842]:800), establishing the official interpretation for subsequent generations. The Word of Wisdom was given originally to show the will of God, though not as a commandment. Abstinence from coffee has been expected of fully participating members since the early twentieth century" (*EM*, under "Coffee").

Some members suggest that the reason that the Lord prohibits drinking coffee is that it contains caffeine. However, the Lord has given no revelation to that effect. Therefore, such thinking must be considered a matter of opinion, not Church doctrine.

COLA DRINKS
See CAFFEINE DRINKS.

COLUMBUS, CHRISTOPHER
Was inspired by the Spirit of the Lord to organize his exploring expedition and continue sailing until he arrived in the New World (1 Nephi 13:12).

Columbus himself spoke of the help he received from the Lord. Quoting from *Columbus, Don Quixote of the Seas*, written in German by Jacob Wassermann and translated into English by Eric Sutton, we read [quoting Columbus]:

" 'From my first youth onward, I was a seaman and have so continued until this day. . . . Wherever on the earth a ship has been, I have been. I have spoken and treated with learned men, priests, and laymen, Latins and Greeks, Jews and Moors, and with many men of other faiths. The Lord was well disposed to my desire, and He bestowed upon me courage and understanding; knowledge of seafaring He gave me in abundance, of astrology as much as was needed, and of geometry and astronomy likewise. Further, He gave me joy and cunning in drawing maps and thereon cities, mountains, rivers, islands, and harbours, each one in its place. I have seen and truly I have studied all books—cosmographies, histories, chronicles, and philosophies, and other arts, for which our Lord unlocked my mind, sent me upon the sea, and gave me fire for the deed. Those who heard of my emprise called it foolish, mocked me, and laughed. But who can doubt but that the Holy Ghost inspired me?' (Boston: Little, Brown, and Co., 1930, pp. 19–20. Italics added.)" (Petersen, *The Great Prologue*, pp. 25–26).

COMFORTER, THE
See HOLY GHOST.

COMMANDMENTS
Rules and laws given to us by God to enable us to use our agency to choose to receive His choicest blessings here on earth and ultimately return to live with Him eternally. They are a great blessing and a demonstration of His love for us (D&C 59:4).

COMMON CONSENT
The act of raising our hands as members in meetings, when invited to do so, to sustain callings, actions, priesthood ordinations, and so forth (D&C 26:2).

COMMON JUDGE IN ISRAEL

Bishops and stake presidents serve as common judges in Israel. They counsel with members as needed and help them "judge" between various courses of action in their lives. Part of the calling of a bishop is to help members in matters of worthiness. When necessary, they counsel with them on matters requiring repentance and even place restrictions on membership privileges if needed. And, when things are again in order, bishops and stake presidents can allow that member full access to blessings of the gospel (D&C 58:17–18). Mission presidents have these same responsibilities and opportunities as judges in Israel.

COMMUNION

A term meaning to partake of the Lord's Supper (Luke 22:19–20; 3 Nephi 18:1–4). Latter-day Saints refer to this ordinance of partaking of the bread and water (D&C 20:75–79) as the "sacrament" (Mormon 9:29; D&C 20:46).

CONCEIVED IN SIN

The false notion that when children are born, they are tainted with so-called "original sin" brought upon all people by the transgression of Adam and Eve in the Garden of Eden. The concept of original sin is false. Those who teach that children are conceived in sin also teach that infants must be baptized, which is another false doctrine (Moroni 8:9–12).

CONCUBINES

As generally used in scripture, these are second class or servant wives (2 Samuel 5:13; D&C 132:37) who were legally married to their husbands but did not have all of the legal rights and privileges of first class wives.

CONDESCENSION OF GOD

Refers to both the Father and the Son. In reference to the Father, it means that God the Father, in spite of the great power and glory which accompany His exalted state, still pays tender attention to His children here on earth, who are so inadequate compared to Him (1 Nephi 11:16).

In reference to the Son, it means the fact that Jesus Christ, a God, humbly came to earth and submitted voluntarily to the insults and tortures inflicted upon him by the wicked in order to provide salvation for us (1 Nephi 11:26).

CONFERENCE, GENERAL

Worldwide meetings of the Church, held twice a year, to which all members and all nonmembers are invited. At this time (summer 2007), five sessions of conference are held: (1) A general session for all members, held Saturday, 10:00 AM MST. (2) A general session for all members, held Saturday, 2:00 PM. (3) A general priesthood meeting for all priesthood holders, held Saturday evening. (4) A general session for all members, held Sunday, 10:00 AM. (5) A general session for all members, held Sunday, 2:00 PM.

During these conference sessions, which generally originate from the Conference Center in Salt Lake City, Utah, addresses are given by General Authorities of the Church and others, including members of the general auxiliary presidencies. The proceedings are broadcast throughout the world by satellite and on the Internet.

These conferences are a time when the members of the Church receive revelation and counsel from the Lord through His "prophets, seers, and revelators," the members of the First Presidency and the Quorum of the Twelve Apostles, as well as from other invited speakers.

The proceedings and addresses given during the conferences are printed for all to read and study in Church magazines, the *Ensign*, and the *Liahona* soon after the conference is broadcast. They are also available online, at lds.org.

CONFESSION OF SINS

As a part of the process of obtaining forgiveness, all sins need to be confessed to the Lord and, if others were affected, the sins must also be confessed to those who have been offended or hurt (Leviticus 5:5; Matthew 3:6; Mosiah 26:29–30; D&C 58:42–43). Generally speaking, sins that could affect a member's worthiness to hold a temple recommend should be confessed to his or her bishop or stake president.

CONFIRMATION

After a person has been baptized, he or she is confirmed a member of The Church of Jesus Christ of Latter-day Saints by the laying on of hands by those holding the Melchizedek Priesthood, and is given the gift of the Holy Ghost (D&C 20:41, 43, 68). Baptism and confirmation are required for membership in the Church.

CONSCIENCE

Every person born is given a conscience to guide and direct and help discern between right and wrong (Moroni 7:16). This "conscience" is a free gift from God and comes from the light of Christ "which lighteth every man that cometh into the world" (John 1:9).

CONSCIENTIOUS OBJECTION

The Church encourages its members to honor and sustain the laws of the land in which they live (D&C 134:5; Articles of Faith 1:12). Honorable military service is supported by the Church as a necessary fact of mortal life when conditions require it (Alma 43:9).

When a member of the Church claims to be a conscientious objector, he or she cannot properly claim to be doing so based on membership in the Church and the teachings of the Church.

CONSECRATED OIL

Pure olive oil which has been consecrated or blessed and dedicated for use in administering to the sick by the elders of the Church. One or more Melchizedek Priesthood holders can consecrate pure olive oil for this purpose by removing the lid from the container of oil, addressing Heavenly Father, and consecrating the oil by the power of the Melchizedek Priesthood and in the name of Jesus Christ.

CONSECRATION

The formal dedicating, as part of temple worship, of all one's time, talents, and possessions to the Church and its purposes (D&C 64:34; 82:19; 88:67–68; 98:12–14).

President John Taylor stated that consecration is a celestial law and, when observed, it leads to becoming a celestial people (*JD* 17:177–81).

John A. Widtsoe, an Apostle, explained that the operation of the law of consecration was quite simple. "Those who joined such an order were to place all their possessions in a common treasury—the rich their wealth, the poor their pittance. Then each member was to receive a sufficient portion—called an 'inheritance'—from the common treasury to enable that person to continue in trade, business, or profession as desired. The farmer would receive land and implements; the tradesman, tools and materials; the merchant, necessary capital; the professional person, instruments, books, and the like. Members working for others would receive proportionate interests in the enterprises they served. No one would be without property. All would have an inheritance (Widtsoe, pp. 302–3 as quoted in *EM*, under "Consecration").

A member's "inheritance" became private property. Land, etc., was dis-tributed by the bishop and a deed was given (D&C 51:3–6). Thus, those who lived the law of consecration had private ownership of property, which they could sell or take with them if they left the group.

CONSTITUTION OF THE UNITED STATES OF AMERICA

An inspired document (D&C 101:77–80) providing the foundation upon which this country was to be administered. It provides for the exercising of individual agency and protection of individual rights, while binding citizens together as needed for the preservation of the country.

CONSTITUTION HANGS BY A THREAD

The prophecy that the Constitution of the United States will hang by a thread was given by both Joseph Smith and Brigham Young. Brigham Young said that it will be saved. "How long will it be before the words of the prophet Joseph will be fulfilled? He said if the Constitution of the United States were saved at all it must be done by this people. It will not be many years before these words come to pass" (*JD* 12:204).

"When the Constitution of the United States hangs, as it were, upon a single thread, they will have to call for the 'Mormon' Elders to save it from utter destruction; and they will step forth and do it" (*JD* 2:182). (Quoted in *Discourses of Brigham Young*, pp. 360–61.)

CONTENTION

In the Savior's first message to the Nephites as He appeared to them after His resurrection, He emphasized four times that "contention is not of me" (3 Nephi 11:22, 28–30). Contention is one of the devil's most effective tools of destruction. In today's media, many popular shows are built around contention and people revel in watching them. Contention drives the Spirit of the Lord away. It is a manifestation of pride (Proverbs 13:10).

Families are counseled by the Lord to live in love and harmony (Mosiah 4:14–15).

CONTINUATION OF SEEDS

Having spirit children in eternal family units, as gods, with no end to the number of such children (D&C 132:19). It is a phrase that refers to those who attain exaltation and thus become gods (D&C 132:20).

CONTRITE

A word that means humble, but includes the additional meaning of desiring correction as needed. The word is often used in concert with "broken heart" (Psalm 34:18). Taken together, the two terms, "broken heart" and "contrite spirit," often mean "humble and willing to take correction, even humbly seeking correction from the Lord as needed." People who have both of these attributes tend to make steady progress toward exaltation.

CONVERSION

The process by which an individual accepts and internalizes the witness of the Holy Ghost (1 Corinthians 12:3) that leads to joining The Church of Jesus Christ of Latter-day Saints and faithful adherence to the laws and commandments of God thereafter.

CORRELATION IN THE CHURCH

The process through which curriculum materials and other materials are reviewed for doctrinal and factual accuracy as well as for appropriateness, prior to publication by the Church.

COUNCIL IN HEAVEN

The premortal council held in heaven, during which the Father's plan to send us to earth was announced. The terms and conditions for our entering into mortal bodies were explained and we "shouted for joy" at hearing the news (Job 38:7).

It was during this council that the Savior was chosen to be our Redeemer and that Satan rebelled (Moses 4:1–3).

We understand that this council was held for all of the spirit children of the Father who were assigned to inhabit this earth (Talmage, *Articles of Faith*, p. 194), and that other similar premortal councils are held and will continue to be held for groups of His spirit children as they progress to the point of being ready for mortality and are assigned to their worlds.

COUNCIL OF THE TWELVE
See TWELVE APOSTLES, THE.

COVENANT
A pact or agreement between God and man, which, when kept by us, brings blessings to us in this life and ultimately leads toward returning to live with the Father forever. The Lord always keeps His part of the agreement when we make covenants with Him, and it is up to us to keep our part (D&C 82:10).

COVENANT ISRAEL
The Lord established a covenant with Abraham (Genesis 12:1–3; 17:1–8; Abraham 2:9–11) and, consequently, his posterity through Isaac and Jacob (Genesis 17:19–21). They became known as "Israel" in the scriptures. When kept, this covenant leads people to the full blessings of the gospel of Jesus Christ available on earth and to exaltation in eternity.

This Abrahamic covenant was renewed with Isaac, Jacob, and Moses as well as through other Old Testament prophets, and again in the New Testament as spoken of by Paul (Galatians 3:7, 27–29), and yet again through the Prophet Joseph Smith as the "new and . . . everlasting covenant" (D&C 22:1).

A person becomes part of "covenant Israel" by being baptized and confirmed and then living in harmony with the laws and commandments of the gospel, entering into and keeping sacred covenants with God.

Being a part of covenant Israel is designed by the Lord to set us apart from the ways of the world and to enable us to enjoy the constant companionship of the Holy Ghost, thus being led to exaltation.

Covenant Israel is to be an example to all, to take the gospel and priesthood blessings to all (Abraham 2:9), and, in short, serve as the Lord's ambassadors under all circumstances. They should be kinder, more pleasant, more patient, more humble, more influential for good, more willing to sacrifice for the comfort and good of their fellow beings, and so forth, than any other people on earth.

Individual members of the Church who understand the concept and doctrine of being covenant Israel have a great advantage in stability and gospel living.

COVENANT PEOPLE
See COVENANT ISRAEL.

COVET
Desiring something that belongs to someone else. The Lord commanded, "Thou shalt not covet . . ." (Exodus 20:17). Coveting is a root cause of much personal misery and dissatisfaction on the part of those who covet. It leads to sin, crime, and mischief, hurting individuals and societies.

CREATION
The world was created by Jesus Christ, under the direction of the Father (John 1:1–3). We don't know how it was

made, but we do know that it was created by God. Genesis chapter 1 has over forty statements testifying to us, in one way or another, that God created it.

All things were made in spirit form before they were created physically (Moses 3:5–7).

We do not know how long it took to create the world, but we know that there were seven time periods involved (Abraham 4:5, 8, 13, 19, 23, 31; 5:2).

The details of creation will be given to us when the Savior comes to rule and reign for the Millennium (D&C 101:32–34).

CREATOR, THE

The premortal Jesus Christ created the earth under the direction of the Father and is thus referred to as the Creator in numerous scripture references (examples: John 1:3; Ephesians 3:9; Hebrews 1:2; Mosiah 3:8; D&C 29:31).

CREED, NICENE

See ATHANASIAN CREED.

CREMATION

The Church discourages the practice of cremation, except in situations where the law of the land requires it. The physical body is the physical home of the spirit and is the "temple of God," and we are taught not to "defile" it (1 Corinthians 16–17). However, the decision whether to cremate or bury the body of a deceased loved one is an individual choice and is not a matter of good vs. evil.

If the body of an endowed member is to be cremated, it can be dressed in temple clothing before cremation, just as would be the case with burial.

CROSS

The Church does not use the symbol of the cross in its chapels or architecture. The reason is that the cross is not the end of the account of the Savior. Rather, His Resurrection and final triumph over death and the world is the emphasis in His gospel.

It is a matter of personal choice as to whether members wear crosses or not. However, most do not, because it can misrepresent our beliefs to others.

CRUCIFIX

See CROSS.

CRUCIFIXION

The method of execution used by the Romans for Jesus Christ (Matthew 27:35). It involved tying or nailing the victim to a cross or tree and letting them hang, dying an unimaginably agonizing death, usually over a period two to three days. They nailed the Savior's hands and feet to the cross and added nails through His wrists to ensure that the nails did not tear through His hands.

The Savior had the power to free Himself (John 10:18) but voluntarily remained on the cross in order to complete His Atonement for us. He uttered the following statements from the cross:

1. Luke 23:34—"Father, forgive them; for they know not what they do."

2. Luke 23:43—"Today shalt thou be with me in paradise."

3. John 19:26–27—"Woman, behold thy son!" "Behold thy mother!"

4. Matthew 27:46—"My God, my God, why hast thou forsaken me?"

5. John 19:28—"I thirst."

6. John 19:30—"It is finished."

7. Luke 23:46—"Father, into thy hands I commend my spirit."

CUMORAH, HILL

The hill near Palmyra, New York, where an angel named Moroni took Joseph Smith to show him where ancient records were buried. In 1827, Joseph was permitted by the angel to take these gold plates home and begin the translation which resulted in the Book of Mormon. It is an account of the ancient inhabitants of America and God's dealings with them.

The Church has built a beautiful visitors' center at the foot of Hill Cumorah, and the hill is the site of the annual Hill Cumorah Pageant, which retells the story of the Savior's visit to America and the coming forth of the Book of Mormon.

· D ·

DAMNATION

The opposite of salvation. Being stopped from progressing. Another name for hell (Matthew 23:33). Actually, there are many different degrees of "damnation" within the teachings of the true gospel, including perdition, telestial glory, terrestrial glory (1 Corinthians 15:39–42; D&C 76), and even the first two categories in celestial glory (D&C 131:1–4), because they all fall short of exaltation on the day of final judgment.

DAMNED

See also DAMNATION. As used in the scriptures, the word means "stopped" (Mark 16:16; 2 Thessalonians 2:12; 2 Nephi 9:24).

DANCING

Appropriate dancing was encouraged by Brigham Young (D&C 136:28) and continues to be sponsored in many settings by the Church.

DANITES

"Following the violence in northwestern Missouri in 1838, the Mormon dissident Sampson Avard, star witness in a court of inquiry weighing evidence against LDS leaders, charged that the Church had organized a band of armed men bound by secret oaths who had engaged in illegal activities against non-Mormon neighbors (*Document,* pp. 97–108). With the 1841 publication of the court proceedings, Avard's account became the foundation for all subsequent non-Mormon 'Danite' accounts. Thus was born the legend of the Danites.

"Though no Danite organization was known in Nauvoo or in Utah, the stereotype persisted, becoming a part of national discussion about Utah and the Latter-day Saints and for decades a staple of dime novels (see MORMONS, IMAGE OF: IN FICTION). By 1900 at least fifty novels had been published in English using the Avard-type Danite to develop story lines of murder, pillage, and conspiracy against common citizens. Arthur Conan Doyle (*A Study in Scarlet*) created Sherlock Holmes to solve a murder committed by Danites. Zane Grey (*Riders of the Purple Sage*) and Robert Louis Stevenson (*The Dynamiter*) were among the authors who found the image of the evil Danites well suited for popular reading audiences who delighted in sensationalism (Cornwall and Arrington). The image became so pervasive that few readers were willing to question the accuracy of such portrayals.

"The reality of Danites in Missouri in 1838 is both less and more than the stereotype. Contemporary records suggest something fundamentally different. In October 1838, Albert Perry Rockwood, an LDS resident of Far West, Missouri, wrote in his journal of a *public* Danite organization that involved the whole Latter-day Saint community. He described in biblical terms companies of tens, fifties, and hundreds (cf. Exodus 18:13–36)— similar to the organization the pioneers later used during the migration to the Great Basin. Here the Danite organization encompassed the full range of activities of a covenant community that viewed itself as a restoration of ancient Israel. Working in groups, with some assigned to defense, others to securing provisions, and still others to constructing dwellings, these Danites served the interests of the whole. This was not the secret organization Avard spoke of; in fact, Rockwood's letters to friends and family were even more descriptive than his journal (Jessee and Whittaker)" (*EM*).

DARK AGES

Brought on by the Great Apostasy, after the crucifixion and resurrection of the Savior, the persecution of His Church, and the killing of the Apostles. The dark ages, which lasted roughly a thousand years, emphasized the abject conditions and lack of progress which results when the true gospel is abandoned by individuals and society.

DAUGHTERS OF GOD

Another term for women who are righteous followers of Jesus Christ (Mosiah 5:7). The implication in the term is that these women are "born again" through Christ and His gospel, thus, symbolically, they are His "daughters."

DAVID, KING

Best known as the shepherd boy who killed Goliath (1 Samuel 17), David became King of Judah, serving for seven years and then king over the united kingdom of Israel for an additional thirty-three years (1 Kings 2:11).

Sadly, David is an example of one who did much good and received much revelation and strength from the Lord, but who did not endure faithfully to the end. He committed adultery with Bathsheba (2 Samuel 11:2–5) and then had her husband murdered in an attempt to cover it up (2 Samuel 11:6–17). We know from modern revelation that "he hath fallen from his exaltation" (D&C 132:39). David's last act, while on his death bed, was to instruct his son, Solomon, the next king, to get revenge for him (1 Kings 2:1–10), effectively breaking his word.

DAY OF JUDGMENT

See JUDGMENT DAY.

DAY OF PENTECOST

A feast celebrated by the children of Israel fifty days (Leviticus 23:16, 21) after the feast of Passover. It had become a major event and celebration among the Jews by the time of Christ's mortal ministry (Acts 2).

DAY OF REST

See SABBATH DAY.

DAY OF THE LORD

Another term for the Second Coming of Christ (2 Peter 3:10; Isaiah 13:9; 2 Nephi 12:12).

DAY OF VENGEANCE

Another term for the Second Coming of Christ (D&C 133:51).

DAY OF VISITATION

Another term for the Second Coming of Christ (D&C 56:16).

DAY OF WRATH

Another term for the Second Coming of Christ (D&C 112:24).

DEACON

An office in the Aaronic Priesthood (D&C 20:57–60). Worthy young men in the Church can have the Aaronic Priesthood conferred upon them and be ordained a deacon when they reach age twelve. Among the duties given to deacons are passing the sacrament to the congregation, serving as messengers for the bishopric, collecting fast offerings, providing assistance to ward members, and caring for the meetinghouse and grounds.

DEAD SEA SCROLLS

A collection of ancient manuscripts discovered near the Dead Sea in 1947. The manuscripts include fragments from all the Old Testament books except Esther and include a number of variations and additional materials. While there is still much interest in these manuscripts among LDS scholars, conclusions are still under consideration as to their overall contribution to our understanding of biblical times and their relevance to the true gospel.

DEAD, BAPTISM FOR

See also BAPTISM FOR THE DEAD. The practice of being baptized by proxy for the dead. It was not done in the Old Testament, because the gospel had not yet been preached in the postmortal spirit world to departed spirits. After His crucifixion, while His body was yet in the tomb, the Savior went to the postmortal spirit world and organized the preaching of the gospel to the dead (1 Peter 3:18–20; 4:6; D&C 138:29–35). After this time, members of the New Testament church began being baptized for the dead (1 Corinthians 15:29) in order to allow "converts" in the spirit world to join the Church,

Latter-day Saints continue this practice today (D&C 128:17). This proxy baptism is not binding on the dead. They have their agency and can accept it or reject it. If they accept it, once it is done for them by mortals here on earth, they can continue progressing in the spirit world and can eventually attain all blessings of the gospel, including exaltation.

DEAF, SPIRITUALLY

Not knowing the gospel (Isaiah 29:18). Also can include being insensitive to the Spirit of the Lord, rejecting the teachings of Jesus Christ, and preferring wickedness over righteousness (2 Nephi 9:31).

DEATH

The temporary separation of the spirit from the body (Alma 40:11). The spirit and body are permanently reunited at the time of resurrection (1 Corinthians 15:22; Alma 40:23). Those who have died miss having their physical bodies (D&C 138:50).

For those who have endured considerable pain and suffering leading to dying, death will be a great relief. Brigham Young spoke of dying, saying, "Why this is the greatest advantage of my whole existence, for I have passed from a state of sorrow, grief, mourning, woe, misery, pain, anguish and disappointment into a state of existence, where I can enjoy life to the fullest extent as far as that can be done without a body. My spirit is set free, I thirst no more, I want to sleep no more, I hunger no more, I tire no more, I run, I walk, I labor, I go, I come, I do this, I do that, whatever is required of me, nothing like pain or weariness, I am full of life, full of vigor, and I enjoy the presence of my Heavenly Father" (*JD* 17:142).

DEATH, SPIRITUAL

See SPIRITUAL DEATH.

DEBT

The Church counsels its members to avoid debt wherever possible, especially consumer debt such as can accrue through unwise use of credit cards. Debt for reasonable housing, adequate transportation, and, sometimes, education, may be necessary, but the sustaining of unnecessary lifestyle through debt should be avoided. Members are encouraged to spend less than they earn and to set money aside as savings for emergencies, thus becoming self-sufficient. "Spending less money than you make is essential to your financial security. Avoid debt, with the exception of buying a modest home or paying for education or other vital needs. If you are in debt, pay it off as quickly as possible" (lds.org, under "Provident Living, 2007").

The First Presidency of the Church counsels: "We encourage you wherever you may live in the world to prepare for adversity by looking to the condition of your finances. We urge you to be modest in your expenditures; discipline yourselves in your purchases to avoid debt. . . . If you have paid your debts and have a financial reserve, even though it be small, you and your family will feel more secure and enjoy greater peace in your hearts" (The First Presidency, *All Is Safely Gathered In: Family Finances*, p. 1).

DEDICATION OF BUILDINGS

It is a common practice in the Church to dedicate buildings such as temples, chapels, visitors' centers, seminaries, institutes of religion, and so forth after they are completed. During the dedication meeting, talks are given, music is sung, and a dedicatory prayer given, in which the building is presented to the Lord for use in His work here on earth.

DEDICATION OF GRAVES

It is a common practice in the Church to dedicate the grave of a deceased loved one as a final resting place for the physical body. The dedication is performed by a Melchizedek Priesthood holder who does it in the name of Jesus Christ, stating his priesthood authority, and saying appropriate things as prompted by the Spirit. His prayer might include dedicating the grave as the final resting place for the deceased and a place of peace for loved ones and friends who visit.

DEDICATION OF HOMES

The Church encourages members to dedicate their homes, whether paid for or not. A worthy Melchizedek Priesthood holder such as the owner, the husband, a home teacher, etc., dedicates the home in the name of Jesus Christ, stating his priesthood authority, and saying things as prompted by the Spirit, which might include such thoughts as dedicating it as a place of peace and as an environment in which members of the household can feel the Spirit, serve and strengthen one another, and grow closer to the Lord.

DEFORMITIES, GONE AFTER RESURRECTION

In the Resurrection, all deformities and imperfections will be taken away and our physical bodies will "be restored to their proper and perfect frame" (Alma 40:23). Since every mortal body has some shortcomings or imperfections, we can look forward to having better bodies than we have ever had. There will no doubt be some pleasant surprises at the time of resurrection.

DEGREES OF GLORY

According to the Apostle Paul, there are four major categories to which a person can be assigned in the next life after the resurrection, namely, perdition, which is not a degree of glory (1 Timothy 6:9, Hebrews 10:39), and three different degrees of glory, which he compares to the stars, the moon, and the sun, respectively (1 Corinthians 15:39–42). These categories, including the three degrees of glory, are confirmed by the Lord in modern revelation, where we are given more detail about perdition (D&C 76:31–35), which is not a degree of glory, and are told that the names of the three degrees of glory, in ascending order are the telestial kingdom (D&C 76:81), the terrestrial kingdom (D&C 76:71), and the celestial kingdom (D&C 76:96). Furthermore, we are told that the celestial glory has three categories within it, and in the highest, family units will continue to exist (D&C 131:1–4). This highest degree in the celestial kingdom is called exaltation, and those who attain it will become gods (D&C 132:19–20).

DEIFICATION OF EARLY CHRISTIANS

The Church does not subscribe to the idea of having "patron saints" to whom one can pray or who intercede with God for mortals. Jesus Christ is the only Mediator between us and God the Father (1 Timothy 2:5). However, there is an element of truth in the false practice of deification itself, namely, that mortals can indeed become gods (John 10:34; D&C 132:20).

DEITY

A term used in reference to members of the Godhead, in other words, the Father, the Son, and the Holy Ghost.

DEMONS

Angels of the devil (Helaman 13:37).

DEPENDENT BRANCHES

Small groups of members who meet together regularly but do not have sufficient numbers or leadership to be organized into an independent branch or ward. They meet under the direction of other leadership, perhaps of an independent branch, ward, mission president, or stake president.

DESERET

A word found in the Book of Mormon which means "a honey bee" (Ether 2:3).

DESERET ALPHABET

A phonetic alphabet developed by the Board of Regents of the University of Deseret, under the direction of Brigham Young. He announced that the project was underway on April 8, 1852.

The alphabet consisted of thirty-eight characters representing the individual sounds of the English language. In a way, the alphabet was similar to shorthand. Some verses of scripture written in the Deseret Alphabet appeared in the *Deseret News* in 1859.

Orson Pratt published additional materials in the alphabet in New York, at a cost of $18,500 for casting new type for the Deseret Alphabet. These materials included first and second school readers in 1868, and the Book of Mormon plus a third reader in 1869.

Even though some illiterate Saints demonstrated that they could learn the Deseret Alphabet and were able to read and write in just a matter of weeks, the project failed to gain real momentum and was basically abandoned with the death of Brigham Young in 1877.

DESERET INDUSTRIES

Established by the First Presidency in August 1938 toward the end of the Great Depression, this program was designed to help members help themselves and become self-sufficient. It included donated household items, volunteer labor, and vocational training.

Since that time, Deseret Industries has expanded to include many beautiful stores where donated goods are sold and employees are trained in work skills and habits of dependability.

DESIRES

Our desires will play a role in our final judgment (D&C 137:9). Those who do their best to keep the commandments, including making temple covenants, but are stopped by forces beyond their control, will still be acceptable to the Lord (D&C 124:49).

DESPAIR

The opposite of faith and hope for the future. One of the prophecies of the last days is that many will be caught up in despair, gloom, doom and pessimism (Luke 21:25–26). The Spirit of the Lord fosters hope and determination despite setbacks and gives the righteous confidence in their standing before God and courage to go on (D&C 123:17).

DESTROYER, THE

Another name for Satan (D&C 61:19).

DEVIL

Another name for Satan (Revelation 12:9). Satan became the devil when he rebelled against the Father's plan during the premortal council in heaven (Moses 4:1–4). He works in constant opposition to all that is good and is completely devoid of any righteous desires.

DEVIL, CHILDREN OF

A term referring to the wicked, those who intentionally give in to Satan's temptations and refuse to repent (1 John 3:10). Satan has no literal children because he does not have a physical body, nor will he ever obtain one.

DEVIL, CHURCH OF THE

Any organization, religious or otherwise, that entices people to distance themselves from God (1 Nephi 14:10). Another term for "church of the devil" is "kingdom of the devil" (1 Nephi 22:22–23).

DEVIL WORSHIP

There are many groups and individuals who engage in devil worship of one form or another. Satan is the supreme master of deception and counterfeits true religion, including covenants and sacred symbols, luring the foolish and the wicked into his traps. His most abominable counterfeit of all is human sacrifice, which is a mockery of the voluntary sacrifice of the Son of God.

DEVILS

The evil spirits who followed Satan during the War in Heaven and who were ultimately cast out with him (Revelation 12:4; D&C 29:36). They will never get physical bodies and are here on earth and in the prison portion of the postmortal spirit world (*Teachings of the Presidents of the Church*— Brigham Young, p. 282)

tempting and striving to lead mortals astray. They will ultimately be cast into perdition with Satan (D&C 88:114).

DILIGENCE

An important character trait of the righteous who continue striving against all odds to serve the Lord and keep His commandments. In the scriptures, emphasis is placed on diligence and direction rather than speed in pursuing exaltation (Mosiah 4:27).

DISCERNING OF SPIRITS

See also GIFTS OF THE SPIRIT. The ability, given by the Holy Ghost, to detect evil spirits, evil in people, and false doctrines and philosophies, whether or not there is obvious evidence to that effect (D&C 46:23). It is one of the gifts of the Holy Ghost, also referred to as "gifts of the Spirit." Another aspect of this gift is the ability to see the good in others, where many people miss it in a particular person.

DISCERNMENT, GIFT OF

The gift of the Spirit which enables a person to tell the difference between good and evil, between wise actions and foolish actions, between inspiration from God and deception from the devil. This gift is an enhancement of the light of Christ as described in the Book of Mormon (Moroni 7:12–18). It includes an increased ability to recognize inspiration and understand the needs of others.

In addition to being a gift given to some members of the Church, this gift is also given to bishops and those who are called to preside (D&C 46:27).

DISCERNMENT OF SPIRITS

See DISCERNING OF SPIRITS.

DISCIPLE

See also DISCIPLES OF CHRIST. The word "disciple" means "a loyal follower."

DISCIPLES OF CHRIST

Loyal followers of the Savior. He had many disciples during His mortal mission, from which were chosen the original Twelve Apostles (Luke 6:13–16). Any faithful member of the Church can properly be referred to as a disciple of Christ. Doctrine and Covenants section 42 is an example of specific instruction in how to be a true disciple of Jesus Christ.

DISCIPLINE, CHURCH

In general, a bishop or stake president is a "judge in Israel" and has the responsibility to administer disciplinary action upon the request of a member or as needed to help members repent and continue progressing toward a pleasant final judgment. Such discipline can include informal discipline, such as requesting that a member not partake of the sacrament for a period of time until a matter is sufficiently cleared up. It could also include taking a member's temple recommend for a while, or simply requesting that the member not attend the temple during a period of informal probation designed to help and encourage getting a life back in harmony with the gospel.

Formal discipline includes the convening of a bishop's disciplinary council, consisting of the bishop, his two counselors, and a clerk, presided over by the bishop, or a stake council consisting of the stake president, his two counselors, plus the twelve high counselors and a clerk, presided over by the stake president. See Disciplinary Council for more information.

DISCIPLINARY COUNCIL

Disciplinary councils are formal councils in which a member is considered for disciplinary action, which could result in no action, informal probation, formal probation, disfellowshipment, or excommunication. They are convened only in the case of serious transgression. In established areas of the Church, such councils are convened by bishops or stake presidents. Mission presidents can convene them in the case of transgressions by missionaries.

DISFELLOWSHIP

See also DISCIPLINARY COUNCIL. Disfellowshipment is a form of disciplinary action, less severe than excommunication, in which the individual retains his or her membership in the Church but has restrictions placed on membership privileges, such as: may not partake of the sacrament, hold a calling, attend the temple, exercise the priesthood (in the case of men), or give a prayer or talk in a public meeting of the Church. The individual is encouraged to attend public meetings of the Church, pay tithing, continue wearing temple garments (if previously endowed), and meet frequently with the bishop or stake president to discuss progress and receive encouragement in returning to full fellowship in the Church.

DISHONESTY

Any type of dishonesty offends the Spirit and leads an individual away from God. Unrepented of, dishonesty will eventually lead to being sent to the telestial kingdom (D&C 76:103; Revelation 22:15).

DISOBEDIENCE

In order to be disobedient, a person must have sufficient knowledge of the gospel to ignore it or intentionally break the laws and commandments of the Lord. However, even without specific knowledge of the gospel, a person can be disobedient to conscience, which is given to everyone born to earth (John 1:9).

DISPENSATION

See also DISPENSATIONS. Generally, as used in the scriptures, a period of time in which the gospel was restored to the earth and actively available to people (D&C 112:31). It is also sometimes used to mean particular

blessings and help from heaven (1 Corinthians 9:17; Ephesians 3:2).

DISPENSATIONS

Periods of time when the gospel has been placed on earth or restored to earth, at the end of which the people went into apostasy (except for our dispensation, which will not go into apostasy—see Dispensation of the Fulness of Times).

There have been many dispensations, including the dispensations of Adam, Enoch, Noah, Abraham, Moses, Jesus Christ, and Joseph Smith. There were many "dispensations" in the Book of Mormon.

DISPENSATION OF THE FULNESS OF TIMES

The last dispensation, the one which is now on earth. It is the final dispensation and will endure up to and including the Second Coming of the Savior. This time, the Church will not go into apostasy (Daniel 2:35, 44).

This last dispensation is called the dispensation of the fulness of times because things from past dispensations have all been restored in this one (Ephesians 1:10; D&C 27:13; 110:11–16; 112:30–32).

DISSOLUTION, FALSE DOCTRINE OF

A false doctrine that claims that sons of perdition will have their physical bodies and their spirit bodies dissolved after their resurrection and thus be reduced down to intelligence only. Then, they will be "recycled," so to speak, and be sent through spirit birth and then mortal birth on another planet. This "recycling" will continue until they eventually attain a kingdom of glory.

Again, this is a false doctrine. The Lord said that all will be resurrected (1 Corinthians 15:22) and that we only die once (Hebrews 9:27). Furthermore, we are told that sons of perdition are resurrected (D&C 88:32) and will go into perdition, sometimes called outer darkness, with the devil (D&C 88:114).

DISTRICT

In developing areas of the Church where there are several members but not yet enough to form a stake, missions are divided into districts. When sufficient numbers and sufficient leadership is in place, the district is made into a stake.

DISTRICT PRESIDENTS

See also DISTRICT. District presidents are the ecclesiastical leaders of districts and are similar in function to stake presidents.

DIVINITY

A term often used when referring to members of the Godhead.

DIVORCE

Latter-day Saints believe that marriage is designed by the Lord to be a permanent, eternal union (Gen-

esis 2:24; Matthew 19:6). However, because people are people, divorce becomes the only reasonable solution to marital incompatibility in some situations. President James E. Faust said: "Divorce can be justified only in the rarest of circumstances. In my opinion, 'just cause' for divorce should be nothing less serious than a prolonged and apparently irredeemable relationship that destroys a person's dignity as a human being" (First Presidency Message, *Ensign*, April 2007).

Members in good standing who have been previously divorced are allowed and encouraged to marry in the temple for time and eternity, when they find a new opportunity for marriage.

In the days of the Savior's mortal mission, many people were taking marriage vows lightly and divorce was very common. Obtaining a divorce was easy. The Master addressed divorce in Matthew 5:31–32. On occasion, well-meaning people use these verses to teach that marrying a divorced person causes one to commit adultery. A careful reading of these verses reveals that the Savior used the word "fornication" rather than "adultery" in reference to a married couple. As used in the scriptures, in addition to sexual transgression between unmarried individuals, "fornication," symbolically, can also mean breaking of covenants and complete disloyalty (Revelation 14:8; BD, under "Adultery"). With this in mind, we might read Matthew 5:32 as "whosoever shall put away [divorce] his wife, saving for extreme breaking of covenants and complete disloyalty and incompatibility . . ."

The safest approach to interpreting Matthew 5:31–32 is to "follow the Brethren." In other words, what do the Brethren (our prophets, seers, and revelators) allow? They speak for the Lord (D&C 1:38). If marriage to a divorced individual automatically made a person an "adulterer," such individuals would be automatically unworthy to enter the temple, let alone to be sealed. Since the Lord allows them to worthily enter the temple and to be sealed, and gain exaltation through continued faithfulness, there is obviously something about Matthew 5:31–32 that we don't understand. In the meantime, we are completely safe in following the Brethren on this matter.

DOCTRINE

The truths, teachings, principles, and ordinances found in the true gospel of Jesus Christ which are necessary to save us in exaltation. Doctrines do not change. Examples include faith, repentance, baptism (for those who attain the age of accountability), the gift of the Holy Ghost, the Atonement of Christ, the Fall of Adam, the sacrament, celestial marriage, the existence of God the Father and His Son, Jesus Christ, premortality, the Second Coming, Millennium, death, resurrection, the law of chastity, the laws of mercy and justice, three degrees of glory, temple work for the dead, continuing revelation, the possibility of becoming gods and living in the family unit forever.

DOCTRINE AND COVENANTS

One of four books considered to be sacred scripture by members of The Church of Jesus Christ of Latter-day Saints. The other three are the Bible, the Book of Mormon, and the Pearl of Great Price. These four books are sometimes called the standard works of the Church.

The Doctrine and Covenants contains modern revelations and instructions given by the Lord through Joseph Smith and others. In its present form (2007), it contains 138 sections plus two official declarations. One hundred thirty-three of the sections were given to Joseph Smith. Oliver Cowdery and Orson Hyde recorded minutes of a meeting which were corrected and added to by Joseph Smith and now appear as section 102. Oliver Cowdery also was the principle author of section 134. John Taylor wrote the tribute to Joseph Smith and his brother Hyrum, known as section 135. Brigham Young received section 136 through revelation. President Joseph F. Smith received the revelation recorded in section 138. Wilford Woodruff received the revelation leading to the writing of Official Declaration—1, and Spencer W. Kimball received the revelation leading to Official Declaration—2.

The first edition of the revelations was the Book of Commandments, containing 65 chapters. It went to press in 1833, but was mostly destroyed by mobs in Missouri. Editions of the Doctrine and Covenants were published in 1835 (103 sections), 1844 (111 sections), 1845 (printed in Liverpool, England, same as the 1844 edition), 1876 (with 26 revelations added and the revelations divided into verses for the first time), 1879 (with footnotes added), 1921 (with revised footnotes and pages arranged in double columns; *Lectures on Faith* was taken out), and 1981 (with completely revised footnotes and revised headings for each section). Sections 137 and 138 were added along with Official Declaration—2 to the 1981 edition. It is the one now in current use.

DOGMA

The beliefs and doctrines of any religious group, individual, or any organization.

DOLE, THE

Handouts by any government organization or private individuals or groups which sustain a person's lifestyle without requiring work on his or her part. Such doles are contrary to the gospel (D&C 42:42) because they tend to stunt personal growth.

DOVE, SIGN OF

Joseph Smith taught about the sign of the dove as he explained the mission of John the Baptist to baptize the Savior. He said, "Whoever led the Son of God into the waters of baptism, and had the privilege of beholding the Holy Ghost descend in the form of a dove, or rather in the *sign* of the dove, in witness of that administration? The sign of the dove was instituted before the creation of the world, a witness for the Holy Ghost, and the devil cannot come in the sign of a dove. The Holy Ghost is a personage, and is in the form of a personage. It does not confine itself to the *form* of the dove, but in *sign* of the dove. The Holy Ghost cannot be transformed into a dove; but the sign of a dove was given to John to signify the truth of the deed, as the dove is an emblem or token of truth and innocence" (*TPJS*, pp. 275–76).

DOVE, SYMBOLISM OF

See also DOVE, SIGN OF. The dove has come to be a universal symbol of peace, especially a dove with an olive branch in its beak.

DRAGON, THE GREAT

Another name for Satan (Revelation 12:9).

DREAMS

The Lord has often communicated with individuals through dreams. For example, Joseph in Egypt had two dreams in which he was shown details about his future (Genesis 37:5–10). The Lord gave Lehi counsel and instruction in a dream (1 Nephi

2:1–2). Many individuals today have dreams in which the Lord communicates with them.

Sometimes people wonder if it is just a dream or a message from God. The Holy Ghost can help, but if they still wonder about it, they can go to their bishop and get counsel from him. Bishops have the gift of discernment for such things (D&C 46:27).

DRUGS, ABUSE OF
See WORD OF WISDOM.

DUST OF THE EARTH
A phrase that is used several different ways in the scriptures. It means "countless" (Genesis 13:16), "soil" (Job 14:19), "earth" (Daniel 12:2), "insignificant" (Mosiah 2:25), and "dependent on nutrition from the earth, as mortals" (D&C 77:12).

· E ·

EARTH
Created as part of the Father's plan for us. It is sometimes called "the University of Earth" because we have been sent away from our premortal heavenly home to gain physical bodies, to be tested, to gain knowledge and experience as we continue our education toward exaltation.

Jesus created the earth for us, under the direction of the Father (John 1:1–3). At the beginning of the Millennium, "the earth will be renewed and receive its paradisiacal glory" (Articles of Faith 1:10). The earth has seven thousand years of being inhabited by mortals, including the Millennium (D&C 77:6). The earth will die and resurrect (D&C 88:26) and will become the celestial kingdom for its worthy inhabitants for eternity (D&C 130:9–11). It will become a Urim and Thummim for those celestial inhabitants and it

will be Christ's (D&C 130:9). When the earth has finished its mortal mission, it will be "rolled back into the presence of God, and crowned with celestial glory" (*TPJS*, p. 181).

EARTHQUAKES
One of the signs of the times (prophecies that will be fulfilled in the last days as signs to us that the Second Coming is getting close) is that there will be an increase in intensity and frequency of natural disasters, including earthquakes (D&C 88:89–91).

EARTHS
There are many earths like this, currently in outer space, which are serving similar missions for other groups of Heavenly Father's children (Moses 1:33, 35). Our Savior's Atonement works for them also (D&C 76:24). The Savior will visit them

also (D&C 88:58 [see verses 50–61]), but will not live on them as a mortal and be crucified, as was the case on our world. These earths will become celestial kingdoms for their worthy inhabitants, and eventually be moved back into the presence of God (*JD* 17:331–32).

EASTER

The Sunday on which the resurrection of the Savior is celebrated by believers throughout the world. Numerous scriptures testify of His resurrection (Matthew 28; Mark 16; Luke 24; John 20–21; 3 Nephi 11:8–11).

Latter-day Saints believe in and testify of the literal resurrection of Jesus Christ, and that he now has a celestialized, glorified body of flesh and bone (Luke 24:36–39; D&C 130:22).

Latter-day Saints hold Easter services annually but do not celebrate Ash Wednesday, Lent, or Holy Week, as is the case with some other Christian churches.

ECCLESIASTICAL

A term which refers to religious organizations or leadership within them. Example: Bishops and stake presidents are ecclesiastical leaders in The Church of Jesus Christ of Latter-day Saints.

EDEN, GARDEN OF

The garden in which Adam and Eve were placed after their physical bodies were created (Genesis 2:7–8; Moses 3:7–8). The garden was a paradise, a place of beauty and peace, with no death and with no option for Adam and Eve to have children (2 Nephi 2:23).

Two trees in the garden are specifically mentioned in scripture, the tree of life and the tree of knowledge of good and evil (Genesis 2:9; Moses 3:9).

Adam and Eve were given two commandments in the garden, to have children (Genesis 1:28; Moses 2:28) and not to partake of the tree of knowledge of good and evil (Genesis 2:17; Moses 3:17). For more about these, see Adam and also see Eve, in this reference work.

EDEN, LOCATION OF

Brigham Young and Heber C. Kimball both said that the Prophet Joseph Smith taught them that the Garden of Eden was located in what is now Jackson County, Missouri (*JD* 10:235).

EDIFY

To edify or be edified means to be taught and uplifted by the Holy Ghost when studying or being taught the gospel (D&C 50:14, 21–24).

EDMUNDS–TUCKER ACT

Legislation directed against the Latter-day Saints, passed in 1887 by the U.S. government, because of the practice of polygamy among them. Among other things, the act disincorporated the Church and its Perpetual Emigration Fund, on the grounds that they fostered polygamy. In addition, it authorized the seizure by the government of all Church property not directly involved in religious purposes. The act placed extreme hardship on the Church and its members. Over 1,300 Latter-day Saints were put in jail during the 1880s because of legislation against the Church.

EDUCATION

The Church is a strong advocate of education for its members, both men and women. Leaders consistently council the members to obtain as much education as they can, including advanced education beyond high school and secondary schools where possible.

EGYPTUS

Wife of Ham, who was a son of Noah (Abraham 1:23). She was a descendant of Cain (Abraham 1:21-22). The daughter of Ham and Egyptus was also named Egyptus (Abraham 1:25). It was she who discovered the land which became known as Egypt (Abraham 1:23–25).

EIGHT WITNESSES

Eight men were invited by the Prophet Joseph Smith, under the direction of the Lord, to view the gold plates from which the Book of Mormon was translated. Their testimony is recorded in the introductory pages to the Book of Mormon. They were shown the plates in a grove of trees near the home of Joseph's parents in Manchester, New York, shortly after the Three Witnesses were shown them in a vision, in June 1829.

The eight men testified that Joseph showed them the plates, that they looked like gold, that they were allowed to lift the plates and handle the individual sheets in the stack of plates from which the Book of Mormon was translated. They described the engravings as having "the appearance of ancient work, and of curious workmanship" (The Testimony of Eight Witnesses).

The eight men were Christian Whitmer (remained faithful to the Church), Jacob Whitmer (left, never returned to the Church), Peter Whitmer Jr. (remained faithful), John Whitmer (left, never returned), Hiram Page (left, never returned), Joseph Smith Sr. (remained faithful), Hyrum Smith (remained faithful), and Samuel H. Smith (remained faithful). The three who left the Church never denied their testimonies of the gold plates.

ELDER

An office in the Melchizedek Priesthood (D&C 20:45). Normally, worthy men in the Church are given the Melchizedek Priesthood and ordained to the office of elder when they are eighteen years old or some time after baptism if they are converts. An elder has all the rights and privileges of the higher priesthood, which officiates in "the spiritual blessings of the church"

(D&C 107:18). This includes confirming newly baptized members and conferring the gift of the Holy Ghost, administering to the sick, giving blessings, participating in the ordinances of the temple, serving as full-time missionaries, and other duties and responsibilities such as serving in elders quorum presidencies.

The title of "elder" is given to all holders of the Melchizedek Priesthood, including General Authorities.

ELDER BROTHER

Another name for Jesus Christ. He is our "Elder Brother" because He was the first born spirit son of our Heavenly Father (Colossians 1:13–15).

ELECT

A term used to refer to members of the Church who are successfully striving to be faithful to the Lord at all costs and, as a result, are on the path toward exaltation (D&C 25:3; 84:33–34). Even the elect need to be constantly on guard against the devil's wiles and temptations in order to avoid falling (D&C 20:31–32; JS—M 1:22).

ELECTION

In the context of the scriptures, "election" means to live in harmony with the gospel of Jesus Christ, especially the Abrahamic Covenant (Abraham 2:9–11) so that God can "elect" or choose such individuals for exaltation on Judgment Day (2 Peter 1:2–19; JS—M 1:22).

ELEMENTS, ETERNAL NATURE OF

Our physical bodies are made of physical elements, and our spirit bodies are made of spirit matter (D&C 131:7–8). By revelation, Joseph Smith learned, "The elements are eternal, and spirit and element, inseparably connected [in the resurrection] receive a fulness of joy" (D&C 93:33–34).

ELEVENTH HOUR

A term meaning the time shortly before the Savior's Second Coming (D&C 33:3). The phrase comes from the "eleventh hour" parable, given by the Master (Matthew 20:6, 9 [the parable is given in verses 1–16]).

ELIAS

Elias has at least three meanings, as used in the scriptures: (1) A man, apparently from the time of Abraham, who appeared to Joseph Smith and Oliver Cowdery in the Kirtland Temple, on April 3, 1836, and "committed the dispensation of the gospel of Abraham" to them (D&C 110:12), (2) A Greek form of the name Elijah (Matthew 17:3), (3) A forerunner in preparing for specific events in the building of God's kingdom. John the Baptist was an example of this (Luke 1:17; Matthew 3:1–3). Gabriel (Noah—*TPJS*, p. 157) was also an "Elias" who was sent to Mary to announce to her that she would be the mother of the Son of God (Luke 1:26–38).

ELIAS, SPIRIT OF

Joseph Smith explained: "The spirit of Elias is to prepare the way for a greater revelation of God, which is the Priesthood of Elias, or the Priesthood unto which Aaron was ordained. And when God sends a man into the world to prepare for a greater work, holding the keys of the power of Elias, it was called the doctrine of Elias, even from the early ages of the world. . . . We find the Apostles endowed with greater power than John [the Baptist]: their office was more under the spirit and power of Elijah than Elias" (*TPJS*, pp. 335–36).

ELIJAH

The name means "Jehovah is my God" (BD, under "Elijah"). He served as a prophet in the Northern Kingdom of Israel, around 900 BC, during the time that Israel was divided into two nations (1 Kings 17–2 Kings 2). He is one of the best known of the Old Testament prophets. At the end of his mortal mission, he was translated (2 Kings 2:11–12) and taken up into heaven.

About six months before His crucifixion, the Savior took Peter, James, and John up on a mountain, where He was transfigured before them. Elijah appeared to Him there (Matthew 17:1–9) along with Moses (who was also a translated being) and conferred the keys of the priesthood on Peter, James, and John. Malachi prophesied Elijah's return to "turn the heart of the fathers to the children, and the heart of the children to their fathers"

(Malachi 4:5–6), which involves the work of family history and sealing families together in temples. Elijah appeared to Joseph Smith and Oliver Cowdery, in the Kirtland Temple, on April 3, 1836, and restored the keys of sealing families together (D&C 110:13–15), as part of the preparation for the Coming of Christ.

Elijah was resurrected at the time of the Savior's resurrection (D&C 133:55).

ELIJAH, SPIRIT OF

A term referring to the influence of the Spirit which can rest mightily upon individuals and inspire them to become engaged in genealogical research and family history, including sealing families in the temples. Since Elijah restored the keys of this work to Joseph Smith and Oliver Cowdery (D&C 110:13–15), this type of inspiration is often called "the Spirit of Elijah."

ELOHIM

As used by members of the Church, this is a name for Heavenly Father. It is a very sacred name and should be spoken of with reverent care. The First Presidency taught: "God the Eternal Father, whom we designate by the exalted name-title 'Elohim,' is the literal Parent of our Lord and Savior Jesus Christ, and of the spirits of the human race" (*MFP* 5:26).

EMBLEMS

Objects which represent something else. For example, the bread and water used in the sacrament are emblems of the Savior's flesh and blood.

EMERGENCY PREPAREDNESS

The Church teaches its members to prepare for emergencies. For example, Latter-day Saints are encouraged to have basic food necessities for survival, along with cash savings which could tide them over during times of emergency. Where possible, and where laws of their country permit, they are encouraged to have a year's supply of basic food (go to lds.org on the Internet, and then go to "Provident Living" for more on this).

EMMANUEL

See also IMMANUEL. A name derived from the Hebrew "Immanuel," meaning "God is with us." The angel told Joseph that the child Mary was going to bear was coming in fulfillment of prophecy that God (Jesus Christ) would come to earth and live among mankind, and the child was to be named Emmanuel (Matthew 1:23).

END

Among many uses of this word in the scriptures, it is often used to mean "goal" or "purpose." Examples: "To this end was I born" (John 18:37). "To the end that" (Leviticus 17:5).

"Endure to the end" (1 Nephi 22:31) can mean "remain faithful until the end of your lives," but it also has the connotation of enduring until you reach the goal of exaltation.

END OF THE EARTH

Technically speaking, the earth will never have an end, because it will eventually become the celestial kingdom for its righteous inhabitants (D&C 130:9–11). The phrase is context sensitive and can mean every part of the earth (Isaiah 48:20; 49:6), the end of the earth's mortal mission (D&C 43:31), the destruction of the wicked at the Second Coming (JS—M 1:55).

END OF THE WORLD

A phrase meaning the destruction of the wicked, as used in JS—M 1:4.

ENDLESS

See also ENDLESS PUNISHMENT. A term that has various meanings according to the context in the scriptures. When used as an adjective, it can mean lasting forever. Example: God is endless (D&C 19:10). However, it can also mean something that is God's. For example, we might say "endless" sunsets, meaning the kind of sunsets God creates. "Endless" is also used as a noun, a name for God. Example: "Endless is my name" (D&C 19:10).

ENDLESS PUNISHMENT

See also ENDLESS. "Endless" can mean "God's punishment," in other words, "the kind of punishment meted out by God." When used in this sense, it does not mean "forever"; rather, it means a "temporary punishment which is the penalty handed out by the Lord in consequence of disobedience." Thus, "endless torment" (D&C 19:6) can be the temporary torment received by the wicked when they are turned over to Satan to suffer for their own sins because they would not repent (D&C 19:15–17). When they have suffered sufficiently, they will be "redeemed from the devil" (D&C 76:85) and placed in telestial glory, which is a kingdom of glory (D&C 76:89).

ENDLESS TORMENT

See ENDLESS PUNISHMENT.

ENDOWMENT

The word itself generally means "a gift intended by the giver to assist the recipient in attaining a specific goal." As used in the vocabulary of the Church, "endowment" means a course of instruction in the Father's plan of salvation for His children, accompanied by ordinances and the making of covenants. This course is given only in temples, and is called "the endowment." The endowment ceremony is designed to help worthy members in their quest to return to live with the Father in exaltation for eternity. Temple garments are worn by endowed members to remind them of the covenants they have made in the temple to live the gospel of Jesus Christ.

ENDOWMENT HOUSE, THE

Before the completion of the Salt Lake Temple in 1893, Latter-day Saints used the Endowment House for temple ordinances. The Endowment House was designed by Truman O. Angel (the chief architect of the Salt Lake Temple) and built on the northwest corner of Temple Square. It was dedicated on May 5, 1855. It was a two-story structure, 34 by 44 feet, with small, one-story additions on both ends. In addition to about 2,500 marriages annually, plus washings and anointings, 54,170 endowments were performed during the thirty-four years it was in use. It was torn down in 1889, as the Salt Lake Temple neared completion.

ENDURE TO THE END

See also END. A frequently used phrase in scripture (1 Nephi 22:31) which can be considered to have two aspects of meaning: (1) To remain faithful to the Lord until death. (2) To remain faithful to the Lord until one reaches the goal of exaltation.

ENOCH

See also CITY OF ENOCH. An ancient prophet who lived approximately 3400–3000 BC. He is perhaps best known for the fact that the city of righteousness, which he founded, was taken up into heaven (Moses 7:21; Genesis 5:24). Most of the writings of Enoch were left out of the Bible, but much was restored through the Prophet Joseph Smith (Moses 6:21–7:69).

ENSIGN MAGAZINE

A monthly magazine, published by the Church, containing articles and messages from Church leaders and members. In other languages, it is called the *Liahona*. In addition to the ten regular monthly issues each year, two special issues containing general conference talks and proceedings come out in November and May for the October and April conferences, respectively.

The title *Ensign* comes from the Bible (example: Isaiah 11:12) and is used in various scriptural settings to mean a signal to gather, a standard, flag, or banner to attract people's attention to the work of the Lord.

ENSIGN PEAK

A prominent peak, north of Temple Square in Salt Lake City, Utah, which Brigham Young had seen in vision before entering the Salt Lake Valley with the advance pioneer company in July 1847.

ENSIGN TO THE NATIONS

Isaiah prophesied that in the last days, preparatory for the Second Coming of Christ, the Lord would set up "an ensign to the nations" (Isaiah 11:12) and signal from it for all people to gather to the true gospel of Jesus Christ, which was restored by the Prophet Joseph Smith. The Church is fulfilling this prophecy.

EONS

Extremely long periods of time. Often used in gospel discussions to refer to our premortal life as spirit sons and daughters of our heavenly parents.

EPHRAIM

One of the tribes of Israel, to whom the birthright was given (Genesis 48:13–20; 1 Chronicles 5:1–2; Jeremiah 31:9). He was a son of Joseph (Genesis 41:50–52), a grandson of Jacob, and a great, great grandson of Abraham. Many members of the Church today trace their lineage through Ephraim, as given in their patriarchal blessings.

Many descendants of Ephraim have been gathered into the gospel first, in the last days, and have the responsibility of preparing the way for others to join the Church (D&C 133:32, 34).

EPISTLE

Another name for "letter." The Apostle Paul's letters to various members of the early church in the New Testament are called "epistles" (see titles of Paul's letters in the New Testament, as given in the Bible).

EPISTLES OF PAUL

See also EPISTLE. Paul wrote fourteen letters or "epistles" which are contained in the New Testament. These letters were written to individual members of the Church as well as to wards and branches of the Church. There is debate among some Bible scholars as to whether or not Paul wrote Hebrews, but Joseph Smith confirmed that he is the author (*TPJS*, p. 59). His letters are arranged in the New Testament according to length (except for Hebrews, which comes last), beginning with the longest. They contain much detailed doctrine and are very valuable to us in studying, teaching, and preaching the gospel.

EQUALITY OF MEN AND WOMEN

The Church teaches that men and women are equal in the sight of God. While the Lord has provided a division of responsibility, such that women are able to bear children and men receive the priesthood, through which they serve others, the scriptures affirm that both men and women can become gods, as husbands and wives. This confirms again that they are equal (D&C 132:20).

In "The Family: A Proclamation to the World," given September 23, 1995, the First Presidency and Quorum of the Twelve Apostles of the Church confirmed doctrinally that husbands and wives are equal. They stated, "Fathers and mothers are obligated to help one another as equal partners."

ESPOUSAL

The basic term used for what we sometimes call the "engagement" of Joseph and Mary, before they were married. Actually, in the culture of that day, "espoused" (Matthew 1:18) was a much more binding agreement than an engagement is in our day. There were strong commitments and strict rules for behavior during the espousal period. For example, during the espousal period, the bride-to-be lived with her

family or friends and communication between her and her husband-to-be was carried on by a friend.

ESTATE, FIRST

See FIRST ESTATE.

ESTATE, SECOND

See SECOND ESTATE. See also FIRST ESTATE.

ETERNAL

Forever.

ETERNAL INCREASE

Those who live worthy to become gods (D&C 132:20) will live as husbands and wives eternally and will have the blessing of "eternal increase," in other words, of having an unlimited number of spirit children. Spirit children will be born to them as offspring (Acts 17:28–29), just as we were to our heavenly parents (Hebrews 12:9). This is also referred to as "a continuation of the seeds forever and ever" (D&C 132:19). As gods, they will create worlds for their spirit children and send them through the same "great plan of happiness" (Alma 42:8) that the Father has in place for us.

ETERNAL LIFE

"The greatest of all the gifts of God" (D&C 14:7). Eternal life is a term which always means "exaltation," when used in the scriptures (John 3:15; Romans 6:23; 1 John 1:2; 2 Nephi 2:28; D&C 5:22; 18:8; 131:5; 138:51; Moses 1:39).

ETERNAL LIVES

In gospel conversations, can refer to those who attain exaltation. However, this phrase usually refers to the spirit children who will be born to those who become gods. It is one of the blessings of exaltation. Those who become gods will continue having "eternal lives" or spirit children eternally (D&C 132:24).

ETERNAL MARRIAGE

See CELESTIAL MARRIAGE.

ETERNAL PROGRESSION

The condition of those who eventually attain exaltation. The concept that, for those who prove willing and worthy, progress will continue forever. God continues to progress in terms of dominion as He adds additional worlds to His realm as a Heavenly Father. However, the exact definition of "eternal progress" has not yet been revealed. Thus, we will have to wait for an authorized explanation of this doctrine.

ETERNAL ROUND

See ONE ETERNAL ROUND.

ETERNITY TO ETERNITY

An expression used in D&C 76:4. In some gospel discussions, this phrase is used to refer to premortal life as an "eternity" in which we lived before coming to earth, coupled with the "eternity" in which we will live after resurrection and final judgment. Thus, in effect, we will have gone from "eternity" to mortality and on to another "eternity" as the Father carries out His plan for us.

The phrase is also used occasionally to describe the work of the Father, as He continues to use the same plan of salvation for additional spirit children, sending them from one "eternity" to the next.

EUNUCHS

In the scriptures, the term generally refers to "a class of emasculated men attached to the courts of eastern rulers" who "were employed to watch over the harems" (BD, under "Eunuch"; see 2 Kings 20:18; Isaiah 39:7; Matthew 19:12; Acts 8:27–38).

EUTHANASIA

The so-called "mercy killing" of someone who is terminally ill. The Church does not condone this practice.

EVANGELISTS

A term for "patriarchs" (Ephesians 4:11, footnote d).

EVE

Wife of Adam, created by the Lord as a "help meet" for Adam (Genesis 2:18). The word "meet," as used in this context, means "essential," "necessary" (compare with D&C 58:26). Some Bible readers make the mistake of combining "help" and "meet" into one word, and coming out with "helpmeet" or "helpmate," which is a sad mistake because it is often translated in people's minds to mean "servant." Such is by no means the case. Together with her husband, Adam, Eve began the process, as mortal parents, of bringing us spirit children of the Father to earth, to take our turn in mortality.

The Church teaches the highest respect for Eve as "the mother of all living" (Genesis 3:20). However, many religions condemn Eve for bringing misery and evil into the world. We are indebted to modern revelation for additional details which are vital to correct understanding of Eve's role in the beginning scenes of the Garden of Eden which led to the Fall. We will provide quotes here which support our respect and appreciation for both Adam and Eve and which support the idea that Eve made an intentional choice, rather than naively making a blunder.

"Satan was present to tempt Adam and Eve, much as he would try to thwart others in their divine missions: 'and he sought also to beguile Eve, for he knew not the mind of God, wherefore he sought to destroy the world' (Moses 4:6). Eve faced the choice between selfish ease and unselfishly facing tribulation and death (Widtsoe, p. 193). As befit her calling, she realized that there was no other way and deliberately chose mortal life so as to further the purpose of God and bring children into the world" (*EM*, under "Eve").

The question comes up as to how Eve could "deliberately" choose, as indicated by Elder Widtsoe in the above quote, when she and Adam were "innocent" in the Garden of Eden. Where would she get the knowledge with which to make such an informed decision? Elder Widtsoe answers this question in the following quote. He said: "Such was the problem before our first parents: to remain forever at selfish ease in the Garden of Eden, or to face unselfishly tribulation and death, in bringing to pass the purposes of the Lord for a host of waiting spirit children. They chose the latter. . . . This they did with open eyes and minds as to consequences. The memory of their former estates [including their premortal spirit existence] may have been dimmed, but the gospel had been taught them during their sojourn in the Garden of Eden. . . . The choice that they made raises Adam and Even to preeminence among all who have come on earth" (Widtsoe, *Evidences and Reconciliations*, p. 193–94).

Elder George Albert Smith, who later became the President of the Church, also taught on this subject. He said: "When God created the earth and placed our first parents upon it, He did not leave them without knowledge concerning Himself. It is true that there had been taken from them the remembrance of their pre-existent life, but in His tender mercy He talked with them and later He sent His choice servants to instruct them in the things pertaining to eternal life" (CR [Oct. 1928]: 90–91).

Thus, Latter-day Saints hold Eve

in a position of highest esteem and respect, being grateful for her sacrifice of her own comforts in the Garden of Eden for the good of mankind.

EVENING AND MORNING STAR

The first newspaper published by the Church. Each issue consisted of eight pages with double columns. It was published monthly in Independence, Missouri, from June 1832 to July 1833, for a total of fourteen issues published in Missouri.

After the press was destroyed by mobs in Missouri, publication was resumed several months later from Kirtland, Ohio. Ten issues were published from December 1833 to September 1834.

EVERLASTING LIFE

Another term for "eternal life," which means "exaltation" (John 3:16; Alma 32:41; D&C 45:5).

EVIL SPIRITS

Spirits who were the "third part of the hosts of heaven" (D&C 29:36) who were cast out of heaven with Satan (Revelation 12:4). They are on the earth today, helping the devil in his efforts to snag more of us in his trap. These evil spirits will eventually go with him permanently into perdition (D&C 88:114), along with any mortals from this earth who become sons of perdition (D&C 76:32–33).

EVOLUTION

There is much yet to be revealed about the creation of the earth and the placement of people and other forms of life on it. We are told by revelation that the details will be revealed when the Savior comes at the beginning of the Millennium (D&C 101:32–34). In the meantime, most arguments between those who believe in evolution and those who do not are probably pointless and fruitless.

However, if arguments for evolution include the theory that there is no God and that life on earth is basically a biological accident, Genesis chapter 1 disagrees completely. That and other passages of scripture bear witness that God created the earth and placed all forms of life on it, including the crowning achievement of creation, that of placing Adam and Eve upon it. It is all part of the Father's plan for us.

A statement by the First Presidency, published in 1909, can be helpful: "It is held by some that Adam was not the first man upon this earth, and that the original human being was a development from lower orders of the animal creation. These, however, are the theories of men. The word of the Lord declares that Adam was 'the first man of all men' (Moses 1:34), and we are therefore in duty bound to regard him as the primal parent of our race. It was shown to the brother of Jared that all men were created in the beginning after the image of God;

and whether we take this to mean the spirit or the body, or both, it commits us to the same conclusion: Man began life as a human being, in the likeness of our Heavenly Father. . . . The Church of Jesus Christ of Latter-day Saints, basing its belief on divine revelation, ancient and modern, proclaims man to be the direct and lineal offspring of Deity. God Himself is an exalted man, perfected, enthroned, and supreme. By His almighty power He organized the earth, and all that it contains, from spirit and element, which exist co-eternally with Himself. He formed every plant that grows, and every animal that breathes . . . . He made the tadpole and the ape, the lion and the elephant but He did not make them in His own image, nor endow them with Godlike reason and intelligence. . . . Man is the child of God, formed in the divine image and endowed with divine attributes, and even as the infant son of an earthly father and mother is capable in due time of becoming a man, so the undeveloped offspring of celestial parentage is capable, by experience through ages and aeons, of evolving into a God" (The First Presidency [Joseph F. Smith, John R. Winder, and Anthon H. Lund], in James R. Clark, comp., *Messages of the First Presidency of The Church of Jesus Christ of Latter-day Saints*, 4:205–6).

One interesting question that comes up if one subscribes to the theory that people developed from lower forms of life is the question of temple work for deceased ancestors. Should temple work be done for lower forms of life in the ancestral chain?

It will indeed be interesting to get the rest of the story from the Savior at the beginning of the Millennium.

EXALTATION

Life in the highest degree of glory in the celestial kingdom (D&C 132:19). It is also referred to in scripture as "eternal life" (Moses 1:39). Those who attain exaltation live in the family unit forever (D&C 131:1–4). They become gods (D&C 76:58; 132:20). "Exaltation" is another way of saying "the type of life that God lives." It is only available to men and women, as husbands and wives, who have the ordinance of celestial marriage and live worthy of it (D&C 132:17, 19–20).

EXCOMMUNICATION

See also DISCIPLINE, CHURCH; DISCIPLINARY COUNCILS; DISFELLOWSHIP. Excommunication is the most severe discipline that can be given by a disciplinary council. It is imposed only for the most serious sins. An individual who is excommunicated from the Church is no longer a member and has lost all membership privileges and accompanying blessings, including temple endowment and sealing. Such an individual may not partake of the sacrament, pray in public meetings of the Church, pay tithing or offerings, wear temple garments, give a public talk or a prayer in church, teach a class, or hold a calling in the

Church. If the individual is a male member who held the priesthood, he no longer has the priesthood. An excommunicated former member is invited to attend public meetings of the Church and to meet frequently with the bishop and stake president, where compassionate help is offered for getting one's life back in order.

After a sufficient period of time has elapsed, the individual can apply through the bishop for readmission into the Church by rebaptism. Temple blessings can be restored under the direction of proper priesthood authorities, including temple marriage if the marriage is still intact.

It is not uncommon for members who are guilty of very serious transgression to request excommunication in order to get their lives in order and start fresh.

EXORCISM

Exorcism, as commonly defined and practiced in other churches, is not practiced in The Church of Jesus Christ of Latter-day Saints. It is, in fact, a counterfeit of the use of the true priesthood of God. The Apostle Paul cast evil spirits out by the power of his priesthood (Acts 19:11–12). Faithful elders in the Church today have the authority to cast out evil spirits if prompted to do so by the Spirit of the Lord.

EXPIATION

A term sometimes used in gospel conversations and teaching that means the cleansing of our sins through the atoning sacrifice of the Savior. For example, one could say that our sins are "expiated" by the Atonement of Jesus Christ.

· F ·

FAITH

Faith is more than belief. A person can believe something but not do anything about it. Faith, on the other hand, implies action. In other words, true faith makes a difference in how you behave.

In the context of gospel teaching and discussion, we always need to think in terms of "faith in the Lord Jesus Christ" (Articles of Faith 1:4), rather than merely the word "faith." Faith in Jesus Christ is the motivating force in all we do as we strive to live the gospel and work toward exaltation. Joseph Smith taught that this type of faith is "the first principle in revealed religion, and the foundation of all righteousness" (*Lectures on Faith*, Lecture First, paragraph 1).

Faith in the Atonement of Jesus Christ is our motivation for seeking forgiveness of sins. Because of our faith, we can repent with full confidence that our sins will be remembered "no more" (D&C 58:42–43) here on earth as well as on the day of final judgment.

"Faith is a principle of action and power" (*TF*, p. 54). The scriptures give many examples of action and power on the part of some who have had great faith (Hebrews 11; Ether 12:6–20). Faith is influential in the healing of the sick (D&C 42:43–52).

In *Lectures on Faith*, Lecture Third (see BD, under "Faith"), we are taught that there are three major requirements for strong faith.

(1) The idea that God actually exists.

(2) A correct idea of who and what He is, including His attributes.

(3) Knowledge that the type of life we are living is in harmony with His will.

Faith is a gift of the Spirit (D&C 46:19–20) and can be developed by all who are willing to do their best to live according to the commandments and teachings of the gospel of Jesus Christ (Alma 32).

FAITH AND WORKS

The scriptures clearly teach that faith and works go together (James 2:17–18).

However, some Christians make the mistake of taking some of Paul's writing out of context, including the context of the whole Bible, and teaching that we are saved by grace, and not by works at all. Example:

Romans 3:27–28

27 Where is boasting then? It is excluded. By what law? of works? Nay: but by the law of faith.

28 Therefore we conclude that a man is justified by faith without the deeds of the law.

On the other hand, Paul teaches:

Romans 2:13

13 (For not the hearers of the law are just before God, but the doers of the law shall be justified.

What is going on here? The answer is simple. We must keep Paul's writings in their context, in their setting in the scriptures. In our example, above, in Romans 3:27–28, Paul is speaking to Jewish members of the Church who, because of their past tradition and culture before their baptism, are going through the motions of religion. They go through the rituals and sacrifices and works but don't have faith and have not internalized the true gospel. Therefore, Paul emphasizes faith to them and downplays empty works, which won't save them. Also, the "law" in verse 28 refers to the law of Moses, which was fulfilled by the Savior.

On the other hand, in Romans 2:13, quoted above, Paul's audience consists of Gentile converts to the Church who are not as concerned as they should be about works. Rather, they are thinking that, since they have been baptized and are members, they don't need much else. Therefore, Paul's emphasis to them is that they must pay much closer attention to righteous works and deeds, including avoiding sin and unrighteous behaviors.

FAITH IN JESUS CHRIST
See FAITH.

FALL OF ADAM AND EVE
The Fall refers to the partaking of the forbidden fruit by Adam and Eve in the Garden of Eden (Genesis 3:6, Moses 4:12). The Fall was good (2 Nephi 2:22–25). It was a vital part of the Father's plan for us. It has been said that rather than "falling down," Adam and Eve "fell forward," meaning that the Fall was a necessary step forward in providing the opportunity for us to progress toward exaltation. The Fall cannot be adequately taught without also teaching the Atonement of Christ. They go hand in hand (Alma 22:12–14). The Fall gives us the opportunity to enter mortality, and the Atonement opens the door for us to progress, in spite of mistakes and shortcomings associated with our mortal probation.

We hold Adam and Eve in highest esteem for their role in opening the door for us to enter mortality. Few, if any other, religions share our respect and appreciation for them. You may wish to read the entry under "Eve" in this book to learn more about Eve and her role in the Fall.

FALLING AWAY
See APOSTASY.

FALSE CHRISTS
Prophecies indicate that in the last days before the Second Coming of Jesus Christ, there will be many "false Christs" whose intention will be to deceive many and draw attention to themselves (Matthew 24:24; Mark 13:22). There are many ways in which these prophecies could be fulfilled. Among other things, people could claim to be Christ. Some could claim that the Second Coming has already taken place and they are Christ (as in the case of Ann Lee—see heading to D&C 49).

In another sense, any who intentionally teach philosophies or doctrines which are in opposition to the true gospel of Jesus Christ might be considered to be "false Christs" (Mormon 1:15). Another term for them would be "false prophets" (Matthew 24:24).

FALSE DOCTRINE
Ideas, teachings, philosophies, and so forth, which oppose or lead away from the truths taught in the pure gospel of Jesus Christ, whether intentional or unintentional, are false doctrines. Satan is a master at inspiring false doctrines (Jacob 7:1–4, 6–7; Alma 1:2–6, 12; 30:6–48).

FALSE GODS
We often think of idols and idol worship as examples of false gods (Leviticus 19:4). Such practices go directly against the first two of the Ten Commandments (Exodus 20:3–4).

However, any priority we set which takes precedence over God and His commandments can properly be considered a "false god."

FALSE PROPHETS

Many prophecies of the last days warn about the abundance of false prophets in the days preceding the Second Coming of Jesus Christ (Mark 13:22). We often think of false prophets in terms of those who teach religious doctrines and philosophies which are contrary to those of the true gospel of Jesus Christ. Such is the case.

However, there are much more influential "false prophets" in the media, in politics, on university campuses, in dictatorships, and countless other positions of influence who lead people away from God.

FALSE RELIGIONS

This can be a sensitive issue, because there are many honest and sincere individuals who are teaching much that is good and honorable in their respective religions. In general, those who adhere sincerely to their teachings are already living on a terrestrial level, which means that they are honorable people (D&C 76:71, 75). And when we invite them to consider the teachings and doctrines of The Church of Jesus Christ of Latter-day Saints, we respect and build up the good they already have (D&C 10:52) as stepping stones to receiving the rest of the gospel of Christ. In other words, we fill in that which is missing as they join the Church.

FALSE REVELATION

Satan is a master of deception, and giving false revelation is one of his well-used tools. Knowing the scriptures and being familiar with the words of our modern prophets is one of the best protections against being deceived by the devil. If we feel that we have been "inspired" to go against the scriptures or the teachings of our living prophets, we can rest assured that the "revelation" is from Satan. One of the important functions of the gift of the Holy Ghost is to warn us against deception. Those who do their best to live righteously and keep the commandments tend to be in tune with the promptings of the Holy Ghost and can sense right or wrong, whether or not they understand the particulars about a given situation.

FALSE SPIRITS

The one-third of our group of premortal spirits who were cast out with the devil as a result of the War in Heaven (Revelation 12:4, 7–9) are literally "false spirits," meaning that they go about working evil of every sort as coworkers and followers of Satan. They do everything they can to support the devil as he attempts to persuade people to do evil (Moroni 7:17). Joseph Smith taught, "Lying spirits are going forth in the earth. There will be great manifestations of spirits, both false and true. . . . Not every spirit, or vision or singing, is of God" (TPJS, p. 161–62).

A loving Father has made sure that we are not left on our own when it comes to detecting the influence of these false spirits. "The Spirit of Christ is given to every man, that he may know good from evil" (Moroni 7:16).

FALSE WITNESS

"Bearing false witness" is another way of saying "lying," and is often used in the context of lying about others. It violates one of the Ten Commandments (Exodus 20:16). Unrepentantant liars go to telestial glory (D&C 76:103).

FAMILIAR SPIRITS

Fortune tellers and other such people who try to contact the dead are said to have "familiar spirits." In other words, they are attempting to contact evil spirits in order to get "revelation" for their clients. Such conduct is against the commandments of God (Leviticus 19:31).

FAMILY: A PROCLAMATION TO THE WORLD, THE

On September 23, 1995, the First Presidency and the Council of the Twelve Apostles of The Church of Jesus Christ of Latter-day Saints issued the following proclamation on the family to all the world. It is titled "The Family: A Proclamation to the World, The First Presidency and Council of the Twelve Apostles of The Church of Jesus Christ of Latter-day Saints."

After presenting the proclamation in its entirety, we will list thirty current issues addressed in this revelation to us and the world from the Lord

through His modern prophets, seers, and revelators.

"We, the First Presidency and the council of the Twelve Apostles of The Church of Jesus Christ of Latter-day Saints, solemnly proclaim that marriage between a man and a woman is ordained of God and that the family is central to the Creator's plan for the eternal destiny of His children.

"All human beings—male and female—are created in the image of God. Each is a beloved spirit son or daughter of heavenly parents, and, as such, each has a divine nature and destiny. Gender is an essential characteristic of individual premortal, mortal, and eternal identity and purpose.

"In the premortal realm, spirit sons and daughters knew and worshiped God as their eternal Father and accepted His plan by which His children could obtain a physical body and gain earthly experience to progress toward perfection and ultimately realize his or her divine destiny as an heir of eternal life. The divine plan of happiness enables family relationships to be perpetuated beyond the grave. Sacred ordinances and covenants available in holy temples make it possible for individuals to return to the presence of God and for families to be united eternally.

"The first commandment that God gave to Adam and Eve pertained to their potential for parenthood as husband and wife. We declare that God's commandment for His children to multiply and replenish the earth remains in force. We further declare that God has commanded that the sacred powers of procreation are to be employed only between man and woman, lawfully wedded as husband and wife.

"We declare the means by which mortal life is created to be divinely appointed. We affirm the sanctity of life and of its importance in God's eternal plan.

"Husband and wife have a solemn responsibility to love and care for each other and for their children. 'Children are an heritage of the Lord.' (Psalm 127:3.) Parents have a sacred duty to rear their children in love and righteousness, to provide for their physical and spiritual needs, to teach them to love and serve one another, to observe the commandments of God and to be law-abiding citizens wherever they live. Husbands and wives—mothers and fathers—will be held accountable before God for the discharge of these obligations.

"The family is ordained of God. Marriage between man and woman is essential to His eternal plan. Children are entitled to birth within the bonds of matrimony, and to be reared by a father and a mother who honor marital vows with complete fidelity. Happiness in family life is most likely to be achieved when founded upon the teachings of the Lord Jesus Christ. Successful marriages and families are established and maintained on principles of faith, prayer, repentance, forgiveness, respect,

love, compassion, work, and wholesome recreational activities. By divine design, fathers are to preside over their families in love and righteousness and are responsible to provide the necessities of life and protection of their families. Mothers are primarily responsible for the nurture of their children. In these sacred responsibilities, fathers and mothers are obligated to help one another as equal partners. Disability, death, or other circumstances may necessitate individual adaptation. Extended families should lend support when needed.

"We warn that individuals who violate covenants of chastity, who abuse spouse or offspring, or who fail to fulfill family responsibilities will one day stand accountable before God. Further, we warn that the disintegration of the family will bring upon individuals, communities, and nations the calamities foretold by ancient and modern prophets.

"We call upon responsible citizens and officers of government everywhere to promote those measures designed to maintain and strengthen the family as the fundamental unit of society." (September 23, 1995)

As noted in the introduction to this topic, we will now list thirty current issues addressed by the Lord in this proclamation. No doubt, there are more. By the way, many members of the Church have inserted copies of this proclamation into their scriptures or scripture carrying cases in order to have quick reference access to it.

If you look at a copy of the official printing of the proclamation, you will see that there are nine paragraphs in it. As we list thirty current issues, we will note which paragraph(s) they appear in so you can find them more easily.

30 Current Issues Addressed

1. The family is central to the Father's plan for us. "Family," in one form or another, is listed thirteen times in this brief proclamation (the title and paragraphs 1, 3, 7–9).

2. The institution of marriage is God-given and is fundamental to society (paragraphs 1, 4, 7).

3. The importance of the traditional family, with a mother and a father (paragraphs 1, 4, 6–7).

4. Same sex marriage. Marriage is to be between a man and a woman (paragraphs 1, 4, 7).

5. The worth of each individual on earth (paragraphs 2–3).

6. Gender is part of our eternal identity (paragraph 2).

7. Premortal existence (paragraphs 2–3).

8. We had agency in premortality and accepted the Father's plan there (paragraph 3).

9. People can progress to the point of being like God (paragraphs 2–3).

10. Families can be together eternally (paragraph 3).

11. The significance of temples and ordinances performed there (paragraph 3).

12. Zero growth population (paragraphs 4, 6).

13. Sexual relationships outside of marriage (paragraphs 2, 4–5, 7–8).

14. The sanctity of life. Abortion. Euthanasia (mercy killing). Suicide. (Paragraphs 2, 5).

15. The seriousness of marriage responsibilities (paragraph 6).

16. The importance of having children (paragraphs 1, 4, 6).

17. Obeying the laws of the land (paragraph 6).

18. Accountability for providing righteous homes (paragraph 6).

19. Ingredients of righteous homes (paragraphs 6–7).

20. Placement of babies born out of wedlock (paragraph 7).

21. The role and responsibilities of fathers (paragraphs 2, 7–8).

22. The role and responsibilities of mothers (paragraphs 2, 7–8).

23. The role of children (paragraphs 6–7).

24. The equality of fathers and mothers (paragraph 7).

25. Adaptation for other circumstances in families (paragraph 7).

26. Violation of the law of chastity (paragraph 8).

27. Spouse abuse (paragraph 8).

28. Child abuse (paragraph 8).

29. The causes of prophesied last days calamities (paragraph 8).

30. The responsibility of citizens and government officials to strengthen the family (paragraph 9).

FAMILY, BASIC UNIT OF SOCIETY

The word of the Lord through His modern prophets, seers, and revelators states clearly that the family is "the fundamental unit of society" ("Proclamation," last paragraph). Furthermore, the sealing of families together for eternity is the fundamental purpose of the gospel of Jesus Christ (Malachi 4:5–6; D&C 2:1–3).

The above-quoted proclamation on the family gives counsel from the Lord as to how to promote and maintain the family in its God-given role. To read the entire proclamation, see "Family: A Proclamation to the World, The" in this reference work.

FAMILY HISTORY

A major emphasis in The Church of Jesus Christ of Latter-day Saints. It has many facets, including genealogical research, the keeping of personal histories, journals, certificates of achievement, family photo journals, scrapbooks of events in the lives of individuals and families, and so forth.

Seeking out the names and histories of one's ancestors and sealing them together as families in temples is one of the main missions of the restored gospel. To support this ongoing work as well as to help nonmembers find information about their family lines and ancestors, the Church has established family history centers and an extensive online program (available at lds.org). These helps have become known worldwide and are accessed by millions of people annually.

FAMILY HOME EVENING

The Church urges families to select one evening each week, usually Monday evening, to get together as a family and spend time in activities such as studying the gospel, reading the scriptures, playing games, chatting, singing, working together on projects, doing service, etc., and generally strengthening family ties. Helps and resources for family home evenings are available for parents and children online at lds.org.

FAMILY PRAYER

The Church encourages parents to gather their children together in daily family prayer. Ideally, this takes place both morning and evening. Where possible, the privilege of saying the prayer is rotated from one family member to another, as the days go by, and includes young children, usually with some coaching and help from a parent or older sibling.

FAMILY REGISTRY

In times past, this has been a service provided by the Family History Department of the Church to help individuals working on the same family lines to get in touch with each other and thus avoid duplication of effort in research. You would do well to go online to lds. org and see what the latest helps from the Church are on this.

FAMILY SEARCH

An automated computer system that was designed to help individuals simplify their family history research. The Church continues to update and improve available helps for groups and individuals seeking assistance in their family history research. Go online to lds. org for the latest programs and helps.

FAMILY UNIT

See FAMILY, BASIC UNIT OF SOCI-ETY. *See also* FAMILY: A PROCLAMA-TION TO THE WORLD, THE.

FAST AND TESTIMONY MEETING

Once a month, usually on the first Sunday of the month, Latter-day Saints go to church fasting from food and drink, and attend a special sacrament meeting called "fast and testimony meeting." After the usual opening exercises, business, and partaking of the sacrament, the rest of the meeting is available for individual members to bear their testimonies of the gospel to the congregation.

FAST DAY

See also FAST OFFERINGS. Once a month, usually in connection with

the first Sunday of the month, members fast for two consecutive meals (see *Church News* article, back page, Saturday, July 21, 2007). They give a fast offering or donation to the Church for use in helping the poor and the needy in the Church as well as outside of the Church. This donation can reflect the actual money saved by not eating, but often is a generous fast offering consisting of much more money than the actual cost of meals missed.

FAST MEETINGS

See FAST AND TESTIMONY MEET-ING.

FAST OFFERINGS

See also FAST DAY. Voluntary donations given by members of the Church which are used to assist the poor and the needy in the Church and outside of the Church. Fast offerings are distributed by the bishops and branch presidents of the Church on the local level to needy members, and by the general leadership of the Church to assist with humanitarian service throughout the world. It is done quietly and often amounts to millions of dollars for a particular natural disaster.

FASTING

See also FAST DAY. Fasting, the abstaining from food and drink for a length of time, is referred to throughout the scriptures as a means of humbling oneself and gaining access to the help and blessings of the Lord (2 Samuel

12:16; Ezra 8:23; Daniel 6:18; Mark 9:29; 1 Corinthians 7:5; Alma 5:46; D&C 59:13).

We often encounter situations that we cannot solve without divine intervention and help. Fasting is a way in which we can give focused effort and sacrifice on our part in order to put extra meaning into our prayers to the Lord for His help and blessing in a particular matter.

FATHER IN HEAVEN

The Supreme Being in the heavens (Ephesians 4:6). The "Father of [our] spirits" (Hebrews 12:9). We are His offspring (Acts 17:28–29). He has a glorified, resurrected body of flesh and bone (D&C 130:22). His work and eternal joy consists in helping us to become like Him (Moses 1:39). His plan of salvation for us is the "great plan of happiness" (Alma 42:8), designed to give us the opportunity to live the happiest lifestyle of all in family units in eternity; in other words, to become like Him and live like He does, eventually receiving all that He has (D&C 84:37–38).

FATHER OF LIES

Another name for Satan (2 Nephi 9:9).

FATHER OF SPIRITS

See also FATHER IN HEAVEN. We are literal spirit offspring of our Heavenly Father (Acts 17:28–29), and as such, we have the potential to become like Him (Matthew 5:48). He is indeed the "Father of spirits" (Hebrews 12:9).

From the above references and many others, we understand that, as literal spirit sons and daughters, we were born and raised in the home of our heavenly parents ("Proclamation," paragraph 2). Our heavenly parents possess glorified, resurrected, exalted bodies of flesh and bone which produce spirit offspring. Thus, when we sing "I am a child of God" (*Hymns*, no. 301), we are singing literal truth.

FATHER'S BLESSINGS

It is the privilege and opportunity of fathers who hold the Melchizedek Priesthood to give father's blessings to their children. This is commonly done at the beginning of the school year, on special occasions when a son or daughter is facing important challenges, or any other time when the need is felt and the request is made.

FEAR OF GOD

A scriptural phrase which is often used two different ways: (1) For the righteous, it means respect and reverence for God (Exodus 18:21). (2) For the wicked, it can mean actual fear of the judgment and punishment of God because they are not living in harmony with His commandments (Luke 23:40).

FEAST OF PASSOVER

A feast celebrated anciently by the Israelites in memory of the fact that the destroying angel "passed over" the dwellings of the children of Israel and did not slay their firstborn, after they put the blood of a lamb on their door posts (Exodus 12:21–29). On the other hand, the firstborn of the Egyptians was slain, thus setting the stage for the children of Israel to be set free from their Egyptian bondage.

Many Jews today celebrate Passover yearly in March or April. It corresponds to Easter season for Christians. You can read more about Passover in the Bible Dictionary, under "Feasts."

FELLOWSHIPPING

A word which commonly denotes the actions of making new members feel welcome in the Church.

FEMINISM

As used in modern society, this term often refers to women who are unusually active in furthering the causes of women's rights. Feminism often comes into play when there are real or perceived inequities in the treatment of women as compared to men. The Church teaches that men and women are equal in the eyes of God, while still recognizing that there are God-given differences between men and women which ought not to be legislated against.

FINAL BATTLE

Often referred to as the Battle of Gog and Magog (Revelation 20:7–9), this is the end of the war which began in heaven during premortality (Revelation 12:7–9). Thus, it is called the "final battle" (of that war). It will take place when Satan is let loose during the "little season" after the Millennium (D&C 88:11–115). You can read a bit more about this in the Bible Dictionary, under "Gog."

FIRE AND BRIMSTONE

Fire is fire, and brimstone is white hot molten sulfur. The phrase is often used in the scriptures to describe the punishments of the wicked (Luke 17:29) and the torment of the wicked who refuse to live the gospel and repent of their sins on earth, and so are turned over to the devil (Revelation 20:10). While there is no literal "lake of fire and brimstone," the imagery is an attempt to let people know that the aftermath of unrepentant sins is not particularly pleasant.

FIRE AND THE HOLY GHOST

In teaching about the mission and function of the Holy Ghost, we often hear that the Holy Ghost "cleanses by fire." The imagery comes from the process of refining gold as used in ancient times. The gold ore is placed in a crucible, and a fire is used to heat the ore until it becomes molten. At that point, the gold, which is heavier than the rock in which it is imbedded, settles to the bottom of the pot and the imperfections and molten rock rise to the top, where they are scraped off or ladled off. As more and more ore is added and heated by the fire, more and more gold is produced. Finally, pure gold is all that remains.

All the impurities have been refined out by fire.

In scriptural symbolism, gold represents the very best, in other words, celestial exaltation (Revelation 4:4). Thus, the Holy Ghost "burns" in our conscience, prompting us to change our ways and repent. He gives us warmth and comfort as He bears witness to us of the truths of the gospel. He guides and directs, inspires and teaches, testifies and warns (John 14:26; 15:26; 16:13). As we heed His promptings, the impurities and imperfections are "burned" out of us and we are cleansed by the Atonement of Jesus Christ, as was the case for Isaiah (Isaiah 6:6–7).

FIRMAMENT

As used in the creation scriptures (Genesis 1:6–7, 14; Moses 2:6–7, 14), firmament means the atmosphere surrounding the earth, the sky, the heavens we see as we look up from the earth, the night sky with the stars and moon.

FIRST AND LAST

See ALPHA AND OMEGA.

FIRST COMFORTER

Another name for the Holy Ghost (John 14:12, 16–17, 26). A second "Comforter" is also spoken of by John (John 14:18, 21, 23, 28), which is the direct presence of the Savior and, sometimes, the Father.

FIRST ESTATE

A term used to refer to our premortal life. Those who proved worthy to be sent to earth kept "their first estate" (Abraham 3:26). Those who were cast out with Satan "kept not their first estate" (Jude 1:6), in other words, did not earn the privilege of coming to earth and receiving a mortal body.

FIRST FLESH

See EVOLUTION.

FIRST MAN

See EVOLUTION.

FIRST PRESIDENCY

The First Presidency is the highest governing body of the Church. The Lord instructed that "three Presiding High Priests . . . form a quorum of the Presidency of the church" (D&C 107:22). They preside over the Quorum of the Twelve Apostles, the Quorums of the Seventy (D&C 107:33–34), and, of course, the entire Church.

FIRST PRINCIPLES OF THE GOSPEL

Joseph Smith defined the first principles of the gospel when he wrote what are now known as the Articles of Faith, which appeared in the Wentworth Letter (see "Wentworth Letter" in this reference work). He wrote, "We believe that the first principles and ordinances of the Gospel are: first, Faith in the Lord Jesus Christ; second, Repentance; third, Baptism by immersion for the remission of sins; fourth, Laying on of hands for the gift of the Holy Ghost" (Articles of Faith 1:4).

FIRST RESURRECTION

A generic term, so to speak, always referring in the scriptures to those who will be resurrected and receive celestial glory (Revelation 20:6). For example, the people who were resurrected with the Savior (D&C 133:54–55) are part of the first resurrection. Another large group—the righteous who have died since the resurrection of Christ (except Peter, James, and Moroni, who have already been resurrected)—will come forth in another big part of the first resurrection as they come forth from the grave at the time of the Second Coming (D&C 88:97–98). And during the Millennium, as righteous mortals reach age one hundred (Isaiah 65:20), they will die and be resurrected in the "twinkling of an eye" (D&C 101:31), thus joining the "first resurrection."

FIRST TO BE LAST

"The last shall be first and the first shall be last" (1 Nephi 13:42) and "that the first shall be last and that the last shall be first" (D&C 29:30) can be explained as follows. At the time of the Savior's mortal ministry, the gospel was taken to the Jews (Matthew 15:24), and then later, after His resurrection, Jesus instructed the Apostles to take the gospel to all the world (Mark 16:15). In this sense, the Jews were first and the Gentiles were last to get the gospel.

In the last days, it is the other way around. The Gentiles are getting the gospel first, and the Jews will get it last (1 Nephi 13:42).

FIRST VISION

This is a reference to the first vision (JS—H 1:5–20) received by the Prophet Joseph Smith. In the spring of 1820, fourteen-year-old Joseph went into a grove of trees, not far from the family home, to pray about which of the many churches in his area to join. He had been earnestly investigating them for about two years, but was unable to decide which to join. In reading the Bible, he came upon a passage that said, "If any of you lack wisdom, let him ask of God" (James 1:5). This verse had great impact on him, and he determined to follow its counsel. During his prayer in the grove, Heavenly Father and His Son Jesus Christ both appeared to him. When he had gained sufficient composure "so as to be able to speak" (JS—H 1:18), he asked his question. The answer surprised him. None of them were true (JS—H 1:19).

We understand this answer not to mean that they had no good in them nor that they had no truth at all. Rather, none of them had the full gospel of Jesus Christ, in its purity, and none of their ministers had the true priesthood that the Master had conferred upon His Apostles and disciples during His New Testament ministry. Thus, none of the existing churches had the power to save mankind in the highest heaven which is the celestial kingdom (1 Corinthians 15:39–42; D&C 76).

Later, on April 6, 1830, the Savior established His restored church once again, through Joseph Smith, and in process of time, the truths of the ancient Church of Jesus Christ were restored, along with the authority to act in the name of God in performing the ordinances of salvation, including baptism. Thus, the First Vision was the beginning of the restoration of The Church of Jesus Christ of Latter-day Saints, as prophesied by Peter (Acts 3:19–21).

FIRSTBORN

Another name for the Savior, who is the "firstborn of every creature" (Colossians 1:15), meaning that He is the firstborn spirit child of Heavenly Father. Thus, He is literally our elder brother.

Another meaning of firstborn, as used in the scriptures, is "the one who receives the birthright," as it is handed down from father to son (*see* BIRTHRIGHT).

FIRSTBORN FROM THE DEAD

The first one resurrected, from this earth. It is a reference to Jesus Christ (Colossians 1:18).

FIRSTBORN OF GOD

See also FIRSTBORN. A reference to Jesus Christ, who is the firstborn of all of Heavenly Father's spirit children (Colossians 1:15).

FIRSTLINGS

The very best. The term is usually used in connection with animal sacrifices (Genesis 4:4; Moses 5:5).

The symbolism involved was that the Father was willing to sacrifice the very best (His only begotten Son) for us. Thus, the animal sacrifices used in the rituals of the law of Moses had to be the firstlings, in other words, the very best, in order to properly symbolize the sacrifice of the Son of God for our sins.

FLESH

The scriptural term for meat, such as beef, lamb, etc., as we use the term today. When the term "meat" is used in the scriptures, it can mean grains, fruits, vegetables, and so forth (Genesis 9:3–4).

FLESH AND BLOOD

A way of saying "mortal" or "mortals," in the scriptures (Matthew 16:17).

FLOOD

The Flood is thought to have taken place sometime between about 2,400 BC and 2,300 BC. Noah preached the gospel up until the time of the Flood, and then he and his family members who were saved boarded the Ark (Genesis 7:7). The flood covered the whole earth (Genesis 6–9). Some people tend to doubt that the Flood was universal, in other words, that it covered the whole earth. Elsewhere in scripture, the Lord confirms that it did (Moses 8:43; Ether 13:2).

The Flood was the baptism of the earth (*MD,* p. 289).

FOLLOWING THE BRETHREN

The term "Brethren," in this context, is generally used to mean the First Presidency and the Quorum of the Twelve Apostles, whom we sustain as prophets, seers, and revelators. There is spiritual safety in following their teachings and council (D&C 1:38). If we follow them, we will not be led astray (D&C 43:3–6).

FORBIDDEN FRUIT

The fruit partaken of by Adam and Eve in the Garden of Eden, which was forbidden by God (Genesis 2:17; Moses 3:17). Partaking of it led to the Fall. We do not know what the forbidden fruit was.

FOREKNOWLEDGE OF GOD

God knows "the end from the beginning" (Abraham 2:8). People have been given agency (2 Nephi 2:27). God's foreknowledge is not predestination. How His foreknowledge works hand in hand with agency has not yet been explained by His prophets. However, through revelation, we are assured that this life is a test and that we are determining our future in the next life by the informed choices we make in this life (Abraham 3:25).

FOREORDINATION

In premortality, many were foreordained to carry out certain responsibilities during mortality. This does not mean we are predestined to do certain things. Foreordination allows for the use of individual agency. The false doctrine of predestination does not.

Abraham was foreordained in premortality to accomplish his mortal mission (Abraham 3:22–23). Jeremiah was likewise foreordained (Jeremiah 1:5). Priesthood holders in the Church here on earth were foreordained (Alma 13:3–6). Joseph Smith taught that "every man who has a calling to minister to the inhabitants of the world was ordained to that very purpose in the Grand Council of heaven before this world was" (TPJS, p. 365).

Some Christians use the term "predestinate" (Romans 8:29–30) and "predestinated" (Ephesians 1:5) as the basis for the false doctrine of predestination, which teaches that God is the ultimate causative factor in all that people do and in all that happens to them. Such false philosophy robs us of God-given agency.

FORGIVE

We are commanded to forgive one another (Matthew 6:14–15; Mosiah 26:31; D&C 64:9). Being willing to forgive others relieves us of the heavy and destructive burden of holding grudges.

Being willing to forgive others does not imply that we must be willing to submit to additional abuse and threats. Nephi, even though he forgave his brothers, was instructed by the Lord to flee from them for his own safety and that of his followers (2 Nephi 5:5).

FORGIVENESS

See also REMISSION OF SINS. The scriptures teach that all sins can be forgiven, with the exception of the sin against the Holy Ghost (Matthew 12:31) as described in D&C 76:31–35. The sin of first degree murder can apparently be forgiven to the extent of being sent to telestial glory rather than perdition on the day of judgment (Revelation 22:15; D&C 76:103; 42:18).

Godly sorrow (2 Corinthians 7:9–11) is an essential ingredient in successfully repenting and thus receiving forgiveness. Alma the younger experienced the cleansing power of the Atonement because of the intensity of his recognition of the evil he had done (Alma 36:11–25). It is sometimes said that when we quit blaming others for our own inappropriate behavior, we are on the path to successful repentance.

Restitution is also an important part of repentance (Exodus 22:12). Forsaking sin (D&C 58:42–43) and filling in with good things (Isaiah 1:16–17) are also vital parts of the changes associated with forgiveness from the Lord. Complete forgiveness and cleansing (Isaiah 1:18) are available to all who come unto Christ, confess their sins, change their ways, and remain faithful to the gospel.

FORNICATION

Sexual intercourse between unmarried people.

Fornication is also used in the scriptures to mean complete disloyalty and breaking covenants made with God (Revelation 14:8; BD, under "Adultery").

FORTUNE TELLING

See also FAMILIAR SPIRITS. As a serious endeavor, such activity violates the commandments of God (Leviticus 19:31).

FOWLS

A scriptural term for birds (Genesis 1:20; 6:7).

FREE AGENCY

See also AGENCY. You may have noticed that, in recent years, Church leaders have tended to use the term "agency" (D&C 29:36; 93:31) or "moral agency" (D&C 107:78) rather than "free agency." The reason is that "agency" and "moral agency" are scriptural terms, whereas, "free agency" is not found in the scriptures. Also, the word "free," associated with agency, sometimes makes people think that use of agency can be free of consequences, which it is not (2 Nephi 2:27).

FREEDOM

An environment of freedom, in which individuals can exercise their moral agency to choose between right and wrong, is essential for the plan of salvation (Alma 42:5) to serve its purposes. Any tyranny, whether governmental or individual, which thwarts such exercise of God-given agency, comes of evil.

FREEMASONRY AND THE TEMPLE

The existence of some similarities between Masonic rites and the rites of Latter-day Saint temples is an accepted fact. Many Masons trace their rites and ceremonies back to Solomon's Temple. Latter-day Saints trace the rites and ceremonies conducted in their temples back to Adam. It is possible that Solomon's Temple would have had some elements of worship, though perhaps somewhat altered over time, whose origins dated back to Adam.

Joseph Smith and a number of other early leaders in the Church joined the Masons when Illinois Grand Master Abraham Jonas visited Nauvoo, Illinois, on March 15, 1842, and organized a Masonic Lodge there. It was a common practice to join the Masons in many surrounding communities at the time.

As Joseph Smith received the temple endowment by revelation, and introduced it in Nauvoo, in 1842, he was probably not surprised to see a few similarities between it and the rites of Freemasonry, since he was receiving the pure endowment through revelation and some of the rites of Masonry had come from original truth, filtered down through the ages to their present form. "Latter-day Saints see their temple ordinances as fundamentally different from Masonic and other rituals and think of similarities as remnants from an ancient original" (*EM*, under "Freemasonry and the Temple").

For more information, see *Encyclopedia of Mormonism*, under "Freemasonry in Nauvoo," and "Freemasonry and the Temple."

FRIEND, THE

A monthly publication of the Church for children.

FRUIT, FRUITS

Scriptural terms which are often used symbolically to mean product (Galatians 5:22–23), the result of one's actions (Matthew 3:8), or end result of one's actions and choices (Matthew 7:16).

FULNESS OF THE FATHER

Another term for exaltation (D&C 76:71, 77).

FULNESS OF THE GENTILES

See also FIRST TO BE LAST. One of the prophecies that is being fulfilled in our day is that the "fulness of the gospel of the Messiah [will] come unto the Gentiles" (1 Nephi 15:13; Romans 11:25). The term "Gentiles," in this context, means "everyone who is not a Jew." Thus, according to prophecy, in the last days, before the Second Coming of Christ, the gospel is to be restored in its fulness to the Gentiles, who will later take it to the Jews (1 Nephi 15:13; D&C 90:9). Therefore, the "fulness of the Gentiles" refers to the restoration of the gospel through Joseph Smith.

FULNESS OF THE GOSPEL

The complete gospel of Jesus Christ, with all of the truths, doctrines, and ordinances necessary for salvation and exaltation (D&C 90:11).

As used to describe the Book of Mormon (D&C 20:9), the phrase has a bit different meaning, focusing on understanding the doctrines of the gospel, along with the accompanying lifestyle that leads to exaltation. Ezra Taft Benson explained that "the Book of Mormon contains the fulness of the gospel of Jesus Christ (D&C 20:9). That does not mean it contains every teaching, every doctrine ever revealed. Rather, it means that in the Book of Mormon we will find the fulness of those doctrines required for our salvation. And they are taught plainly and simply so that even children can learn the ways of salvation and exaltation" (Benson, pp. 18–19).

FULNESS OF TIMES

See also DISPENSATION OF THE FULNESS OF TIMES. "Fulness of times" is usually used in conjunction with the word "dispensation" in the phrase "dispensation of the fulness of times."

"Fulness of times" also refers to the final scenes of this earth, when the Savior will have finished up His work and turned things over to the Father (D&C 76:106–08).

FUNDAMENTALISTS

A term used to describe groups or individuals who have broken off from the main body of the Church, claiming that it has departed from the fundamental teachings of Joseph Smith. There are a number of these so-called Mormon Fundamentalist groups today. They are not affiliated with or representative of the present Church of Jesus Christ of Latter-day Saints, and any attempt to lump them all together in presentations, including journalism and media productions, is either naive or dishonest.

·G·

GABRIEL

The name of the angel sent to Zacharias to announce the coming birth of John the Baptist to him and Elizabeth, in their old age (Luke 1:11–19). The same angel later announced to Mary that she was to be the mother of the Son of God (Luke 1:26–38). The Lord revealed to Joseph Smith that Noah, the Old Testament prophet who built the Ark, is the angel Gabriel (*TPJS*, p. 157).

GADIANTON ROBBERS

A group of wicked men in the Book of Mormon, originally organized about 50 BC, by Kishkumen, and then taken over by Gadianton (Helaman 2:4). This band, who robbed, murdered, and plundered for personal gain, maintained their power through the use of secret pacts or secret combinations. Gadianton was given secret oaths and covenants by the devil (Helaman 6:26).

Over the next four hundred plus years, the Gadianton Robbers, thriving through their evil secret combinations, wreaked untold misery upon society. Mormon informed us that "in the end of this book [the Book of Mormon] ye shall see that this Gadianton did prove the overthrow, yea, almost the entire destruction of the people of Nephi" (Helaman 2:13).

GAMBLING

"The Church of Jesus Christ of Latter-day Saints is opposed to gambling, including lotteries sponsored by governments. Church leaders have encouraged Church members to join with others in opposing the legalization and government sponsorship of any form of gambling" (2007 statement by the Church on lds.org/Gospel Topics/Gambling).

GARDEN OF EDEN

See EDEN, GARDEN OF.

GARDEN OF EDEN, LOCATION OF

See EDEN, LOCATION OF.

GARDEN OF GETHSEMANE

The garden in which the Savior began the final suffering that would culminate in His Atonement for our sins (Matthew 26:36). According to tradition, it is located on a slope of the Mount of Olives, outside the east wall of Jerusalem. Here, the Master prayed to the Father, saying, "O my Father, if it be possible, let this cup pass from me: nevertheless not as I will, but as thou wilt" (Matthew 26:39). His suffering in the Garden caused Him to bleed from every pore (Luke 22:44; D&C 19:18).

We understand that the suffering in the Garden of Gethsemane recurred on the cross. "To this we add, if we interpret the holy word aright, that all of the anguish, all of the sorrow, and all of the suffering of Gethsemane recurred during the final three hours on the cross, the hours when darkness covered the land. Truly there was no sorrow like unto his sorrow, and no anguish and pain like unto that which bore in with such intensity upon him" (McConkie, *The Mortal Messiah*, 4:232 p. 22).

The word "Gethsemane" means "oil press," and comes from the Hebrew "Gat Shemanim" (see Wikipedia, the free online encyclopedia, under "Gethsemane"). There is much significant symbolism here. For example, The Jews put olives into bags made of mesh fabric and placed them in a press to squeeze olive oil out of them. The first pressings yielded pure olive oil which was prized for many uses, including healing and giving light in lamps. Priesthood holders consecrate it and use it to administer to the sick. The final pressing of the olives, under the tremendous pressure of additional weights added to the press, yielded a bitter, red liquid which can remind us of blood and the "bitter cup" of which the Savior partook. Symbolically, the Savior is going into the "oil press" (Gethsemane) to submit to the "pressure" of all our sins which will "squeeze" His blood out in order that we might have the healing "oil" of the Atonement to heal and cleanse us from our sins.

GARMENTS

Special underclothing worn by members of The Church of Jesus Christ of Latter-day Saints who have participated in the ordinances of the temple. The garments serve as a reminder to them of the covenants they have made in the temple with the Lord, to live pure and virtuous lives. In addition, garments provide protection understood by the worthy wearer, and promote modesty in clothing styles.

GATES OF HELL

A symbolic phrase meaning the temptations and efforts of the devil to take us away from God (Matthew 16:18; 2 Nephi 4:32; D&C 17:8).

GATHERING OF ISRAEL

One of the most important missions of The Church of Jesus Christ of Latter-day Saints is to "gather Israel." The last days' gathering of Israel is one of the most repeated and constant themes in prophecy (Isaiah 5:26;

10:22; 54:7; Ezekiel 28:25; Ephesians 1:10; 1 Nephi 10:14; D&C 39:11; Articles of Faith 1:10). Abraham was given the promise that through him and his posterity, all people of the earth would be blessed (Abraham 2:9–11). The overall sense of this mission is to gather people to Christ. It is being done through the preaching of the gospel throughout the world, giving individuals the opportunity to hear the full gospel of Jesus Christ, receive a testimony through the Holy Ghost, and be baptized and remain faithful to the end. Those who are "gathered" receive the blessings of the gospel in this life and can look forward to returning to live with the Father and the Son in celestial glory forever.

GAYS AND LESBIANS

See SAME GENDER ATTRACTION.

GAZELAM

A code name for Joseph Smith, used in some versions of early revelations as a means of protecting him from his enemies. When the need for such substitute names was no longer necessary, the Prophet's name was again used in the revelations (see heading to D&C 78).

GENEALOGY

See FAMILY HISTORY.

GENERAL AUTHORITIES

A term, currently used in referring to members of the First Presidency, the Quorum of the Twelve Apostles, and the First and Second Quorums of the Seventy (*TF*, p. 35).

GENERAL AUXILIARIES

See also AUXILIARY ORGANIZATIONS OF THE CHURCH. General auxiliary officers of the Church support the General Authorities in the work of strengthening the members of the Church. Currently, there are five auxiliary presidencies serving at Church headquarters in Salt Lake City: the Relief Society, Young Women, Primary, Young Men, and Sunday School presidencies. Each presidency consists of a president and two counselors. Secretaries and board and committee members serve with these presidencies as needed and as called by General Authorities.

Those serving in these five presidencies are "general officers of the Church," not "general auxiliary officers." The implication of this careful wording is that, overall, they work together to further the work of the Lord, rather than more or less isolating themselves to their own focus and emphasis.

GENERAL HANDBOOK OF INSTRUCTIONS

"The *General Handbook of Instructions* is the official book of instruction for Church leaders, mainly stake presidents and bishops. Church leaders who receive the handbook include General Authorities, Church department heads, general auxiliary presidencies, temple presidents, and officers in stakes, wards, missions, districts, and branches. It is a handbook of Church policy and practices, not doctrine. The First Presidency and Quorum of the Twelve Apostles prepare the handbook to provide uniform procedures and methods for local leaders as they minister to the members and direct Church affairs in their areas throughout the world. Other Church handbooks, such as those for priesthood and auxiliary organizations, are based on the *General Handbook of Instructions*.

"Handbooks have included such things as instruction on (1) Church administration and meetings; (2) calling members to Church positions and releasing them from such calls; (3) ordaining members to priesthood offices; (4) performing ordinances and giving blessings; (5) doing sacred temple work and family history; (6) responding to calls for missionary service; (7) keeping records, reports, and accounting for finances; (8) applying Church discipline; and (9) implementing Church policies on such matters as buildings and property, moral issues, and medical and health issues" (*EM*, under "General Handbook of Instructions").

GENERATION

This term can have several different meanings in the scriptures, depending on the context. For example, it can mean the offspring of a given set of parents. Genesis chapter 5 gives several "generations." It can also mean about a hundred years (Helaman 13:9–10).

Furthermore, it can mean "the period of time in which specific prophecies are fulfilled," which could cover many years (example: D&C 45:30–31). In this sense, the dispensation of the fulness of times is a generation.

GENTILES

The definition of this term is very context sensitive. In the broadest scriptural use, Gentiles are non-Jews (2 Nephi 10:16; 26:33).

In non-religious and non-scriptural contexts, it can mean "anyone who is not a member of our group."

"In the Bible, the Hebrew and Greek words translated into English as 'Gentile' signified other peoples; i.e., 'not Israelite' and later 'not Jewish.' For Latter-day Saints, 'Gentile' generally means 'not Latter-day Saint,' although the meaning also extends to include 'not Jewish' and 'not Lamanite.' These latter senses are rooted partly in scripture, where the distinction between Gentiles and Israelites or Jews is firmly maintained, and partly in the language adopted by early leaders of The Church of Jesus Christ of Latter-day Saints. In the LDS scriptural view, Gentiles play an important role in the restoration of the gospel in the latter days (1 Nephi 13:38–39; 22:6–11; 3 Nephi 21:1–6) and in the latter-day work of gathering Israel (1 Nephi 22:12; 3 Nephi 21:6, 22–9)" (*EM*, under "Gentiles").

GENTILES, FULNESS OF

See FULNESS OF THE GENTILES.

GERMAN BIBLE

Speaking of the German New Testament available to him in his day, Joseph Smith said, "I have been reading the German, and find it to be the most [nearly] correct translation, and to correspond nearest to the revelations which God has given to me for the last fourteen years" (*TPJS*, p. 349).

GETHSEMANE

See GARDEN OF GETHSEMANE.

GETHSEMANE, GARDEN OF

See GARDEN OF GETHSEMANE.

GIFT OF THE HOLY GHOST

See also GIFTS OF THE SPIRIT. The gift of the Holy Ghost is the privilege of having the constant companionship of the Holy Ghost. As part of the ordinance of confirmation, after baptism, new members of the Church are instructed to "receive the Holy Ghost."

Parley P. Pratt described the blessings and benefits of this gift. He taught: "The gift of the Holy Spirit . . . quickens all the intellectual faculties, increases, enlarges, expands and purifies all the natural passions and affections; and adapts them, by the gift of wisdom, to their lawful use. It inspires, develops, cultivates and matures all the fine-toned sympathies, joys, tastes, kindred feelings and affections of our nature. It inspires virtue, kindness, goodness, tenderness, gentleness and charity. It develops beauty of person, form and features. It tends to health, vigor, animation and social feeling. It develops and invigorates all the faculties of the physical and intellectual man. It strengthens, invigorates, and gives tone to the nerves. In short, it is, as it were, marrow to the bone, joy to the heart, light to the eyes, music to the ears, and life to the whole being" (Pratt, *Key to the Science of Theology*, pp. 100–101).

GIFT OF PROPHECY
See GIFTS OF THE SPIRIT.

GIFT OF TONGUES
See GIFTS OF THE SPIRIT.

GIFTS OF THE SPIRIT
Spiritual gifts which are given by the Holy Ghost (D&C 46:11, 13). The most often-used scriptural references which list these spiritual gifts are D&C 46:13–27; 1 Corinthians 12:3–11; Moroni 10:9–18 (which mentions the gift of seeing angels—verse 14—a gift not mentioned in either of the other two references). In addition, a number of gifts of the Holy Ghost are mentioned in Romans 12:6–13 as well as elsewhere.

A major purpose of spiritual gifts is to help us avoid deception (D&C 46:8). Another major reason for these gifts is to help members grow and progress in the gospel (D&C 46:9) and serve one another (D&C 46:12). Every member of the Church is given at least one spiritual gift (D&C 46:10–11). We are encouraged to seek to develop gifts of the Spirit, in addition to the ones we

have been given (D&C 46:8). A brief review of some of the better-known gifts of the Spirit follows, using D&C 46:13–27:

Gifts of the Spirit

1. Knowing that Jesus is the Christ (D&C 46:13). This is the gift of having one's own testimony.

2. Believing the testimony of those who have their own testimony. Members who have this gift can also attain eternal life, meaning exaltation (D&C 46:14).

3. The differences of administration. The ability to lead others appropriately, including understanding and skillfully using the various organizations within the Church to save souls (D&C 46:15).

4. The diversities of operations. Being able to distinguish between true philosophies and false philosophies, good ideas and bad ideas, wise counsel and foolish counsel, whether something is from God or from some other source (D&C 46:16). Sometimes a person with this gift will sense something wrong with a philosophy or idea being taught in a class at school or elsewhere, even if a complete understanding of what is wrong is not yet in place. This gift, along with other gifts of the Spirit, can be most valuable in distinguishing between the things of God and counterfeits.

5. Wisdom (D&C 46:17). The "word of wisdom" spoken of in verse 17 is not the Word of Wisdom, known as section 89 of the Doctrine and

Covenants. Rather, it is the gift of having wisdom, seeing through false fronts and getting to root causes, etc. It includes the gift of seeing ahead to the ultimate consequences of a particular course of action.

6. Knowledge (D&C 46:18). The ability to learn and retain knowledge.

7. The ability to teach (D&C 46:18). Paul lists good teachers as being right after apostles and prophets, in order of importance (1 Corinthians 12:28). Perhaps you have had the experience of having an instructor who had the gift of knowledge but who did not have the gift of teaching.

8. Faith to be healed (D&C 46:19). This is a marvelous gift for those who posses it. There are many healings because of this gift of the Spirit. Yet, many righteous members do not have it. Under such circumstances, it might be easy for one not possessing it to feel less important than one who has it. The Lord addressed this situation in D&C 42:43–44, 48–52.

9. Faith to heal (D&C 46:20). This gift applies both to physical healings as well as spiritual healings. Being healed spiritually, gaining a testimony, conversion to the Church, being healed of bitterness and anger, and so forth are no doubt even more important than physical healing, in the eternal perspective. The gift of healing is not limited to priesthood holders. Faithful women, including mothers, are often blessed with this gift and use it through their prayers of faith in behalf of the sick. The Prophet Joseph Smith spoke of faithful sisters healing the sick. He said: "If the sisters should have faith to heal the sick, let all hold their tongues, and let everything roll on" (*TPJS*, p. 224).

10. Working miracles (D&C 46:21). Here, as with the gift of healing, we may tend to think more in terms of the spectacular such as stopping rain or calming the water on a stormy sea, rather than the less conspicuous daily helps and miracles associated with this gift. For example, the gift of working miracles could be seen in the lessening of contention, the calming of a soul during difficult times, the impression to call someone who has an urgent need to talk, the sudden inspiration to solve a problem on an assembly line, the avoidance of a traffic accident, the calming of a child in discomfort, and so forth.

11. Prophecy (D&C 46:22). In John 16:13, we are taught that the Holy Ghost "shall shew you things to come." Therefore, we understand that, among other things, this gift (which all members can have, and which must be kept within proper stewardship and realm of influence) can include the gift of knowing the future. The First Presidency and the members of the Quorum of the Twelve have this gift for their responsibilities over the whole world. Indeed, we sustain them as "prophets, seers, and revelators." Other

leaders within the Church can have this gift for those within their direct responsibilities. Parents can have it for their families. A faithful member could have the gift of prophecy by way of a good feeling or uncomfortable feeling dealing with an important upcoming decision. The gift of prophecy could be helpful in choosing a career path in college, a topic for a sacrament meeting talk, choosing between employment options, deciding whether or not to relocate, and so forth.

12. Discerning of spirits (D&C 46:23). Elder Stephen L. Richards explained that, in addition to sensing hidden evil or good, this gift also enables one who possesses it to see the good in others. This is perhaps one of the most important manifestations of this gift. Elder Richards said that this gift consists largely "of an acute sensitivity to impressions—spiritual impressions, if you will—to read under the surface as it were, to detect hidden evil, and more important, to find the good that may be concealed. The highest type of discernment is that which perceives in others and uncovers for them their better natures, the good inherent within them. It's the gift every missionary needs when he takes the gospel to the people of the world. He must make an appraisal of every personality whom he meets. He must be able to discern the hidden spark that may be lighted for truth. The gift of discernment will save him from

mistakes and embarrassment, and it will never fail to inspire confidence in the one who is rightly appraised" (CR [April 1950]: 162).

13. Tongues (D&C 46:24). The gift of speaking in other languages. This gift was manifest on the day of Pentecost when Peter and the Apostles spoke to the multitudes in their own language and those in the crowds (from many different countries) heard the preaching in their own languages (Acts 2:4–13). The most common manifestation of this gift is found in how fast and effectively our missionaries learn to speak foreign languages, as part of their missionary work. This happens much to the amazement of people outside the Church. It is a gift of the Holy Ghost (D&C 46:13).

On occasions, this gift is manifest in the sudden ability of someone to understand or to speak and understand a foreign language that they do not know.

On the other hand, speaking in tongues is perhaps one of the most misunderstood gifts of the Holy Ghost, and is often used by Satan and his evil spirits to deceive and to divert and detour people from the true gospel of Jesus Christ. The Prophet Joseph Smith taught, "Be not so curious about tongues, do not speak in tongues except there be an interpreter present; the ultimate design of tongues is to speak to foreigners, and if persons are very anxious to display their intelligence, let them speak to such in their own tongues. The gifts of God are all useful in their place, but when they are applied to that which God does not intend, they prove an injury, a snare and a curse instead of a blessing" (*HC* 5:31–32).

14. Interpretation of tongues (D&C 46:25). This gift usually appears in conjunction with the gift of tongues. Elder Bruce R. McConkie taught, "Tongues and their interpretation are classed among the signs and miracles which always attend the faithful and which stand as evidences of the divinity of the Lord's work (Mormon 9:24; Mark 16:17; Acts 10:46; 19:6). In their more dramatic manifestations they consist in speaking or interpreting, by the power of the Spirit, a tongue which is completely unknown to the speaker or interpreter. Sometimes it is the pure Adamic language which is involved" (McConkie, *Doctrinal New Testament Commentary*, 2:383).

This gift, as is the case with the gift of tongues, is most often found in the work of spreading the gospel to all the earth. Those who work with translating the scriptures and Church curriculum materials into foreign languages for use as the Church spreads forth into all nations would certainly experience this gift.

As mentioned at the beginning of this topic, there are other gifts of the Spirit that are perhaps not as commonly spoken of as those given above. We will give Romans 12:7–13 with a few notes added in brackets, as an example of many other spiritual gifts spoken of in the scriptures. We will use **bold** to point out specific gifts.

Romans 12:7–13

7 Or **ministry** [*the gift of serving others*], let us wait on [*attend to*] our ministering [*let us serve others*]: or he that **teacheth** [*the gift of teaching*], on teaching [*let him teach*];

8 Or he that **exhorteth** [*the gift of speaking and encouraging others to do right*], on exhortation: he that **giveth** [*the gift of generosity*], let him do it with simplicity [*without drawing much attention to himself*]; he that **ruleth** [*the gift of leadership*], with diligence [*let him be diligent in leading and fulfilling his duties*]; he that **sheweth mercy** [*the gift of mercy*], with **cheerfulness** [*the gift of being cheerful*].

9 Let **love** be without dissimulation [*let the gift of love be used sincerely, without hypocrisy*]. **Abhor that which is evil** [*the gift of shunning evil*]; **cleave to that which is good** [*the gift of deeply desiring to be involved with good*].

10 Be **kindly affectioned** [*the gift of being kind*] one to another with **brotherly love**; in honour **preferring one another** [*the gift of leading by good example and honor*];

11 **Not slothful in business** [*the gift of being skilled in business*]; **fervent in spirit** [*the gift of spirituality*]; **serving the Lord** [*the gift of enjoying church and service in it*];

12 Rejoicing in **hope** [*the hope and confidence which comes through living Christ's gospel*]; **patient** in

tribulation [*the gift of patience*]; **continuing instant in prayer** [*the gift of being in constant communication with God*];

13 **Distributing** [*the gift of sharing*] to the necessity of saints [*sharing according to the needs of the saints*]; given to **hospitality** [*the gift of being hospitable*].

GNASHING OF TEETH

A scriptural phrase referring to the extreme anguish and misery of the wicked when they receive the punishments demanded by the eternal law of justice, which they could have avoided had they chosen to repent (Matthew 8:12; 13:50; D&C 19:5; 101:90–91).

GNOLAUM

Another word for "eternal" (Abraham 3:18).

GNOSTICISM

A system of philosophy that considers people to be spirits trapped in physical bodies, and God to be a completely unknowable Supreme Being. Over the centuries, Gnosticism has mixed in with the dogmas of a number of Christian religions, creating false doctrines about God and His plan of salvation for us.

GOATS, SYMBOLISM OF

The imagery of separating the sheep from the goats (Matthew 5:32) is that of separating the righteous from the wicked.

GOD

See also GOD THE FATHER; GOD, ATTRIBUTES OF; GODHEAD. "We believe in God, the Eternal Father, and in His Son, Jesus Christ, and in the Holy Ghost" (Articles of Faith 1:1). Thus, The Church of Jesus Christ of Latter-day Saints teaches that there are three distinct members of the Godhead, namely, the Father (the Supreme God), the Son (the Redeemer), and the Holy Ghost (the Testifier and Comforter).

The Father and Son both have resurrected bodies of flesh and bone, but the Holy Ghost is a personage of spirit (D&C 130:22–23).

The scriptures teach that God can be known (John 17:3) but that we will not be able to comprehend Him until the next life, if we are faithful (D&C 88:49).

Joseph Smith taught, "If men do not comprehend the character of God, they do not comprehend themselves" (*TPJS*, p. 343).

GOD AS A SPIRIT

Because John 4:24, as given in the Bible, states that "God is a Spirit," many Christian religions have developed false teachings about the nature of God. Joseph Smith corrected this verse to read, "For unto such hath God promised his Spirit. And they who worship him, must worship in spirit and in truth" (JST, John 4:26).

GOD, ATTRIBUTES OF

Joseph Smith taught, "If men do not comprehend the character of God, they do not comprehend themselves" (*TPJS*, p. 343). We are taught that "He is perfect, has all power, and knows all things. Our Heavenly Father is a God of judgment and strength and knowledge and power, but He is also a God of perfect mercy, kindness, and charity. Even though we 'do not know the meaning of all things,' we can find peace in the sure knowledge that He loves us (see 1 Nephi 11:17). As children of God, we have a special relationship with Him, setting us apart from all His other creations. We should seek to know our Father in Heaven. He loves us, and He has given us the precious opportunity to draw near to Him as we pray. Our prayers, offered in humility and sincerity, are heard and answered. We can also come to know our Father by learning about His Beloved Son and applying the gospel in our lives. The Savior taught His disciples: 'If ye had known me, ye should have known my Father also. . . . He that hath seen me hath seen the Father' (John 14:7, 9). We draw near to God the Father as we study the scriptures and the words of latter-day prophets and as we give service. When we follow God's will and live as He would have us live, we become more like Him and His Son. We prepare ourselves to return to live in Their presence" (*TF*, p. 74–76).

GOD OF ABRAHAM, ISAAC, AND JACOB

Jehovah, the premortal Jesus Christ, is the "God of Abraham, Isaac, and Jacob" (BD, under "Jehovah"). He is the God who appeared to Abraham (Abraham 3:11), Isaac (Genesis 26:1–2), and Jacob (Genesis 32:30), to Moses (Exodus 33:11), Isaiah (Isaiah 6:1), and other Old Testament prophets. Thus, Jesus Christ, as a personage of spirit (since He had not yet received a mortal body) is the God of the Old Testament (Ether 3:16).

Joseph Fielding Smith explained, "All revelation since the fall has come through Jesus Christ, who is the Jehovah of the Old Testament. In all of the scriptures, where God is mentioned and where he has appeared, it was Jehovah who talked with Abraham, with Noah, Enoch, Moses and all the prophets. He is the God of Israel, the Holy One of Israel; the one who led that nation out of Egyptian bondage, and who gave and fulfilled the law of Moses" *(DS* 1:27).

GOD OF ISRAEL

See GOD OF ABRAHAM, ISAAC, AND JACOB.

GOD OF JACOB

See GOD OF ABRAHAM, ISAAC, AND JACOB.

GOD OF OUR FATHERS

See GOD OF ABRAHAM, ISAAC, AND JACOB.

GOD OF THIS WORLD

As used in scripture, this is a reference to Satan (2 Corinthians 4:3–4).

GOD THE FATHER

See also ELOHIM. Heavenly Father is God the Father. He is the Supreme God, the "supreme Governor of the universe" (BD, under "God"), who is "above all" (Ephesians 4:6). He is the Father of our spirits (Hebrews 12:9), thus making all of us on earth brothers and sisters. We are His literal spirit offspring (Acts 17:28–29), and thus, the term "Father" applies literally to our relationship with Him. We pray to Him, in the name of Jesus Christ (2 Nephi 32:9; 3 Nephi 18:19; Moroni 4:2). He has a resurrected, tangible body of flesh and bone (D&C 130:22). Jesus Christ was the creator of our world (John 1:10) and has created "worlds without number" under the direction of the Father (Moses 1:33).

GOD, THE LIVING

A scriptural phrase (Deuteronomy 5:26; 1 Nephi 17:30) used to differentiate the true God from idols, which are not "living" or "real" gods.

GOD'S LIFE

See also GOD THE FATHER; GOD, ATTRIBUTES OF. "God's life" is another term for "exaltation," which means attaining the highest degree of glory in the celestial kingdom and living in the family unit forever (D&C 131:1–4; 132:19–20), thus, living as God does now.

GOD'S TIME

The phrase comes from the question, "Is not the reckoning of God's time, angel's time, prophet's time, and man's time, according to the planet on which they reside? I answer, Yes" (D&C 130:4–5). Abraham informs us that "the Lord's time . . . was after the time of [the planet] Kolob" (Abraham 5:13). He also instructs us that "one day in Kolob is equal to a thousand years according to the measurement of this earth" (Abraham, Facsimile No. 2, Explanation, Fig. 1).

GODHEAD

As witnessed at the baptism of the Savior by John the Baptist, there are three separate and distinct personages in the Godhead, the Father, the Son, and the Holy Ghost. John heard the Father's voice, he baptized the Son, and the Holy Ghost was present (Matthew 3:13–17).

"We believe in God, the Eternal Father, and in His Son, Jesus Christ, and in the Holy Ghost" (Articles of Faith 1:1). The Father and the Son both have resurrected, physical bodies of flesh and bone (Luke 24:36–39; D&C 130:22), but the Holy Ghost is a personage of spirit (D&C 130:22). The three members of the Godhead work in complete harmony with each other (John 14:26; Acts 7:55–56; 2 Nephi 31:18), and thus the scriptures refer to them as being "one" (John 17:21; Mosiah 15:4; Mormon 7:7).

GODHOOD

The final status of those who attain

exaltation and thus become gods (D&C 132:19–20).

GODS

The scriptures teach that there are many people from other worlds who have already become gods (1 Corinthians 8:5; *TPJS*, pp. 370–71). Many gods will be added in the universe when worthy mortals from this world become gods (D&C 132:20). However, for us, there is only one God (1 Corinthians 8:6), namely, our Heavenly Father, who is the literal father of our spirits (Hebrews 12:9, Acts 17:28–29), and whose plan of salvation we are invited to follow in order to become like Him (Matthew 5:48).

GOG AND MAGOG, BATTLE OF

See BATTLE OF GOG AND MAGOG. *See also* BATTLE OF THE GREAT GOD.

GOLD, SYMBOLISM OF

See also SYMBOLISM IN THE SCRIPTURES. As used in the scriptures, gold symbolizes the very best, and thus often symbolizes exaltation in the celestial kingdom (Revelation 4:4).

GOLD PLATES

See BOOK OF MORMON PLATES.

GOLGOTHA

Another name for the place on the hill outside Jerusalem where they crucified the Savior (Matthew 27:32–33; John 19:16–18).

GOMORRAH

A city in the Old Testament, generally associated with the city of Sodom, both of which were destroyed by fire from heaven because of extreme wickedness, including widespread homosexuality (Genesis 19:5; 24).

GOOD SHEPHERD

Another name for the Savior (John 10:11).

GOOD WORKS

See also GRACE. Good works are required, along with faith, in order to have the Savior's grace save us from our sins (Titus 2:7; James 2:17, 20, 26; 2 Nephi 25:23).

GOSPEL

Comes from an Old English word which means "good tidings" or "good news" (see online Wickipedia Encyclopedia). The word is also used to refer to the first four books in the New Testament. Thus, the Gospels are Matthew, Mark, Luke, and John in the New Testament.

GOSPEL COVENANTS

See also COVENANT. Covenants are binding agreements between people. Gospel covenants are thus binding agreements between God and man (D&C 43:9; 82:10). Some examples are making formal covenants with God at the time of baptism (Mosiah 18:8–10), partaking of the sacrament (D&C 20:77, 79), men receiving the priesthood (D&C 84:33–41), receiving our endowments in the temple, and being married or sealed in the temple.

GOSPEL DISPENSATIONS
See DISPENSATIONS.

GOSPEL HOBBIES ·
A term which refers to members who emphasize one aspect of the gospel far out of proportion to the emphasis they place on other important teachings of the Church. For example, members could get so caught up in the study of the signs of the times that they begin to get caught up in gloom and doom and constantly attempt to spread it to others. Another example might be members who get caught up in dietary fads and begin to look down on other members who use white flour, white sugar, processed foods, and so forth, as if they are less righteous.

The danger in gospel hobbies is that they can and do occasionally lead to apostasy. Sometimes it is because people with such hobbies begin to feel that Church leaders are out of tune with the Spirit because they do not teach or emphasize the same "hobby" topics sufficiently.

GOSPEL OF JESUS CHRIST
All of the teachings, truths, principles, laws, ordinances, covenants, commitments, actions, forgiveness, blessings, and so forth, embodied in the gospel taught by Jesus Christ, which enable men and women to come unto Him so that He can take them into the Father's kingdom with Him (D&C 45:3–5). This full gospel of Jesus Christ was restored to earth for the final time before the Second Coming (Daniel 2:35, 44–45), in this dispensation of the fulness of times, through the Prophet Joseph Smith.

Since God is completely fair, all people who are past the age of accountability (D&C 137:10; 68:25, 27) will have the opportunity to hear and understand the complete and pure gospel of Jesus Christ before they are brought to final judgment. Thus, they can, under completely fair circumstances, either here on earth, in the postmortal spirit world (D&C 138), or during the Millennium, accept or reject the gospel and thus receive a fair judgment (1 Peter 4:6).

GOSPEL ORDINANCES
In a general sense, the term "ordinances" can encompass all of the laws, principles, commandments, and ordinances of the gospel (D&C 136:2–4; 52:15–16).

In a more limited and specific sense, "ordinances" are rites and ceremonies performed for members by holders of the priesthood. These include baptism, confirmation, sacrament, having the priesthood conferred upon them (in the case of male members of the Church), being ordained to various offices in the Aaronic and Melchizedek priesthood, naming and blessing of children, dedication of graves, dedicating buildings, washings and anointings, endowments, temple marriage, sealings, administering to the sick, consecrating oil, blessings of counsel and comfort, father's blessings, and patriarchal blessings.

GOSPELS

Matthew, Mark, Luke, and John are often referred to as "the Gospels" or "the four Gospels," because they report the "glad tidings" or "good news" (the original meaning of "gospel") brought and taught by Jesus Christ. Among members of the Church, Third Nephi is sometimes referred to as "the fifth Gospel."

GOSSIP

Unofficial talking and chatting about the personal lives of others in ways that discredit or damage them or their reputation (Leviticus 19:16; Proverbs 11:12–13; 18:7–8).

GOVERNMENT OF GOD

"Theocracy" is the term commonly used for "government by God." When the Savior rules and reigns during the Millennium, as "Lord of lords and King of kings" (Revelation 17:14), the inhabitants of the earth will live under a theocracy as their form of government.

GOVERNMENTS

The teachings of the gospel stress the importance of being loyal to our respective governments (Titus 3:1; 1 Peter 2:13–17; D&C 58:22).

The Church teaches "that governments were instituted of God for the benefit of man; and that he holds men accountable for their acts in relation to them, both in making laws and administering them, for the good and safety of society" (D&C 134:1).

GRACE

See also GOOD WORKS; JUSTIFICATION. A very simple definition of grace is "the help of Christ." Without the grace of Jesus Christ, all of our efforts to gain salvation would get us nowhere and we would be completely lost (2 Nephi 9:7–9).

Various definitions of "grace" have created much contention and controversy in the Christian world. Paul's writings are often used in the debate. For example, his statement that "a man is justified by faith without the deeds of the law" (Rom 3:28) is used to suggest that "deeds" are not required for salvation and that grace is all we need. What Paul is actually saying here is that we cannot be saved by the deeds of the law of Moses. Rather, one must accept and live the gospel of Jesus Christ. James clearly teaches that "faith, if it hath not works, is dead, being alone" (James 2:17).

The Church teaches the simple truth that both grace and works are necessary for salvation (2 Nephi 25:23). "It is by grace that we are saved, after all we can do" (2 Nephi 25:23).

It may be helpful to consider the fact that, in some significant ways, we are indeed saved by grace alone. Using the writings of Paul (Romans 4:16; 5:15; 11:16; Ephesians 2:5, 8) in the context of all the scriptures, resurrection is not dependent on works at all. Everyone will be resurrected (1 Corinthians 15:22) through the grace of Christ.

Also, using Paul's description of three different categories of "heaven" (1 Corinthians 15:40–42) to which people will be sent on Judgment Day, we note that, since no ordinances are required for entrance to the telestial kingdom in the afterlife (which Paul compared to the stars) or the terrestrial glory (which Paul compared to the moon), people are, in a real sense, saved by grace to these categories of heaven.

However, when it comes to going to the heaven (the celestial) where God and Christ dwell (D&C 76:112), specific works are required, including baptism (Mark 16:16) and faithfully living the gospel of Jesus Christ.

GRACE, DOCTRINE OF
See GRACE.

GRACE OF GOD
See GRACE.

GRANITE MOUNTAIN RECORD VAULT

Created by excavating six hundred feet into the north face of a granite mountain, the vault serves as a storage area for rolls of microfilm which contain genealogical and historical infor-mation collected by the Church. The excavation and construction began in 1958 and was completed in 1963, at a cost of approximately two million dollars. The vault is located about twenty miles southeast of downtown Salt Lake City, Utah, and is about one mile up from the mouth of Little Cottonwood Canyon.

In addition to an office and laboratory section, the vault has six chambers, each 190 feet long, 25 feet wide, and 25 feet high. Because of the approximately 700 feet of granite above it as well as the granite surrounding it, temperature and humidity are naturally maintained at the ideal for preserving such microfilm records. Because of modern electronic developments in storing such data, further expansion of the vault is no longer needed. The records are currently being transferred to modern forms of electronic media.

GRATITUDE

Interestingly, the Lord compares the importance of gratitude against all other commandments combined. "And in nothing doth man offend God, or against none is his wrath kindled, save those who confess not his hand in all things, and obey not his commandments" (D&C 59:21). Among other things, this may be because gratitude is one of the most healing and stabilizing of all attributes. Those who possess it fare better under conditions of trial and stress. They exhibit more compassion and love toward others. They tend to remain constant and loyal to God under all circumstances. Thus, having sincere and genuine gratitude is one of the most influential qualities leading to exaltation.

GRAVEN IMAGES

Idols, statues, and objects used by people throughout history in idol worship. Such worship violates the second of the Ten Commandments (Exodus 20:4).

GRAVESIDE PRAYERS

See DEDICATION OF GRAVES.

GREAT AND ABOMINABLE CHURCH

See also CHURCH OF THE DEVIL; DEVIL, CHURCH OF. Another name for the Church of the Devil (1 Nephi 14:10). In vision, Nephi saw some of the prominent aspects of this church (1 Nephi 13:6–9). The "great and abominable church" is a collective term for any and all of the devil's so-called "front" organizations through which his schemes to entrap us are promoted. It is not limited to one specific organization.

GREAT AND DREADFUL DAY

In its most common contexts in the scriptures, this phrase refers to the time of the Second Coming, and conveys the message that it will be a frightening and terrible day for the wicked (Malachi 4:5; Alma 45:14).

GREATER PRIESTHOOD

Another name for the Melchizedek Priesthood (D&C 84:19–21).

GREAT I AM, THE

Another name for Jehovah, the pre-mortal Jesus Christ (Exodus 3:13–14; D&C 29:1).

GROVES

Referred to quite often in the Old Testament in connection with pagan idol worship (Exodus 34:13; Deuteronomy 7:5; 1 Kings 14:23, 18:19; Micah 5:14). It was common for the Lord to command His people to destroy such groves. These groves were commonly used, in pagan temple worship, as places for sexual immorality associated with idol worship (see BD, under "Grove").

GUARDIAN ANGELS

It is not true that all people have guardian angels who are assigned to be with them constantly. Such notions have been around for a long time and come from many sources. However, there is much activity "behind the veil," and we understand that angels are assigned temporarily as "guardian angels" for mortals, often relatives, for specific situations and needs. Such "guardian angels" are sometimes mentioned in priesthood blessings, including patriarchal blessings.

Joseph Fielding Smith taught, "We have often heard of guardian angels attending us and many patriarchs have spoken of such protection. There are times no doubt when some unseen power directs us and leads us from harm. However, the true guardian angel given to every man who comes into the world is the Light of Truth or Spirit of Christ.

"The Holy Ghost is given to faithful members of the Church to guard and direct them: theirs is the privilege, through their faithfulness, to have such guidance and protection.

"There is no angel following us about like a stenographer taking notes and making a record of our lives. The Lord has a more perfect way by which the acts of our lives are recorded" (*DS* 1:54).

·H·

HADES

See HELL.

HALLELUJAH

Derived from Hebrew, the word basically means "Praise ye the Lord." It is found at the beginning or the end of several of the Psalms (example: Psalm 146:1).

HAND, THE RIGHT

In scriptural symbolism, the right hand is the covenant hand and represents making covenants with God (Acts 2:33). To be found on the "right hand of God" symbolically represents having attained exaltation (Moses 7:56).

HANDCART COMPANIES

From 1856 to 1860, ten handcart companies brought 2,962 immigrants the approximately 1,300 miles from the end of the western railroad at Iowa City to Utah. About 250 died along the way, with all but 30 of those being from the Willie and Martin companies.

The first two companies, with a total of 486 immigrants pulling 96 handcarts, arrived safely in Salt Lake City on September 26, 1856, having made the trek in less than 16 weeks. A third company arrived safely on October 2, 1856. Two more companies, the Willie company and the Martin company, totaling 980 people and 233 handcarts, had been delayed until dangerously late in the season. They were caught by early snows in Wyoming and about 220 of them died. Rescue parties from Salt Lake City were dispatched by Brigham Young as soon as news reached the valley of the plight of the Willie and Martin companies. Rescuers led the Willie company into the Salt Lake Valley on November 9, 1856, and the

Martin party arrived three weeks later on November 30.

Five additional companies of handcarts, totaling 1,076 immigrants with 223 handcarts, came west with little difficulty, two in 1857, one in 1859, and two in 1860.

HARLOT

Generally used in the scriptures to mean a prostitute (Genesis 38:15). "Harlot" can also symbolize breaking of covenants and "stepping out on God" as was often the case with apostate Israel (Jeremiah 3:8; Revelation 14:8).

HARMONY, PENNSYLVANIA

The town in upper Pennsylvania where Joseph and Emma Smith went to live after they were married. They lived in a cabin on thirteen acres of the farm purchased from Emma's father, Isaac Hale. Harmony is known in Church history, among other things, because it was there that Joseph Smith met his future wife, Emma Hale (JS—H 1:57). It is also well known because it was there that Oliver Cowdery joined Joseph Smith and began his service as scribe during the translation of the Book of Mormon from the gold plates (JS—H 1:66). Additionally, John the Baptist restored the Aaronic Priesthood near Harmony, on the banks of the Susquehanna River (D&C 13).

HARRIS, MARTIN

One of the Three Witnesses to the fact that the Book of Mormon came forth under the direction and power of God (see Testimony of Three Witnesses in introductory pages to the Book of Mormon). He was a farmer, a weaver, and successful businessman in Palmyra, New York, known for his honesty and integrity, and was active and respected in local government and community affairs.

Martin was born May 18, 1783, which made him about twenty-two years older than Joseph Smith. He died in Clarkston, Utah, on July 10, 1875, at age 92.

Martin Harris was about five feet, eight inches tall, and had blue eyes and brown hair. He married his first cousin, Lucy Harris, and they had at least six children. Sometime after the Smith family moved to the Palmyra area, in 1816, Martin Harris became acquainted with young Joseph Smith Jr. By 1824, Joseph had told Martin about the angel Moroni's visits to him, and later, Martin agreed to finance the publication of the Book of Mormon. When persecution against Joseph Smith intensified in the Palmyra area, Joseph and Emma determined to move to her parents' farm in Harmony, Pennsylvania. Martin provided money for them to settle their debts and also gave Joseph fifty dollars (JS—H 1:61) for the trip to Harmony. They arrived in Harmony in late December 1827.

In February 1828, Martin Harris visited Joseph in Harmony, obtained a copy of some characters off the gold plates, and took them to New

York to have their authenticity verified by scholars there (see JS—H 1:63–65). He later returned to Harmony and served as scribe during the translation of the plates, from April 12 to June 14, 1828, during which time a total of 116 manuscript pages was produced. At that point, Martin requested to take the 116 pages home to Palmyra in order to show family and friends what he was doing, and to stop unkind rumors about him. In the course of events, the 116 pages were lost, resulting in considerable pain for Martin and Joseph both (D&C 3, 10).

Oliver Cowdery took over as scribe, beginning on April 5, 1829. After the translation was completed, three witnesses, including Martin Harris, were shown the plates by an angel and had testimony born to them by a voice from on high that the work was true.

Martin eventually left the Church in 1837, but never did deny his testimony. He returned to the Church and was rebaptized on November 7, 1842. In 1870, he joined the Saints in Utah, arriving by train in Salt Lake City on August 30, 1870. He died, faithful to his testimony and faithful to the Church on July 10, 1875, in Clarkston, Utah.

HARVEST OF THE EARTH

In reference to the time of the Second Coming of Christ, this "harvest" is the gathering of the righteous, who are taken up to meet the Coming Lord (D&C 88:96) and the burning of the wicked (D&C 86:7), in preparation for the Millennium.

HATE

The term "hate," when used by the Lord in the scriptures referring to the wicked, carries the sense that He cannot bless them as He would like to because of their lifestyles and the evil desires of their hearts (Malachi 1:2–3; Romans 9:13).

HAUN'S MILL MASSACRE

On October 27, 1838, Governor Lilburn W. Boggs, of Missouri, issued the infamous Extermination Order against the Mormons in Missouri. On October 30, 1838, a mob of some 200 to 250 armed men, under the auspices of being members of the Missouri militia, attacked a small settlement of thirty to forty Mormon families around Jacob Haun's mill, located on Shoal Creek in eastern Caldwell County, Missouri.

As the mob approached the village, a few men and most of the women and children fled into the woods while others, including some men and boys ran into the blacksmith's shop. The mob fired mercilessly at everyone in sight, including women and children, as well as into the shop through the widely spaced logs of the structure, and brutally murdered seventeen Latter-day Saints and one friendly non-Mormon. Another thirteen were wounded, including one woman and a seven-year-old boy.

During the massacre, seventy-eight-year-old Thomas McBride surrendered to militiaman Jacob Rogers, who then shot him and hacked his body up with a corn knife. Another militiaman, William Reynolds, discovered a ten-year-old boy, Sardius Smith, hiding under the blacksmith's bellows. He placed the muzzle of his gun against the boy's head and fired. He later explained, "Nits will make lice, and if he had lived he would have become a Mormon" (Jenson, Historical Record, p. 673).

Jacob Haun, who was injured during the massacre but recovered, had founded the mill in 1835. Just a few days prior to the tragedy, after the Battle of Crooked River, on Thursday, October 25, Joseph Smith had asked all members of the Church in surrounding areas to come to Far West because of dangers to outlying settlements as violence against the Saints increased. Brother Haun visited with the Prophet and requested that the people in his small settlement not be required to go to Far West. Joseph insisted, but Jacob still resisted. Finally, the Prophet answered that he could do as he pleased. Years later, Joseph said, "At Haun's Mill the brethren went contrary to my counsel; if they had not, their lives would have been spared" (*HC* 5:137).

HEALING, GIFT OF

See GIFTS OF THE SPIRIT.

HEALTH IN THE NAVEL

This phrase, as used in the scriptures, conveys the sense of having the blessings and support of the Lord (Proverbs 3:8–10; D&C 89:18).

HEALTH, SCRIPTUAL LAWS OF

It is not unusual for the Lord to give His people laws of health. Two prominent examples are the law of health given through Moses to the children of Israel (Leviticus 11) and the law of health known as the Word of Wisdom, given by the Lord to the Latter-day Saints through Joseph Smith (D&C 89).

HEART

Among many other uses in scripture, "heart" is often used to mean "courage" (Luke 21:26). In the context of receiving personal revelation, "heart" is often used to mean general impressions and feelings, whereas "mind" is used to mean rather specific thoughts and words (D&C 8:2).

HEATHEN

People and nations who do not believe in or worship the true God of Israel (2 Chronicles 36:14; D&C 45:54).

HEATHEN NATIONS

Nations, referred to in the scriptures, who did not have any knowledge of or belief in the true God and the gospel of Jesus Christ. They will yet have their opportunity to hear the truth and be converted (D&C 90:10).

HEAVEN

The place where God the Father lives and where Christ and all faithful Saints will eventually dwell (Genesis 28:12; Psalm 11:4; Matthew 6:9; Mosiah 2:41). The scriptures teach that heaven is called the celestial kingdom (D&C 76:50–53, 70, 92). There are three major categories in celestial glory (D&C 131:1–4), and the highest is known as exaltation (D&C 132:19). Those who attain it live in the family unit.

HEAVENLY FATHER

See GOD THE FATHER.

HEAVENLY MOTHER

In 1909 the First Presidency, under President Joseph F. Smith, issued a statement on the origin of man that teaches that "man, as a spirit, was begotten and born of heavenly parents, and reared to maturity in the eternal mansions of the Father . . . [as] . . . offspring . . . of celestial parentage." The statement goes on to say that "all men and women are in the similitude of the universal Father and Mother, and are literally the sons and daughters of Deity" (*MFP* 4:203; see also *EM*, under "Mother in Heaven").

Thus we know that we have a Mother in Heaven. Furthermore, each of us "is a beloved spirit son or daughter of heavenly parents" ("Proclamation," paragraph 2). This inspired statement from our modern prophets, seers, and revelators further confirms the fact that we have a Heavenly Mother.

In the scriptures, we are taught that worthy husbands and wives from this earth, who have entered into celestial marriage and kept their covenants, can eventually enter into exaltation and become heavenly parents with "the continuation of the seeds forever and ever" (D&C 132:19). Thus, these worthy husbands and wives become gods (D&C 132:20), that is to say, Heavenly Fathers and Heavenly Mothers.

Other than these revealed facts, we know nothing more about Heavenly Mother. For whatever purposes, Heavenly Father has chosen not to give further revelation on this subject, and so we would do well to appreciate what we do know and avoid inappropriate speculation on the matter.

HEBREWS

As used in the scriptures, the word means "descendants of Abraham, through Isaac and Jacob." One of Paul's epistles (letters) was addressed to the Hebrews. It is contained in the New Testament.

HEIRS OF GOD

A scriptural phrase which refers to those who attain exaltation (Romans 8:16–17). Such faithful Saints become "joint heirs with Christ" (Romans 8:17) and thus become "heirs" or "inheritors" of "all that my Father hath" (D&C 84:38).

HELAMAN, SONS OF

The two thousand stripling warriors, spoken of in the Book of Mormon known for their faith, courage, and loyalty, taught them by their mothers (Alma 56:3, 9; 46–49, 56). They were joined by sixty additional faithful young men (Alma 57:6).

HELL

As used in the scriptures, this term can have several meanings: (1) The most common meaning among Christian churches is to be turned over to Satan to be punished for sins, or to be cast out to live with him forever. In the doctrine of The Church of Jesus Christ of Latter-day Saints, this would be termed perdition (D&C 76:26, 30–49), and is sometimes called outer darkness; (2) The prison portion of the postmortal spirit world (1 Peter 3:19); (3) For Latter-day Saints, who know of exaltation and desire to attain it, but who fail to live worthy, anything short of exaltation could be considered to be a type of "hell" for them, personally.

HERESY

False doctrines. Any opinion, doctrine, or philosophy which is not in harmony with the teachings of the true gospel of Jesus Christ. Paul warns against being part of teaching heresies (1 Corinthians 11:19; Galatians 5:20).

HIGH COUNCIL

A "high council," consisting of twelve high priests, serves under the direction of a stake presidency.

The basic local ecclesiastical unit of the Church, in areas where it is well-established, is the ward. Several wards together make up a stake. Each stake is presided over by a high priest who serves as the stake president. The stake president has two counselors who are likewise high priests. Members of the high council meet in counsel with the stake presidency and other stake officers, and carry out any number of assignments from the presidency.

One of the responsibilities of a high council is to serve with the stake presidency as a disciplinary council when needed. Such councils are convened in cases of serious transgression when a member's status in the Church is in jeopardy. See more on this under Disciplinary Council.

HIGH COUNCILORS

See HIGH COUNCIL.

HIGH PRIEST

Jesus Christ is the High Priest, spelled with uppercase initial letters, meaning that He presides over the Church under the direction of the Father (Hebrews 3:1).

One of the offices in the Melchizedek Priesthood is that of high priest. High priests are called to minister in the spiritual things of the Church (D&C 107:10–12). Worthy men in the Church are ordained to the office of high priest for many reasons, including to serve as a bishop, stake president, counselor to a bishop or stake president, or to serve on the high council.

HIGH PRIESTESS

There is no such office in the true Church of Jesus Christ of Latter-day Saints.

HILL CUMORAH

See CUMORAH, HILL.

HISTORY OF THE CHURCH

An official publication of the Church, in seven volumes. The first six volumes primarily cover the history of the Church during the Joseph Smith period. They were compiled under the direction of Joseph Smith and are rich in historical detail and doctrine. The seventh volume continues on after the martyrdom of the Prophet.

HISTORY, PERSONAL

The Church believes in and teaches record keeping. Individual members are counseled to keep a personal history. Adam and Eve began this practice by keeping a "book of remembrance" (Moses 6:5).

HOLINESS

See HOLY.

HOLY

The term "holy" is used in many ways within the gospel. For example, it is used to refer to things, such as temples, chapels, and scriptures, which are dedicated to the Lord.

Through the Atonement of Jesus Christ, people can become "holy" (Moroni 10:33). In other words, they can become clean and pure and qualified to be in the presence of God. In effect, the Sacred Grove, the site of Joseph Smith's first vision, was made holy by the presence of the Father and the Son. The ground on which Moses walked to get closer to the burning bush was made holy by the presence of the Lord (Exodus 3:5).

HOLY GHOST

The third member of the Godhead (Matthew 28:19; 1 John 5:7). Whereas the Father and the Son have resurrected bodies of flesh and bone, the Holy Ghost does not, but is a personage of spirit (D&C 130:22). We know nothing from the scriptures about the personal circumstances of the Holy Ghost, who He is, where He comes from, and so forth. We do have one tiny hint from the journal of George Laub, an early member of the Church, who informs us that the Prophet Joseph Smith said the Holy Ghost is still waiting to get a body (see *Ensign,* Jan. 1989, p. 29).

The scriptures teach us much about the mission and function of the Holy Ghost. Among other things, He testifies of the Father and the Son, teaches us, brings things to our remembrance, and guides us in finding truth (John 14:26; 15:26, 16:13).

The Holy Ghost may come upon non-members of the Church and testify of the truth of the gospel when they hear it (D&C 130:23). He gives the gifts of the Spirit (D&C 46:11, 13). He is often referred to as the Comforter (John 14:26; D&C 21:9). The Holy Ghost has all knowledge, and can thus help us in all matters (D&C 35:19).

We are taught that "by the Spirit ye are justified" (Moses 6:60). Justified, as used in this context, can mean "to be lined up in harmony with God." In a sense, it is the same use as in the case of a word document on a computer. When we justify the margins in a document, the computer lines them all up. Thus, an important function of the Holy Ghost is to "line us up in harmony with the gospel of Jesus Christ" so that the Atonement can heal and cleanse us and make us holy and fit to be in the presence of God (in other words, "sanctified").

The Holy Ghost is also known as "the Holy Spirit of Promise" (D&C 76:53; 132:7). This name-title denotes the role of the Holy Ghost in sealing and ratifying ordinances upon the heads of the faithful.

HOLY KISS

As used by Paul, this phrase means a greeting (Romans 16:16; 1 Thessalonians 5:26). In the Joseph Smith Translation of the Bible (JST), the Prophet changed the phrase to "holy salutation" (JST, 1 Thessalonians 5:26).

HOLY LAND

Another name for the land of Israel, Palestine—the land in which the Savior served His mortal mission.

HOLY OF HOLIES

Also known as "the most holy place" (Exodus 26:34; 1 Kings 6:16), the name refers to the most sacred inner sanctuary of the Tabernacle and later the Temple in Jerusalem (BD, under "Holy of Holies"). It was a sacred room which could be entered by the High Priest only on Yom Kippur.

The Salt Lake Temple has a Holy of Holies, just off of the celestial room.

HOLY ONE

A term which refers to Jesus Christ (Job 6:10).

HOLY ONE OF GOD

See also HOLY ONE. Another name for Jesus Christ, with the added sense that He came forth from God, in other words, from Heavenly Father (Luke 4:34).

HOLY ONE OF ISRAEL

Another name for Jesus Christ (Isaiah 1:4; 17:7; 1 Nephi 19:15).

HOLY ONE OF JACOB

See also HOLY ONE OF ISRAEL. "Israel" is another name for "Jacob" (Genesis 32:28). Therefore, "Holy One of Jacob" is the same as "Holy One of Israel." It means "the God of Israel."

HOLY ONE OF ZION

Another name for Jesus Christ (D&C 78:15).

HOLY PRIESTHOOD AFTER THE ORDER OF THE SON OF GOD

The original name of the Melchizedek Priesthood. Before the days of Melchizedek (the great high priest to whom Abraham paid tithing (Genesis 14:20), this priesthood was called "the Holy Priesthood, after the Order of the Son of God" (D&C 107:3). "But out of respect or reverence to the name of the Supreme Being, to avoid the too frequent repetition of his name, they, the church, in ancient days, called that priesthood after Melchizedek, or the Melchizedek Priesthood" (D&C 107:4).

HOLY SCRIPTURES

In The Church of Jesus Christ of Latter-day Saints, four books are considered to be scripture. They are sometimes referred to as "the standard works." They are the Bible, the Book of Mormon, the Doctrine and Covenants, and the Pearl of Great Price.

HOLY SPIRIT

See HOLY GHOST.

HOLY SPIRIT OF PROMISE

See also HOLY GHOST. Another name for the Holy Ghost. This name-title is indicative of the role of the Holy Ghost in sealing and ratifying ordinances (Ephesians 1:13; D&C 132:7, 18–19). When a member participates in an ordinance that is performed by proper authority, and does so worthily, or later becomes worthy of it, the Holy Ghost seals or validates that ordinance. This way, no one "sneaks by" by lying to a bishop or stake president.

The phrase "Holy Spirit of Promise" means, in effect, "the Spirit that the Savior promised would come upon His disciples after His ascension." In other words, it comes from the promise the Savior made to His disciples that the gift of the Holy Ghost would come powerfully upon them after His ascension into heaven (John 14:26; Acts 1:8; 2:1–13).

HOLY WRIT

Another name for the scriptures, the word of God, the holy scriptures, and so forth.

HOME

The Church teaches that the home is, or can be, one of the most sacred places on earth. In gospel-centered homes, the gospel of Jesus Christ can be lived and taught, thus making such homes "a defense, and . . . a refuge from the storm" (D&C 115:6); a place of security and peace. The Church encourages members to have their homes dedicated as a place where the Spirit of the Lord can dwell and family members can serve one another in love and kindness. King Benjamin gave counsel to parents on this matter (Mosiah 4:14–15). Families who endeavor to create such homes have the assurance that the Lord will bless them, despite the ups and downs that inevitably accompany their righteous efforts.

HOME TEACHERS

Priesthood brethren who are assigned as a companionship to regularly visit and teach the gospel in the homes of assigned members. In addition to teaching, they are to watch out for the members and assist them where possible in difficulties or concerns facing them. As needed, the home teachers enlist the aid of others, including the bishop, in helping and blessing the families to whom they are assigned.

HOME TEACHING

See HOME TEACHERS.

HOMICIDE

See MURDER.

HOMOSEXUALITY

See SAME GENDER ATTRACTION.

HONESTY

Honesty is a requirement for stable individuals, societies, governments, and nations. It is a requirement of the Lord for those who strive to be worthy in His sight (D&C 51:9; 97:8). It is a requirement of members of the Church who hold a temple recommend. Dishonesty, if not repented of, will lead individuals to the telestial kingdom (D&C 76:103; Revelation 22:15).

HOPE

As used in the scriptures, hope is not a weak sister to faith, for example, when a member sort of hopes he or she makes it to heaven. Rather, hope is a strong assurance, based on faith in Jesus Christ, that one's personal righteousness and commitment to living the gospel will lead to celestial glory (Alma 58:11). We are invited to "press forward with a steadfastness in Christ, having a perfect brightness of hope" (2 Nephi 31:20).

Faith, hope, and charity (Moroni 7), or faith, "confidence," and charity, are a powerful combination in saving our souls.

HOPE OF ISRAEL

This phrase appears three times in the scriptures: Jeremiah 14:8; 17:13; and Acts 28:20. In each of these references it means Jehovah, in other words, the premortal Jesus Christ, who is the God of the Old Testament.

"Hope of Israel" can also mean the "anticipation of obtaining exaltation," held in the hearts of faithful members of the Church (who are covenant Israel) as they strive to keep the commandments.

HOREB

Another name for Sinai (BD, under "Horeb"; Exodus 3:1; Deuteronomy 1:6; 4:10).

HORNS OF THE ALTAR

A place of safety. In ancient Israel, if someone had made an enemy and could make it to the altar of sacrifice and grab onto the horns of the altar before the enemy caught up to him, the enemy was not allowed to touch him. If he could manage to hang onto the horns of the altar long enough for the enemy to tire or negotiate peace with him, his life was saved (1 Kings 1:50–51).

HOROSCOPES

See ASTROLOGY; FORTUNE TELL-ING.

HOSANNA

Comes from the Hebrew "hoshana" and means, in effect, "save now" or "Lord, save us now." We see a tender illustration of its use in the following from the Bible: "Save now, I beseech thee, O Lord: O Lord, I beseech thee, send now prosperity" (Psalm 118:25; see also BD, under "Hosanna.")

HOSANNA SHOUT

A shout used by participants in temple dedications today. Joseph Smith described it as it was used in the dedication of the Kirtland, Ohio, Temple, Sunday, March 27, 1836. "President Rigdon then made a few appropriate closing remarks, and a short prayer, at the close of which we sealed the proceedings of the day by shouting hosanna, hosanna, hosanna to God and the Lamb, three times, sealing it each time with amen, amen, and amen" (*HC* 2:427–48).

In biblical times, the waving of palm branches (palm fronds) was symbolic of triumph and victory. The hoped-for victory over enemies was demonstrated with palm fronds during the triumphal entry of the Savior into Jerusalem (Matthew 21:9). Spiritually, palm branches are used to symbolize triumph and victory over sin and imperfection, because of the Savior's Atonement. An example of this is seen in Revelation 7:9.

White handkerchiefs used in the Hosanna Shout at temple dedications today are symbolic of the waving of palm fronds, and represent our humble and enthusiastic plea that the Savior and His Atonement give us victory over sin and save us in His Father's kingdom forever.

HOT DRINKS

This term means "tea and coffee" (*TF*, p. 186). This phrase (D&C 89:9) is used in what is known in the Church as the Word of Wisdom (D&C 89). When some confusion arose among the early members of the Church as to the meaning of hot drinks, the Prophet Joseph Smith explained, "I understand that some of the people are excusing themselves in using tea and coffee, because the Lord only said 'hot drinks' in the revelation of the Word of Wisdom. Tea and coffee are what the Lord meant when he said 'hot drinks' " (in Widtsoe, *Word of Wisdom*, pp. 85–86).

Another concern regarding the term "hot drinks" is that some members tend to think that, since the word "hot" is used, it may be permissible to drink these products cold, or iced. This is not so. "Hot drinks" was a common phrase in Joseph Smith's day which simply meant tea or coffee. Also, some members tend to believe that any "hot drink," including hot chocolate, is against the Word of Wisdom. This also is not the case.

HOUSE OF ISRAEL

The twelve nations formed by the twelve sons of Jacob (Genesis 29–30). Jacob was the son of Isaac, and the grandson of Abraham. Jacob's name was changed to Israel by the Lord (Genesis 32:28). Thus, the "house of Israel" came to mean "the descendants of Abraham, Isaac, and Jacob through Jacob's twelve sons." They are "covenant Israel" and inherit the blessings and responsibilities of Abraham (Abraham 2:9–11).

HOUSE OF JACOB

Another name for the house of Israel.

HOUSE OF THE LORD

A name which generally refers to temples. It is also occasionally used to refer to chapels.

HUMAN SACRIFICES

A devil-inspired mockery of the sacrifice of the Son of God for our sins.

HUMANITARIAN SERVICE

A program of the Church organized for the specific purpose of rendering voluntary humanitarian aid to individuals, groups, or nations throughout the world. Members donate gener-

ously to this fund, often by using the same form used for paying tithing and other donations to the Church. The humanitarian services of the Church are well known throughout the world and continue to increase in scope. The Church is often the first on the scene of a natural disaster, organizing and distributing goods and services to those who have been devastated by the situation. Millions upon millions of dollars in aid have been given thus far in this charitable service.

HUMILITY

The quiet recognition of one's imperfection and dependency upon God. It is a prerequisite for genuine service in the work of the Lord. It includes the quality of gratitude and the attribute of charity. It is necessary for receiving direction and correction from the Spirit and the Lord's representatives on earth. It is a vital element of repentance (Mosiah 4:10). It is a defense against pride (1 Peter 5:5; 2 Nephi 9:42). The Savior Himself is the perfect example of humility (Ether 12:39).

HUSBANDMEN

A scriptural term which usually means "farmers" or those engaged in agricultural pursuits such as tending olive orchards or vineyards (2 Kings 25:12; Matthew 21:33).

HYMNS

Sacred music sung by groups and individuals in their worship of God. Hymns have been important in the

Church since the beginning. In July 1830, Emma Smith, wife of Joseph Smith, was given the assignment by the Lord to make a selection of sacred hymns for use by the Saints (D&C 25:11). She completed the assignment, and it was printed by the Church in 1835.

HYPNOTISM

Bishops and stake presidents have materials from Church leaders indicating that the use of hypnosis by competent medical professionals in treating and diagnosing patient conditions is a matter to be left up to authorities in that field. However, the Church has discouraged its members from involvement in hypnosis when it is used for demonstrations or for entertainment purposes.

HYPOCRISY

Intentionally trying to appear righteous to others while secretly being involved in intentional wickedness (Matthew 23:13–15; D&C 50:6–8).

· I ·

I AM

Another name for Jehovah, who is the premortal Jesus Christ, the Creator, the God of the Old Testament (Ether 3:16). Jehovah introduced himself to Moses as "I AM" (Exodus 3:14). When the Jews challenged Jesus, saying that He could not possibly have seen Abraham (John 8:56–57), the Master responded by telling them that He was involved on earth long before Abraham was (as the God of the Old Testament). He said, "Before Abraham was, I am" (John 8:58), in effect saying that I AM was there before Abraham came to earth. It might help if the punctuation in the Bible were changed so that the phrase would read "Before Abraham, was I am."

I AM, THE GREAT
See I AM.

I AM THAT I AM
See I AM.

IDOLATERS

People who worship idols (1 Corinthians 10:7, referring to Exodus 32:4–6).

IDOLATRY

The practice of worshipping idols (Acts 17:16).

IDOLS

See also IMAGE, GRAVEN. Objects, whether man-made or natural, to which people assign mystical powers, and which people then turn around and worship (Leviticus 19:4; Isaiah 2:8). The practice of idol worship is strictly forbidden by the Lord (Exodus 20:3–5).

IDUMEA

Another name for the world (D&C 1:36).

IGNORANCE

In its most important scriptural sense, ignorance means lack of knowledge of the gospel of Jesus Christ (D&C 131:6).

ILLEGITIMACY

See OUT OF WEDLOCK BIRTHS.

ILLITERACY

Not being able to read and write. Adam and Eve were literate and taught their children to read and write (Moses 6:6).

IMAGE, GRAVEN

See also IDOLS. A graven image is a carved or sculpted idol, used in idol worship. The practice of idol worship is strictly forbidden by God as stated in the Ten Commandments (Exodus 20:3–5).

IMMACULATE CONCEPTION

"The belief of some Christians that from her conception in her mother's womb, Jesus' mother was free from original sin. Original sin holds that Adam's sinful choice in the Garden of Eden, made for all his descendants, led to a hereditary sin incurred at conception by every human being and removed only by the sacraments of the church. From this view arose the concept of Mary's immaculate conception. By a unique grace, Mary was preserved from the stain of original sin, inheriting human nature without taint in order that she be a suitable mother for Jesus. This teaching was defined as obligatory dogma by Pope Pius IX in 1854" (*EM*, under "Immaculate Conception).

Latter-day Saints do not subscribe to the dogma of the Immaculate Conception, as described above. Rather, they hold to the doctrine that Mary was a choice virgin, highly favored of the Lord, chosen to become the mother of the Son of God, as described by Luke (Luke 1:26–38).

IMMANUEL

The Hebrew form of "Emmanuel." The angel who appeared to Joseph and told him to wed Mary instructed him to call Mary's child "Emmanuel" (Matthew 1:23). Since Jesus Christ was the Old Testament Jehovah, the ancient "El," the name "Emmanuel" or "Immanuel," meaning "El with us" or "God with us" (Matthew 1:23) fits perfectly.

IMMERSION

See also BAPTISM. As used in relation to baptizing, the term means to place completely under water. Any other form of baptism fails to fulfill the symbolism of burying the old self and coming forth a new person in

Christ, as described by Paul (Romans 6:4–6).

IMMODESTY

See also MODESTY; MODESTY IN DRESS. Any form of dress for women or men which calls undue attention to private parts of the body and intentionally elicits lustful thoughts is immodesty. Temple garments are designed to promote modesty in dress.

Immodesty can also extend to language and behavior that calls inappropriate attention to self.

IMMORALITY

As used in gospel teaching and discussions, the term usually means "sexual immorality."

IMMORTAL

Living forever with a physical body after being resurrected. Sometimes people confuse immortality with eternal life (Moses 1:39). Eternal life is the type of life God lives, in other words, exaltation. All people will become immortal because all will be resurrected (1 Corinthians 15:22). But not all will attain exaltation on Judgment Day.

IMMORTAL BODY

See also INCORRUPTION; RESURRECTED BODIES. The type of permanent body of flesh and bone that all will have (1 Corinthians 15:22) after the spirit and body are reunited at the time of resurrection (Alma 40:23).

IMMORTALITY

See IMMORTAL.

IMMORTALITY AND ETERNAL LIFE

See IMMORTAL.

IMPROVEMENT

One of the simple keys to having a successful and pleasant day of final judgment (2 Nephi 9:14, last half of verse) is "improvement." In Alma 34:33, we are warned that if we "do not improve" during our life here in mortality, we will reap the result. It follows, then, that if we do "improve," through sincere and honest consistent effort in living the gospel, our "garments [*symbolic of our lives*] should be made white through the blood of the Lamb" (Alma 33:36). In other words, we will stand before God on the Day of Judgment and be allowed to enter into exaltation (D&C 45:3–5). We will not be perfect at that time. However, we will qualify to be saved by grace, "after all we can do" (2 Nephi 25:23), and thus continue progressing in the next life.

IMPROVEMENT ERA

See also MAGAZINES, CHURCH. From 1897 to 1970, the *Improvement Era* was an official magazine published by the Church. In January 1971, it was replaced by the *Ensign*, for adults in English speaking areas of the Church, and the *Liahona* (which includes material for members of all ages), in non-English speaking areas. The *New Era* became the official magazine for youth, and the *Friend* the official magazine for children.

INCARNATE

A term referring to Christ, meaning "took upon Himself a body of flesh and blood." In other words, He, a God, the premortal Jehovah, took upon Himself a mortal body and served His mortal mission (John 1:14; D&C 93:4).

INCARNATE GOD

See INCARNATE.

INCORRUPTION

See also IMMORTAL BODY.

Refers to resurrected bodies (1 Corinthians 15:42). Whereas our mortal bodies are subject to decay or "corruption," when we die, they will be "incorruptible" and perfect when we are resurrected (Alma 40:23).

INCREASE, ETERNAL

Having an unlimited number of spirit children. Refers to those who attain exaltation, thus becoming gods. As gods, they will have "a continuation of the seeds forever" (D&C 132:19–20). In other words, they will be heavenly parents to spirit offspring (Acts 17:28–29), will create worlds, and send their own spirit children through the same plan of salvation that we are being sent through by our Father in Heaven.

INDEPENDENCE, MISSOURI

The "center place" for Zion (D&C 57:1–3), and the New Jerusalem, which will eventually be built upon the American continent (Articles of Faith 1:10).

INDEX

The topical reference section at the back of the Book of Mormon as well as the Triple Combination (the Book of Mormon, Doctrine and Covenants, and Pearl of Great Price, bound together as one book).

INDIGNATION, RIGHTEOUS

A term used often in the scriptures in association with the righteous anger or wrath of the Lord because of wickedness (Deuteronomy 29:28; Ezekiel 22:31; Alma 40:14; D&C 29:17; 87:6).

INFANT BAPTISM

The Church does not practice infant baptism. In fact, it teaches strongly against it (Moroni 8:9). Baptism is for "those who are accountable and capable of committing sin" (Moroni 8:10). The Lord has established the earliest age for baptism at age eight (D&C 68:25, 27). A beautiful gospel truth teaches "that all children who die before they arrive at the years of accountability are saved in the celestial kingdom of heaven" (D&C 137:10).

INFIDELITY

A term generally associated with breaking marriage covenants by engaging in sexual relations outside of one's marriage.

INIQUITY

Another word for wickedness and sin.

INSPIRATION

See also REVELATION. Inspiration is a form of revelation, which can come from sources such as the Light of Christ (John 1:9) and the Holy Ghost. Inspiration is sometimes called the "still small voice" (1 Kings 19:12; 1 Nephi 17:45; 85:6). It can come into our minds (D&C 8:2) as sudden thoughts, ideas, phrases, and so forth. It can come into our hearts (D&C 8:2) as feelings and general impressions. Inspiration is properly called revelation, but revelation, as defined in the scriptures, can be more than inspiration because it can be stronger and more direct than inspiration. For example, dreams, visions, voices, and appearances of angelic beings would be forms of revelation which go beyond the normal definition of inspiration.

Inspiration, as we go about our normal daily pursuits, keeps us in constant contact with heaven.

INSPIRED VERSION OF THE BIBLE

See also JOSEPH SMITH TRANSLA-TION OF THE BIBLE. Another name for the Joseph Smith Translation of the Bible (JST).

INSTITUTES OF RELIGION

See CHURCH EDUCATIONAL SYSTEM.

INSTRUCTOR, THE

An official publication of the Church from 1929 to 1970, *The Instructor* was primarily the voice of the Sunday School of the Church, but included articles from other Church auxiliaries. Its publication came to an end in 1971, when the *Ensign*, the *New Era*, and the *Friend* became the official magazines of the Church.

INTEGRITY

A description of moral character in a person, which includes honesty, dependability, virtue, modesty of speech, and loyalty to principle (Job 2:3; D&C 124:15).

INTELLIGENCE

See INTELLIGENCES.

INTELLIGENCES

In premortality, before we were born as spirit children of our heavenly parents (Hebrews 12:9; Acts 17:28–29; "Proclamation," paragraph 2), we existed as "intelligence" or "intelligences" (we don't know yet what the exact and correct term is) We are taught that "the intelligence of spirits had no beginning" (*HC* 6:311; see also D&C 93:29). We know nothing more about this aspect of our premortal existence, but it is significant that we have existed eternally, and that we will continue to exist eternally, after our mortal lives end and we are resurrected. One of Satan's effective tools of destruction is to convince people that they have no eternal purpose. Rather, they came into existence at birth, and they will cease to exist at death. Such false doctrine thwarts the purposes which the Father has for us.

INTELLECTUAL RESERVE

The department in the Church which copyrights materials and intellectual property owned by the Church.

INTERCESSOR

See also ADVOCATE WITH THE FATHER; REDEEMER. An intercessor is one who comes between someone and someone else, to work out an agreement, to overcome trouble or difficulty. Jesus Christ is our Intercessor (Mosiah 15:8). He atoned for our sins, thus interceding between us and the law of Justice. He is our Intercessor or Advocate with the Father (D&C 45:3–5). He intercedes in our lives to help us overcome sins, imperfections, inadequacies, and so forth. He is the Great Intercessor, who makes salvation possible for us. Without Him, we would be lost (2 Nephi 9:10, 19–22).

INTERCESSORY PRAYER

Recorded in John 17, this is the prayer given by the Savior on the Mount of Olives just before going with His Apostles to the Garden of Gethsemane, prior to His arrest and crucifixion. It is known as the great intercessory prayer (see heading to John 17 in the LDS Bible).

In the first three verses of John 17, Jesus formally offers Himself as the great sacrifice for our sins, in order that we might have eternal life (exaltation). He is the one who intercedes for us, allowing the law of mercy to act on our behalf. Thus, it is called the intercessory prayer.

INTERNATIONAL GENEALOGICAL INDEX

A vital records index, containing millions of names, made available by the Church for genealogical research by anyone who is interested in searching for their ancestors. It is generally referred to as the IGI, and has been made available to the public through the Church's family history centers.

INTERPRETATION OF TONGUES

See GIFTS OF THE HOLY SPIRIT.

ISAIAH

The name Isaiah means "the Lord is salvation" (BD, under "Isaiah"). Isaiah was a major Old Testament prophet who served in Jerusalem from about 740 BC to 701 BC. The Savior commanded us to "search" his writings, "for great are the words of Isaiah" (3 Nephi 23:1). Isaiah used much symbolism in his writing, which often makes it difficult for people to understand his messages. The Book of Mormon contains about 35 percent of Isaiah's writings and provides help in understanding them. For example, 1 Nephi 20 is the equivalent of Isaiah 48 in the Bible. However, every verse in 1 Nephi 20 reads differently than in Isaiah 48.

Among several important themes, two major messages found in Isaiah are that Jesus is the Redeemer, and that there is hope for all. These messages are emphasized by Nephi as he counsels his brothers Laman and Lemuel to study Isaiah. Nephi said, "But that I might more fully persuade them to believe in the Lord their Redeemer I did read unto them that which was written by the prophet Isaiah; for I did liken all scriptures unto us, that it might be for our profit and learning. Wherefore I spake unto them, saying: Hear ye the words of the prophet, ye who are a remnant of the house of Israel, a branch who have been broken off; hear ye the words of the prophet, which were written unto all the house of Israel, and liken them unto yourselves, that ye may have hope as well as your brethren from whom ye have been broken off; for after this

manner has the prophet written" (1 Nephi 19:23–24).

According to tradition, Isaiah was "sawn asunder" during the reign of wicked King Manasseh (BD, under "Isaiah").

ISHMAEL

Son of Abraham and Hagar the Egyptian (Genesis 16:11–16). Ishmael had twelve sons (Genesis 25:12–13). The descendants of Ishmael are the Ishmaelites. Arabs today trace their genealogy back to Abraham through Ishmael and his twelve sons, and thus belong in the Holy Land, along with the descendants of Abraham through Isaac and the twelve sons of Jacob (Genesis 17:8).

ISHMAELITES
See ISHMAEL.

ISRAEL
See COVENANT ISRAEL.

ISRAEL, COVENANT
See COVENANT ISRAEL.

ISRAELITES
See COVENANT ISRAEL.

· J ·

JACK MORMONS

A term sometimes used in referring to members of the Church who are not active in practicing the religion.

JACKSON COUNTY, MISSOURI

See ZION.

JACOB, SON OF ISAAC

See also COVENANT ISRAEL. Jacob, the twin son of Isaac and Rebekah (Genesis 25:23–27), had twelve sons (Genesis 29 and 30). He was the son through whom the Abrahamic covenant was perpetuated (Genesis 25:29–34). His name was changed to Israel (Genesis 32:28). The extended families or tribes formed, as his twelve sons married and had children, became known as the children of Israel.

JAHWEH

Another name for Jehovah, the premortal Jesus Christ, who is the God of the Old Testament. See similar forms of the spelling in BD, under "Jehovah."

JAMES, THE APOSTLE

Two of the Savior's original Apostles were named James. One was the brother of John the Apostle (Matthew 10:2). The other was the son of Alphaeus (Matthew 10:3).

JARED

Lived at the time of the Tower of Babel (Ether 1:33). He and his brother, Mahonri Moriancumer, with their families and friends, were led by the Lord to the Americas. Their civilization became known as the Jaredites, in the Book of Mormon.

JAREDITES

See JARED.

JEALOUS

This word, when used to describe the Lord (Exodus 20:5), means that, for our own good, He commands us to worship Him exclusively. It is not the same jealousy which is a weakness in humans.

JEHOVAH

The God of the Old Testament, the God of Israel. He is the premortal Jesus Christ (Ether 3:14, 16; BD, under "Jehovah").

JEREMIAH

A major Old Testament prophet who served in and around Jerusalem for about forty years, from 626 BC to 586 BC. He was a contemporary of Lehi (1 Nephi 5:13).

JERUSALEM

Members of the Church view Jerusalem to be a holy city, as do other Christians, as well as Jews, and Muslims. It is the focus of much prophecy, ancient and modern. Its significance dates back to King David, who made it his capital. And, going farther back in history, it appears that the city was named Salem at the time Melchizedek reigned as its righteous king (Alma 13:17–18). Abraham paid tithing to Melchizedek (Genesis 14:20), and it was to Mount Moriah, in the Jerusalem area, that he brought his son, Isaac, to sacrifice him, as commanded by the Lord (Genesis 22:2).

Significant portions of the Savior's earthly ministry took place in and around Jerusalem, and it was just outside the walls of the city that He suffered in the Garden of Gethsemane (Matthew 26:36–45). Likewise, it was just outside the walls of Jerusalem that He was crucified (Luke 22:33).

Jerusalem was destroyed by the Romans, about AD 70, as prophesied (Matthew 24:2), and it will be a major focus of conflict in the last days, prior to the Second Coming of Christ (JS—M 1:32) when Jerusalem will again be under siege (BD, under "Abomination of Desolation). During a terrible battle in the last days, called the Battle of Armageddon (Revelation 16:14–21), the Savior will appear on the Mount of Olives, just outside of Jerusalem, and will save the Jews (Zechariah 14:4–5).

Jerusalem will finally be restored and become a holy city again (Ether 13:5).

JERUSALEM, NEW

See NEW JERUSALEM.

JESUS

The Greek form of the Hebrew name, Joshua. It means "God is help" or "Savior" (BD, under "Jesus"). It was a rather common name among the Jews, and is a somewhat common name today in some languages and cultures.

JESUS CHRIST

Jesus Christ is the central focus of the doctrine and teachings of The Church of Jesus Christ of Latter-day Saints. Joseph Smith taught that "the fundamental principles of our religion are the testimony of the Apostles and Prophets, concerning Jesus Christ, that He died, was buried, and rose again the third day, and ascended into heaven; and all other things which pertain to our religion are only appendages to it" (*TPJS*, p. 121).

On average, the Book of Mormon mentions Jesus Christ every 1.7 verses. Indeed, "we talk of Christ, we rejoice in Christ, we preach of Christ, we prophesy of Christ, and we write according to our prophecies, that our children may know to what source they may look for a remission of their sins" (2 Nephi 25:26).

Joseph Smith and Sidney Rigdon bore witness of Jesus Christ. They testified, "And now, after the many testimonies which have been given of him, this is the testimony, last of all, which we give of him: That he lives! For we saw him, even on the right hand of God; and we heard the voice bearing record that he is the Only Begotten of the Father—That by him, and through him, and of him, the worlds are and were created, and the inhabitants thereof are begotten sons and daughters unto God" D&C 76:22–24).

On January 1, 2000, the First Presidency and Quorum of the Twelve Apostles issued the following declaration. Titled "The Living Christ," this declaration bears witness of the Lord Jesus Christ and summarizes His identity and divine mission:

"As we commemorate the birth of Jesus Christ two millennia ago, we offer our testimony of the reality of His matchless life and the infinite virtue of His great atoning sacrifice. None other has had so profound an influence upon all who have lived and will yet live upon the earth.

"He was the Great Jehovah of the Old Testament, the Messiah of the New. Under the direction of His Father, He was the creator of the earth. 'All things were made by him; and without him was not any thing made that was made' (John 1:3). Though sinless, He was baptized to fulfill all righteousness. He 'went about doing good' (Acts 10:38), yet was despised for it. His gospel was a message of peace and goodwill. He entreated all to follow His example. He walked the roads of Palestine, healing the sick, causing the blind to

see, and raising the dead. He taught the truths of eternity, the reality of our premortal existence, the purpose of our life on earth, and the potential for the sons and daughters of God in the life to come.

"He instituted the sacrament as a reminder of His great atoning sacrifice. He was arrested and condemned on spurious charges, convicted to satisfy a mob, and sentenced to die on Calvary's cross. He gave His life to atone for the sins of all mankind. His was a great vicarious gift in behalf of all who would ever live upon the earth.

"We solemnly testify that His life, which is central to all human history, neither began in Bethlehem nor concluded on Calvary. He was the First-born of the Father, the Only Begotten Son in the flesh, the Redeemer of the world.

"He rose from the grave to 'become the firstfruits of them that slept' (1 Corinthians 15:20). As Risen Lord, He visited among those He had loved in life. He also ministered among His 'other sheep' (John 10:16) in ancient America. In the modern world, He and His Father appeared to the boy Joseph Smith, ushering in the long-promised 'dispensation of the fulness of times' (Ephesians 1:10).

"Of the Living Christ, the Prophet Joseph wrote: 'His eyes were as a flame of fire; the hair of his head was white like the pure snow; his countenance shone above the brightness of the sun; and his voice was as the sound of the rushing of great waters, even the voice of Jehovah, saying:

" 'I am the first and the last; I am he who liveth, I am he who was slain; I am your advocate with the Father' (D&C 110:3–4).

"Of Him the Prophet also declared: 'And now, after the many testimonies which have been given of him, this is the testimony, last of all, which we give of him: That he lives!

" 'For we saw him, even on the right hand of God; and we heard the voice bearing record that he is the Only Begotten of the Father—

" 'That by him, and through him, and of him, the worlds are and were created, and the inhabitants thereof are begotten sons and daughters unto God' (D&C 76:22–24).

"We declare in words of solemnity that His priesthood and His Church have been restored upon the earth—'built upon the foundation of apostles and prophets, Jesus Christ himself being the chief corner stone' (Ephesians 2:20).

"We testify that He will someday return to earth. 'And the glory of the Lord shall be revealed, and all flesh shall see it together' (Isaiah 40:5). He will rule as King of Kings and reign as Lord of Lords, and every knee shall bend and every tongue shall speak in worship before Him. Each of us will stand to be judged of Him according to our works and the desires of our hearts.

"We bear testimony, as His duly ordained Apostles, that Jesus is the Living Christ, the immortal Son of God. He is the great King Immanuel, who stands today on the right hand of His Father. He is the light, the life, and the hope of the world. His way is the path that leads to happiness in this life and eternal life in the world to come. God be thanked for the matchless gift of His divine Son" (*TF*, pp. 87–89).

JEWS

As used in the Bible, the word first was used to mean members of the tribe of Judah, that is, literal descendents of Judah who was one of the twelve sons of Jacob (2 Kings 16:6). In a broader sense, Lehi and his family were Jews, meaning politically and geographically that they came from the Jerusalem area (1 Nephi 1:4), even though Lehi was from the tribe of Manasseh (Alma 10:3). In this same sense, the Lamanites in the Missouri area were also referred to as Jews (D&C 57:4).

In the days of the Savior's mortal mission, He took the gospel first to the Jews (Matthew 15:24). Then, after His resurrection, He commanded His disciples to take the gospel also to the Gentiles (Mark 16:15). In the last days, the gospel is to come to the Gentiles first and then the Jews (1 Nephi 13:42). Apparently, there will be a great conversion among the Jews when the Savior appears to them on the Mount of Olives, prior to the Second Coming (D&C 45:48, 51–53).

JOHN

One of the original twelve Apostles (Matthew 10:2). Also known as John the Beloved because he does not refer directly to himself in his writings, rather, as the "disciple whom Jesus loved" (John 13:23; 20:2; 21:7). He is also known as John the Revelator because he wrote the book of Revelation. He is the author of five books in the New Testament: the Gospel of John, 1 John, 2 John, 3 John, and the book of Revelation. He wrote Revelation before he wrote the gospel of John.

He was translated (D&C 7:1–3) and continues to minister on earth as a translated being. Thus, his continuing mission is similar to that of the Three Nephites (3 Nephi 28). As a translated being, John joined Peter and James (who have been resurrected) in appearing to Joseph Smith and Oliver Cowdery to restore the Melchizedek Priesthood (D&C 128:20). John will be resurrected at the time of the Savior's Second Coming (D&C 7:3).

JOHN, REVELATION OF

See also SYMBOLISM IN THE SCRIPTURES. John the Apostle, also known as John the Revelator, received the vision which led to the book of Revelation, while he was on the Isle of Patmos (Revelation 1:9), approximately AD 95. The book of Revelation is also known as the Apocalypse, which comes from the Greek *Apocalypsis*, meaning "an uncovering" or "unveiling." This fits, since Revelation, especially chapters 4–22, is an "unveiling" of the future up to the end of the world.

John's vision includes much symbolism, which can make it difficult for people to understand. Joseph Smith helped by answering several questions about Revelation, including the "question and answer" session in D&C 77 and by making changes in over eighty verses in the book of Revelation in the Joseph Smith Translation of the Bible (JST) version of it.

JOHN THE BAPTIST
See BAPTIST, JOHN THE.

JOHN THE REVELATOR
See JOHN.

JOINING THE CHURCH

In order to join The Church of Jesus Christ of Latter-day Saints, an individual must be taught the basics of the gospel of Jesus Christ, be willing to live the restored gospel, and keep the commandments of the Lord. Once they arrive at this point in their personal commitment and testimony, they must be baptized by immersion by an authorized priesthood holder of the Church, and confirmed a member of the Church by the laying on of hands, again, by authorized priesthood holders.

The Lord explained that "all those who humble themselves before God, and desire to be baptized, and come forth with broken hearts and contrite spirits, and witness before the church that they have truly repented of all their sins, and are willing to take upon them the name of Jesus Christ, having a determination to serve him to the end, and truly manifest by their works that they have received of the Spirit of Christ unto the remission of their sins, shall be received by baptism into his church" (D&C 20:37).

The covenants made at baptism include those spoken of by Alma as he addressed his followers on the subject. "And it came to pass that he said unto them: Behold, here are the waters of Mormon (for thus were they called) and now, as ye are desirous to come into the fold of God, and to be called his people, and are willing to bear one another's burdens, that they may be light; Yea, and are willing to mourn with those that mourn; yea, and comfort those that stand in need of comfort, and to stand as witnesses of God at all times and in all things, and in all places that ye may be in, even until death, that ye may be redeemed of God, and be numbered with those of the first resurrection, that ye may have eternal life—Now I say unto you, if this be the desire of your hearts, what have you against being baptized in the name of the Lord, as a witness before him that ye have entered into a covenant with him, that ye will serve him and keep his commandments, that he may pour out his Spirit more abundantly upon you?" (Mosiah 18:8–10).

JOINT-HEIRS WITH CHRIST

See HEIRS OF GOD.

JOSEPH OF EGYPT

One of the twelve sons of Jacob, Joseph was sold by his brothers into Egyptian bondage (Genesis 37:12–36). Through his faithfulness and integrity, including fleeing from the lustful enticings of Potiphar's wife (Genesis 39:7–23), the Lord "prospered" him (Genesis 39:1–4) in Egypt. He eventually became second in command, directly under Pharaoh, in all of Egypt (Genesis 41:40–41). Under his direction, the Egyptians saved food during seven years of plenty and thus survived seven years of famine (Genesis 41:47–49, 53–57). He saved his father's family from the famine, including the brothers who had sold him, after tenderly forgiving the brothers for what they did to him (Genesis 42–45).

Joseph was a great prophet, but his prophecies have been left out of the Bible. The Book of Mormon gives us a sample of his prophecies (2 Nephi 3).

JOSEPH SMITH

Paul foretold that the church which Jesus established on earth during His mortal ministry would apostatize, in other words, fall away (2 Thessalonians 2:2–3). It would no longer exist in its pure form (Ephesians 2:20; 4:11–14). Peter prophesied that in the last days, before the Second Coming of the Savior, the full gospel of Jesus Christ would be restored again to earth (Acts 3:19–21). Joseph Smith was called of God to be the prophet of the prophesied restoration. Through him, the Lord restored His true church. It is now once again available on the earth as The Church of Jesus Christ of Latter-day Saints (D&C 115:4).

From age twelve to age fourteen, young Joseph Smith sought to find one church to join, among the many who were actively seeking members in the Palmyra, New York, area where he lived. As he attended their many meetings and heard their claims to be the church that he and others should join, he found that he was still unable to determine which one was right. Finally, while reading in the Bible, he came across a verse which inspired him to pray for an answer to his dilemma. "If any of you lack wisdom, let him ask of God, that giveth to all men liberally, and upbraideth not; and it shall be given him" (James 1:5).

He went into a grove of trees not far from his parent's house and prayed. In answer to his prayer, and in answer to the New Testament prophecies of a latter-day restoration, the Father and Son appeared to him. He asked which church he should join. The answer he was given startled him. He was to join none of them (JS—H 1:11–20). The stage was now set for the restoration of the true church of Jesus Christ. It was to be the "marvelous work and a wonder" in the last days prophesied by Isaiah (Isaiah 29:14).

Over the next years, Joseph Smith was schooled and prepared for the work of restoring the Church, by many heavenly messengers. He brought forth the Book of Mormon, which is another Testament of Jesus Christ. Through him, the priesthood was restored, which is the authority to act for God in the salvation of His children. On April 6, 1830, the Church was officially organized, according to the laws of the state of New York, with six members.

Over the next years, additional revelations were given and heavenly messengers came and restored priesthood keys necessary for the complete restoration of Christ's New Testament church.

On June 27, 1844, in Carthage Jail, Carthage, Illinois, Joseph Smith and his brother Hyrum were martyred by an angry mob who sought to stop the growth of the Church. Joseph was thirty-eight years old when he and his brother sealed their testimonies with their blood (D&C 135:1–3). Since then, the Church has grown to some thirteen million members and continues to grow steadily, as it takes the gospel to all the world.

Members of the Church do not worship Joseph Smith. They revere and honor him as a prophet of God. But they worship the Father and seek to return to live with Him eternally through the true gospel of His Son Jesus Christ.

JOSEPH SMITH—MATTHEW

The third book in the Pearl of Great Price. It is an inspired revision of the last verse of Matthew chapter 23, and all of Matthew, chapter 24, in the Bible, which deal with the signs of the times. It is taken from the JST (the Joseph Smith Translation of the Bible). In Joseph Smith—Matthew, the Prophet added about 450 new words to the Bible text and rearranged some verses.

JOSEPH SMITH TRANSLATION OF THE BIBLE

Under the direction of the Lord, the Prophet Joseph Smith made inspired changes to 3,410 verses of the King James Version of the Bible. He worked fairly regularly on this project from June 1830 until July 1833, and continued making a few more changes and corrections to the Bible until his martyrdom on June 27, 1844. This work on the Bible gave rise to many questions in his mind, which in turn led to asking God, which in turn led to many revelations. An example of this is section 76 of the Doctrine and Covenants (see D&C 76:15–19), which gives revelation on the three degrees of glory and perdition.

Manuscript documents provide evidence that the Prophet considered every book of the Bible even though there are some books in which he made no changes. Based on other published revelations given to the Prophet Joseph Smith, it appears that there are some additional verses that he could have changed. But many LDS scholars feel that he had substantially completed his work on "translating" the Bible by the time of his death.

The JST (Joseph Smith Translation of the Bible), as we now know it, was accurately published by the Reorganized Church of Jesus Christ of Latter-Day Saints as "Joseph Smith's 'New Translation' of the Bible," and is available in many LDS bookstores. Many of the JST revisions are included in the current LDS King James Version of the Bible, as footnotes and in a special "Joseph Smith Translation" section at the back of that Bible.

JOURNAL OF DISCOURSES

A series of twenty-six volumes containing a collection of "1,438 speeches given by fifty-five people, including Presidents of the Church, members of the Quorum of the Twelve Apostles, members of the seventy, and sixteen other speakers. Brigham Young gave 390; John Taylor, 162; Orson Pratt, 127; Heber C. Kimball, 113; and George Q. Cannon, 111. Twenty-one people gave a single speech, and the rest gave from 2 to 66 speeches" (*EM*, under "Journal of Discourses"). This collection was originally published in England, from 1854–1886, for members of the Church there who did not have ready access to Church materials published in the *Deseret News* in Salt Lake City, Utah.

While there can be much value in studying *Journal of Discourses*, there is also the potential to be led astray if one does not keep things in doctrinal and historical context. "While the *Journal* most often published sermons of Church leaders, these speeches were not always considered to be official statements of doctrine. Many different kinds of speeches were printed, including the prayer given at the laying of a cornerstone of the Salt Lake Temple, a report of a high council court decision, a funeral sermon, and a plea for the defendant and the charge to the jury in a murder trial" (*EM*).

JOURNALS

See BOOK OF REMEMBRANCE.

JUDAH

One of the twelve sons of Jacob. He was the fourth son of Jacob and Leah (Genesis 29:35). From him came the tribe of Judah, and thus, the Jews.

JUDEANS

Generally speaking, the inhabitants of the southern portion of the Holy Land in biblical times.

JUDGES

The term has several uses in the context of the scriptures. Among the various meanings are (1) The seventh book of the Old Testament; (2) The leaders of the Israelites from the time of Joshua's death until the time of Samuel. It was about two hundred years, during which time Israel was without a prophet; (3) The period of time among the Nephites, known as the "reign of the judges (Mosiah 29:44) when they were led by chief judges, beginning with Alma the Younger (Mosiah 29:41–42); (4) Bishops and stake presidents are "judges in Israel," meaning that they have the responsibility to judge the worthiness of members in matters such as extending callings, giving temple recommends, conducting disciplinary councils, helping members repent, interviewing for priesthood advancements, missions, and so forth; (5) Jesus Christ is the "Judge of all" (John 5:22; Hebrews 12:23; D&C 76:68).

JUDGES IN ISRAEL

See JUDGES.

JUDGING

Sometimes individuals take "judge not that ye be not judged" (Matthew 7:1) to such an extreme that they believe that they should never use any kind of judging at all in their dealings with others. The JST clarifies this verse. It reads "Judge not unrighteously, that ye be not judged; but judge righteous judgment." This doctrine was further clarified by the Lord when He said, "Judge not according to the appearance, but judge righteous judgment" (John 7:24). Obviously, one must judge what kind of company to keep, with whom to do business, which political candidates to support, whom to date and marry, etc. An important message here is to avoid being prejudiced or biased because of race, color, social status, financial status, and so forth, where "unrighteous judgment" tends to flourish.

JUDGMENT

See also JUDGE; JUDGING. The final judgment will be presided over by Jesus Christ. He is the final judge (John 5:22; 3 Nephi 27:16). He will be assisted by others in ways that have not yet been fully explained in the revelations. His Apostles will be involved (1 Nephi 12:9–10; D&C 29:12) as will bishops and stake presidents.

JUDGMENT BAR

Another term for standing before the Lord to be judged, at the day of final judgment (2 Nephi 33:15).

JUDGMENT DAY

In the context of the scriptures, as well as gospel conversations and class discussions, this term usually means the day of final judgment, after the Millennium and the "little season" (D&C 88:111) which follows. At that time, all will receive their final judgment from Jesus Christ (John 5:22; Revelation 20:12), following which they will enter the kingdom assigned to them (1 Corinthians 15:39–42; D&C 76; 131:1–4).

By the time of final judgment, everyone ever born on earth will have had a completely fair chance to hear, understand, and accept or reject the pure gospel of Jesus Christ, whether on earth, in the postmortal spirit world, or during the Millennium. Thus, the final judgment will be completely fair.

JUDGMENT SEAT OF CHRIST

See also JUDGMENT BAR. A phrase which means the final judgment day, when all will stand before Jesus Christ, who sits as our final judge (John 5:22).

JUDGMENTS OF GOD

In the general context of the scriptures, this phrase usually refers to the punishments from God which come upon the wicked after they have continually ignored His commandments (1 Nephi 18:15; 2 Nephi 25:6; Mosiah 29:27; Mormon 4:5).

JUST ONE, THE

Another name for Jesus Christ (Acts 7:52). The word "just" means "fair" and also means "exact in living the gospel."

JUSTICE

See LAW OF JUSTICE.

JUSTICE AND MERCY

See LAW OF JUSTICE; LAW OF JUSTICE AND MERCY; LAW OF MERCY.

JUSTIFICATION

Being placed in a position where the grace of Jesus Christ can be extended to us such that we can enter celestial glory and dwell with the Father forever. The scriptures inform us that "by the Spirit ye are justified" (Moses 6:60). In basic terms, being "justified" means being lined up in harmony with God, by the Holy Ghost. The term "justified" is used similarly in word processing, when we prompt the computer to "justify" (align) the left margins or right margins or both.

As we listen to the promptings of the Holy Ghost, and thereby live the gospel, we qualify for the Atonement of Christ to cleanse us and "sanctify" us (Moses 6:60). When we are thus "justified" and "sanctified," we are prepared to be in the presence of God in celestial glory forever.

JUVENILE INSTRUCTOR

Published privately from 1866 to 1901 by Elder George Q. Cannon, and by the Church from 1901 to 1929, it was initially published as a children's magazine and also, over time, became a major voice for the Sunday Schools of the Church, with articles directed to children, youth, and adults.

·K·

KEEPER OF THE GATE

Another name for Jesus Christ. In this use, "keeper of the gate" refers to Christ's role as our final Judge (John 5:22), and thus, the keeper of the "gate to heaven" because He determines who will enter the Father's kingdom (celestial glory) and who will be sent elsewhere.

KEY OF DAVID

A term used in reference to Christ's power to pronounce final judgment (Revelation 3:7; Isaiah 22:22; John 5:22). The reference to David is actually to the "throne of David," which, symbolically, is the power to rule and reign over Israel. Ultimately, Jesus Christ is the "King of kings, and Lord of lords" (Revelation 17:14) over the whole world.

KEYS

See also KEYS OF THE PRIESTHOOD. The power and authority to control and direct the work of the Lord.

KEYS OF THE KINGDOM

See KEYS OF THE PRIESTHOOD.

KEYS OF THE MINISTERING OF ANGELS

See also MINISTERING OF ANGELS. One of the powers and rights attending the ministry of the Aaronic Priesthood (D&C 13:1; 107:20).

KEYS OF THE PRIESTHOOD

A phrase referring to the right to preside over a priesthood function, a priesthood quorum, or an organization of the Church, and, in general, to control the correct functioning of the Church. Such keys are held by the president of the Church, his two counselors, and the Quorum of Twelve, all of whom are Apostles. "The president of the church, who is the senior apostle, holds all the keys presently on earth and presides over all the organizational and ordinance work of the Church (D&C 107:8–9, 91–92). He delegates authority by giving the keys of specific offices to others (D&C 124:123). Only presiding priesthood officers (including General Authorities, stake presidents, mission presidents, temple presidents, bishops, branch presidents, and quorum presidents) hold keys pertaining to their respective offices" (*EM*, under "Keys of the Priesthood). These officers receive their keys by the laying on of hands by those who are in authority to give such keys.

In a typical ward, there are only four men who hold keys. They are the bishop, the elders quorum president, the teachers quorum president, and the deacons quorum president. The high priests quorum is organized on a stake basis, with the stake president as its president and with groups of its members meeting in each ward under the direction of a high priest group leader and two assistants. The bishop is the president of the priests quorum in each ward.

In summary, these keys provide the means of maintaining order and correctness in the Church. They ensure a channel, both on the general level and on the local level, through which authorized guidance and direction comes from the Lord through the General Authorities of the Church.

KEYSTONE OF MORMONISM

See also BOOK OF MORMON. Joseph Smith referred to the Book of Mormon as "the keystone of our religion," and taught that "a man would get nearer to God by abiding by its precepts, than by any other book." This statement by the Prophet is found in the Introduction to the Book of Mormon, and is a quote from Joseph Smith, given in Brigham Young's home in Nauvoo, Illinois, on November 28, 1841 (*HC* 4:461; *TPJS*, p. 194).

KIMBALL, SPENCER W.

The twelfth president of the Church. He served as the president from 1973 to 1985.

KINDRED

A group of related people. Extended families (Genesis 12:1; 24:4; Acts 7:14; Revelation 5:9; Mosiah 3:13; D&C 10:51; 77:8).

KING FOLLETT DISCOURSE

The name of a two hour and fifteen minute address given by Joseph Smith to the Saints at a general conference of the Church in Nauvoo, Illinois, on April 7, 1844. The sermon was, in effect, a funeral address, given in memory of Brother King Follett, and focused on the subject of the dead. King Follett was a respected member of the Church who had died in an accident on March 9, 1844. The talk was given to several thousand members of the Church who had gathered for the conference in a grove west of the Nauvoo Temple, in a natural amphitheater.

This sermon was the last conference address given by the Prophet before his martyrdom on June 27, 1844. It was recorded by four scribes and is printed in *History of the Church*, volume 6, pages 302–17, as well as in *Teachings of the Prophet Joseph Smith*, pages 342–62.

This sermon is considered by many to be the greatest ever given by Joseph Smith, because in it he brought together so many of the major truths and doctrines of the gospel. Among other things, he spoke of the condition of the dead, the character of God, the Creation, the intelligence of spirits, the power of knowledge, man's relationship to God, the salvation of the dead, the unpardonable sin, baptism, and repentance.

One example of the power and doctrine contained in this sermon is the following statement by the Prophet: "If men do not comprehend the character of God, they do not comprehend themselves" (*TPJS*, p. 343). The Prophet explained more about God the Father and who He is. He taught, "God himself was once as we are now, and is an exalted man, and sits enthroned in yonder heavens! That is the great secret. If the veil were rent today, and the great God who holds this world in its orbit, and who upholds all worlds and all things by his power, was to make himself visible,—I say, if you were to see him today, you would see him like a man in form—like yourselves in all the person, image, and very form as a man; It is the first principle of the Gospel to know for a certainty the Character of God, and to know that we may converse with him as one man converses with another" (*TPJS*, p. 345–46).

KING IMMANUEL
See also IMMANUEL. Another name for Jesus Christ (D&C 128:22).

KING JAMES VERSION OF THE BIBLE
The version of the Bible used by the Church in English-speaking areas. The King James Version was produced by fifty-four scholars under the sponsorship of King James I of England. The work took from 1604 to 1611 to complete.

Joseph Smith used the King James Version. Among other things, he used it for his basic text as he made his inspired translation of the Bible (known today as the Joseph Smith Translation of the Bible, or JST). Since his time, the presidents and General Authorities of the Church have continued to endorse the King James Version as the official Bible to be used in English-speaking areas of the Church, even though it has imperfections, as expressed in the eighth Article of Faith.

Some have wondered why the Church does not use the JST as the official Bible of the Church. The answer is simple. Among other things, it is much easier to use the King James Version in missionary work, rather than our own version, because the King James Bible is well accepted among other Christians. They would be suspicious of a Mormon version of the Bible if used in the initial teaching of the gospel.

KING OF GLORY

Another name for Jesus Christ (Psalm 24:7–10).

KING OF HEAVEN

Another name for Jesus Christ (Daniel 4:37; 2 Nephi 10:14; Alma 5:50). This title does not imply that Christ is above the Father. The Father is above all (Ephesians 4:6). Therefore, this name/title indicates that the Savior has power and authority both in heaven and earth to save the faithful. He is, in effect, King of our salvation, both on earth and in heaven, where He now resides (Acts 1:11) until the Second Coming.

KING OF ISRAEL

Another name for Jesus Christ, the Lord, who was the Jehovah of the Old Testament (Isaiah 44:6).

KING OF KINGS

Another name/title for Jesus Christ (Revelation 17:14; 19:16). This one has special reference to the Millennium. It is interesting to note in Revelation 17:14 that uppercase "King" is used to mean the Savior, and lowercase "king" refers to the resurrected Saints who will eventually be kings and priests (Revelation 5:10), in other words, exalted beings who will reign with Christ during the Millennium (Revelation 20:4).

KING OF THE JEWS

Jesus Christ. The Jews were looking forward to a King who would save them from their enemies and give them victory and political status, as prophesied in the Old Testament (Zechariah 9:9–10). Pilate asked Jesus, "Art thou the King of the Jews?" (John 18:33). And the Master's answer affirmed that He was (John 18:34–37). Even though the Jews rejected Him, Pilate had a sign placed on the cross, saying, "Jesus of Nazareth the King of the Jews" (John 19:19).

KINGDOM OF GOD

See also KINGDOM OF HEAVEN. As used in section 65 of the Doctrine and Covenants, this phrase means "The Church of Jesus Christ of Latter-day Saints" (D&C 65:6). Daniel prophesied that this church will go forth to fill the whole earth (Daniel 2:35, 44–45; D&C 65:2, 5–6).

In a general sense, the kingdom of God is the celestial kingdom, where God and Christ dwell (Matthew 19:24; 21:31; 2 Nephi 9:18; 3 Nephi 11:33; D&C 6:13).

KINGDOM OF HEAVEN

See also KINGDOM OF GOD. As used in section 65 of the Doctrine and Covenants, this phrase means Christ's millennial kingdom, which will begin at the time of the Second Coming (D&C 65:5–6).

The "kingdom of heaven" is often used in the scriptures to mean "celestial glory" (Matthew 18:3; 3 Nephi 12:20; D&C 6:37).

KINGDOM OF ISRAEL

When Saul became king, the nations or tribes of Israel became the kingdom of Israel (1 Samuel 8:4–5, 22; 9:15–17). Later, when the nation of Israel split in two (1 Kings 12), the northern kingdom, consisting of the northern ten tribes, became known as the kingdom of Israel (sometimes called Ephraim—see Isaiah 7:5). The southern kingdom, consisting of the tribe of Judah and part of the tribe of Benjamin, became known as the kingdom of Judah.

KINGDOM OF JUDAH

See KINGDOM OF ISRAEL.

KINGDOM OF THE DEVIL

See also CHURCH OF THE DEVIL. Satan is well organized in his evil attempts to lead people away from God. Any individuals, organizations, false philosophies, views, or pressures which influence us to commit sin or distance ourselves from God are part of the kingdom of the devil (1 Nephi 22:22–23).

The devil's goal is to make all people "miserable like unto himself" (2 Nephi 2:27), and his ultimate goal is to gain all power over the souls of men (Alma 34:35).

KINGDOMS OF GLORY

See also DEGREES OF GLORY; EXALTATION. We are told in the scriptures that there are three basic kingdoms of glory, plus perdition (which is not a kingdom of glory), to which we can be assigned on the day of final judgment (1 Corinthians 15:39–42; D&C 76). These degrees of glory are compared (1 Corinthians 15:41; D&C 76:96–98) to the sun (celestial), moon (terrestrial), and stars (telestial).

The lowest of these three kingdoms of glory is the telestial kingdom (D&C 76:81–89, 98–106, 109–12; 88:100–101). The people who will be assigned to this glory are those who, on final Judgment Day, are still "liars, and sorcerers, and adulterers, and whoremongers, and whosoever loves and makes a lie" (D&C 76:103). Elsewhere, we are told that murderers also fit in this category (Revelation 22:15; D&C 42:18). No one going to telestial glory will be resurrected until the end of the Millennium (D&C 88:100–101). Although this is the lowest kingdom of glory, it is so wonderful that we cannot even imagine it (D&C 76:89), which is a reminder of how tender and merciful God is.

The terrestrial kingdom of glory (D&C 76:71–80, 87, 91, 97) fits between the telestial and the celestial kingdoms. Those who will be assigned to the terrestrial glory are basically those who were good and honorable people but who chose not to become valiant and faithful members of the Lord's Church despite having a fair opportunity to do so.

The celestial glory (D&C 76:50–70, 92–96) is what is often thought of as heaven. Those who attain it "shall dwell in the presence of God and his Christ forever and ever" (D&C 76:62).

In order to go to the celestial kingdom, individuals must accept the gospel, be baptized, receive the gift of the Holy Ghost, strive to keep the commandments in order to be cleansed from their sins, and overcome obstacles to righteousness by faith in Jesus Christ, so that, ultimately, they can be sealed by the Holy Spirit of Promise (D&C 76:50–53).

Within the celestial glory there are three "heavens or degrees" (D&C 131:1–4), the highest of which is called exaltation. Exaltation is the type of life that Heavenly Father lives. Celestial marriage is a requirement for exaltation (D&C 132:19–20). Husbands and wives who attain exaltation will become gods, have spirit children, make worlds for them, and send them through the same plan of salvation used for us by the Father (First Presidency statement, *Improvement Era*, August 1916, p. 942).

KINGDOMS OF THIS WORLD

A phrase referring to the nations of the world with man-made governments (Revelation 11:15; D&C 105:32).

KIRTLAND, OHIO

A major gathering place for the Saints from 1831 to early 1838. During this same basic time period, Zion, in Jackson County, Missouri, was also a gathering place for members of the Church. In effect, there were two headquarters of the Church during this time and Joseph Smith made several trips between the two locations.

The Kirtland period was a time of significant doctrinal development for the Church. Just a little less than half of the revelations in the Doctrine and Covenants were given in Kirtland and the surrounding area.

One of the highlights of the Kirtland period was the construction and dedication of the Kirtland Temple. The Savior appeared in the temple, as did Moses, Elias, and Elijah (D&C 110).

Early in 1838, amidst apostasy and financial woes, along with threats and mob action by non-LDS enemies, more than 1,600 Saints left the Kirtland area, abandoning their temple and moving westward toward Missouri.

KIRTLAND TEMPLE

The first temple to be built by the Church in this dispensation. At the end of December 1832, the Lord commanded the Saints to build a temple (D&C 88:119). It was a time of great poverty for the early members of the Church, many of whom had left homes and property of considerable value in order to gather with the Saints in Ohio. By June of 1833, they still had not begun the actual construction of the temple. Consequently, the Savior chastised them (D&C 95:2–3) and said, "Let the house be built" (D&C 95:13). Four days later, they began digging foundation trenches and hauling stones for construction of the temple.

Over the next three years, the temple was constructed, at a cost estimated to be between $40,000 and

$60,000. It was dedicated on Sunday, March 27, 1836 (D&C 109).

Many miraculous manifestations were received in conjunction with the dedication. For example, Sunday evening, after the actual dedication, Joseph Smith reported, "Brother George A. Smith arose and began to prophesy, when a noise was heard like the sound of a rushing mighty wind, which filled the Temple, and all the congregation simultaneously arose, being moved upon by an invisible power; many began to speak in tongues and prophesy; others saw glorious visions; and I beheld the Temple was filled with angels, which fact I declared to the congregation. The people of the neighborhood came running together (hearing an unusual sound within, and seeing a bright light like a pillar of fire resting upon the Temple), and were astonished at what was taking place. This continued until the meeting closed at eleven p.m." (*HC* 2:428).

KOLOB

The name of the planet that is "nearest to the celestial, or the residence of God" (Pearl of Great Price, Abraham, Facsimile No. 2, Explanation). This same source of information tells us that one day on Kolob is equal to a thousand years on earth.

·L·

LAKE OF FIRE AND BRIMSTONE

See BRIMSTONE.

LAMANITES

Descendants of Laman and Lemuel and their followers, in the Book of Mormon. Over time, the term came to refer to those who did not follow the ways of God (2 Nephi 5:14; Jacob 1:13–14). However, there were times in the Book of Mormon when the Lamanites were righteous and the Nephites were wicked (Helaman 13:1). A great prophecy contained in the Doctrine and Covenants foretells that the day would come when the "Lamanites shall blossom as the rose" (D&C 49:24). This prophecy is being fulfilled in our day.

LAMB

A male lamb, without blemish, was used in animal sacrifices anciently, symbolizing the Savior, who was to be the "sacrificial Lamb" for our sins (Leviticus 23:12; 1 Peter 1:19).

LAMB OF GOD

Another name for the Savior, symbolizing His role as the "sacrifice for our sins" (John 1:29; 1 Nephi 10:10; D&C 88:106).

LAMB'S BOOK OF LIFE
See BOOK OF LIFE.

LAMENTATION
A term which means "great mourning and expression of grief" (Jeremiah 9:20–21; Mosiah 21:9). There is a book in the Old Testament called Lamentations, in which Jeremiah laments the downfall of his people because of sin.

LANGUAGE OF ADAM
See ADAMIC LANGUAGE.

LANGUAGES
See also BABEL, TOWER OF. It appears that for the approximately 1,750 years from the time of Adam and Eve until the Tower of Babel, everyone on earth spoke the same basic language, at least sufficiently so that they could understand each other (Genesis 11:1). However, as a means of stopping work on the Tower of Babel, the Lord "confounded" the language of the people such that many different languages were spoken (Genesis 11:6–9).

LARGE PLATES OF NEPHI
See BOOK OF MORMON PLATES.

LASCIVIOUSNESS
Any type of sexual immorality, including lustful thinking and pornography (Mark 7:22; Galatians 5:19; Jacob 3:12; Alma 16:18).

LAST DAY, THE
This term seems to be context sensitive, with at least two different basic meanings in the scriptures: (1) The time of the Second Coming of Christ, when the righteous dead will be resurrected (John 11:24); (2) The final scenes of this earth, including the final Day of Judgment (1 Nephi 13:37; 2 Nephi 9:44; Jacob 1:19; Alma 22:18).

LAST DAYS, THE
See also SIGNS OF THE TIMES. We live in the last days, which are the prophesied final scenes on earth prior to the Second Coming of the Savior (Isaiah 2:2; 2 Timothy 3:1–7; D&C 77:15; 89:2–4; 112:30; JS—H 1:54). There are many "signs of the times" which bear witness to us that we are in the last days.

LAST JUDGMENT
The last judgment or final judgment is so named because we have had a number of "judgment days" already. For example, at the time of the War in Heaven, we had a type of judgment day to determine whether we would come to earth or be cast out with Satan (Revelation 12:4). When we die, we will undergo a partial judgment to determine whether we go to paradise or prison (Alma 40:11–14). When we are resurrected, we will be judged to determine what kind of resurrected body we receive, celestial, terrestrial, telestial, or perdition (D&C 88:28–32). Therefore, when the last judgment comes (Revelation 20:12), we will have already undergone a number of partial judgments.

164

·L·

LAST SUPPER

See also SACRAMENT. On Thursday evening, before His crucifixion on Friday, the Savior gathered with His Twelve Apostles and ate the Passover meal. He informed them that this would be His last meal or "supper" with them (Luke 22:14–16). During this Passover meal, he taught them about the sacrament and blessed and administered it to them (Luke 22:19–20; Matthew 26:26–28). Therefore, this Passover meal and the sacrament which was introduced with it, is called the Last Supper.

LAST TO BE FIRST

See FIRST TO BE LAST.

LATIN VULGATE

A Latin version of the Bible commissioned by the Pope in AD 382. It was in common use for about a thousand years. When Gutenberg printed the Bible and published it, in AD 1452, it was the Latin Vulgate version.

LATTER DAYS

A phrase which means "in the last days." "The latter days" refers to the time of the earth's history from the restoration of the gospel by Joseph Smith up to the Second Coming of Christ. It is also known as "the dispensation of the fulness of times" (Ephesians 1:10; D&C 112:30).

LATTER-DAY SAINTS

A short form of the full name of the Church, which is The Church of Jesus Christ of Latter-day Saints. The Lord told Joseph Smith that this full name was to be the official name of the Church in the last days (D&C 115:4).

LAW OF CARNAL COMMANDMENTS

Another name for the law of Moses (D&C 84:23–27).

LAW OF CONSECRATION

See CONSECRATION.

LAW OF FORGIVENESS

Simply put, the law of forgiveness requires that we forgive others in order to be forgiven ourselves by the Lord. The Sermon on the Mount states this clearly: "For if ye forgive men their trespasses, your heavenly Father will also forgive you: But if ye forgive not men their trespasses, neither will your Father forgive your trespasses" (Matthew 6:14–15).

Forgiving others does not require allowing them to keep "walking" on someone. Nephi is an example of this. He "did frankly forgive" his brothers (1 Nephi 7:21) time and time again. But the time came when he had to flee from them because of their behavior toward him (2 Nephi 5:4–5). Forgiving does not mean condoning the abusive behavior, or suggesting that it was not evil (D&C 1:31–32). In cases where it becomes extremely difficult to forgive, the Savior invites us to lift the burden from ourselves by shifting the burden to Him (D&C 64:9–11).

LAW OF JUSTICE

See also LAW OF MERCY; LAWS OF JUSTICE AND MERCY. The law of justice (Alma 42:13–26, 30) is the eternal law which requires that a penalty be paid for any law that is broken. This includes sins. It also requires that the designated reward be given for a law that is kept (D&C 82:10). The law of justice keeps equilibrium in the universe. Without it, there would be chaos. Nothing would be stable and we could trust nothing, not even God.

LAWS OF JUSTICE AND MERCY

See also LAW OF JUSTICE; LAW OF MERCY. The universe is run according to laws. The laws of justice and mercy work together in harmony (Alma 42:22–24) to preserve the equilibrium of the universe. They make all things completely fair for us, ultimately. The Atonement of Jesus Christ makes it possible for us to be saved and still have the demands of justice satisfied (Alma 42:22).

LAW OF MERCY

See also LAW OF JUSTICE; LAWS OF JUSTICE AND MERCY. The law of mercy is an eternal law. It allows the Savior, through His Atonement, to pay the penalties that we owe to the law of justice because of our sins. His payment for us (2 Nephi 9:21) satisfies justice, and the equilibrium of the universe is preserved. In return, He requires "payment" by us to Him. The payment He requires is "merciful" and consists of nothing but things which are good for us, such as faith, repentance, baptism, the gift of the Holy Ghost, keeping the commandments, and being kind to others, all of which lead to personal growth and happiness here and exaltation in the hereafter. If we choose not to take advantage of His Atonement by living the gospel, then His merciful payment for our sins (2 Nephi 9:21) is cancelled, in our case (2 Nephi 9:24; Alma 42:25), and we become subject to the full demands of the law of justice (2 Nephi 9:19–24; D&C 19:15–19).

LAW OF MOSES

The law of Moses was given to the children of Israel as a "schoolmaster law" (Galatians 3:24) because of their failure to live the higher laws of the Abrahamic Covenant. This law consisted of additional laws and rules which would enable the children of Israel to live in peace and harmony with each other. It was a preparatory law which was designed by the Lord to prepare His people for the higher law given by Him during His mortal mission.

The central focus of the law of Moses was found in animal sacrifices, which were symbolic of the sacrifice of the Son of God for our sins. These sacrifices and rituals were filled with types and symbols of Christ and His Atonement. As an example, consider these verses from Leviticus, with notes added:

Leviticus 14:1–9

1 And the LORD spake unto Moses, saying,

2 This shall be the law of the leper [*the rules for being made clean; symbolic of serious sin and great need for help and cleansing*] in the day of his cleansing [*symbolic of the desire to be made spiritually clean and pure*]: He shall be brought unto the priest [*authorized servant of God, bishop, stake president, who holds the keys of authority to act for God*]:

3 And the priest shall go forth out of the camp [*the person with leprosy did not have fellowship with the Lord's people and was required to live outside the main camp of the children of Israel; the bishop, symbolically, goes out of the way to help sinners who want to repent*]; and the priest shall look, and, behold, if the plague of leprosy be healed in the leper [*the bishop serves as a judge to see if the repentant sinner is ready to return to full membership privileges*];

4 Then shall the priest command to take for him that is to be cleansed [*the person who has repented*] two birds [*one represents the Savior during His mortal mission, the other represents the person who has repented*] alive and clean, and cedar wood [*symbolic of the cross*], and scarlet [*associated with mocking Christ before his crucifixion; see Mark 15:17*], and hyssop [*associated with Christ on the cross; see John 19:29*]:

5 And the priest shall command that one of the birds [*symbolic of the Savior*] be killed in an earthen vessel [*Christ was sent to earth to die for us*] over running water [*Christ offers "living water," the gospel of Jesus Christ—see John 7:37–38, which cleanses us when we come unto*]:

6 As for the living bird [*representing the person who has repented*], he [*the priest; symbolic of the bishop, stake president, one who holds the keys of judging*] shall take it [*the living bird*], and the cedar wood, and the scarlet, and the hyssop [*all associated with the Atonement*], and shall dip them and the living bird in the blood of the bird that was killed over the running water [*representing the cleansing power of the Savior's blood which was shed for us*]:

7 And he shall sprinkle upon him that is to be cleansed from the leprosy [*symbolically, being cleansed from sin*] seven times [*seven is the number which, in Biblical numeric symbolism, represents completeness, perfection*], and shall pronounce him clean [*he has been forgiven, and shall let the living bird (the person who has repented) loose into the open field [representing the wide open opportunities again available in the kingdom of God for the person who truly repents*].

8 And he that is to be cleansed shall wash his clothes [*symbolic of cleaning up your life from sinful ways and pursuits—compare with Isaiah 1:16*], and shave off all his hair [*symbolic of becoming like a newborn baby; fresh start*], and wash himself in water [*symbolic of baptism*], that he may be clean [*cleansed from sin*]: and after that he shall come into the camp [*rejoin the Lord's covenant people*], and shall tarry

abroad out of his tent seven days.

9 But it shall be on the seventh day, that he shall shave all his hair off his head and his beard and his eyebrows, even all his hair he shall shave off [*symbolic of being born again*]: and he shall wash his clothes [*clean up his life*], also he shall wash his flesh in water [*symbolic of baptism*], and he shall be clean [*a simple fact, namely that we can truly be cleansed and healed by the Savior's Atonement*].

The law of Moses was fulfilled at the time of the Savior's mortal mission, meaning that the ceremonial laws, including animal sacrifice, were done away with. The Ten Commandments remain in force today, as do many aspects of moral and ethical behavior contained in the law of Moses.

You may be surprised at how "high" many of the laws of Moses were. An example of how "high" the laws were is found in Exodus 22:1–4. They included many of the laws and moral principles of the gospel of Jesus Christ, including faith, repentance, baptism by immersion, and the remission of sins (see BD, under "law of Moses"). They were filled with types and symbols of Christ and His Atonement. They required very high levels of behavior toward others.

Sometimes people confuse the law of Moses with the "traditions of the elders," which consisted of almost countless rules and nitpicky laws, established over the centuries, as religious leaders added unauthorized details to the law of Moses. Jesus and His disciples were constantly subjected to these "laws of the Jews."

LAW OF WITNESSES

This law states that there must be at least two or more witnesses for official ordinances and actions of the Church (Deuteronomy 17:6; 2 Corinthians 13:1; Matthew 18:15–16; D&C 42:81).

LAW, DIVINE

A term which means "God's law." "Divine" means "having to do with God."

LAWGIVER

Jesus Christ is our "lawgiver" (D&C 38:22).

LAWS OF THE LAND

The Church teaches its members to obey the laws of the land. "We believe in being subject to kings, presidents, rulers, and magistrates, in obeying, honoring, and sustaining the law" (Articles of Faith 1:12).

Furthermore, "We believe that all men are bound to sustain and uphold the respective governments in which they reside, while protected in their inherent and inalienable rights by the laws of such governments; and that sedition and rebellion are unbecoming every citizen thus protected, and should be punished accordingly; and that all governments have a right to enact such laws as in their own judgments are best calculated to secure the public interest; at the same time, however, holding sacred the freedom of conscience" (D&C 134:5).

LAY MINISTRY

The Church of Jesus Christ of Latter-day Saints does not have what is normally called a paid ministry in which local ministers are paid for their service. Instead, they have a lay ministry in which laymen, meaning men who are not paid ministers, lead local church units, volunteering their time and service. Bishops and stake presidents are lay ministers.

LAYING ON OF HANDS, THE

"We believe that a man must be called of God, by prophecy, and by the laying on of hands by those who are in authority, to preach the Gospel and administer in the ordinances thereof" (Articles of Faith 1:5).

The "laying on of hands" means that priesthood holders place their hands upon the head of an individual who is receiving an ordinance or blessing. For example, when a person is confirmed a member of the Church and given the gift of the Holy Ghost, it is done by the laying on of hands (D&C 20:41). When a person receives a blessing, it is done by the laying on of hands.

The laying on of hands provides for the orderly and definite transfer of keys, power, and authority in the Church. It leaves no doubt as to what was done and provides basis for keeping written records of the event as needed.

The scriptures confirm that the laying on of hands has been used for ordinations and blessings in the Lord's Church from earliest times (Numbers 27:18; Deuteronomy 34:9; Matthew 9:18; 1 Timothy 4:14; Alma 6:1; D&C 20:58).

LECTURES ON FAITH

A collection of seven lectures which were presented in the School for the Elders early in the winter of 1834–35, in Kirtland, Ohio. The school was established for the instruction of Church leaders and missionaries. The collection was included in the 1835 edition of the Doctrine and Covenants, and most subsequent editions until the 1921 edition, which did not include the lectures because "they were never presented to nor accepted by the Church as being otherwise than theological lectures or lessons" (from a note in 1921 edition of Doctrine and Covenants).

No clear evidence exists as to who actually wrote the lectures, but some studies suggest that Sidney Rigdon was the principle author with considerable involvement by Joseph Smith.

Perhaps one of the best-known lectures is "Lecture Third," in which these early brethren were taught three major requirements for being able to exercise faith in God: "First, the idea that he actually exists. Secondly, a correct idea of his character, perfections, and attributes. Thirdly, an actual knowledge that the course of life which he is pursuing is according to his will."

As a separate publication, *Lectures on Faith* was published by Deseret Book in 1985 and by the Religious Studies Center at Brigham Young University in 1990.

LEE, HAROLD B.

The eleventh president of the Church. He was born in 1899 and died in 1973. He became the president on July 7, 1972, and served until his death on December 26, 1973. He served as the prophet for 538 days, which is the shortest term of service for any modern president of the Church.

He was well known for, among many other things, having started the welfare system of the Church, many years earlier, in 1935, under the direction of the First Presidency. As one of the youngest stake presidents in the Church at the time, at age thirty-one, he had been faced with severe welfare needs in his stake, the Salt Lake Pioneer Stake, as a result of the Great Depression. His effective handling of the needs of his stake members led to his appointment to organize this system for the whole Church.

LEHI

A prophet in the Book of Mormon who was called by the Lord to preach to the wicked inhabitants of Jerusalem in 600 BC (1 Nephi 1:18). When he was rejected and the Jews sought to kill him, the Lord directed him to take his family and flee into the wilderness (1 Nephi 2:2–4). He and his family were eventually led by the Lord to the Americas. The account of him and his descendants composes the bulk of the Book of Mormon.

LESBIANS

See SAME GENDER ATTRACTION.

LESSER PRIESTHOOD

Another name for the Aaronic Priesthood (D&C 84:25–26, 30; 107:13–14).

LEVI

See also LEVITICAL PRIESTHOOD. One of the twelve sons of Jacob (Genesis 29:34). His descendants became known as the tribe of Levi. Among the children of Israel, it was only the men of the tribe of Levi who held the Aaronic Priesthood (BD, under "Aaronic Priesthood"). Moses and his brother were of the tribe of Levi, and it was upon Aaron and his male descendants that the Aaronic Priesthood was conferred (D&C 84:18).

LEVITES

See also LEVI; LEVITICAL PRIESTHOOD. Members of the tribe of Israel who were descendants of Levi were called Levites. The men of the tribe of Levi were the only ones given the Aaronic Priesthood.

LEVITICAL PRIESTHOOD

See also LEVI. The "Levitical Priesthood" is sometimes used as simply another name for the Aaronic Priesthood. But a distinction is often made in the scriptures (1 Kings 8:4; D&C

107:1). The men of the tribe of Levi held the Aaronic Priesthood, which was first conferred upon Aaron and his sons (D&C 107:18). Within the Aaronic Priesthood, as it functioned among the Israelites of the Old Testament, there were those who were priests and high priests, and there were men who held the "Levitical" priesthood. The priests and high priests had greater privileges, including offering sacrifices for the people, burning incense on the altar, and giving instructions about the law of Moses. Those holding the Levitical Priesthood functioned in lesser tasks, such as cleaning the tabernacle, keeping oil in the lamps, transporting the Ark of the Covenant, taking down and setting up the tabernacle as travel required, and so forth.

LEVITY

Not taking serious things seriously (JS—H 1:28).

LEWDNESS

As used in the scriptures, this term generally refers to sexual immorality (Jeremiah 13:27).

LIAHONA

A compass or director, in the shape of a ball, which the Lord prepared to guide Lehi and his family as they journeyed in the wilderness (1 Nephi 16:10). It worked "according to the faith and diligence and heed" which they gave to it (1 Nephi 16:28–29). The name of this compass or director was given in Alma 37:38.

The Liahona was shown to Joseph Smith and the Three Witnesses in 1829 (D&C 17:1).

Liahona is also the name of the international magazine published by the Church.

LIARS

The fate of liars who refuse to repent and become honest is to be sent to the telestial kingdom on Judgment Day (D&C 76:103; Revelation 22:15).

LIBERTY JAIL

The name of the jail in Liberty, Missouri, in which Joseph Smith was imprisoned during the winter of 1838–1839. He was there from December 1, 1838 until April 6, 1839. With him in the jail were his brother Hyrum, who served as his second counselor in the presidency of the Church; Sidney Rigdon, his first counselor; and three other members of the Church: Lyman Wight, Alexander McRae, and Caleb Baldwin.

The jail was a miserable dungeon. It was 22 feet square on the outside and about 14 feet by 14 feet by 12 feet high on the inside. Its walls were approximately four feet thick. It had two inside levels. The basement level was accessible only through a trap door in the floor of the upper level. Joseph Smith, who was six feet tall, could not stand up straight in the basement level. The building had two narrow slits which served as the only windows.

Near the end of his time in Liberty Jail, the Prophet received a revelation, known today as sections 121–23 of the Doctrine and Covenants. The jail is sometimes referred to as "the temple prison" because of the sublime beauty of this revelation compared to the dismal circumstances in which it was received. The jail is owned by the Church today, and has been partially rebuilt in cutaway form, surrounded by a beautiful visitor's center.

LICENTIOUSNESS

Actions and thoughts that focus on sexual immorality.

LIES

See LIARS.

LIFE

Has several meanings within the scriptures: mortality (Genesis 2:7; Acts 8:33), spirituality (2 Corinthians 3:6), eternal life or exaltation (Acts 11:18; Helaman 14:31).

LIFE AND DEATH, SPIRITUAL

We have very little control, relatively speaking, over physical life and death. However, our agency coupled with the Atonement of Jesus Christ provide for us to have final control over spiritual life or death for us personally. "Wherefore, men are free according to the flesh; and all things are given them which are expedient unto man. And they are free to choose liberty and eternal life, through the great Mediator of all men, or to choose captivity and death, according to the captivity

and power of the devil; for he seeketh that all men might be miserable like unto himself" (2 Nephi 2:27).

LIFE OF THE WORLD

A phrase which refers to the mission of the Savior (John 6:51; Mosiah 16:9; D&C 34:2).

LIGHT

A word often used in the scriptures to represent truth, knowledge, and intelligence which come to us from God (John 1:4, 9; D&C 45:9, 28–29; 88:11). "Light" is also used to describe the power of Christ which holds all things in the universe in proper position, including keeping the planets in orbit (D&C 88:7–13). Light often represents God, and darkness represents Satan and his kingdom (Helaman 13:29).

LIGHT OF CHRIST

See CHRIST, LIGHT OF.

LIGHT OF THE WORLD

Another name for Jesus Christ (John 8:12). The phrase is also used in the scriptures to mean our responsibility to be an example of the gospel to others (Matthew 5:14).

LIGHT OF TRUTH

This phrase has three main meanings, as used in the scriptures: (1) The Savior (D&C 88:6). (2) Intelligence (D&C 93:29). (3) The light and truth of the gospel of Jesus Christ (D&C 124:9).

LIGHT SPEECHES

The phrase comes from D&C 88:121, and is used in the context of temple worship (D&C 88:119), where serious and sacred things are discussed and taught. Speech and conversation which take away from the sacredness and reverence of such worship is called "light speech." "Light speeches" could likewise destroy the spirit of the occasion if used in the middle of an especially spiritual sacrament meeting, a class, or even when someone is sharing a sacred experience and the Spirit is strongly present.

LIGHT-MINDEDNESS

Speaking lightly of serious and sacred things. The phrase comes from D&C 88:121.

LIMBO

The Church does not teach a belief in Limbo. It is considered to be a false doctrine.

It is defined by some Christian churches as an in-between state in the afterlife, between heaven and hell, to which individuals who lived good lives but were not baptized will go. Some Christian denominations have taught that babies who die without being baptized will be in eternal Limbo.

The Church of Jesus Christ of Latter-day Saints teaches that all children who die before the age of accountability (eight years old— D&C 68:25, 27) are saved in heaven (D&C 137:10).

The Church likewise teaches that all who die on this earth without a completely fair opportunity to hear and understand the gospel of Jesus Christ will have that opportunity in the postmortal spirit world (1 Peter 3:18–20; 4:6; D&C 138). Baptisms for them can be performed by proxy (1 Corinthians 15:29), and thus, they will have had a chance to hear and respond to the gospel of Jesus Christ before the day of final judgment. God is completely fair to all.

LINEAGE

The ancestral line from which an individual is descended. Lineage is important to Latter-day Saints, since they inherit the right, through personal faithfulness, to the blessings of Abraham, Isaac, and Jacob (Abraham 2:9–11), which are the blessings of the Lord to Covenant Israel.

Also, members of the Church are taught to study their lineage in order to seek out their ancestors and have the ordinances of salvation performed for them in the temples of the Church (D&C 128:15–18).

LION OF THE TRIBE OF JUDAH

Another name for Jesus Christ, containing the connotation that the Master was the powerful Savior from the tribe of Judah (Revelation 5:5). In the Jewish culture, a lion was considered to be unstoppable as it went forth to accomplish its goals (Numbers 23:24; Micah 5:8).

LIQUOR

A type of alcoholic drink. Such beverages are forbidden by the Word of Wisdom (D&C 89:7).

LIVES

This term almost always refers to our mortal existence as used in the scriptures (Acts 27:10; Mormon 2:14)

However, in the special context of becoming gods and having our own spirit children, it means "spirit children" or "spirit offspring" (D&C 132:22, 24; Acts 17:28–29).

LIVING CHRIST, THE

On January 1, 2000, the First Presidency and Quorum of the Twelve Apostles issued the following declaration. Titled "The Living Christ," this declaration bears witness of the Lord Jesus Christ and summarizes His identity and divine mission:

"As we commemorate the birth of Jesus Christ two millennia ago, we offer our testimony of the reality of His matchless life and the infinite virtue of His great atoning sacrifice. None other has had so profound an influence upon all who have lived and will yet live upon the earth.

"He was the Great Jehovah of the Old Testament, the Messiah of the New. Under the direction of His Father, He was the creator of the earth. 'All things were made by him; and without him was not any thing made that was made' (John 1:3). Though sinless, He was baptized to fulfill all righteousness. He 'went about doing good'

(Acts 10:38), yet was despised for it. His gospel was a message of peace and goodwill. He entreated all to follow His example. He walked the roads of Palestine, healing the sick, causing the blind to see, and raising the dead. He taught the truths of eternity, the reality of our premortal existence, the purpose of our life on earth, and the potential for the sons and daughters of God in the life to come.

"He instituted the sacrament as a reminder of His great atoning sacrifice. He was arrested and condemned on spurious charges, convicted to satisfy a mob, and sentenced to die on Calvary's cross. He gave His life to atone for the sins of all mankind. His was a great vicarious gift in behalf of all who would ever live upon the earth.

"We solemnly testify that His life, which is central to all human history, neither began in Bethlehem nor concluded on Calvary. He was the Firstborn of the Father, the Only Begotten Son in the flesh, the Redeemer of the world.

"He rose from the grave to 'become the firstfruits of them that slept' (1 Corinthians 15:20). As Risen Lord, He visited among those He had loved in life. He also ministered among His 'other sheep' (John 10:16) in ancient America. In the modern world, He and His Father appeared to the boy Joseph Smith, ushering in the long-promised 'dispensation of the fulness of times' (Ephesians 1:10).

"Of the Living Christ, the Prophet Joseph wrote: 'His eyes were as a flame of fire; the hair of his head was white like the pure snow; his countenance shone above the brightness of the sun; and his voice was as the sound of the rushing of great waters, even the voice of Jehovah, saying:

" 'I am the first and the last; I am he who liveth, I am he who was slain; I am your advocate with the Father' (D&C 110:3–4).

"Of Him the Prophet also declared: 'And now, after the many testimonies which have been given of him, this is the testimony, last of all, which we give of him: That he lives!

" 'For we saw him, even on the right hand of God; and we heard the voice bearing record that he is the Only Begotten of the Father—

" 'That by him, and through him, and of him, the worlds are and were created, and the inhabitants thereof are begotten sons and daughters unto God' (D&C 76:22–24).

"We declare in words of solemnity that His priesthood and His Church have been restored upon the earth—'built upon the foundation of apostles and prophets, Jesus Christ himself being the chief corner stone' (Ephesians 2:20).

"We testify that He will someday return to earth. 'And the glory of the Lord shall be revealed, and all flesh shall see it together' (Isaiah 40:5). He will rule as King of Kings and reign as Lord of Lords, and every knee shall bend and every tongue shall speak in worship before Him. Each of us will stand to be judged of Him according to our works and the desires of our hearts.

"We bear testimony, as His duly ordained Apostles, that Jesus is the Living Christ, the immortal Son of God. He is the great King Immanuel, who stands today on the right hand of His Father. He is the light, the life, and the hope of the world. His way is the path that leads to happiness in this life and eternal life in the world to come. God be thanked for the matchless gift of His divine Son" (*TF*, pp. 87–89).

LIVING GOD, THE

Throughout history, many individuals and cultures have engaged in the practice of worshipping idols. Such idols are man-made objects and are not "living" (Isaiah 2:8). In contrast to such inanimate objects of worship, the "Living God" (Jeremiah 10:10–11) is real and has all power over heaven and earth.

Jesus Christ is the Son of the "living God" (John 6:69).

LIVING ORACLES

There are two main uses of the term "oracle" or "oracles" in the scriptures: (1) Oracles are the revelations of God (D&C 90:4 footnote a). (2) Oracles are also the prophets themselves who receive revelations from God for us (2 Samuel 16:23).

LORD

See also LORD GOD. Spelled with capital "L" and small capitals "ORD," the word "LORD" means "Jehovah" in the King James Version of the Bible (Genesis 18:14; Exodus 3:7; BD, under "Jehovah"). Jehovah is the pre-mortal Jesus Christ (Ether 3:14, 16). However, the Bible is not consistent in using "LORD" to mean Jehovah, and sometimes uses "Lord" (Isaiah 6:1) and sometimes "LORD God" (Exodus 3:18).

LORD ALMIGHTY

A term that means "all powerful" and can refer to both the Father and the Son (2 Corinthians 6:18; D&C 84:118).

LORD GOD

Generally means "Jesus Christ" as used throughout the scriptures. However, in some scriptural pas-sages relating to the creation of man, it refers to the Father (Genesis 2:7; 3:8–19).

LORD GOD ALMIGHTY

See LORD ALMIGHTY.

LORD GOD OF THE HEBREWS

Means "Jehovah," in other words, Jesus Christ, who is the God of the Old Testament and the God who led the children of Israel (the Hebrews) out of Egyptian bondage (Exodus 7:16; 9:1).

LORD JEHOVAH

Another name for Jesus Christ (Isaiah 12:2).

LORD JESUS

Using the fact that "Lord" gener-ally means "Jehovah" as used in the Old Testament, we see that "Lord Jesus" (Acts 4:33; 11:20) is a way of saying, in effect, "Jehovah of the Old Testament is Jesus Christ of the New Testament."

LORD OF GLORY

Another name for Jesus Christ (James 2:1).

LORD OF HOSTS

Another name for Jehovah, in other words, Jesus Christ (1 Samuel 15:2; Isaiah 24:23; Malachi 3:10; 2 Nephi 26:6; D&C 29:9; 107:60).

LORD OF LORDS

Another name for Jesus Christ, with the connotation that Jesus is "Lord" over all other "lords" (Revela-tion 17:14), including the resurrected Saints who will rule with Him during the Millennium (Revelation 20:4).

LORD OF SABOATH

Another name for Jesus Christ, with the added meaning that He is "the creator of the first day, the begin-ning and the end" (D&C 95:7).

LORD OF THE HARVEST

Another name for Jesus Christ (Matthew 9:36–38).

LORD OF THE SABBATH

Another name for Jesus Christ (Luke 6:5).

LORD OF THE VINEYARD

This can mean either Heavenly Father or the Savior, depending on context. In the parable of the laborers in the vineyard, Jesus is the "Lord of the Vineyard" (Matthew 20:1–16). In the parable of the wicked husbandmen, the Father is the "Lord of the Vineyard" (Matthew 21:33–46).

LORD OMNIPOTENT

Another name for Jesus Christ (Mosiah 3:5). "Omnipotent" means "all powerful."

LORD'S DAY

See also SABBATH DAY. The Lord's Day is another way of saying the Sabbath Day. In Old Testament times, what we know as Saturday was the Sabbath (Exodus 20:10–11). However, after the resurrection of Christ, what we know as Sunday became the Sabbath (Acts 20:7).

The Lord's Day is to be a holy day, dedicated to worshipping Him in church (D&C 59:9) and to drawing closer to Him through other appropriate activities, including "praying, meditating, studying the scriptures, and the teachings of latter-day prophets, writing letters to family members and friends, reading wholesome material, visiting the sick and distressed" (*TF*, p. 146). It is designed by the Lord for our benefit. In the Ten Commandments, the Lord gave strict instructions for keeping the Sabbath Day holy (Exodus 20:8–11). Isaiah gave counsel for making the "sabbath a delight" (Isaiah 58:13–14).

LORD'S PRAYER

A prayer given by the Savior as an example of how to pray (Matthew 6:9; Luke 11:1). It appears twice in the Bible (Matthew 6:9–13; Luke 11:2–4) and once in the Book of Mormon (3 Nephi 13:9–13).

Before He gave this as an example of how to pray, He cautioned His disciples, "Thou shalt not be as the hypocrites are; for they love to pray standing in the synagogues and in the corners of the streets, that they may be seen of men" (Matthew 6:5). He also instructed them, "Use not vain repetitions" (Matthew 6:7). These cautions about prayer indicate that the Lord's Prayer was given only as an example, and not as something to memorize and say over and over in place of personal, individualized prayer.

LORD'S SUPPER

See also LAST SUPPER. The Lord's Supper is another term for the sacrament. The sacrament was introduced by the Savior during the Passover meal or "supper" which He ate with His Apostles on the Thursday evening before His suffering in Gethsemane (Matthew 26:26–28).

LORD'S TIME

Abraham informs us that the Lord's time is "after the time of Kolob" (Abraham 5:13). He also tells us that "one day in Kolob is equal to a thousand years" on the earth (Abraham, Facsimile No. 2, Explanation, Fig. 1). Peter teaches that one day with the

Lord is like a thousand years on earth (2 Peter 3:8).

Another phrase sometimes seen in the scriptures and in gospel discussions is "in the due time of the Lord" which means "when the Lord is ready for it to happen" (D&C 68:14; 76:38).

LOST 116 MANUSCRIPT PAGES

See MANUSCRIPT, LOST 116 PAGES.

LOST SCRIPTURE

See MISSING SCRIPTURE.

LOST SOULS

This term generally refers to those who have not yet found the gospel of Jesus Christ or to those who have but who choose not to live it. The scriptures teach that there will be no "accidentally" lost souls. Everyone will get a perfect opportunity to hear, understand, and then accept or reject the gospel, whether here on earth (Mark 16:15), in the postmortal spirit world (1 Peter 3:18–20; 4:6), or during the Millennium (D&C 84:98). Therefore, the only so-called "lost souls" on Judgment Day (Revelation 20:12–13) will be those who use their God-given agency to intentionally reject the gospel.

LOST TEN TRIBES

All twelve tribes of Israel were united as a nation in the Holy Land at the time that Solomon succeeded David as King (1 Kings 2:12). Solomon raised taxes and created excessive burdens upon his people in order

to support his goals as king, as well as to support his own lifestyle, which included seven hundred wives and three hundred concubines (1 Kings 11:3). When Solomon died (1 Kings 11:43), the people approached his son, Rehoboam, who was to be the next king, and requested relief from the heavy burdens placed upon them by King Solomon (1 Kings 12:3–4).

After thinking it over and counseling with older men, he talked with his young friends about the people's request. He decided to refuse the people's pleas and threatened them with higher taxes and burdens (1 Kings 12:6–14). As a result, Israel split in two (1 Kings 12:16–17) about 925 BC. Ten of the tribes of Israel formed a nation, known as, among other names, the Northern Kingdom, Ephraim, the Northern Ten Tribes, or Israel, with headquarters in Shechem in Samaria. The Southern Kingdom was formed, with the tribes of Judah and Benjamin as the main population. It was generally known as Judah, with headquarters in Jerusalem.

The Northern Kingdom soon went into apostasy, and after about 200 years, in about 721 BC, its people were carried away captive into the north, by the Assyrians (2 Kings 15:29). They thus became the Lost Ten Tribes.

The resurrected Christ mentioned "other sheep" during His visit to the Nephites, which were neither in America nor in Jerusalem (3 Nephi

16:1–3), and told them that He was going to visit the "lost tribes of Israel" (3 Nephi 17:4). It will be interesting to someday read their record of His visit to them (2 Nephi 29:13).

The gospel will be taught to the Lost Ten Tribes (3 Nephi 21:26), and it appears that the Three Nephites will minister to them, along with us and others of the house of Israel (3 Nephi 28:29). Prophecies about the return of the Lost Ten Tribes are among the signs of the times. The keys of "the leading of the ten tribes from the land of the north" (D&C 110:11) were conferred upon Joseph Smith and Oliver Cowdery by Moses when he appeared to them in the Kirtland Temple on April 3, 1836. These keys reside with the president of the Church today. One of the major prophecies about their return is found in D&C 133:26–34.

LOTTERIES

See GAMBLING.

LUCIFER

See also DEVIL; SATAN. Lucifer is another name for Satan. The name "Lucifer" means "light bearer" in Latin. Lucifer was "an angel of God who was in authority" in our premortal life (D&C 76:25). He was "a son of the morning" (D&C 76:26) and fell from being a glorious and influential bearer of light as a son of the morning to a being of perdition, meaning complete, irreparable loss or "utter ruin" (Free Online Dictionary definition of "perdition"). He is called Perdition in the scriptures (D&C 76:26). Those who join him and follow him completely are partakers of this utter ruin. The phrase lends stark meaning to the term "sons of perdition" (D&C 76:32), in other words, "followers of Perdition."

His position as a powerful influence for good and a bearer of light in our premortal life made his rebellion (Moses 4:3) very hard on us. In fact, we "wept over him" (D&C 76:26). His influence was such that one-third of the spirits followed him and were cast out with him (Revelation 12:4).

LUSTS

Unwholesome physical and emotional desires which can lead mortals away from God (Mark 4:19; Romans 13:14; Ephesians 2:2–3; 2 Timothy 4:3). The most damaging of lustful desires and behaviors often have to do with sexual immorality (Romans 1:24; 2 Peter 2:18). If lustful thoughts are entertained in the mind, the Spirit is driven away (D&C 42:23).

LUSTS OF THE FLESH

See LUSTS.

·M·

MAGAZINES, CHURCH

See also IMPROVEMENT ERA. Since 1971, the Church has published three magazines for its English-speaking members: the *Ensign* for adults, the *New Era* for youth, and the *Friend* for children. The Church also publishes the *Liahona*, in several different languages, with material for members of all ages.

Prior to 1971, a number of magazines and periodicals were published over a period of many years.

MAGI

See WISE MEN.

MAGIC

Magic can be a part of harmless entertainment. However, when those using magic claim to be doing it by supernatural powers, it becomes something to avoid because it can lead people away from God as their source of inspiration and guidance. "Latter-day Saints reject magic as a serious manipulation of nature and are advised to avoid any practice that claims supernatural power apart from the priesthood and spiritual gifts of the Church. They are also counseled against using any fortune-telling devices. Both so-called white and black magic can be Satanic.

"True miracles are done by the power of Jesus Christ. Devils may be cast out, but only in humility and by fasting, faith, and prayer, and the power of the true priesthood, with no fanfare or public acclaim (Matthew 17:21; D&C 84:66–73). Regarding the discernment of true spirits from evil ones, the Prophet Joseph Smith taught that without the priesthood and 'a knowledge of the laws by which spirits are governed,' it is impossible to discover the difference between the miracles of Moses and the magicians of the pharaoh or between those of the apostles and Simon the sorcerer (*TPJS*, pp. 202–6). A test of a godly spirit is to discern whether there is 'any intelligence communicated' or 'the purposes of God developed' (*TPJS*, p. 204)" (*EM*, under "Magic").

In ancient times, the Lord instructed His people to avoid those who claimed magical powers, especially for contacting the dead and foretelling the future (Exodus 22:18; Leviticus 19:31; Isaiah 8:19).

MAGICIANS

See MAGIC.

MAGNIFICANT

A term referring to Mary's humble and prophetic response to the angel Gabriel's announcement to her that she was to be the mother of the Son of God (Luke 1:46–55).

MAGNIFY THE PRIESTHOOD

A phrase, derived from such scriptures as Romans 11:13 and D&C 84:33. It means to take seriously and fulfill one's priesthood callings and duties. Priesthood holders who do this find many opportunities for service such that the blessings of the priesthood are magnified or enlarged in their own lives and in the lives of God's children.

MAGNIFYING ONE'S CALLING

See also MAGNIFY THE PRIESTHOOD. This phrase means to carry out the duties and responsibilities of a calling with sincerity and diligence (D&C 88:80).

MAGOG

See also BATTLE OF GOG AND MAGOG. Magog was a country or people in ancient times, located near the Black Sea (BD, under "Magog"). Gog was the king of Magog. The Battle of Gog and Magog is spoken of in Ezekiel 38 and 39.

MAHONRI MORIANCUMER

See BROTHER OF JARED, NAME OF.

MAJOR PROPHETS

Bible scholars sometimes categorize the Old Testament prophets who have books named after them as major prophets and minor prophets. They consider Isaiah, Jeremiah, Ezekiel, and Daniel to be major prophets, and Hosea, Joel, Amos, Obadiah, Jonah, Micah, Nahum, Habakkuk, Zephaniah, Haggai, Zechariah, and Malachi to be minor prophets.

An obvious problem with such categorizing of the Lord's prophets is that it tends to make some sound more important than others. Another problem is that Abraham, Moses, Elijah, Elisha, and others are left off of the list.

MALACHI, PROPHECIES OF

Malachi is the last book in the Old Testament. The prophecies and teachings of Malachi have major impact in the lives of Latter-day Saints. For example, the prophecy that the Lord's name "shall be great among the Gentiles" (Malachi 1:11) is being fulfilled in our day. The prophecy that John the Baptist, who prepared the way for the Savior's mortal mission, would come again in the last days as preparation for the Second Coming (Malachi 3:1) has been fulfilled (D&C 13). The prophecy that the Lord will come to His temple (Malachi 3:1) continues to be fulfilled over and over in our day.

The priesthood will again be on earth so that valid priesthood ordinances can be performed (Malachi 3:3; D&C 13:1). The Jews will receive and accept the gospel (Malachi 3:4). The wicked will be destroyed (Malachi 3:5–6; 4:1). Malachi explains the law of tithing (Malachi 3:8–11). The Church will become well known throughout the world (Malachi 3:12). The Millennium will be a time of peace and great blessings (Malachi 4:2). Elijah will appear in the last days and restore the keys of sealing, including doing the work for our dead (Malachi 4:5–6).

MAN OF HOLINESS

Another name for Heavenly Father (Moses 6:57). Therefore, "Son of Man of Holiness" is another name for the Savior. It is sometimes shortened to "Son of man" in the scriptures (Matthew 16:27).

MAN OF SIN

Another name for Satan (2 Thessalonians 2:3).

MAN'S TIME

See GOD'S TIME.

MANIFESTO

A name sometimes used to refer to the revelation given by President Wilford Woodruff putting an end to the practice of plural marriage among members of The Church of Jesus Christ of Latter-day Saints. It was dated September 24, 1890, and was presented to the members of the Church in the general conference held October 6, 1890 (Official Declaration—1). The revelation is located at the end of the Doctrine and Covenants and is called "Official Declaration—1." More information about the circumstances surrounding the receiving of this revelation is printed immediately following Official Declaration—1 in the Doctrine and Covenants.

MANKIND

A general term referring to all people (past, present, and future), during the mortal phase of this earth (Job 12:10; 1 Nephi 10:6; 2 Nephi 2:18).

However, in the context of homosexuality, it means men (Leviticus 18:22; 20:13; 1 Corinthians 6:9; 1 Timothy 1:10).

MANNA

Food from heaven, provided by the Lord for the children of Israel during their time of wandering in the wilderness. We find a description of manna in Exodus, and a description of it and how it was prepared for food, in Numbers. "It was like coriander seed, white; and the taste of it was like wafers made with honey" (Exodus 16:31). "And the people went about, and gathered it, and ground it in mills, or beat it in a mortar, and baked it in pans, and made cakes of it: and the taste of it was as the taste of fresh oil" (Numbers 11:8).

Symbolically, manna is nourishment and help from heaven.

MANSIONS

A term used by the Savior to represent the heavenly homes prepared for the righteous (John 14:2).

MANUSCRIPT, LOST 116 PAGES

Early on in the translation of the Book of Mormon from the gold plates, 116 pages of manuscript were lost by Martin Harris, who was then serving as scribe for the Prophet Joseph Smith during the translation process. It was a major setback and very discouraging for Joseph as well as Martin. Doctrine and Covenants 3 and 10 are revelations relating to the lost pages.

Some details of circumstances leading up to the loss are as follows: Martin Harris came to Harmony, Pennsylvania, in February 1828, and served as scribe for Joseph Smith as he translated from the gold plates. By June 14, 1828, they had 116 handwritten pages (called "manuscript pages") containing the translation of the Book of Mormon plates up to that point. After repeated requests by Martin, and contrary to the Lord's initial instruction, Joseph finally let him take the manuscript back to Palmyra, New York. Martin's hope, among other things, was to convince his wife and others that he was not wasting his time with a false prophet.

Martin broke serious promises made, with respect to safeguarding the precious manuscript pages, and they were lost. After about three weeks, when Martin had not returned to Joseph and Emma's home in Harmony with the 116 pages, Joseph went to Palmyra to check concerning the manuscript. Upon finding that the pages had been lost, he returned to Harmony, dejected and very discouraged.

After returning home, the Urim and Thummim was taken from the Prophet by an angel (see Smith, *History of Joseph Smith by His Mother*, pp. 133–36). Shortly thereafter, it was returned to Joseph, at which point he received the revelation we now have as section 3 of the Doctrine and Covenants. Afterward, both the Urim and Thummim as well as the gold plates were taken from him.

After a time, both the plates and the Urim and Thummim were returned to him. Of this, the Prophet's mother wrote the following, quoting Joseph: " 'After the angel left me," said he, "I continued my supplications to God, without cessation, and on the twenty-second of September, I had the joy and satisfaction of again receiving the Urim and Thummim, with which I have again commenced translating, and Emma writes for me, but the angel said that the Lord would send me a scribe [Oliver Cowdery], and I trust his promise will be verified. The angel seemed pleased with me when he gave me back the Urim and Thummim, and he told me that the Lord loved me, for my faithfulness and humility' " (Smith, *History of Joseph Smith by His Mother*, p. 135).

At first glance, it might appear that the disappearance of the 116 pages was a tragic loss. But we actually came out ahead. The Lord had prepared far in advance for the loss, by having Mormon include the small plates of Nephi in the stack of plates which Moroni buried and Joseph Smith received (Words of Mormon 1:3–7). As a result, the translation on the lost 116 pages, which came from the large plates of Nephi, was replaced with the books of 1 Nephi, 2 Nephi, Jacob, Enos, Jarom, and Omni, which contain more spiritual things (D&C 10:38–42) than were in the lost pages.

MARRIAGE

Marriage is defined in the scriptures and by the Church as the legal union of a man and a woman, thus creating a family unit (Genesis 2:24; Matthew 19:5; Mark 10:6–9; 1 Corinthians 11:11; "Proclamation," paragraphs 1, 4, 6–7).

Marriage is intended by the Lord to be eternal (Matthew 19:6). Eternal marriage is one of the principle doctrines of the Church. It is required for exaltation (D&C 131:1–4; 132:19–20).

MARRIAGE SUPPER OF THE LAMB

This phrase comes from Revelation 19:9. The symbolism is that, at the Second Coming, the righteous will be caught up to meet the Savior (D&C 88:96–98). The occasion is called "the marriage supper of the Lamb." Previously, He has invited them to come and "sup" with Him (Revelation 3:20), and they have "come" so to speak, through living the gospel. Now, at the time of the Second Coming, Christ, the Bridegroom (see Matthew

25:6), and the righteous Saints, the bride (Revelation 21:2), have finally come together to celebrate their wedding supper, in other words, to feast together on the rewards of living the gospel.

MARTYR

One who is killed by enemies because of his or her religious beliefs (Acts 22:20; Revelation 2:13; D&C 138:40).

MARTYRDOM

See MARTYR.

MARTYRDOM OF JOSEPH AND HYRUM SMITH

See also CARTHAGE JAIL. Both Joseph Smith and his brother Hyrum suffered martyrdom at the hands of a mob at the jail in Carthage, Illinois, on June 27, 1844.

MARY

A number of women named Mary are mentioned in the scriptures: (1) The mother of Jesus (Matthew 1:18). (2) The sister of Martha and Lazarus (Luke 10:38–39; John 11:1–46). (3) The other woman named Mary who came to the Savior's tomb Sunday morning (Matthew 28:1). (4) Mary Magdalene (Matthew 28:1) out of whom seven devils were cast (Luke 8:2).

MARY, MOTHER OF JESUS

See also IMMACULATE CONCEPTION. The virgin, to whom Jesus Christ, the Son of God, was born

(Luke 1:26–33). King Benjamin, an ancient Book of Mormon prophet, prophesied about her by name (Mosiah 3:8). Nephi saw her in vision and described her as "a virgin, most beautiful and fair above all other virgins" (1 Nephi 11:15).

The New Testament speaks of Mary at the time of the "Annunciation" (Luke 1:26–38), at the time when Mary visits her cousin Elizabeth (Luke 1:39–41), at the time of the Savior's birth (Luke 2:16), at the time of her ritual purification (Luke 2:22), at the time Joseph and Mary brought Jesus to Jerusalem to present Him to the Lord (Luke 2:22–39), and at the time of the visit of the Wise Men (Matt 2:11). She is also mentioned when she and Joseph found Jesus in the temple at age twelve, teaching the elders of the Jews (Luke 2:41–51), at the marriage at Cana when she asked Jesus to provide more wine for the feast (John 2:1–11), on an occasion when Jesus was teaching (Matthew 12:46), and at the crucifixion of the Savior (John 19:26–27). We have no reliable information about Mary after the crucifixion.

Latter-day Saints hold Mary in highest esteem but do not pray to her nor regard her as an intercessor with her Son for others. The Savior gave no permission to pray to anyone other than the Father (1 Timothy 2:5) and taught that we should pray in the name of Jesus Christ (John 14:13–14; 16:23).

The Church teaches the virgin birth but does not teach the traditional view of an immaculate conception. Nor does the Church teach that Mary was miraculously taken up into heaven.

MASONS AND MORMONISM
See FREEMASONRY AND THE TEMPLE.

MASTER
Another name for Jesus Christ, when spelled with an uppercase *M* (Mark 9:5).

MASTER MAHAN
A name by which Cain was known, after he killed his brother Abel (Moses 5:31).

MASTURBATION
The Apostle Paul taught that this is considered to be a form of sexual immorality. He said:

Romans 1:24
Wherefore God also gave them up [*allowed them to use their agency and thus turned them over*] to uncleanness [*immorality*] through the lusts [*evil, immoral desires*] of their own hearts, to dishonour their own bodies between themselves [*by themselves; see Strong's Concordance #1722; in other words, masturbation*].

MEAT
As used in the King James Version of the Bible, this word generally means "food" (Genesis 1:29; Matthew 6:25; Luke 8:55). When the King James translators meant meat, as we use the word today (to mean beef, lamb, and

so forth), they used the word "flesh" (Leviticus 17:14; 1 Kings 17:6).

MEDIATOR

Jesus Christ is the Mediator between man and God (1 Timothy 2:5; Hebrews 9:15; 12:24; 2 Nephi 2:27). In other words, through His Atonement, He mediates or negotiates our salvation and places us in a position to enter the presence of the Father and dwell with Him eternally, if we live the gospel.

MEDIUMS

See FAMILIAR SPIRITS; FORTUNE TELLERS.

MEEK

A character trait which consists of being voluntarily humble, kind, forgiving, and gentle, even in a position of strength (Psalm 25:9; Zephaniah 2:3; Matthew 5:5; Mosiah 3:19). The Savior was meek (Matthew 21:5).

MEETINGHOUSES

Another name for buildings, churches, or chapels, in which members of The Church of Jesus Christ of Latter-day Saints assemble to worship.

MEETINGHOUSE LIBRARIES

Resource centers for media and other teaching and learning materials, housed in church buildings.

MEETINGS

The main church meetings held on Sunday by the Latter-day Saints consist of a three-hour meeting block. This allows the building to be used by more than one ward (church unit). During this meeting block, the following meetings are held: (1) Sacrament meeting; (2) Sunday School; (3) concurrent priesthood quorum meetings for men and Relief Society for women, with children under twelve years of age simultaneously attending Primary. Also during this concurrent time, young women meet in their own sessions, while young men of equivalent age are in priesthood meeting.

In addition to these weekly Sunday meetings, other meetings are held regularly during the week, such as activities for Primary children, young men and young women, and Relief Society sisters.

Among other meetings held for larger groups of church members are stake conferences (held twice a year) and general conference (held twice a year at Church headquarters in Salt Lake City, Utah, and broadcast throughout the world).

MELCHIZEDEK

A name which means "King of Righteousness" (BD, under "Melchizedek"). Melchizedek was a great high priest (D&C 107:2) and king of Salem, later called Jerusalem (Genesis 14:18). Abraham paid tithing to Melchizedek (Genesis 14:20). We gain additional knowledge about Melchizedek from the Book of Mormon (Alma 13:17–19). The

Melchizedek Priesthood was named after him (D&C 107:1–4).

MELCHIZEDEK PRIESTHOOD

"There are, in the church, two priesthoods, namely, the Melchizedek and Aaronic, including the Levitical Priesthood" (D&C 107:1). "The Melchizedek Priesthood holds the right of presidency and has power and authority over all the offices in the church in all ages of the world, to administer in spiritual things" (D&C 107:8). "The power and authority of the higher, or Melchizedek Priesthood, is to hold the keys of all the spiritual blessings of the church" (D&C 107:18).

Once a male member of the Church has the Melchizedek Priesthood conferred upon him by the laying on of hands, he holds all the priesthood there is. It is the same priesthood that the Savior has (D&C 107:3). The offices (elder, seventy, high priest, patriarch, Apostle) within the Melchizedek Priesthood are used for organizational matters, including presiding (D&C 107:8; 21–26, 33–34).

Among the duties and privileges of Melchizedek Priesthood holders are naming and blessing babies, confirming new members of the Church and bestowing the gift of the Holy Ghost, administering to the sick, giving blessings of counsel and comfort, and giving father's blessings.

MEMBERSHIP

Membership in The Church of Jesus Christ of Latter-day Saints requires baptism by immersion by an authorized priesthood holder of the Church, and being confirmed by the laying on of hands and given the gift of the Holy Ghost (Articles of Faith 1:4; D&C 20:37, 41, 43, 72–74).

MEMBERSHIP RECORDS

By commandment of God, the Church is a record-keeping organization. Thus, a record of the names of all members is kept (D&C 20:82).

MENTALLY HANDICAPPED

Baptism is not required by the Lord for the mentally handicapped. They come under the same category as children who have not arrived at the age of accountability (D&C 29:50). Thus they are saved in the celestial kingdom of God (D&C 29:50; 137:10).

Many intellectually handicapped members are nevertheless baptized, after consultation with their bishop, and are able to serve in the Church. Some male members who are mentally handicapped are sufficiently high functioning as to be able to receive the priesthood and serve within its ranks. Some male and female members are able to function well enough to attend the temple, receive their own endowments, and do temple work for the dead thereafter.

MERCY

See LAW OF MERCY.

MERCY KILLING
See EUTHANASIA.

MERIDIAN OF TIME
A phrase used in the scriptures in reference to the Savior's mortal ministry (Moses 5:57; D&C 20:26). "Meridian" is sometimes used to mean "high point." For example, when the sun is at its highest point of the day in the sky, it is at its meridian. Thus, "meridian of time," as used in the scriptures, can mean "the high point" or "the central focus" of the earth's mortal time, which was the Savior's mortal mission (see *EM*, under "Meridian of Time).

MESSENGER AND ADVOCATE
A periodical, published by the Church from October 1834 to September 1837. The official name was the *Latter Day Saints' Messenger and Advocate.* Thirty-six issues were published.

MESSIAH
"Messiah" is a Hebrew term as well as a word transliterated from Aramaic that means "anointed one" (BD, under "Messiah"). In the context of the scriptures, the "Anointed One" is Jesus Christ. Among many other uses of "anointed," it can mean "to be prepared in advance" for an office, usually the office of king. Some examples are Saul (1 Samuel 10:1) and David, who was anointed to be king years before he actually became the king of Israel (1 Samuel 16:13; 2 Samuel 5:3–4).

The word "Messiah," when used as the title of an office, such as "the Messiah," carries with it the connotation of being a king and a deliverer for the people (BD, under "Messiah").

The Greek equivalent of "Messiah" is *Christos,* which is where the name Christ comes from.

MESSIANIC PROPHECIES
A phrase meaning "prophecies about Jesus Christ." There were many prophecies about the Messiah in the Old Testament as well as in the Book of Mormon and in the book of Moses in the Pearl of Great Price. The fact that there were many such prophecies in the Old Testament is evidenced by the fact that the resurrected Savior discussed prophecies about Himself at length with the two disciples on the road to Emmaus (Luke 24:13–35, especially verse 27).

For an extensive listing of these prophecies, see Topical Guide, under "Jesus Christ, Prophecies about."

MESSIAS
The Greek form of "Messiah" (John 1:41; 4:25).

METAPHYSICS
The attempt by some philosophers and theologians to combine philosophy and scripture into a unified description of the ultimate nature of reality. Based on the writings of Paul, this is an impossible quest. He wrote, "But God hath revealed them unto us by his Spirit: for the Spirit searcheth all things, yea, the deep things

of God. For what man knoweth the things of a man, save the spirit of man which is in him? even so the things of God knoweth no man, but the Spirit of God" (1 Corinthians 2:10–11).

MICHAEL

See ADAM.

MICHAEL THE ARCHANGEL

See also ADAM. Michael, which means "one who is like God" (BD, under "Michael"), is another name for Adam. An archangel is an angel who holds high power and priesthood authority in heaven. Michael is immediately under Jesus Christ in the hierarchy of authority over this earth. Joseph Smith taught that Adam, who, with Eve, started the human family on earth, "is the father of the human family, and presides over the spirits of all men" (*TPJS*, p. 157).

Michael led the forces of the righteous in casting the devil and his evil followers out in the War in Heaven (Revelation 12:7–9).

Michael (Adam) called a meeting of the righteous three years before his death, in "the valley of Adam-ondi-Ahman" at which he was addressed as "Michael, the prince, the archangel" (D&C 107:53–56).

During the "little season" after the Millennium, Michael the Archangel will "gather together his armies, even the hosts of heaven" and will "overcome" the devil and his armies, who will be "cast away into their own place," in other words, perdition, or outer darkness" (D&C 88:111– 15).

MIGHTY ONE OF ISRAEL

Another name for the Savior (Isaiah 1:24; 1 Nephi 22:12). The name indicates that He is the God of Israel and has the "mighty" power to save them.

MILITARY AND THE CHURCH

See also CHAPLAINS; CONSCIENTIOUS OBJECTION. The Church teaches its members to honor and sustain the laws of the land. "We believe in being subject to kings, presidents, rulers, and magistrates, in obeying, honoring, and sustaining the law" (Articles of Faith 1:12). When the law of the land requires military service on the part of its citizens, members are sustained in that service by the Church.

The Book of Mormon teaches the following about honorable military service:

Alma 43:45–48

45 Nevertheless, the Nephites were inspired by a better cause, for they were not fighting for monarchy nor power but they were fighting for their homes and their liberties, their wives and their children, and their all, yea, for their rites of worship and their church.

46 And they were doing that which they felt was the duty which they owed to their God; for the Lord had said unto them, and also

unto their fathers, that: Inasmuch as ye are not guilty of the first offense, neither the second, ye shall not suffer yourselves to be slain by the hands of your enemies.

47 And again, the Lord has said that: Ye shall defend your families even unto bloodshed. Therefore for this cause were the Nephites contending with the Lamanites, to defend themselves, and their families, and their lands, their country, and their rights, and their religion.

48 And it came to pass that when the men of Moroni saw the fierceness and the anger of the Lamanites, they were about to shrink and flee from them. And Moroni, perceiving their intent, sent forth and inspired their hearts with these thoughts—yea, the thoughts of their lands, their liberty, yea, their freedom from bondage.

MILLENNIAL STAR

A publication of the Church in the British Isles from 1840 to 1970. Its full title was *The Latter-day Saints' Millennial Star*. Its mission was absorbed into the *Ensign*, the official publication of the Church for English-speaking adults, which began publication in 1971.

Apostle Parley P. Pratt was the first editor of the *Millennial Star*. In the first issue, May 1840, he explained its purpose: "The *Millennial Star* will stand aloof from the common political and commercial news of the day. Its columns will be devoted to the spread of the fulness of the gospel—the restoration of the ancient princi-

ples of Christianity—the gathering of Israel—the rolling forth of the kingdom of God among the nations—the signs of the times— . . . in short, whatever is shown forth indicative of the coming of the 'Son of Man,' and the ushering in of his universal reign on the earth."

MILLENNIUM

See also ADAM-ONDI-AHMAN. The word "millennium" means "one thousand years." The Millennium is the one-thousand-year period which will be ushered in by the Second Coming (D&C 29:11). During the Millennium, the Savior and the resurrected Saints will rule and reign upon the earth (Revelation 20:4). It will be a time of peace and righteousness (Isaiah 11:6–9). The purposes of the Millennium include missionary work (D&C 84:98) and the finishing up of temple work for any of the worthy who have not yet had all the ordinances of salvation and exaltation (D&C 138:58).

Many wonderful conditions will exist during the Millennium. Some of them are as follows:

1. All of the inhabitants of the earth will speak the same language. It will be a "pure language" (Zephaniah 3:9).

2. The earth will be a paradise, like it was before the fall of Adam and Eve (Articles of Faith 1:10).

3. The City of Enoch will return to earth (Moses 7:63).

4. Satan will be bound, not even allowed to try to tempt people (D&C 88:110; 101:28; Revelation 20:1–3).

5. All violence between man and the animal kingdom will cease (D&C 101:26; Isaiah 2:4; 11:6–9; 65:25).

6. People will be in tune with the Spirit such that whatever they pray for will be given (D&C 101:27).

7. Children will "grow up without sin unto salvation" (D&C 45:58).

8. The government of the earth will be a theocracy (government by God) with Christ as the King (D&C 45:59).

9. There will be no infant deaths (Isaiah 65:20).

10. Mortals will live to the age of one hundred (Isaiah 65:20; D&C 101:29).

11. When mortals reach the age of one hundred, they will die and be resurrected "in the twinkling of an eye" (D&C 101:31).

12. All things will be revealed, including how the earth was created, information about dinosaurs, how long it took to create the earth, and all other things which haven't yet been revealed (D&C 101:32–34).

13. There will be good people on the earth at the beginning of the Millennium who are not mem-

bers of the Church (Micah 4:3–5) and who were not destroyed with the wicked at the time of the Second Coming. Virtually all of them will be converted in due time as the thousand years continue (Jeremiah 31:31–34; D&C 84:98).

14. The land masses will be moved together and there will be one continent and one ocean (D&C 133:23–24).

15. Resurrected Saints will be coming and going on the earth, visiting and helping as needed, as well as ruling and reigning with Christ (Revelation 20:4). Joseph Smith taught, "Christ and the resurrected saints will reign over the earth during the thousand years. They will not probably dwell upon the earth, but will visit it when they please or when it is necessary to govern it" (*TPJS*, p. 268).

16. Righteous parents (whether resurrected or still mortal) will raise their children who died before the age of accountability. The children will be resurrected at the age they died and will be raised until they are full grown. President Joseph F. Smith taught this wonderful doctrine. He taught what Joseph Smith said, saying, "Joseph Smith declared that the mother who laid down her little child, being deprived of the privilege, the joy, and the

satisfaction of bringing it up to manhood or womanhood in this world, would, after the resurrection, have all the joy, satisfaction and pleasure, and even more than it would have been possible to have had in mortality, in seeing her child grow to the full measure of the stature of its spirit . . . and when the mother is deprived of the pleasure and joy of rearing her babe to manhood or to womanhood in this life, through the hand of death, that privilege will be renewed to her hereafter, and she will enjoy it to a fuller fruition than it would be possible for her to do here. When she does it there, it will be with the certain knowledge that the results will be without failure; whereas here, the results are unknown until after we have passed the test" (Smith, *Gospel Doctrine*, pp. 453–54).

17. Bruce R. McConkie gave a summary of living conditions during the Millennium. He wrote, "Mortality as such will continue. Children will be born, grow up, marry, advance to old age, and pass through the equivalent of death. Crops will be planted, harvested, and eaten; industries will be expanded, cities built, and education fostered; men will continue to care for their own needs, handle their own affairs, and enjoy the full endowment of free agency. Speaking a pure

language (Zephaniah 3:9), dwelling in peace, living without disease, and progressing as the Holy Spirit will guide, the advancement and perfection of society during the millennium will exceed anything men have supposed or expected" (*MD* pp. 496–97).

18. During the Millennium, there will be two world capitals, Old Jerusalem and Zion or New Jerusalem (Moses 7:62; Ether 13:3; 3 Nephi 20:22), in Independence, Jackson County, Missouri (Isaiah 2:3).

MINISTERING OF ANGELS

As John the Baptist conferred the Aaronic Priesthood upon Joseph Smith and Oliver Cowdery, he spoke of "the ministering of angels" (D&C 13:1). There are numerous references to ministering angels in the Topical Guide, under "Angels, Ministering." Elder Dallin H. Oaks addressed this topic in a general conference address in October 1998. He taught, "The word 'angel' is used in the scriptures for any heavenly being bearing God's message" (Cannon, *Gospel Truth*, p. 54). The scriptures recite numerous instances where an angel appeared personally. Angelic appearances to Zacharias and Mary (see Luke 1) and to King Benjamin and Nephi, the grandson of Helaman (see Mosiah 3:2; 3 Nephi 7:17–18) are only a few examples. When I was young, I thought such personal appearances were the only meaning of the ministering of angels. As a young holder of the Aaronic Priesthood, I did not think I would see an angel, and I wondered what such appearances had to do with the Aaronic Priesthood.

"But the ministering of angels can also be unseen. Angelic messages can be delivered by a voice or merely by thoughts or feelings communicated to the mind. President John Taylor described "the action of the angels, or messengers of God, upon our minds, so that the heart can conceive . . . revelations from the eternal world" (*Gospel Kingdom,* p. 31).

Nephi described three manifestations of the ministering of angels when he reminded his rebellious brothers that (1) they had "seen an angel," (2) they had "heard his voice from time to time," and (3) that an angel had "spoken unto [them] in a still small voice" though they were "past feeling" and "could not feel his words" (1 Nephi 17:45). The scriptures contain many other statements that angels are sent to teach the gospel and bring men to Christ (see Hebrews 1:14; Alma 39:19; Moroni 7:25, 29, 31–32; D&C 20:35). Most angelic communications are felt or heard rather than seen.

"How does the Aaronic Priesthood hold the key to the ministering of angels? The answer is the same as for the Spirit of the Lord.

"In general, the blessings of spiritual companionship and communication are only available to those who are clean. As explained earlier,

through the Aaronic Priesthood ordinances of baptism and the sacrament, we are cleansed of our sins and promised that if we keep our covenants we will always have His Spirit to be with us. I believe that promise not only refers to the Holy Ghost but also to the ministering of angels, for 'angels speak by the power of the Holy Ghost; wherefore, they speak the words of Christ' (2 Nephi 32:3). So it is that those who hold the Aaronic Priesthood open the door for all Church members who worthily partake of the sacrament to enjoy the companionship of the Spirit of the Lord and the ministering of angels" (CR [Oct. 1998]).

MINOR PROPHETS
See MAJOR PROPHETS.

MIRACLES
A miracle from God is a blessing, sign, or event brought about by His power which cannot be duplicated by man. There are many types of miracles (Mark 16:17; Mormon 9:24; John 2:1–11; D&C 84:65–72).

The greatest miracle of all is the Atonement of Jesus Christ. Within it, the miracle of forgiveness is one of the most prominent. It is often a private, rather quiet miracle which brings healing to the soul.

Miracles do not bring conversion unless sufficient faith and humility already exist in the heart of the recipient (John 12:37; 2 Nephi 26:13; 27:23). When such qualities do exist in an individual, conversion is indeed a wonderful miracle.

The devil and his angels can work miracles which can deceive (Revelation 16:14; 19:20). Sometimes, the only means of discerning between miracles from God and miracles from the devil is the power of the Holy Ghost.

MISSING SCRIPTURE

There are a number of books that are mentioned in the Bible itself, but which we do not have. This is evidence that the Bible is not complete and that there is a need for continuing revelation from God.

The following are books mentioned in, but not included in the Bible: the book of the Wars of the Lord (Numbers 21:14); the book of Jasher (Joshua 10:13; 2 Samuel 1:18); the book of the acts of Solomon (1 Kings. 11:41); the book of Samuel the seer (1 Chronicles 29:29); the book of Gad the seer (1 Chronicles 29:29); the book of Nathan the prophet (1 Chronicles 29:29; 2 Chronicles 9:29); the prophecy of Ahijah (2 Chronicles 9:29); the visions of Iddo the seer (2 Chronicles 9:29; 12:15; 13:22); the book of Shemaiah (2 Chronicles 12:15); the book of Jehu (2 Chronicles 20:34); the sayings of the seers (2 Chronicles 33:19); an earlier epistle of Paul to the Corinthians, which Paul himself mentions in 1 Corinthians (1 Corinthians 5:9); and possibly an earlier epistle to the Ephesians, written by Paul (Ephesians 3:3); an epistle of Paul to the Church at Laodi-cea (Colossians 4:16); prophecies of Enoch mentioned by Jude (Jude 1:14); the rest of the acts of Uzziah written by Isaiah (2 Chronicles 26:22).

The Book of Mormon also mentions Old Testament writings that we do not have in the Bible. They are the writings of Zenock, Zenos, and Neum (1 Nephi 19:10; Alma 33:3–17); the prophecies of Joseph in Egypt (2 Nephi 3:4–22); and a prophecy of Jacob, which is not in the Bible, concerning the preservation of a portion of Joseph's coat of many colors (Alma 46:24–26).

MISSIONARIES

In response to the Lord's commandment, "Go ye into all the world, and preach the gospel to every creature" (Mark 16:15), the Church has a large force of missionaries teaching and preaching the gospel throughout the world. Male missionaries are called elders, and female missionaries are called sisters.

Young single elders and sisters, as well as older sisters and couples, pay their own mission expenses, often with help from family and friends. Currently, the Church extends mission calls for two years to young men ages nineteen to twenty-six, and for eighteen months to single women, ages twenty-one and over. Older couples with no dependent children at home are generally called for twelve, eighteen, or twenty-four month missions. There are some seasonal missions and special-occasion missions that have couples and older sisters serving for shorter periods of time.

Missionaries are trained at any one of several Missionary Training Centers throughout the world. If foreign language training is needed, the stay at an MTC is longer.

A typical daily schedule in the mission field for young single sisters and elders might be somewhat as follows:

6:30 AM Get up
7:00 AM Study with companion
8:00 AM Breakfast
8:30 AM Personal study
9:30 AM Teaching and contacting
12:00 PM Lunch
1:00 PM Teaching and contacting
5:00 PM Dinner
6:00 PM Teaching and contacting
9:30 PM Plan tomorrow's schedule
10:30 PM Go to bed

For senior sisters and couples, the daily schedule is flexible, since their assignments vary widely, as do their health and energy needs.

Available missions for older sisters and senior couples, with accompanying costs and requirements, are posted and updated frequently on the Church's website, lds.org. When applying, senior missionaries are invited to suggest missions that would interest them, but they should be willing to serve wherever called.

MISSIONARY TRAINING CENTERS

The Church has missionary training centers in many locations throughout the world. Missionaries attend these training centers as part of their missions and pay their own expenses while there. A variety of training in gospel topics, teaching, culture, and language, as needed, are offered to assist missionaries in getting off to a good start on their missions.

MISSIONARY WORK

See MISSIONARIES; MISSIONARY TRAINING CENTERS.

MISSOURI

See also INDEPENDENCE, MISSOURI.
Missouri holds special interest to Latter-day Saints for several reasons. According to revelation, the Garden of Eden was located in Missouri. Brigham Young and Heber C. Kimball both stated that the Prophet Joseph Smith taught them the Garden of Eden was located in what is now Jackson County, Missouri (*JD* 10:235).

Several early Saints of this dispensation settled in what was known as Zion (D&C 57:2–3), Jackson County, Missouri, and other locations in that state. They were driven out, but members still consider it to be a future gathering place for some who will be called to return to it. This gathering is to be done only by call from the prophet.

New Jerusalem will eventually be built in the Jackson County, Missouri, area (Ether 13:6; 3 Nephi 21:23–24), and this area will become one of two headquarters for the Savior during the Millennium (Isaiah 2:3; 3 Nephi 21:25).

MODERN REVELATION

Just as God spoke in times past to His prophets, so also does He speak today through true prophets. Amos assured us that "the Lord God will do nothing, but he revealeth his secret unto his servants the prophets" (Amos 2:7).

This modern revelation through prophets of God began with the calling of the Prophet Joseph Smith to restore the true Church of Jesus Christ again to the earth (JS—H 1:1–74). Peter prophesied of this restoration (Acts 3:19–21). Such revelation has continued in the Church through present day. It comes today to modern prophets, seers, and revelators who serve as the leaders of the Church and as prophets of God for the whole world. These "prophets" consist of the First Presidency and the Quorum of the Twelve Apostles. The president of the Church is *the* prophet.

MODESTY

See also IMMODESTY. Modesty is more than dress style. It is an indicator of deeper personal qualities and attributes, including strength and humility, which do not call undue attention to self. "It includes humility and decency in dress, grooming, language, and behavior" (*TF*, p. 106).

Modesty in dress plays a significant role in preserving chastity for one's self as well as in the actions and thoughts of those around us. Modern prophets have given the counsel of the Lord on this aspect of modesty. "Your clothing expresses who you are. It sends messages about you, and it influences the way you and others act. When you are well groomed and modestly dressed, you can invite the companionship of the Spirit and exercise a good influence on those around you" (*TF*, p. 107).

The Brethren have explained some problems associated with immodest clothing. They wrote: "Revealing and sexually suggestive clothing, which includes short shorts and skirts, tight clothing, and shirts that do not cover the stomach, can stimulate desires and actions that violate the Lord's law of chastity. . . . You should avoid extremes in clothing, appearance, and hairstyle. In dress, grooming, and manners, always be neat and clean, never sloppy or inappropriately casual. Do not disfigure yourself with tattoos or body piercings. If you are a woman and you desire to have your ears pierced, wear only one pair of modest earrings" (*TF*, p. 107).

Immodesty of dress, language, and behavior are well-used and effective tools of destruction sponsored by the devil. Members of the Church are constantly reminded to avoid these common and obvious (except to those who are immodest) offenses to the Spirit.

MODESTY IN DRESS

See IMMODESTY; MODESTY.

MONEY

There is nothing inherently wrong with money itself. The problem comes with how one pursues it and how one uses it after gaining it (Jacob 2:18–19). Paul is often misquoted on this subject. The misquote is "money is the root of all evil." The correct quote is "the love of money is the root of all evil" (1 Timothy 6:10).

MONOTHEISM

The belief in and worship of one God. Polytheism is the belief in and worship of multiple gods.

MOONS, NEW

The phrase, as used in the scriptures, has reference to special sacrifices that were to be offered at the time of the new moon, according to the law of Moses (1 Chronicles 23:31; 2 Chronicles 2:4; Ezra 3:5; BD, under "New Moon"). Isaiah spoke for the Lord and chastised the people for hypocrisy because they continued with authorized worship services and rites but otherwise lived wickedly (Isaiah 1:13–14).

MORE SURE WORD OF PROPHECY

This phrase comes from the teachings of the Apostle Peter, when he was teaching how to assure one's exaltation, in other words, how to "make your calling and election sure" (2 Peter 1:10). He said, "We have also a more sure word of prophecy; whereunto ye do well that ye take heed, as unto a light that shineth in a dark place, until the day dawn, and the day star arise in your hearts" (2 Peter 1:19).

Joseph Smith explained the phrase as follows: "The more sure word of prophecy means a man's knowing that he is sealed up unto eternal life, by revelation and the spirit of prophecy, through the power of the Holy Priesthood" (D&C 131:5).

MORMON

See also BOOK OF MORMON; MORMONS. "Mormon" is a nickname given to The Church of Jesus Christ of Latter-day Saints because of the Book of Mormon, a sacred book of scripture which serves as "another testament" or witness of Jesus Christ. The definition of the word "Mormon" is "more good." This was explained by Joseph Smith when he said, "The word Mormon, means literally, more good" (*HC* 5:399–400).

Mormon himself was a great prophet and historian who lived on the American continent from about AD 310 to AD 385. He quoted and abridged the records of the ancient inhabitants of America and the Lord's dealings with them, creating a record on gold plates which was turned over to his son, Moroni. Moroni later buried the plates (Moroni 10:2). In 1823, Moroni appeared to Joseph Smith, as a resurrected being, and showed him the gold plates. When Joseph later translated a portion of the plates, the result was called the Book of Mormon as given on the title page of the record on the gold plates (see title page at the front of the Book of Mormon).

MORMON BATTALION

Members of the Mormon Battalion made the longest military march in the history of the United States. It was a distance of over 2,030 miles. Enlisted on July 16, 1846, at Council Bluffs, Iowa, by the United States government, the Battalion consisted of 541 volunteer soldiers accompanied by 35 women, including 20 who were laundresses, and 42 children. They departed on July 21, 1846, and arrived at San Diego, California, on January 29, 1847. They were recruited to help in the campaign against Mexico.

Because so many men volunteered to join the Battalion, the main body of Latter-day Saints emigrating west was forced to delay their westward migration for one year.

Even though the march was difficult, the Battalion was never engaged by the enemy in battle. They built roads as they traveled through to Santa Fe, New Mexico; Tucson, Arizona; and on to San Diego, California, which were later used by many others traveling west. When they arrived at San Diego, they contributed significantly to the building up of that community.

At first look, it might seem unusual for the Mormon men to volunteer to assist the U.S. government when the Saints had been so poorly treated by the United States, including being recently driven out of Illinois. But there was a great benefit to the westward migration of the Church. Near the beginning of their journey, at Fort Leavenworth, Kansas, the Battalion members were outfitted at government expense with supplies, guns, and forty-two dollars per man as clothing allowance, but were not required to purchase military uniforms. Thus, a portion of the money was sent to their families and the Church and was used to help the westward trek of the Saints.

After their discharge on July 16, 1847, when the one-year enlistment was up, a number of the single men remained and worked in California during the winter of 1847–48, while the married men returned to their families, most of whom had arrived in the Salt Lake Valley or were underway. Some of the men who remained assisted with the discovery of gold at Sutter's Fort on the Sacramento River, which began the California Gold Rush of 1848.

MORMON PIONEER TRAIL

The approximately 1,300-mile route of the Mormon westward migration from Nauvoo, Illinois, to the Salt Lake Valley. It was used for twenty-three years by an estimated 70,000 members of the Church as they came to the Utah Territory.

MORMON PIONEERS

See PIONEERS.

MORMON TABERNACLE

At the April 1863 general conference of the Church, plans were announced to build a tabernacle in which a large number of Saints could gather for meetings, including conferences (*JD* 10:139). The building was to be 150 feet wide, 250 feet long, and 80 feet high, with a unique dome-shaped roof. The building was completed in time for the October 1867 general conference. A magnificent pipe organ was built for the tabernacle by master organ builder Joseph Harris Ridges. The building is still world famous for its acoustics and unusual architectural style.

MORMON TABERNACLE CHOIR

The now world-famous Mormon Tabernacle Choir had its first broadcast on July 15, 1929. The 300-plus voice choir, now joined by the Orchestra at Temple Square, continues to inspire people of all faiths and walks of life with its weekly broadcasts from the Tabernacle on Temple Square. Choir members are all volunteers and are set apart as missionaries for the Church.

In addition to weekly broadcasts, the Choir performs at numerous special events and continues to do occasional tours, drawing record crowds as they teach the gospel and bring the Spirit through music.

MORMONISM

See MORMONS.

MORMONS

See also BOOK OF MORMON; MORMON. A nickname for The Church of Jesus Christ of Latter-day Saints. Members are often called Mormons because of their belief in a sacred volume of scripture named the Book of Mormon. The Book of Mormon is subtitled "Another Testament of Jesus Christ" (see introductory notes to Book of Mormon) and goes hand in hand with the Bible in bearing witness of the Savior.

The Church of Jesus Christ of Latter-day Saints (D&C 115:4) was established by the Lord through the Prophet Joseph Smith on April 6, 1830, in Fayette, New York.

A brief at-a-glance summary of many of the things Mormons believe and do not believe follows. Most of these topics are covered in more detail elsewhere in this book.

Mormons do:

1. Believe in Heavenly Father.

2. Believe in Jesus Christ.

3. Believe in the Holy Ghost.

4. Believe that the Godhead consists of three separate, distinct members: the Father, the Son, and the Holy Ghost (Matthew 3:13–17; Acts 7:55–56).

5. Believe that God the Father is the Supreme God who is above all (Ephesians 4:6).

6. Believe that Jesus Christ is the Only Begotten Son of God the Eternal Father in the flesh (John 1:14).

7. Believe that the Atonement of Christ is the central focus of the

gospel (John 3:16; 17:3).

8. Believe "that the first principles and ordinances of the Gospel are: first, Faith in the Lord Jesus Christ; second, Repentance; third, Baptism by immersion for the remission of sins; fourth, Laying on of hands for the gift of the Holy Ghost" (Articles of Faith 1:4).

9. Believe that we all lived in a pre-mortal life, as spirit children of Heavenly Father (Hebrews 12:9), before we came to earth (Jeremiah 1:5).

10. Believe that the Father and Son have resurrected bodies of flesh and bone (John 14:9; 1 John 3:2).

11. Believe that the Holy Ghost is the third member of the Godhead and is a personage of Spirit (D&C 130:22).

12. Believe that baptism by immersion (Matthew 3:16), by proper authority, is the only mode of baptism acceptable to God (1 Corinthians 1:11–14).

13. Believe in continuing revelation through modern prophets.

14. Believe in keeping the Lord's law of chastity, which means no premarital sex, under any circumstances, and no sexual relationships outside of marriage.

15. Believe in the sanctity of marriage and that the family is the basic unit of society.

16. Believe that marriage should only be between a man and a woman.

17. Believe that children who die before age eight go to heaven and do not need baptism (D&C 137:10).

18. Believe the Bible to be the word of God as far as it is translated correctly (Articles of Faith 1:8).

19. Believe the Book of Mormon to be the word of God (Articles of Faith 1:8).

20. Believe that the Savior established one authorized church during His earthly mission (Ephesians 4:5), and that he restored that church in our day through the Prophet Joseph Smith.

21. Believe in the eternal nature of families, in other words, that families can be together forever through marriages performed in LDS temples (D&C 131:1–4; 132:19).

22. Believe in getting as much education as possible for both men and women.

23. Salute the flag.

24. Celebrate Christmas on December 25.

25. Believe in military service when necessary to defend freedom, country, wives, and children (Alma 43:45–48).

26. Believe in abstaining from tea, coffee, alcohol, and tobacco (D&C 89).

27. Believe in performing saving ordinances for the dead, such as baptism (1 Corinthians 15:29) and sealing families together as family units for eternity (D&C 138:58).

28. Believe that all people will be resurrected, regardless of whether they were righteous or wicked (1 Corinthians 15:22).

29. Believe that, as Paul taught, there are various "heavens" to which people will be sent on Judgment Day, depending on how they lived their lives (1 Corinthians 15:39–42).

30. Believe that all people will get a perfect opportunity to hear, understand, accept, or reject the pure gospel of Jesus Christ, whether on the earth or in the postmortal spirit world (1 Peter 3:18–20). Thus, the final judgment will be completely fair for everyone (1 Peter 4:6).

31. Believe that people who faithfully live the gospel of Jesus Christ can become like Heavenly Father (Matthew 5:48); in other words, they can become gods (Psalm 82:6; John 10:34; 1 Corinthians 8:5).

32. Believe in a literal Satan, also called Lucifer or the devil (Matthew 4:10; Isaiah 14:12), who opposed God in the War in Heaven (Revelation 12:7–9) and who is now on earth with the one-third of spirits who followed him as a result of the War in Heaven (Revelation 12:4).

33. Pay tithing (Genesis 14:20).

34. Believe in the Savior's command to take the gospel to all the world, baptizing those who believe (Mark 16:15–16).

35. Believe in the separation of Church and state, but not in taking God out of all public dealings.

36. Believe in keeping the Sabbath Day holy (Exodus 20:8–11).

37. Believe that the Ten Commandments are still in force (Exodus 20:3–17).

38. Believe that both grace and works, including baptism, are required to be saved in the sense of living with God forever (see "Grace" in this reference book).

39. Believe that there is one true church when it comes to attaining the celestial heaven spoken of by Paul (1 Corinthians 15:40-42). This true church is the church established by Jesus Christ when He was on earth (Mark 16:15–16; Ephesians 4:5–6; 1 Corinthians 1:12–13) and which He restored through the Prophet Joseph Smith in our day. All other religions that teach good and honorable living can lead their members to the middle (terrestrial) heaven spoken of by Paul (1 Corinthians 15:40–41). And all the rest, except those who follow Satan

completely, in other words, who become "sons of perdition" (D&C 76:32), will go to the telestial kingdom, which is the lowest heaven (1 Corinthians 15:40–41; D&C 76:89, 103; Revelation 22:15).

40. Believe in the literal Second Coming of Jesus Christ (Acts 1:11; 2 Thessalonians 2:8), which will usher in the one-thousand-year Millennium (Revelation 20:4).

41. Believe in a literal Adam and Eve, who were the first humans on earth (Genesis 1:27; 2:18–25).

42. Believe that Adam and Eve were highly intelligent individuals who knew how to read and write and who taught their children to do likewise (Moses 6:5–6).

43. Believe that the Fall of Adam was good and that it was a part of God's plan for His children on earth (2 Nephi 2:22–25).

44. Revere Adam and Eve and honor them as our "first parents."

Mormons do not:

1. Worship Joseph Smith.

2. Practice polygamy.

3. Have any fundamentalist groups affiliated with the Church at all, including those who practice polygamy.

4. Pray to Mary.

5. Believe in infant baptism.

6. Believe that premarital sex is appropriate under any circumstances.

7. Believe in predestination.

8. Believe in being saved by grace alone, when it comes to living with God forever in the afterlife (see "Grace" in this reference work).

9. Believe that the Bible is complete (see "Missing Scripture" in this reference work).

10. Believe in limbo (see "Limbo" in this reference work).

11. Believe in patron saints.

12. Drink tea (herbal tea is permitted), coffee, alcohol, or use tobacco.

13. Believe that God has stopped speaking to prophets on earth.

MORNING STAR

Symbolic of the best (Revelation 2:28). Also, another name for the Savior (Revelation 22:16).

MORNING STARS

Symbolic of the premortal spirit children of God during the council in heaven (Job 38:7).

MORONI

See also ANGEL MORONI. There are two Moronis in the Book of Mormon: (1) A righteous military leader named Captain Moroni, who led the Nephite armies against the Lamanites (Alma 43:16). Studying his life (Alma 43–63) is of great value because, among other things, we are taught how to survive spiritually in times of war and difficulty and are taught when war is justified and how to conduct it honorably. (2) The last prophet in the Book of Mormon. He became the Angel Moroni who appeared to Joseph Smith, instructed him about the gold plates and many other things, and eventually delivered the gold plates to him.

MORONI, ANGEL

See ANGEL MORONI; MORONI.

MORONI, VISITATIONS OF

From 1823 to 1829, the angel Moroni made at least twenty appearances to Joseph Smith and others. Joseph was, in effect, called by God and then taught and prepared by Moroni during the early scenes of the Restoration. There were five separate appearances on September 21 and 22, 1823, as Moroni introduced Joseph to the gold plates and to his role in the restoration of the gospel (JS—H 1:30, 44, 46, 49, 50–53). Following these first appearances, Moroni met Joseph Smith each September 22 for the next four years (JS—H 1:53–54). During these four years, Joseph reported that he "received many visits from the angels of God unfolding the majesty and glory of the events that should transpire in the last days" (*HC* 4:537).

Joseph's mother wrote about what her son learned and taught the family during these years: "From this time

forth, Joseph continued to receive instructions from the Lord, and we continued to get the children together every evening for the purpose of listening while he gave us a relation of the same. . . . He would describe the ancient inhabitants of this continent, their dress, mode of traveling, and the animals upon which they rode; their cities, their buildings, with every particular; their mode of warfare; and also their religious worship. This he would do with as much ease, seemingly, as if he had spent his whole life among them" (Smith, *History of Joseph Smith by His Mother*, pp. 82–83).

When Martin Harris lost the 116 manuscript pages, Moroni took the plates and Urim and Thummim from him. Later, Moroni returned them to him so he could resume translating (Smith, *History of Joseph Smith by His Mother*, pp. 149–50).

Moroni took the plates for safekeeping, when Joseph, Emma, and Oliver moved from Harmony, Pennsylvania, to the Whitmer farm in Fayette, New York, where he then met Joseph and returned the plates to him (*Church History in the Fulness of Times*, p. 57). It was during the trip to Fayette that David Whitmer, who was driving the wagon carrying Joseph and Oliver (Emma came later), saw Moroni. He later described the event:

"A very pleasant, nice-looking old man suddenly appeared by the side of our wagon and saluted us with, 'good morning, it is very warm,' at the same time wiping his face or forehead with his hand. We returned the salutation, and, by a sign from Joseph, I invited him to ride if he was going our way. But he said very pleasantly, 'No, I am going to Cumorah.' This name was something new to me, I did not know what Cumorah meant. We all gazed at him and at each other, and as I looked around enquiringly of Joseph, the old man instantly disappeared. . . . It was the messenger who had the plates, who had taken them from Joseph just prior to our starting from Harmony" (*Church History in the Fulness of Times*, p. 57).

Moroni showed the plates to the Three Witnesses (*HC* 1:54–55), took them when the translation was completed (JS—H 1:60), and returned them to Joseph briefly so he could show the gold plates to the Eight Witnesses (see The Testimony of Eight Witnesses in this reference book).

In addition, it is believed that Moroni was the angel who showed the plates to David Whitmer's mother, Mary Whitmer, as reported by her grandson. He said:

"One evening, when (after having done her usual day's work in the house) she went to the barn to milk the cows, she met a stranger carrying something on his back that looked like a knapsack. At first she was a little afraid of him, but when he spoke to her in a kind, friendly tone, and began to explain to her the nature of the work which was going on in her house, she was filled with unexpressible joy and satisfaction. He then untied his knapsack and showed her a bundle of plates, which in size and appearance corresponded with the description subsequently given by the witnesses to the Book of Mormon. This strange person turned the leaves of the book of plates over, leaf after leaf, and also showed her the engravings upon them; after which he told her to be patient and faithful in bearing her burden a little longer, promising that if she would do so, she should be blessed and her reward would be sure, if she proved faithful to the end. The personage then suddenly vanished with the plates, and where he went, she could not tell. From that moment my grandmother was enabled to perform her household duties with comparative ease, and she felt no more inclination to murmur because her lot was hard. I knew my grandmother to be a good, noble and truthful woman, and I have not the least doubt of her statement in regard to seeing the plates being strictly true. She was a strong believer in the Book of Mormon until the day of her death" (*Juvenile Instructor* 24 [1899]: 23). The above quote is also found in Richard Lloyd Anderson, *Investigating the Book of Mormon Witnesses* [Salt Lake City: Deseret Book, 1981], 31.

MORONI'S PROMISE

At the end of the Book of Mormon, Moroni made a promise to all who read it. He wrote:

Moroni 10:3–5

3 Behold, I would exhort you that when ye shall read these things, if it be wisdom in God that ye should read them, that ye would remember how merciful the Lord hath been unto the children of men, from the creation of Adam even down until the time that ye shall receive these things, and ponder it in your hearts.

4 And when ye shall receive these things, I would exhort you that ye would ask God, the Eternal Father, in the name of Christ, if these things are not true; and if ye shall ask with a sincere heart, with real intent, having faith in Christ, he will manifest the truth of it unto you, by the power of the Holy Ghost.

5 And by the power of the Holy Ghost ye may know the truth of all things.

MORTAL

A term which means "subject to death." It refers to people and to all life on earth. It is a temporary state and will be done away with through resurrection (D&C 29:24).

MORTAL LIFE

See MORTAL.

MORTALITY

See MORTAL.

MOSAIC DISPENSATION

See also DISPENSATION; DISPENSA-

TIONS. The Mosaic dispensation is the period of time from Moses to the time of Christ, when the Israelites were living, for the most part, under the law of Moses.

MOSAIC LAW

See LAW OF MOSES.

MOSES

See also LAW OF MOSES. One of the greatest prophets of the Old Testament, Moses led, in effect, "three lives." (1) From birth to age 40, he was a prince of Egypt. (2) From age 40–80, he was a shepherd. (3) From age 80 to 120, he was the Lord's prophet, leading the children of Israel from Egyptian bondage.

Moses was perhaps the most revered of all Old Testament prophets by the Jews in the days of the Savior's mortal ministry. They were constantly saying that Jesus was undermining what Moses had said, and comparing the Savior's teachings against the teachings of Moses (Matthew 19:7; 22:24).

Moses gave the law of Moses, which was a schoolmaster law (Galatians 3:24) to prepare the Israelites for the higher law that Christ would bring during His mortal ministry.

Moses was translated (taken to heaven without tasting death) at age 120 (Alma 45:19; BD, under "Moses"). The Bible reports that he died but no one knew where he was buried (Deuteronomy 34:5–6). This is not correct, and the reason nobody knew of his burial site was that he did not die; rather, he was translated.

With his physical, translated body, he ministered to the Savior on the Mount of Transfiguration, about six months before the crucifixion (Matthew 17:1–3). While on the mount, he, along with Elijah, conferred the keys of the priesthood upon Peter, James, and John (BD, under "Moses").

Moses was resurrected with Christ (D&C 133:54–55). As a resurrected being, he appeared to Joseph Smith and Oliver Cowdery in the Kirtland Temple and conferred the keys of the "gathering of Israel" and the "leading of the ten tribes from the land of the north" (D&C 110:11).

He wrote Genesis, Exodus, Leviticus, Numbers, and Deuteronomy. Writings of his that are missing from the Bible are found in the Book of Moses in the Pearl of Great Price.

MOSES, BOOK OF

One of the five books contained in the Pearl of Great Price. The exact title of this book of scripture is Selections from the Book of Moses, but we usually just call it Moses. Moses consists of eight chapters, which were given to Joseph Smith by direct revelation, from June 1830 to February 1831.

The material in chapter 1, which deals with the time from the burning bush to before Moses returns to Egypt to lead the children of Israel out of bondage (see Moses 1:17, 25–26) is completely missing from the Bible. The other seven chapters contain much that is in the Bible, from Genesis 1 through Genesis 6:13, as well as much that was left out of this part of Genesis.

MOST HIGH

A term that can refer either to the Father or the Son in the scriptures. For examples pertaining to the Father, see Isaiah 14:14; Mark 5:7; for the Son, 2 Samuel 22:14.

MOTHER IN HEAVEN

See HEAVENLY MOTHER.

MOTHERS IN ISRAEL

A phrase often used in patriarchal blessings given to sisters in the Church, which can mean "motherhood in mortality as a faithful member of the Church" or "motherhood in eternity" as an exalted being (D&C 132:19–20).

MOUNT OF TRANSFIGURATION

The mountain upon which the Savior was transfigured about six months before His crucifixion (Matthew 17:1–9). It probably took place in October, about a week after the Savior promised Peter that he would receive the keys of the kingdom of heaven (Matthew 16:19). The exact location of the mountain is not known for sure, but many Bible scholars believe it was Mount Hermon (BD, under "Transfiguration, Mount of").

Bruce R. McConkie summarized the transfiguration of the Savior as follows:

"From the New Testament accounts and from the added light revealed through Joseph Smith it appears evident that:

" (1) Jesus singled out Peter, James, and John from the rest of the Twelve; took them upon an unnamed mountain; there he was transfigured before them, and they beheld his glory. Testifying later, John said, 'We beheld his glory, the glory as of the only begotten of the Father' (John 1:14); and Peter, speaking of the same event, said they 'were eyewitnesses of his majesty' " (2 Pet. 1:16).

" (2) Peter, James, and John were themselves 'transfigured before him' (*Teachings,* p. 158), even as Moses, the Three Nephites, Joseph Smith, and many prophets of all ages have been transfigured, thus enabling them to entertain angels, see visions and comprehend the things of God (*Mormon Doctrine,* pp. 725–26).

" (3) Moses and Elijah—two ancient prophets who were translated and taken to heaven without tasting death so they could return with tangible bodies on this very occasion, an occasion preceding the day of resurrection—appeared on the mountain; and they and Jesus gave the keys of the kingdom to Peter, James, and John (*Teachings,* p. 158).

" (4) John the Baptist, previously beheaded by Herod, apparently was also present. It may well be that other unnamed prophets, either coming as translated beings or as spirits from paradise, were also present.

" (5) Peter, James, and John saw in vision the transfiguration of the earth, that is, they saw it renewed and returned to its paradisiacal state—an event that is to take place at the Second Coming when the millennial era is ushered in (D&C 63:20–21; *Mormon Doctrine,* pp. 718–19).

" (6) It appears that Peter, James, and John received their own endowments while on the mountain (*Doctrines of Salvation,* vol. 2, p. 165). Peter says that while there, they 'received from God the Father honour and glory,' seemingly bearing out this conclusion. It also appears that it was while on the mount that they received the more sure word of prophecy, it then being revealed to them that they were sealed up unto eternal life (2 Peter 1:16–19; D&C 131:5).

" (7) Apparently Jesus himself was strengthened and encouraged by Moses and Elijah so as to be prepared for the infinite sufferings and agony ahead of him in connection with working out the infinite and eternal atonement (*Jesus the Christ,* p. 373). Similar comfort had been given him by angelic visitants after his forty-day fast and its attendant temptations (Matthew 4:11), and an angel from heaven was yet to strengthen him when he would sweat great drops of blood in the Garden of Gethsemane (Luke 22:42–44).

" (8) Certainly the three chosen apostles were taught in plainness 'of his death and also his resurrection' (JST Luke 9:31), teachings which would be of inestimable value to them in the trying days ahead.

" (9) It should also have been apparent to them that the old dispensations of the past had faded away, that the law (of which Moses was the symbol) and the prophets (of whom Elijah was the typifying representative) were subject to Him whom they were now commanded to hear.

" (10) Apparently God the Father, overshadowed and hidden by a cloud, was present on the mountain, although our Lord's three associates, as far as the record stipulates, heard only his voice and did not see his form" (McConkie, *Doctrinal New Testament Commentary,* 1:399).

MOUNTAIN MEADOWS MASSACRE

The massacre, on September 11, 1857, in southern Utah, of a westbound wagon train of emigrants who were heading for California. The party consisted of two companies, the Baker company, who called themselves the Missouri Wildcats (*Church History in the Fulness of Times,* p. 371), and the Fancher Company, consisting of families from Arkansas, who had previously combined to travel together.

The basic details of the massacre are as follows: "On September 11, 1857, some 50 to 60 local militiamen in southern Utah, aided by American Indian allies, massacred about 120 emigrants who were traveling by wagon to California. The horrific crime, which spared only 17 children age six and under, occurred in a highland valley called the Mountain Meadows, roughly 35 miles southwest of Cedar City. The victims, most of them from Arkansas, were on their way to California with dreams of a bright future" (Richard E. Turley Jr., "The Mountain Meadows Massacre" [quote from the Church website, lds.org, under Gospel Topics, Mountain Meadows Massacre, dated 2007]. Go to this website for an entire September 2007 *Ensign* article posted on the subject).

Collecting accurate information on events leading up to the tragedy and on the massacre itself has proven difficult at best. However, information provided in the *Encyclopedia of Mormonism* gives helpful background.

"A large contingent of United States troops was marching westward toward Utah Territory in the summer of 1857. Despite having been the federally appointed territorial governor, Brigham Young was not informed by Washington of the army's purpose and interpreted the move as a renewal of the persecution the Latter-day Saints had experienced before their westward hegira. 'We are invaded by a hostile force who are evidently assailing us to accomplish our overthrow and destruction,' he proclaimed on August 5, 1857. Anticipating an attack, he declared the territory to be under martial law and ordered '[t]hat all the forces in said Territory hold themselves in readiness to March, at a moment's notice, to repel any and all such threatened invasion' (Arrington, p. 254).

"Part of Brigham Young's strategy in repelling the approaching army was to enlist local Indian tribes as allies. In an August 4 letter to southern Utah, for example, he urged one Latter-day Saint to '[c]ontinue the conciliatory policy towards the Indians, which I have ever recommended, and seek by works of righteousness to obtain their love and confidence, for they must learn that they have either got to help us or the United States will kill us both' (Brooks, p. 34).

"Meanwhile, owing to the lateness of the season, a party of emigrants bound for California elected to take the southern route that passed through Cedar City and thirty-five miles beyond to the Mountain Meadows, which was then an area of springs, bogs, and plentiful grass where travelers frequently stopped to rejuvenate themselves and their stock before braving the harsh desert landscape to the west. Led by John T. Baker and Alexander Fancher, the diverse party consisted of perhaps 120 persons, most of whom left from Arkansas but others of whom joined the company along their journey.

"As the Baker-Fancher party traveled from Salt Lake City to the Mountain Meadows, tensions developed between some of the emigrants, on the one hand, and Mormon settlers and their Native American allies, on the other. Spurred by rumors, their own observations, and memories of atrocities some of them had endured in Missouri and Illinois, Mormon residents in and around Cedar City felt compelled to take some action against the emigrant train but ultimately decided to dispatch a rider to Brigham Young, seeking his counsel. Leaving September 7, 1857, the messenger made the nearly 300-mile journey in just a little more than three days.

"Approximately one hour after his arrival [in Salt Lake City], the messenger was on his way back with a letter from Brigham Young, who said he did not expect the federal soldiers to arrive that fall because of their poor stock. 'They cannot get here this season without we help them,' he explained. 'So you see that the Lord has answered our prayers and again averted the blow designed for our heads.' Responding to the plea for counsel, he added, 'In regard to the emigration trains passing through our settlements, we must not interfere with them until they are first notified to keep away. You must not meddle with them. The Indians we expect will do as they please but you should try and preserve good feelings with them' (Brooks, p. 63). The messenger arrived back in Cedar City on September 13.

"By that time, however, it was too late, and nearly all the men, women, and children of the Baker-Fancher party lay dead. Besides a few persons who left the party before the attack, only about eighteen small children were spared. Two years later, seventeen of the children were returned to family members in northwestern Arkansas. Two decades after the tragedy, one of the Mormon settlers who was present at the massacre, John D. Lee, was executed by a firing squad at the Mountain Meadows, symbolically carrying to the grave the responsibility for those who 'were led to do what none singly would have done under normal conditions, and for which none singly can be held responsible' " (Brooks, p. 218).

MOUNTAIN OF THE LORD'S HOUSE

This has multiple meanings as used in the scriptures. For example, as used in Isaiah 2:3, it can mean, among other things, (1) the headquarters of the Church in Salt Lake City, (2) the Salt Lake Temple, or (3) the restoration of the Church. President Harold B. Lee taught, "The coming forth of his church in these days was the beginning of the fulfillment of the ancient prophecy when 'the mountain of the Lord's house shall be established in the top of the mountains' " (CR [Apr. 1973]: 5).

President Lee also noted, regarding Isaiah 2:2–3, that "with the coming of the pioneers to establish the Church in the tops of the mountains, our early leaders declared this to be the beginning of the fulfillment of that prophecy" (*Ensign*, Nov. 1971, p. 15).

Elder LeGrand Richards said, "How literally [Isaiah 2:3] has been fulfilled, in my way of thinking, in this very house of the God of Jacob right here on this block! This temple [Salt Lake], more than any other building of which we have any record, has brought people from every land to learn of his ways and walk in his paths" (CR [Apr. 1971]: 143).

MULEK

Mulek was one of the sons of wicked King Zedekiah, who was the King of Judah (1 Nephi 1:4) at the time Lehi and his family left Jerusalem in 600 BC. Zedekiah refused to listen to the prophets, especially Jeremiah (see Jeremiah, chapter 38). We know from Jeremiah chapter 39 that Nebuchadnezzar, King of Babylon, attacked Jerusalem and captured Zedekiah as he was trying to escape. Zedekiah was forced to watch as his sons were killed (Jeremiah 39:6), but the killers obviously missed Mulek (Helaman 8:21). Mulek and others were brought by the Lord to the Americas (Helaman 6:10), where they settled north of where Lehi and his people settled. Mulek and his people are known as Mulekites.

MULEKITES

See MULEK.

MURDER

The intentional and unjustified taking of human life for selfish purposes, generally referred to as "first degree murder." Cain was guilty of this when he killed his brother, Abel, to "get gain" (Moses 5:31). Regarding this type of killing, the Doctrine and Covenants teaches, "He that kills shall not have forgiveness in this world, nor in the world to come" (D&C 42:18).

In cases of members of the Church who desire rebaptism after having been excommunicated for murder, the First Presidency of the Church makes the final decision. Likewise, for convicted murderers who have studied the Church and desire baptism, the First Presidency makes the final decision on a case by case basis.

Ultimately, the decision on the eternal fate of murderers rests with the Lord, who knows all things.

MURDERERS

See also MURDER. Revelation 22:15, in combination with D&C 76:103 (speaking of the telestial kingdom), indicates that murderers can be forgiven to the extent of being sent to telestial glory on Judgment Day, rather than remaining in perdition with Satan.

MUTUAL IMPROVEMENT ASSOCIATION

The organization of the Church in past years for youth ages 12–18. It is now called Mutual. It consists of two divisions: Young Women and Young Men.

MYSTERIES

Generally, as used in the scriptures, "mysteries" refers to the simple basics of the gospel, including faith, repentance, baptism, the gift of the Holy Ghost, and the saving principles and ordinances of the gospel of Jesus Christ that were "hidden" from the world because of apostasy but which are now available to all because of the restored gospel (BD, under "Mystery"; 1 Corinthians 15:51; Ephesians 5:22; Colossians 1:26–27;).

However, there are times when "mysteries" is used in the sense of things that are not known or cannot be comprehended by the human mind (Alma 40:3).

· N ·

NAME EXTRACTION

A program sponsored by the Church whereby names of ancestors are transferred from original records, such as birth records, marriage certificates, military service records, death certificates, and so forth, to a database in the Family History program. This allows researchers to find their ancestors more easily.

NAME OF THE CHURCH

The official name of the Church was given by the Lord through direct revelation to Joseph Smith on April 26, 1838. The Lord said, "For thus shall my church be called in the last days, even The Church of Jesus Christ of Latter-day Saints" (D&C 115:4). Prior to this revelation, several names were used, including 'The Church of Christ,' 'The Church of the Latter Day Saints,' and 'The Church of Christ of Latter Day Saints' " (*EM*, under "Name of the Church").

NAMING OF CHILDREN

The ordinance of naming and blessing babies is practiced in the Church (D&C 20:70). Holders of the Melchizedek Priesthood take the baby in their arms, and the one serving as voice addresses Heavenly Father, stating that it is by the power of the Melchizedek Priesthood that they are acting. He goes on to give the full name chosen for the child and then proceeds to pronounce a blessing upon him or her, according to the promptings of the Spirit. Sometime during the ordinance or at the end, he states that it is done in the name of Jesus Christ.

The ordinance of naming and blessing of children is not required for salvation.

NATURAL MAN

Anyone, male or female, who fails to repent, and thus lives in opposition to God's laws and commandments (Mosiah 3:19), is a "natural man." The phrase "natural man" does not mean that people are naturally evil or that by nature they are depraved or wicked. All people are innocent when they are born (D&C 93:38). They become a "natural man" by going "contrary to the nature of God" (Alma 41:11). In other words, they go

against their conscience (John 1:9) and make agency choices that lead to becoming "carnal, sensual, and devilish" (Moses 6:49).

NAUVOO

The word "Nauvoo" comes from the Hebrew language and means "beautiful" (*Church History in the Fulness of Times*, p. 217). Joseph Smith said that it is a word "carrying with it also the idea of rest" (*HC* 2:11). Thus, combining these insights together, one could say that "Nauvoo" means "a place of beauty and rest."

In April 1839, leaders of the Church purchased 660 acres in an area known as Commerce, Illinois, on a bend of the Mississippi River, on the western edge of Illinois. The Saints, who had been driven out of Missouri, built a new city here and named it Nauvoo. It would be home for about seven years, until they were again driven out.

Nauvoo rapidly became a thriving community, with beautiful homes on one-acre lots and a temple under construction. They had their own city charter and militia and their own public schools with over 1,800 students enrolled. They also had their own University of the City of Nauvoo, with classes taught in private homes and public buildings. In addition, they had their own newspapers, the *Times and Seasons*, devoted mainly to religious matters, and the *Nauvoo Neighbor*, dealing mostly with agriculture, business, science, art, and community matters.

After the martyrdom of the Prophet Joseph Smith and his brother Hyrum on June 27, 1844, in Carthage, Illinois, pressure continued building against the members of the Church in Nauvoo. Under threats and some mob violence, the Saints once again left a beloved city and this time headed west. The first major groups crossed the Mississippi River, heading for the Rocky Mountains, in February 1846.

NAUVOO CHARTER

The state of Illinois granted the Church in Nauvoo a liberal charter, known as the Nauvoo Charter. It allowed the Saints to have their own government in many significant ways, including having their own militia, a municipal court system, and a university. Under the provisions of this charter, the city council of Nauvoo established their own police force and passed ordinances and laws guaranteeing the right of assembly and freedom of worship for all religions. They established plans to drain the swamps and set up a public works program which provided jobs building homes, stores, hotels, and so forth.

NAUVOO EXPOSITOR

The *Nauvoo Expositor* was a Nauvoo newspaper run by apostates who were determined to destroy the Church and Joseph Smith. On June 7, 1844, the first and only issue of the newspaper was published. Joseph was martyred less than three weeks later.

Among other things in the paper was a statement by one of the apostate owners of the *Nauvoo Expositor*, Francis Higbee. He wrote that Joseph Smith was "the biggest villain that goes unhung." The false claims and accusations in the paper fueled fears of riot and violence in the city, and the city council declared it a "public nuisance." For the safety of the citizens, the council directed the mayor of Nauvoo to remove the paper and its press. He carried out the orders. That action was seen by apostates and violent enemies of the Church in surrounding communities as justification for having Joseph Smith arrested in Carthage Jail and later murdering him and Hyrum.

NAUVOO HOUSE

A hotel built by the Saints in Nauvoo, on the eastern bank of the Mississippi River, in which to receive guests and visitors to the City of Nauvoo.

NAUVOO LEGION

The name of a division of the Illinois state militia, which was housed in Nauvoo and was under the control of Joseph Smith and others in Nauvoo. It grew to three thousand enlistees.

NAUVOO NEIGHBOR

The name of one of the newspapers in Nauvoo. It was published by the Church. It chronicled community events and treated a wide variety of topics, including agriculture, science, business, and art.

NAUVOO TEMPLE

A temple built by the early members of the Church in Nauvoo, and rebuilt by the Church in our day. Construction on the original temple began in the fall of 1840. Delays and financial setbacks caused continual problems right up to the time of completion and public dedication on May 1, 1846.

Prior to its completion, portions of it were dedicated for ordinance work, including baptisms for the dead. Endowments for the living and dead, as well as sealings, were performed, especially in the months just prior to the exodus of the Saints for the West.

The rebuilt Nauvoo Temple, using the same architectural style as the original and built on the same site, was dedicated near the end of June 2002 by President Gordon B. Hinckley.

NAZARENE

A person from Nazareth (Matthew 2:23).

NAZARITE

A man who had taken a vow to avoid wine, to abstain from any cutting of the hair, and to avoid any contact with the dead (Judges 13:5; 16:17; Numbers 6). The vow might be for a lifetime or for just a short period of time with a particular goal in mind. Numbers chapter 6 gives more details about such vows.

NECKING

Excessive kissing and making out which elicits and sustains lustful thoughts. The Lord counsels against such behavior (D&C 59:6).

NEUTRALS IN HEAVEN

Joseph Fielding Smith taught, "There were no neutrals in the war in heaven. All took sides either with Christ or with Satan" (*DS* 1:65–66).

The War in Heaven became a judgment day of sorts, with one-third going with Satan (Revelation 12:4) and all the others being sufficiently righteous to be sent to earth, where all would start over again, innocent (D&C 93:38).

NEW AND EVERLASTING COVENANT

A phrase meaning all doctrines, principles, covenants, and ordinances contained in the gospel of Jesus Christ. In other words, it is the full gospel of Jesus Christ. It was in the beginning, on this earth (D&C 22:1), and it was restored again in the last days through the Prophet Joseph Smith.

Joseph Fielding Smith explained it this way: "The new and everlasting covenant is the fulness of the gospel. It is composed of 'All covenants, contracts, bonds, obligations, oaths, vows, performances, connections, associations, or expectations' that are sealed upon members of the Church by the Holy Spirit of Promise, or the Holy Ghost, by the authority of the President of the Church who holds the keys. The President of the Church holds the keys of the Melchizedek Priesthood. He delegates authority to others and authorizes them to perform the sacred ordinances of the priesthood.

"Marriage for eternity is a new and everlasting covenant. Baptism is also a new and everlasting covenant, and likewise ordination to the priesthood, and every other covenant is everlasting and a part of the new and everlasting covenant which embraces all things" (*Answers to Gospel Questions*, 1:65; see also *Doctrine and Covenants Student Manual*, p. 46).

NEW BIRTH

See BORN AGAIN.

NEW CREATURES

See also BORN AGAIN. "New creatures" (Mosiah 27:25–26; 2 Corinthians 5:17; Galatians 6:15) is a scriptural phrase used to describe the process of becoming "children of Christ" (Mosiah 5:7). It is similar in meaning to "born again" (John 3:3, 7) and "walk in newness of life" (Romans 6:3–6).

NEW EARTH

See NEW HEAVEN AND NEW EARTH. "New earth" has two distinct definitions, as used in the scriptures: (1) the earth during the Millennium, which will be a paradise (Articles of Faith 1:10; Isaiah 65:17–25; 66:22; D&C 101:23–31); (2) the earth when it becomes the celestial kingdom for its worthy inhabitants (D&C 29:22–24; 88:16–20; 130:9–11).

NEW ERA

The name of the official English-language magazine published by the Church for youth ages 12–18. It has been published monthly since 1971.

NEW HEAVEN

See NEW HEAVEN; NEW EARTH.

NEW HEAVEN AND NEW EARTH

See also NEW EARTH. Depending on context, this phrase can refer to the Millennium (Ether 13:9) or to the earth and its heaven when it becomes the celestial kingdom for its worthy inhabitants (Revelation 21:1; D&C 29:23), at which time it will also have a "new heaven" or sky because it will have been "rolled back into the presence of God" (*TPJS*, p. 181).

NEW JERUSALEM

There seem to be a number of closely related but different uses of "New Jerusalem" in the scriptures. We will quote from the Book of Mormon student manual, 1996 edition, used by the Institutes of Religion of the Church for help:

"Ether 13:1–12 describes what a great seer Ether was. Ether was shown many marvelous things by the Lord, including the establishment of a New Jerusalem prior to the Second Coming. Note what Ether said about the New Jerusalem:

1. It would be 'the holy sanctuary of the Lord' (v. 3).

2. It would be built on the American continent for the remnant of the seed of Joseph (see vv. 4–6).

3. It would be a holy city like the Jerusalem built unto the Lord (see vv. 8–9).

4. It would stand until the earth is celestialized (see v. 8).

5. It would be a city for the pure and righteous (see v. 10).

"President Joseph Fielding Smith wrote the following about the New Jerusalem:

"The prevailing notion in the world is that this [the New Jerusalem] is the city of Jerusalem, the ancient city of the Jews which in the day of regeneration will be renewed, but this is not the case. We read in the Book of Ether that the Lord revealed to him many of the same things which were seen by John. Ether, as members of the Church will know, was the last of the prophets among the Jaredites, and the Lord had revealed to him much concerning the history of the Jews and their city of Jerusalem which stood in the days of the ministry of our Savior.

"In his vision, in many respects similar to that given to John, Ether saw the old city of Jerusalem and also the new city which has not yet been built, and he wrote of them as follows as reported in the writings of Moroni: [Ether 13:2–11]. . . .

" 'In the day of regeneration, when all things are made new, there will be three great cities that will be holy. One will be the Jerusalem of old

which shall be rebuilt according to the prophecy of Ezekiel. One will be the city of Zion, or of Enoch, which was taken from the earth when Enoch was translated and which will be restored; and the city Zion, or New Jerusalem, which is to be built by the seed of Joseph on this the American continent [Moses 7:62–64].

" 'After the close of the millennial reign we are informed that Satan, who was bound during the millennium, shall be loosed and go forth to deceive the nations. Then will come the end. The earth will die and be purified and receive its resurrection. During this cleansing period the City Zion, or New Jerusalem, will be taken from the earth; and when the earth is prepared for the celestial glory, the city will come down according to the prediction in the Book of Revelation' (*Answers to Gospel Questions*, 2:103–6)" (*Book of Mormon Student Manual*, p. 143).

NEW NAME

This term is used five times in the scriptures (Isaiah 62:2; Revelation 2:17; 3:12; D&C 130:11 [used twice]). Each time it is used, it is in the context of favor with God and being worthy to be in His presence.

In the scriptures, new names are given in conjunction with making covenants with God. Abram's name was changed to Abraham in connection with the covenants he made with God (Genesis 17:2–7). Jacob's name was changed to Israel under similar circumstances (Genesis 32:28). King

Benjamin promised to give his people "a name . . . because they [had] been a diligent people in keeping the commandments of the Lord" (Mosiah 1:11), and the name he gave them was "the name of Christ" (Mosiah 5:8).

NEW TESTAMENT

The portion of the Bible which deals with the earthly mission of the Savior (Matthew, Mark, Luke, and John), and the missions and writings of some of the Apostles, after the ascension of Christ into heaven (Acts through Revelation).

The New Testament, in its current form with twenty-seven books, came into being as follows: "The writings of the New Testament were likely all produced within the first Christian century of the Christian era. Even so, its collection of texts went through three centuries of changes, and acceptance or rejection, before it acquired its recognized and current form, first listed in the Easter letter of Athanasius in Egypt in AD 367. The third synod of Carthage (AD 397) canonized the books of the New Testament as represented in the letter of Athanasius because each writing had three qualifications: apostolic authority, support of a major Christian community, and an absence of false teachings" (*EM*, under "New Testament").

NEW YORK, PROPHECY ABOUT

Those who read this prophecy, found in D&C 84:114, should prob-

ably read the whole thing and then pay special attention to the last phrase in it. The prophecy reads, "Nevertheless, let the bishop go unto the city of New York, also to the city of Albany, and also to the city of Boston, and warn the people of those cities with the sound of the gospel, with a loud voice, of the desolation and utter abolishment which await them if they do reject these things" (D&C 84:114).

There are a great many faithful and righteous members of the Church in these areas today who have not "reject[ed] these things." In addition, the Church has temples in these areas, which indicates that many faithful Saints live in these areas.

NICENE CREED

See also GODHEAD. The Nicene Creed was produced by the council of Nicaea under the sponsorship of Constantine, emperor of Rome, about AD 325 in an attempt to promote unity between Christians and non-Christians in his empire. The original creed was as follows:

"We believe in one God the Father Almighty, Maker of all things visible and invisible; and in one Lord Jesus Christ, the only begotten of the Father, that is, of the substance of the Father, God of God, light of light, true God of true God, begotten not made, of the same substance with the Father, through whom all things were made both in heaven and on earth; who for us men and for our salvation descended, was incarnate, and was made man, suffered and rose again the third day, ascended into heaven and cometh to judge living and dead. And in the Holy Ghost. Those who say: There was a time when He was not, and He was not before He was begotten; and that He was made out of nothing; or who maintain that He is of another hypostasis or another substance [than the Father], or that the Son of God is created, or mutable, or subject to change, [them] the Catholic Church anathematizes."

Obviously, this creed has much false doctrine that confuses a sincere seeker of truth about the Godhead. It would seem to be the type of creed spoken of by the Savior to Joseph Smith during the First Vision (JS—H 1:19).

NOBLE AND GREAT ONES

Spirits who had progressed in premortality to the point that they were among the most valiant and faithful spirit children of God. Abraham spoke of these when he said, "Now the Lord had shown unto me, Abraham, the intelligences that were organized before the world was; and among all these there were many of the noble and great ones; And God saw these souls that they were good, and he stood in the midst of them, and he said: These I will make my rulers; for he stood among those that were spirits, and he saw that they were good; and he said unto me: Abraham, thou art one of them; thou wast chosen before thou wast born" (Abraham 3:22–23).

President Ezra Taft Benson taught that many of these "noble and great ones" have been reserved to come to earth in the last days (CR [Oct. 1989]: 48).

·O·

OATH

See also OATH AND COVENANT OF THE PRIESTHOOD. As used in the scriptures, an oath is a "most solemn promise." It adds strength and absolute surety to a promise. In ancient cultures, when a person "swore an oath," that was the end of the matter. It was a sure thing that the promise would be kept. Personal honor and cultural expectation demanded that the promise be kept.

An example of such an oath is found in the Book of Mormon when Nephi swore an oath to Zoram that, if he would remain with Lehi's company in the wilderness, he would have complete freedom and would be treated as an equal. Zoram "made an oath that he would tarry with us" and thus, any concerns about the matter were completely over (1 Nephi 4:31–35).

The most powerful oath of all, anciently, was one sworn using words that in one way or another used the "living God" as the basis for the oath (1 Nephi 4:32). God Himself uses this type of oath in affirming His promises to His children (Jeremiah 22:5; Amos 6:8; D&C 97:20).

In our day, the Lord gives the Melchizedek Priesthood to worthy men by an "oath and covenant" (D&C 84:39–40). A proper understanding of the definition of "oath" gives additional impact to this sacred ordinance.

OATH AND COVENANT OF THE PRIESTHOOD

See also OATH. The Oath and Covenant of the Priesthood is found in section 84 of the Doctrine and Covenants. It is defined and described in verses 33–42. It consists of a set of promises made between God and those who receive the Melchizedek Priesthood. Obligations are involved and blessings are promised to those who honor and magnify this priesthood.

The obligation for worthy men is:

1. To obtain the Aaronic and the Melchizedek Priesthood (v. 33).

2. To magnify, in other words, faithfully fulfill, their calling (v. 33).

3. To receive the Melchizedek Priesthood, in other words, internalize it and make it an active part of daily living and

service, thus reflecting the Savior and the Father in their lives and into the lives of others (v. 35).

4. To faithfully support and follow Church leaders (v. 36).

5. To receive Christ as the Savior (v. 36).

6. To receive the Father and His plan by accepting the Savior and His gospel (vs. 37).

The promised blessings include:

1. Being "sanctified by the Spirit" (v. 33), which includes being guided and purified by the Holy Ghost in order to effectively use the priesthood in the service of others. "Sanctified" can be defined as "being made pure and holy and capable of being in the presence of God."

2. "The renewing of their bodies" (vs. 33) includes two specifics: (1) receiving celestial bodies in the resurrection (D&C 88:28–29), and (2) receiving extra energy to continue in service to others during mortality.

3. Becoming "the sons of Moses and of Aaron and the seed of Abraham, and the church and kingdom, and the elect of God" (v. 34), which are terms meaning exaltation. For example, if you are the seed of Abraham, you are an heir to his blessings (Abraham 2:9–11). Since he has

already become a god (D&C 132:29, 37), faithful Melchizedek Priesthood holders will likewise become gods.

4. Receiving "all that my Father hath" (v. 38), in other words, exaltation, becoming gods (D&C 132:20).

We understand that the oath is the promise that "all that my Father hath shall be given unto him" (v. 38). In other words, it is the Father's promise to faithful Melchizedek Priesthood holders.

The covenant (v. 40) is what the faithful priesthood brethren promise in return, in order to qualify for the Father's oath. By way of review, these men covenant to receive, to magnify, to serve others, and to keep the commandments.

The terms "oath" and "covenant," used together here, are a reminder of the serious nature of receiving the Melchizedek Priesthood. A stern warning is attached (v. 41).

One additional thought: While verse 35 is generally understood to pertain to men, as they accept the call to hold the Melchizedek Priesthood and serve others with it, it can, in a very important sense, pertain to all faithful members, male and female, who enter into, that is, who "receive" Melchizedek Priesthood covenants. D&C 132:19 makes it clear that when faithful men and women enter into covenants performed by "him who is anointed, unto whom I have appointed

this power and the keys of this priesthood," and live worthily thereafter, they will enter exaltation and become gods (D&C 132:20).

OBEDIENCE

"Obedience is the first law of heaven" (MD, p. 539). Through obedience, the door is opened for blessings from heaven (D&C 130:20–21). The kind of obedience meant by this topic is faith obedience. Faith obedience is different from blind obedience. Faith obedience means obedience to God's laws and commandments because of faith in the Savior and His gospel. "Blind obedience" generally means obeying without any idea as to why it is necessary or even important.

Obedience to God's commandments opens the door to additional knowledge and understanding. Adam is an example of this gospel principle. When Adam and Eve were cast out of the Garden of Eden, they were commanded to offer sacrifices (Moses 5:5). No other explanation was given other than to do it. Adam obediently built an altar and did it.

After "many days" of obedience, an angel of the Lord appeared and asked, "Why dost thou offer sacrifices unto the Lord?" Adam's answer was simple and to the point: "I know not, save the Lord commanded me" (Moses 5:6), which is a perfect example of obedience, based on faith in the Lord. Watch what happens next.

As a result of this obedience, the angel gave them much additional knowledge, explaining the symbolism of the sacrifice Adam was offering (Moses 5:7–8). The Holy Ghost came, and both Adam and Eve received a marvelous testimony coupled with understanding about the blessings of mortality (Moses 5:9–11). All of this came because of faithful obedience.

The same principle applies in our lives. Obedience puts us in a position to learn. Keeping the commandments brings the Spirit. The Spirit teaches us all things (John 14:26; 15:26; 16:13). For the faithful, this process will repeat itself over and over until they enter exaltation and "comprehend even God" (D&C 88:49).

OBEISANCE

To bow down and worship someone or something, or to show respect and honor to someone or something (Genesis 37:7; 43:28; Exodus 18:7; 1 Kings 1:16; 2 Chronicles 24:17).

OBLATIONS

Sacrifices and offerings given in worshipping the Lord (Leviticus 7:38; Isaiah 1:13; Ezekiel 20:40). In our day, the Lord spoke of oblations to Him (D&C 59:12). For us, "oblations" means "offerings, whether of time, talents, or means, in service of God and fellowman" (footnote 12b for D&C 59).

OCCULT

A term that refers to so-called magic, sorcery, black magic, fortunetelling, astrology, Ouija boards, and so forth, to which people go for revelation, inspiration, power, and glory, instead of approaching the Lord for guidance. Occult sources do not require humility and righteous living, whereas obtaining guidance and help from God does. Therefore, the occult leads away from God.

OFFICES IN THE PRIESTHOOD

Offices in the Aaronic Priesthood are deacon, teacher, priest, and bishop. Offices in the Melchizedek Priesthood are elder, seventy, high priest, patriarch, and Apostle.

OFFSPRING OF GOD

We are the literal spirit offspring of God (Acts 17:28–29). He is the Father of our spirits (Hebrews 12:9). We are spirit sons and daughters of "heavenly parents" ("Proclamation," paragraph 2).

We were literally born as spirit children and then raised to maturity as spirits in premortality. "Man, as a spirit, was begotten and born of heavenly parents, and reared to maturity in the eternal mansions of the Father, prior to coming upon the earth" ("The Mormon View of Evolution," First Presidency Statement, *Improvement Era*, Sept., 1925).

OIL, CONSECRATED

See CONSECRATED OIL.

OLD TESTAMENT

The portion of the Bible that deals with the time period from the Creation and Adam and Eve down to Malachi, who was a prophet about 400 BC.

The Old Testament consists of thirty-nine books. The Church accepts it to be the word of God, "as far as it is translated correctly" (Articles of Faith 1:8).

OLIVE OIL

See also CONSECRATED OIL. Olive oil was prized for many uses in biblical times, including healing and giving light in lanterns. There is much symbolism attached to olive oil. Among other things, it was used in lamps to make light. Olive oil came from olive trees, which symbolized Israel or the Lord's covenant people. Thus, the Lord's people are commanded to "let [their] light . . . shine" (Matthew 5:16) to light the way for others to come unto Christ.

OMEGA

See ALPHA AND OMEGA.

OMNIPOTENT

A term that means "all powerful." It is used in reference to God (Revelation 19:6; Mosiah 3:17; 5:2).

OMNIPOTENT GOD

See OMNIPOTENT.

OMNIPRESENCE

A term that means "everywhere present." There is a false doctrine held by many religions that God, personally, is omnipresent. And this leads to a false belief that He is indefinable and completely indescribable, is everywhere present, fills the immensity of space, and is yet so small that He dwells in everyone's heart, etc.

In reality, God the Father is an individual personage, with a resurrected body of flesh and bone (D&C 130:22), and is thus limited to being in just one particular place at a time. However, just as is the case with the light and warmth of the sun, His influence can be everywhere present.

OMNISCIENCE

A term which means having unlimited knowledge that God is omniscient.

ONE ETERNAL ROUND

See also ETERNITY TO ETERNITY. A scriptural phrase (1 Nephi 10:19; D&C 35:1) meaning that the same laws, rules, and gospel always apply in God's work for the salvation and exaltation of His children. It is another way of saying that He is always reliable. We can trust Him completely. If we follow His teachings and commandments, we can always plan on the same results, in terms of attaining exaltation.

ONE FLESH

The primary meaning of this phrase in the scriptures is that a man and woman, when married, should live together in unity and harmony, serving and being a blessing to each other (Genesis 2:24; Matthew 19:4–6).

ONE HUNDRED AND FORTY-FOUR THOUSAND

This phrase comes from Revelation 7:4–8. Joseph Smith defined it, in question/answer format, as follows: "Q. What are we to understand by sealing the one hundred and forty-four thousand, out of all the tribes of Israel—twelve thousand out of every tribe? A. We are to understand that those who are sealed are high priests, ordained unto the holy order of God, to administer the everlasting gospel; for they are they who are ordained out of every nation, kindred, tongue, and people, by the angels to whom is given power over the nations of the earth, to bring as many as will come to the church of the Firstborn" (D&C 77:11).

Thus, it appears, among other things, that they are part of a great missionary force which will be involved in getting the gospel to everyone, before the end of the world and the day of final judgment.

ONLY BEGOTTEN OF THE FATHER

Another name for Jesus Christ (John 1:14; Alma 5:48; D&C 76:23). "Begotten" means "conceived by" or "son of" or "daughter of." Since we are all "begotten" spirit sons and daughters of the Father (Hebrews 12:9), in other words, we were born to Him in the premortal life, this phrase needs a little more explanation.

Jesus is literally our elder brother and was the firstborn spirit child of Heavenly Father (Colossians 1:12–15). We were all born as spirits, after He was born in premortality. He is also the "only begotten Son of God in the flesh," meaning that He is the only one born into mortality whose father is Heavenly Father. Mary was His mortal mother. All the rest of us have an earthly father and mother.

ONLY BEGOTTEN SON OF GOD

See ONLY BEGOTTEN OF THE FATHER.

ONLY BEGOTTEN SON

See ONLY BEGOTTEN OF THE FATHER.

OPEN REBELLION

A phrase meaning to know and understand the gospel of Jesus Christ but refusing to live it (Mosiah 2:36–37).

OPPOSITION IN ALL THINGS

Opposition is part of the Father's plan for us. It helps us gain strength and perspective in living the gospel regardless of personal cost. Lehi set the stage for teaching his sons about the Fall and the Atonement by explaining the role of opposition in the plan He taught:

2 Nephi 2:11–16

11 For it must needs be, that there is an opposition in all things. If not so, my first-born in the wilderness, righteousness could not be brought to pass, neither wickedness,

neither holiness nor misery, neither good nor bad. Wherefore, all things must needs be a compound in one; wherefore, if it should be one body it must needs remain as dead, having no life neither death, nor corruption nor incorruption, happiness nor misery, neither sense nor insensibility.

12 Wherefore, it must needs have been created for a thing of naught; wherefore there would have been no purpose in the end of its creation. Wherefore, this thing must needs destroy the wisdom of God and his eternal purposes, and also the power, and the mercy, and the justice of God.

13 And if ye shall say there is no law, ye shall also say there is no sin. If ye shall say there is no sin, ye shall also say there is no righteousness. And if there be no righteousness there be no happiness. And if there be no righteousness nor happiness there be no punishment nor misery. And if these things are not there is no God. And if there is no God we are not, neither the earth; for there could have been no creation of things, neither to act nor to be acted upon; wherefore, all things must have vanished away.

14 And now, my sons, I speak unto you these things for your profit and learning; for there is a God, and he hath created all things, both the heavens and the earth, and all things that in them are, both things to act and things to be acted upon.

15 And to bring about his eternal purposes in the end of man, after he had created our first parents, and the beasts of the field and the fowls of the air, and in fine, all things which are created, it must needs be that there was an opposition; even the forbidden fruit in opposition to the tree of life; the one being sweet and the other bitter.

16 Wherefore, the Lord God gave unto man that he should act for himself. Wherefore, man could not act for himself save it should be that he was enticed by the one or the other.

ORACLES
See LIVING ORACLES.

ORDAIN
In terms of ordinances, the use of this word today is limited to priesthood ordinations. However, in the early days of the Church, before gospel vocabulary had been "fine-tuned," so to speak, "they used the term *ordain . . .* for everything" (*DS* 3:106), including for being "set apart." An example of this is found in D&C 25:7, where Emma Smith was to be ordained, in other words, set apart, to teach in the Church.

ORDAINED PATRIARCHS
Patriarch is an office in the Melchizedek Priesthood. All patriarchs who are called to give patriarchal blessings are ordained patriarchs. This title differentiates between such patriarchs and the use of the word

"patriarch" to mean head of a family, or in reference to ancient "patriarchs" such as Adam and Abraham (Hebrews 7:4; Abraham 1:31).

ORDINANCES

Ordinances are rites and ceremonies performed for members of the Church by holders of the priesthood. These include naming and blessing of children, baptism, confirmation, sacrament, having the priesthood conferred upon them (in the case of male members of the Church), being ordained to various offices in the Aaronic and Melchizedek priesthood, being set apart for callings, dedication of graves, dedicating buildings, washings and anointings, endowments, temple marriage, sealings, administering to the sick, consecrating oil, blessings of counsel and comfort, father's blessings, and patriarchal blessings.

No ordinances are required for entrance into the telestial or terrestrial kingdoms. No ordinances are required for entrance into the celestial kingdom for children under age eight (D&C 137:10) or for intellectually handicapped individuals (D&C 29:50).

However, for those over age eight, the ordinances of baptism and confirmation are required for entrance into the celestial kingdom (John 3:3–5; D&C 76:51–52). And for those desiring to attain the highest degree of glory within the celestial kingdom, Melchizedek Priesthood (for men) is required, plus the ordinances of temple endowments and temple marriage or sealing (D&C 131:1–4; 132:19–20).

ORDINATION

The laying on of hands by those in authority to bestow the priesthood office of deacon, teacher, priest, bishop, elder, seventy, high priest, patriarch, or Apostle upon a worthy male member of the Church.

ORDINATIONS
See ORDINATION.

ORDINATIONS TO THE PRIESTHOOD
See ORDINATION.

ORGAN DONATIONS
See BODY PARTS, DONATION OF.

ORGAN TRANSPLANTS

Bishops and stake presidents are in possession of information from the Church on this matter. Basically, the policy of the Church is that donating organs and tissue, or receiving such, is an individual decision and is not a matter of right or wrong.

ORGANIC EVOLUTION
See EVOLUTION.

ORGANIZATION OF THE CHURCH

As an official organization, The Church of Jesus Christ of Latter-day Saints came into being on April 6, 1830 (D&C 20:1; 21, heading). It was organized with six official members, according to the laws of the state of New York, at the Peter Whitmer Sr. home in Fayette, New York. About fifty people were in attendance at the organization.

ORIGIN OF MAN

See EVOLUTION.

ORIGINAL SIN

A false doctrine that all who are born, except Jesus Christ and his mother, Mary, are "tainted" with sin and evil at birth because of the transgression of Adam and Eve. John Calvin taught, "We believe that all the posterity of Adam is in bondage to original sin, which is a hereditary evil" (Reed, *The Gospel as Taught by Calvin*, p. 33). As a result of such beliefs and dogmas, some churches have taught that infants who are not baptized and die remain unholy and are excluded forever from heaven and the presence of God.

The teaching of The Church of Jesus Christ of Latter-day Saints on this matter was summarized by Joseph Smith as follows: "We believe that men will be punished for their own sins, and not for Adam's transgression" (Articles of Faith 1:2). And, as far as children under age eight are concerned, "all children who die before they arrive at the years of accountability are saved in the celestial kingdom of heaven" (D&C 137:10).

OTHER SHEEP

This phrase comes from John 10:16, where it refers to the people on the American continent to whom the Savior appeared after His resurrection (3 Nephi 15:21).

During the Savior's visit to the Nephites on the American continent, He spoke of yet other "sheep" whom He would also visit (3 Nephi 16:1–3). These were the lost tribes of Israel (3 Nephi 17:4).

OUIJA BOARDS

See OCCULT.

OUT OF WEDLOCK BIRTHS

In "The Family: A Proclamation to the World," the First Presidency and the Quorum of the Twelve Apostles made the following statement: "Children are entitled to birth within the bonds of matrimony, and to be reared by a father and a mother who honor marital vows with complete fidelity." Thus, in cases where it is highly unlikely that the birth parents can marry successfully, the Church counsels them to place the baby for adoption, preferably to an LDS married couple where the infant can be reared in a gospel-centered home.

The following statement is from the LDS Family Services website, in August 2007:

"Numerous studies show that children do better in stable, loving families with both a mother and a father. Most important, children who are adopted by temple-worthy Latter-day Saint couples can be sealed to their parents.

"But children are not the only

ones who benefit from adoption. Studies show that single mothers who place their children for adoption are more likely to finish school, are less likely to live in poverty, and have fewer physical or emotional health problems.

"Contrary to what some may believe, unwed parents who place their children for adoption are not taking 'the easy way out' or abandoning their responsibility. Instead, they are placing the needs of their children before their own feelings and desires—the essence of true parenthood. Such a decision is deserving of the highest commendation and respect."

OUTER DARKNESS

A term commonly used in gospel discussions to mean "perdition or the place where Satan and the sons of perdition will go" (D&C 88:114). The final dwelling place of these individuals is described in D&C 76:36–37, 44–48. The term "perdition" is used in the book of Revelation to explain their final condition (Revelation 17:8, 11).

The phrase "outer darkness," as used in the Bible, Book of Mormon, and Doctrine and Covenants, means hell, or being turned over to Satan in the prison portion of the spirit world (Matthew 8:12; 22:13; Alma 40:13; D&C 101:91).

·P·

PAGAN

See also HEATHEN. Depending on context, the term "pagan," as used today, can mean one who is not a Christian, a Muslim, or a Jew. The word "pagan" does not appear in our scriptures. Rather, the term "heathen" is used. Idol worship was common among heathen nations during the time of the children of Israel.

PAGAN CHURCHES

See also PAGAN. So-called pagan churches are those that do not believe in or worship the true God.

PAGAN GODS

See also PAGAN; PAGAN CHURCHES. The phrase "pagan gods" is a term used in referring to idols and false gods worshiped by heathen nations.

PAGANISM

See PAGAN; PAGAN CHURCHES; PAGAN GODS.

PAGANS

See PAGAN.

PAGEANTS

"In the Church, pageants are outdoor theatrical productions that celebrate a place, person, or event in religious history. Some pageants depict the earthly mission of the Savior and his dealings with covenant peoples in Jerusalem and the New World, both before and after his resurrection. Other pageants dramatize some historical aspect of how the Church in this dispensation fulfills its mission of taking the gospel of Jesus Christ to every nation, kindred, tongue, and people" (*EM*, under "Pageants").

A number of pageants are sponsored annually by the Church or by local Church units. Information about these events can usually be located on the Church website, lds. org, under "News and Events."

PALESTINE

A general term often used in gospel lessons and discussions in referring to the Holy Land.

PALM READING

See also OCCULT. This type of occult activity was strictly forbidden by the law of Moses (Leviticus 19:31; 20:6; 1 Samuel 28:3; Isaiah 8:19).

Participating in palm reading is discouraged by the Church today. Those who get caught up in it tend to seek guidance from this and other evil sources, rather than keeping their lives in order such that they can receive correct guidance from God.

PALM, SYMBOLISM OF

See also HOSANNA SHOUT. Palm leaves or fronds are symbolic, in bib-lical cultures, of triumph and victory (Revelation 7:9).

PALM SUNDAY

The Sunday before Easter Sunday, on which some churches celebrate the Savior's triumphal entry into Jerusalem (Matthew 21:111). When Jesus arrived in Jerusalem, riding on a donkey, the people cheered Him and welcomed Him by laying their cloaks on the ground as a pathway for Him. They also cut "branches of palm trees" (John 12:13) to wave as they "went forth to meet him." The waving of palm branches symbolized triumph and victory in their culture. They hoped that Jesus would exercise His miraculous power and give them triumph and victory over the Romans.

PANTHEISM

The false doctrine that there are many gods who are worshiped in many different forms by different cults and religious groups. Another form or variation of pantheism is that God is not a person or personality, rather that all of nature, including the universe, is God. Yet another variation of pantheism is spoken of by Paul when he notes that apostates have "changed the truth of God into a lie; and worshipped and served the creature more than the Creator" (Romans 1:25). In other words, they worship the creations of God rather than God.

PAPYRI, JOSEPH SMITH

"The term 'Joseph Smith papyri' refers narrowly to twelve extant pieces of the Egyptian papyrus that the Prophet Joseph Smith acquired from Michael H. Chandler in July 1835. Located in the Church Archives, these fragments range in size from 7.5 in. x 12.5 in. to 6.5 in. x 4.5 in. Facsimile No. 1 in the book of Abraham came from one of these fragments. Broadly, the term also refers to Facsimiles Nos. 2 and 3 in the same book and to papers and all the Egyptian materials of the Kirtland period of Church history containing small sections of copied papyrus text" (*EM*, under "Papyri, Joseph Smith").

For a few additional historical details about the papyri, we will quote from the Institute of Religion Church history manual: "In a tomb on the west bank of the Nile River across from the ancient Egyptian city of Thebes (now called Luxor), Antonio Lebolo, a French-speaking explorer from the Piedmont (a region of north-western Italy), discovered several mummies and along with them some papyrus scrolls. Following the death of Lebolo in 1830, the mummies and papyri were shipped to the United States, where Michael H. Chandler, who identified himself as Lebolo's nephew, came into possession of them in 1833. In 1835 Chandler displayed his artifacts in several eastern cities.

"When he came to Kirtland at the end of June, the Saints showed great interest in the mummies and papyri. Chandler had heard that Joseph Smith claimed he could translate ancient records. He asked Joseph if he could translate the papyri. Orson Pratt recalled, 'The Prophet took them and repaired to his room and inquired of the Lord concerning them. The Lord told him they were sacred records' and revealed the translation of some of the characters. Chandler had previously submitted a few characters from the records to scholars in order to deter-mine their probable meaning. Upon receiving the Prophet's translation, he provided a signed testimonial that it corresponded 'in the most minute matters' with those of the scholars.

"Greatly interested in their content, the Saints purchased the mummies and scrolls for twenty-four hundred dollars. Joseph immediately began working with the scrolls and found that they contained the writings of Abraham and the writings of Joseph who was sold into Egypt. 'Truly we can say, the Lord is beginning to reveal the abundance of peace and truth.' During the rest of his time in Kirtland he maintained an active interest in working with these ancient writings. The fruit of his efforts, the book of Abraham, was not printed, however, until 1842 after more trans-lating was completed in Nauvoo. In February 1843 the Prophet promised to supply more of the translation of the book of Abraham, but his demanding schedule did not allow him time to complete the work before he was assassinated" (*Church History in the Fulness of Times*, p. 159).

PARABLES

The Savior used at least forty parables in His teaching during His mortal mission, as recorded in the Bible. "Parable" comes from a Greek word and basically means "placing two things side by side." Thus, the Savior placed the spiritual message He was teaching "side by side" with something in the daily lives of His listeners that they could easily relate to. For example, in the parable of the pearl of great price (Matthew 13:45–46), the message is that the gospel is worth everything we have. This message "is laid side by side" with a real life situation where a man finds a most valuable pearl for sale and sells everything he has to purchase it.

The Prophet Joseph Smith gave us a "key" for understanding parables. He said: "I have a key by which I understand the scriptures. I enquire, what was the question which drew out the answer, or caused Jesus to utter the parable?" (*TPJS*, pp. 276–77).

The Bible Dictionary explains why the Savior used parables: "From our Lord's words (Matthew 13:13–15; Mark 4:12; Luke 8:10) we learn the reason for this method. It was to veil the meaning. The parable conveys to the hearer religious truth exactly in proportion to his faith and intelligence; to the dull and uninspired it is a mere story, 'seeing they see not,' while to the instructed and spiritual it reveals the mysteries or secrets of the kingdom of heaven. Thus it is that the parable exhibits the condition of all true knowledge. Only he who seeks finds" (BD, under "Parables").

The Gospel of John has no actual parables, by strict definition, although it does have two allegories, the good shepherd (John 10:1–16), and the vine and the branches (John 15:1–7).

Several of the Savior's parables are found in two or more of the Gospels besides John (Matthew, Mark, and Luke). But several are found only in Matthew or Mark or Luke. A list of those that appear only once follows:

Matthew

1. The wheat and the tares (Matthew 13:24–30).
2. The hidden treasure (Matthew 13:44).
3. The pearl of great price (Matthew 13:45–46).
4. The net (Matthew 13:47–50).
5. The unmerciful servant (Matthew 18:23–35).
6. The laborers in the vineyard (Matthew 20:1–16).
7. The two sons (Matthew 21:28–32).
8. The marriage of the king's son (Matthew 22:1–10).
9. The ten virgins (Matthew 25:1–13).
10. The talents (Matthew 25:14–30).

Mark

1. The seed growing secretly (Mark 4:26–29).

Luke

1. The two debtors (Luke 7:41–43).
2. The good Samaritan (Luke 10:30–37).

3. The importuned friend (Luke 11:5–8).

4. The foolish rich man (Luke 12:16–21).

5. The barren fig tree (Luke 13:6–9).

6. The lost piece of silver (Luke 15:8–10).

7. The prodigal son (11–32).

8. The unjust steward (Luke 16:1–12).

9. Lazarus and the rich man (Luke 16:19–31).

10. The unjust judge (Luke 18:1–7).

11. The Pharisee and the Publican (Luke 18:9–14).

12. The parable of the pounds (Luke 19:11–27).

We will include one parable and provide notes giving a possible interpretation. Remember, at the beginning of this topic, we said that "parable" means "placing two things side by side," in other words, using familiar things from daily life to be symbolic of a gospel message. We will use the parable of the barren fig tree as our example:

The Parable of the Barren Fig Tree

6 He spake also this parable [*a story that teaches a particular point*]; A certain man [*the Father*] had a fig tree [*the Jews*] planted in his vineyard [*on earth*]; and he came and sought fruit [*looked for righteous lives*] thereon [*among the Jews*], and found none.

7 Then said he unto the dresser of his vineyard [*symbolic of Christ; see*

Talmage, Jesus the Christ, *p. 443*], Behold, these three years [*the three years of Christ's mission*] I come seeking fruit [*righteousness*] on this fig tree [*among the Jews*], and find none: cut it down [*John the Baptist said, "Now . . . the axe is laid unto the root of the trees" (Luke 3:9); in other words, destruction is almost here for the wicked Jews*]; why cumbereth it the ground [*why let it keep cluttering the earth*]?

8 And he [*Jesus*] answering said unto him, Lord, let it alone this year also, till I shall dig about it [*cultivate it*], and dung it [*nourish it; in other words, let's give the Jews one more chance to repent*]:

9 And if it bear fruit, well [*if they do, wonderful!*]: and if not, then after that [*this one more chance*] thou shalt cut it down [*destroy their nation*].

The Jews did not take advantage of this last opportunity, at that time, to repent. They crucified Christ and persecuted His followers. The Romans completed the destruction of Jerusalem and the Jews as a nation about AD 70–73.

PARADISE

See also SPIRIT PRISON; SPIRIT WORLD. Paradise is the place in the postmortal spirit world where the righteous go when they die. The Book of Mormon describes paradise as follows: "The spirits of those who are righteous are received into a state of happiness, which is called paradise, a state of rest, a state of peace, where they shall rest from all their troubles and from all care, and sorrow" (Alma 40:12).

The term "paradise" is not used in the Old Testament but is used three times in the New Testament. As used in Luke 23:43, where the Savior is speaking to the thief on the cross, it means the postmortal spirit world. As used in 2 Corinthians 12:2–4, it can mean celestial glory or perhaps even the highest degree of glory in the celestial kingdom. As used in Revelation 2:7, it means the celestial kingdom.

"Paradise" is used five times in the Book of Mormon (2 Nephi 9:14; Alma 40:12, 14; 4 Nephi 1:14; Moroni 10:34) and each time, it means the part of the postmortal spirit world where the spirits of the righteous go when they die. The word "paradise" is also used in D&C 77:2, 5, in explaining Revelation 2:6.

When the scriptures say that the "righteous" go to paradise, the reference is to baptized, faithful members of the Church, as well as to children who die before the age of accountability (D&C 137:10) and also to the intellectually handicapped who are still childlike in their mental capabilities (D&C 29:50). Speaking of the postmortal spirit world and those who are accountable, who go to paradise after dying, Joseph Fielding Smith taught: "As I understand it, *the righteous—meaning those who have been baptized and who have been faithful*—are gathered in one part and all the others in another part of the spirit world. This seems to be true from the

vision given to President Joseph F. Smith [see D&C 138]" (*DS* 2:230).

The above teaching about those who are accountable and who go to paradise is confirmed in *True to the Faith*: "Paradise . . . is a place of peace and happiness in the postmortal spirit world, reserved for those who have been baptized and who have remained faithful (see Alma 40:12; Moroni 10:34). Those in spirit prison have the opportunity to learn the gospel of Jesus Christ, repent of their sins, and receive the ordinances of baptism and confirmation through the work we do in temples (see D&C 138:30–35). When they do, they may enter paradise" (*TF*, p. 111).

This doctrine pertaining to who goes to paradise can appear to be a contradiction to what the Savior said to the thief on the cross. He said, "To day shalt thou be with me in paradise" (Luke 23:43). However, the Bible Dictionary clarifies this. In it we read, "Paradise is that part of the spirit world in which the righteous spirits who have departed from this life await the resurrection of the body. It is a condition of happiness and peace. However, the scriptures are not always consistent in the use of the word [paradise], especially in the Bible. For example, when Jesus purportedly said to the thief on the cross, 'To day shalt thou be with me in paradise' (Luke 23:43), the Bible rendering is incorrect. The statement would more accurately read, 'Today shalt thou be with me in the world of spirits' since the thief was not ready for paradise (see *HC* 5:424–25)" (BD, under "Paradise").

Brigham Young described what it will be like for those who die and go to paradise: "We shall turn round and look upon it [the valley of death] and think, when we have crossed it, why this is the greatest advantage of my whole existence, for I have passed from a state of sorrow, grief, mourning, woe, misery, pain, anguish and disappointment into a state of existence, where I can enjoy life to the fullest extent as far as that can be done without a body. My spirit is set free, I thirst no more, I want to sleep no more, I hunger no more, I tire no more, I run, I walk, I labor, I go, I come, I do this, I do that, whatever is required of me, nothing like pain or weariness, I am full of life, full of vigor, and I enjoy the presence of my heavenly Father" (*JD* 17:142; see also *Doctrines of the Gospel Student Manual*, p. 83).

Our understanding about the qualifications for those who enter paradise upon dying leads to the conclusion that there is a large variety of people who enter spirit prison upon their death in mortality. This would include a wide range of individuals, from the good and honorable to the vilest of sinners. They are in "prison" (1 Peter 3:19), in other words, the spirit world mission field (D&C 138), because they do not have the redeeming ordinances of the gospel, which can "set them free" (John 8:32) to enter paradise.

It becomes clear that the spirit world mission field, or spirit prison, is much like being on this earth. There are many good and honorable people who are not members of the Church who desire truth but who have not yet had a complete opportunity to hear and understand the gospel. Likewise, there are many wicked who are intentionally evil. The sincere and good spirits who accept the gospel when they hear and understand it in the spirit prison, as well as the wicked postmortal spirits who repent (see D&C 138:32), will receive every privilege and blessing of the gospel, through the proxy temple work which is done for them by mortals.

This doctrine is very comforting to those who worry about good and honorable loved ones and friends who have died but are not yet in paradise. They realize that these loved ones are not being punished by being sent to the spirit prison, or mission field. Rather, they are being given an opportunity to hear, understand, and accept the gospel, just as is the case with people on the earth. Furthermore, they must accept it in an environment of opposition and diversity of thinking and belief systems, just as we here on earth must. If they accept it and are faithful there in the spirit world mission field, they have every opportunity of obtaining the highest degree of glory in the celestial kingdom, just as we have here on earth, once their temple work is done by mortals, either here now, or during the Millennium.

The question arises as to whether or not Satan and the evil spirits who were cast down to earth with him

(Revelation 12:4) can also tempt in the postmortal spirit world. They can tempt in the prison portion of the postmortal spirit world. However, they cannot tempt in paradise. Brigham Young summarized this doctrine as follows: "If we are faithful to our religion, when we go into the spirit world, the fallen spirits—Lucifer and the third part of the heavenly hosts that came with him, and the spirits of wicked men who have dwelt upon this earth, . . . will have no influence over our spirits. . . . All the rest of the children of men are more or less subject to them, and they are subject to them as they were while here in the flesh" (*Teachings of the Presidents of the Church—Brigham Young*, p. 282. Church study course for 2000).

PARADISIACAL EARTH

When the Savior comes at the time of the Second Coming, He will usher in the Millennium (D&C 29:11). The righteous will be taken up to meet Him as he comes (D&C 88:96), and the wicked will be burned (2 Nephi 12:10, 19, 21; D&C 133:41, 64). The earth will be cleansed from wickedness and "will be renewed and receive its paradisiacal glory" (Articles of Faith 1:10). This "paradisiacal earth" will be like the Garden of Eden, and peace will prevail (Isaiah 65:25) for a thousand years (D&C 29:11; Revelation 20:4).

PARENTS, OUR FIRST

This phrase is a reference to Adam and Eve (1 Nephi 5:11).

PASCHAL LAMB

The lamb slain and eaten during the Passover. It was symbolic of Christ and His Atonement for us.

PASSION OF CHRIST

The suffering and agony of the Savior in the Garden of Gethsemane and His death on the cross.

PASSIONS

Some beliefs and systems of religion teach that passions are evil and should be eliminated as far as possible in our mortal lives. They believe that God is "without body, parts, or passions" and that mankind should eliminate personal passions in order to be more pleasing to God. This is false doctrine. The Book of Mormon teaches to "bridle all your passions" (Alma 38:12), rather than eliminating them.

PASSOVER

A commemoration and feast celebrated anciently by the Israelites in memory of the fact that the destroying angel "passed over" the dwellings of the children of Israel and did not slay their firstborn, after they put the blood of a lamb on their door posts (Exodus 12:21–29). On the other hand, the firstborn of the Egyptians was slain, thus setting the stage for the children of Israel to be set free from their Egyptian bondage.

Many Jews today celebrate Passover yearly in March or April. It corresponds to Easter season for Christians. You can read more about

Passover in the Bible Dictionary, under "Feasts."

PASTORS

A term that can mean any church leaders who are in charge of a group, class, congregation, ward, branch, stake, and so forth (Ephesians 4:11). It is not a commonly used term in the Church.

PATRIARCH

As used in the scriptures, "patriarch" has two main meanings: (1) An ancient ancestor such as David (Acts 2:29) or Abraham (Hebrews 7:4). (2) A worthy priesthood holder who has been ordained to the office of patriarch and who gives patriarchal blessings, such as Hyrum Smith (D&C 124:91).

PATRIARCHS, STAKE

See also PATRIARCHAL BLESSINGS. Each stake in the Church has at least one worthy man who has been ordained to the office of patriarch in the Melchizedek Priesthood and who gives patriarchal blessings to worthy members of the stake.

The New Testament uses the term "evangelists" to mean "patriarchs" (Ephesians 4:11). Joseph Smith taught, "An Evangelist is a Patriarch, even the oldest man of the blood of Joseph or of the seed of Abraham. Wherever the Church of Christ is established in the earth, there should be a Patriarch for the benefit of the posterity of the Saints, as it was with Jacob in giving his patriarchal

blessing unto his sons, etc." (*HC* 3:379–381; *TPJS*, p. 151).

PATRIARCH TO THE CHURCH

We will use a quote from the *Encyclopedia of Mormonism* to explain this office. "Before 1979, Patriarch to the Church was a Church officer whose chief duty was to confer patriarchal blessings on Church members who generally did not have the service of stake Patriarchs readily available to them. The Prophet Joseph Smith explained that an 'evangelist' (as in Ephesians 4:11) is a 'patriarch' (*TPJS*, p. 151); that is, he confers the blessings of a patriarch upon members of the Church. Patriarchs are currently ordained in individual stakes of the Church, but for many years there was a patriarch to the entire Church. He was considered one of the General Authorities.

"On December 18, 1833, in Kirtland, Ohio, Joseph Smith, Sr., was ordained the first Patriarch to the Church (D&C 107:39–56), with jurisdiction throughout the Church. Upon his death, he was succeeded by his oldest living son, Hyrum Smith, who served until he was martyred on June 27, 1844. William Smith, a younger brother, was ordained Patriarch to the Church on May 24, 1845, by the Quorum of the Twelve Apostles, but William was rejected by the Church on October 6, 1845, for misconduct. The office was vacant until January 1, 1849, when John Smith, brother of Joseph Smith, Sr., was called. He served until his death on May 23, 1854.

"A second John Smith, son of Hyrum Smith, was Patriarch to the Church from February 18, 1855, until November 6, 1911. Hyrum Gibbs Smith, grandson of the second John Smith, then served from May 9, 1912, until February 4, 1932. For ten years Acting Patriarchs were called who were not in the direct hereditary line. They included Nicholas G. Smith (October 1932 to October 1934), Frank B. Woodbury (June 1935 to October 1937), and George F. Richards (October 1937 to October 1942).

"The call returned to the hereditary line on October 3, 1942, with the call of Elder Joseph Fielding Smith (1899–1964), a great-grandson of Hyrum Smith. He was released at his own request on October 7, 1946, because of poor health. Eldred G. Smith, eldest son of Hyrum Gibbs Smith, was called in April 1947.

"In 1979 the office of Patriarch to the Church was retired 'because of the large increase in the number of stake Patriarchs and the availability of patriarchal service throughout the world.' Eldred G. Smith was designated 'a Patriarch Emeritus, which means that he is honorably relieved of all duties and responsibilities pertaining to the office of Patriarch to the Church' (CR [Oct. 1979]:25)" (*EM*, under "Patriarch").

PATRIARCHAL BLESSINGS

See also LINEAGE. It is the privilege of every baptized and worthy member of the Church to obtain a patriarchal blessing from an ordained patriarch in his or her stake. Such blessings designate the person's lineage and pronounce blessings of guidance and counsel from Heavenly Father to the individual.

Obviously, a patriarchal blessing will not outline everything which will happen during the lifetime of the individual. However, such blessings usually have guidance and counsel which will be quite specific. If something significant is not mentioned at the time of the blessing (example: marriage, mission), it should not necessarily be interpreted to mean that it will not happen.

Members are counseled to read their patriarchal blessings often, so that the Holy Ghost can confirm insights already given as well as inspire and direct to new understanding of some aspects of the blessing.

PATRIARCHAL LINEAGE

See LINEAGE.

PAUL

See also EPISTLES OF PAUL. Paul was a powerfully influential Apostle and a missionary to the Gentiles. He wrote fourteen of the books of the New Testament as "epistles" (letters) to individuals and to groups of Saints in the early Church. These epistles are Romans, 1 Corinthians, 2 Corinthians, Galatians, Ephesians, Philippians, Colossians, 1 Thessalonians, 2 Thessalonians, 1 Timothy, 2 Timothy, Titus, Philemon, and Hebrews. Except for Hebrews, his letters are arranged in the New Testament according to length.

Details of Paul's early life and conversion are found in Acts 7:58, where he is known as Saul, through Acts 9:19. His missionary journeys are detailed in Acts. His first missionary journey is covered by Acts 13:1–14:26. His second journey is reported in Acts 15:36–18:22. And his third missionary journey is detailed in Acts 18:23–21:15.

Paul died as a martyr about AD 65.

PEARL OF GREAT PRICE

See also ABRAHAM, BOOK OF; ARTICLES OF FAITH; JOSEPH SMITH—MATTHEW; MOSES, BOOK OF. The Pearl of Great Price is one of the four standard works or books accepted as scripture by The Church of Jesus Christ of Latter-day Saints. It contains five books: (1) Moses, (2) Abraham, (3) Joseph Smith—Matthew, (4) Joseph Smith—History, and (5) The Articles of Faith.

The Pearl of Great Price was first published in England in 1851 by Apostle Franklin D. Richards. It was officially accepted by the Church as scripture in general conference, on October 10, 1880, in Salt Lake City, Utah.

PEARLY GATES

The phrase comes from Revelation 21:21, where the Apostle John describes the gates leading to the celestial city or the celestial kingdom of heaven which he saw in vision.

PEC

An acronym or abbreviation for Priesthood Executive Committee.

The ward PEC includes leaders of Melchizedek Priesthood quorums and leaders responsible for youth priesthood programs. A ward executive secretary prepares each meeting's agenda, and the ward clerk records its minutes.

The stake PEC includes the stake presidency and high council.

PECULIAR PEOPLE

This phrase comes from Deuteronomy 14:2 and elsewhere. It carries with it the connotation of being a covenant people, a people especially dedicated to the Lord.

PEEP STONE

Hiram Page, one of the Eight Witnesses to the Book of Mormon, came into possession of a peep stone through which he claimed to be receiving revelations about the building up of Zion and the proper order of the Church (see heading to D&C 28). His teachings, received through the stone, were at odds with those of Joseph Smith. Oliver Cowdery was among those who believed Hiram's claims.

In a revelation given to Joseph Smith in September 1830, the Lord said, "No one shall be appointed to receive commandments and revelations in this church excepting my servant Joseph Smith, Jun., for he receiveth them even as Moses" (D&C 28:2).

In that same revelation, Oliver Cowdery was instructed to take his brother-in-law Hiram Page aside, "between him and thee alone, and tell him that those things which he hath written from that stone are not of me and that Satan deceiveth him; For, behold, these things have not been appointed unto him, neither shall anything be appointed unto any of this church contrary to the church covenants. For all things must be done in order, and by common consent in the church, by the prayer of faith" (D&C 28:11–13).

Hiram and others, including Oliver, heeded the Lord's counsel and renounced the stone and the false revelations from Satan which had come by that means.

PENTATEUCH

A Greek word meaning "the five-fold book" (BD, under "Pentateuch"). The five books in the Pentateuch, which were written by Moses, are Genesis, Exodus, Leviticus, Numbers, and Deuteronomy.

PENTECOST

See DAY OF PENTECOST.

PENTECOST, DAY OF

See DAY OF PENTECOST.

PERDITION

See also OUTER DARKNESS; PERDITION, SONS OF. "Perdition" is basically defined as the final destination of Satan and the sons of perdition, as mentioned in Revelation 17:8, 11. The phrase "outer darkness" is often used by members of the Church in place of "perdition."

A description of what it takes to be cast into perdition forever is found in D&C 76:30–35.

Satan and the evil spirits who were cast out of heaven with him (Revelation 12:4, 7–9), along with mortals who became sons of perdition here on earth, will finally be cast into perdition after the "little season" at the end of the Millennium (D&C 88:111–15).

PERDITION, SONS OF

Those who become complete followers of Satan are called sons of perdition. They think like he does, and have the same evil desires and bitter hatred toward God and anything good and decent that he does. They have become completely devoid of any goodness or desire to do right, just as is the case with the devil. Information about perdition, about sons of perdition, and what is required to become a son of perdition is given in D&C 76:30–49. We will use verses 31–35 as a basic outline for this topic.

Qualifications

1. "Know my power" (D&C 76:31).

In order to "know" God and His power, one must have the witness of the Holy Ghost, concerning God and His power. Joseph Smith taught this as follows: "What must a man do to commit the unpardonable sin?

He must receive the Holy Ghost, have the heavens opened unto him, and know God, and then sin against Him. After a man has sinned against the Holy Ghost, there is no repentance for him. He has got to say that the sun does not shine while he sees it; he has got to deny Jesus Christ when the heavens have been opened unto him, and to deny the plan of salvation with his eyes open to the truth of it; and from that time he begins to be an enemy. This is the case with many apostates of The Church of Jesus Christ of Latter-day Saints" (*TPJS*, p. 358).

2. "Have been made partakers thereof" (D&C 76:31).

They are members of the Church and have all ordinances, endowments, etc., that we have available here in this life to prepare for exaltation, as explained by President Joseph F. Smith in the following quote: "And he that believes, is baptized, and receives the light and testimony of Jesus Christ . . . receiving the fulness of the blessings of the gospel in this world, and afterwards turns wholly unto sin, violating his covenants. . . will taste the second death" (Smith, *Gospel Doctrine*, pp. 476–77).

3. "Suffered themselves [*allowed themselves, through agency choices*] through the power of the devil to be overcome" (D&C 76:31).

In other words, they must intentionally allow themselves to be overcome by Satan.

4. "Deny the truth" (D&C 76:31).

They become complete liars, completely lacking integrity; in other words, they become totally dishonest, like Satan is, denying the truth when they fully know it.

5. "Defy my power" (D&C 76:31).

They don't just go inactive, but fight against God and the Church, against all that is good, with the same evil energy with which Satan and his evil hosts fight truth and right.

6. "They are vessels of wrath" (D&C 76:33).

They become full of anger, bitterness, and hatred of that which is good. In other words, they actually become like Satan. They think like he does, act like he does, and react against good like he does. This is the full opposite of becoming like Christ, through following His commandments and living His gospel.

7. "Having crucified him unto themselves and put him to an open shame" (D&C 76:35).

They become so bitter that they would gladly crucify Christ themselves if they had the opportunity. In other words, as stated above, they have become like Satan. They think like he does, hate like he does, and have the same desires and goals as he does.

Brigham Young summarized this topic (becoming sons of perdition) as follows: "How much does it take to prepare a man, or woman . . . to become angels to the devil, to suffer with him through all eternity? Just as much as it does to prepare a man to go into the Celestial Kingdom, into the presence of the Father and the Son, and to be made an heir to his kingdom and all his glory, and be crowned with crowns of glory, immortality, and eternal lives" (*JD* 3:93).

PERFECTION

We can be perfect in some things, such as not taking the name of God in vain (Exodus 20:7), paying an honest tithing, keeping the Word of Wisdom, and so forth. However, Joseph Smith taught the comforting doctrine that complete perfection will not come until long after we have departed from this life. He said, "When you climb up a ladder, you must begin at the bottom, and ascend step by step, until you arrive at the top; and so it is with the principles of the Gospel—you must begin with the first, and go on until you learn all the principles of exaltation. But it will be a great while after you have passed through the veil before you will have learned them. It is not all to be comprehended in this world; it will be a great work to learn our salvation and exaltation even beyond the grave" (*TPJS*, p. 348).

Elder Dallin H. Oaks taught, "Another idea that is powerful to lift us from discouragement is that the work of the Church . . . is an eternal work. Not all problems . . . are fixed in mortality. The work of salvation goes on beyond the veil of death, and we should not be too apprehensive about incompleteness within the limits of mortality" (CR [October 1995]).

And Joseph Fielding Smith counseled, "Salvation does not come all at once; we are commanded to be perfect even as our Father in heaven is perfect. It will take us ages to accomplish this end, for there will be greater progress beyond the grave, and it will be there that the faithful will overcome all things, and receive all things, even the fulness of the Father's glory.

"I believe the Lord meant just what he said: that we should be perfect, as our Father in heaven is perfect. That will not come all at once, but line upon line, and precept upon precept, example upon example, and even then not as long as we live in this mortal life, for we will have to go even beyond the grave before we reach that perfection and shall be like God" (*DS* 2:18–19).

PERPETUAL EDUCATION FUND

A special fund announced by President Gordon B. Hinckley on March 31, 2001, which provides loans to members of the Church seeking additional education, especially in the field of vocational education. The loans are made from the interest earned on the Perpetual Education Fund (PEF), to which members of the Church continue to donate.

One of the principles of the fund is that those who take out loans from the fund give back generously when their education is completed.

PERPETUAL IMMIGRATION FUND

A special fund set up by the Church in 1849 to assist converts to immigrate into the Salt Lake Valley and elsewhere where the Saints were settling. The funds were a combination of Church funds and private funds. Loans were made with the idea that those receiving them would pay all or part back as soon as they were able, in order for others to receive similar loans. It is estimated that about 30,000 Saints were assisted by this fund. It was discontinued in 1887.

PERSONAL ANCESTRAL FILE

A software package produced by the Church for genealogical research. With it, users can organize, store, and search information, contribute genealogies to an Ancestral File database, and match and merge information from other genealogical databases with their own files.

PERSONAL JOURNALS

See also BOOK OF REMEMBRANCE. The Church encourages members to keep personal journals. Some things that might be considered for entries include the recording of significant events such as births, baptisms, gradu-

ations, spiritual experiences, family outings, and inspiration received during scripture reading and church meetings.

PESTILENCE

A scriptural term for plagues, natural disasters, widespread disease, and so forth. The word is often used in association with the punishments of God because of wickedness (Exodus 5:3; 9:15; Jeremiah 27:13; Mosiah 12:4; Alma 10:23; D&C 97:25–26).

PETTING

See also NECKING. "Petting" is a term for touching and fondling the sexual parts of another person's body. It is a form of sexual immorality (D&C 59:6), as are all other sexual activities outside of marriage.

PHARISEES

One of the main religions among the Jews at the time of the Savior's mortal mission. The Pharisees believed in the resurrection of the dead, whereas their main opposition, the Sadducees, did not (Acts 23:8). The Pharisees were prominent in their opposition against Jesus and His work (Matthew 22:15). The Master gave the Pharisees a scathing rebuke in Matthew 23.

PHYLACTERIES

Phylacteries were small leather boxes, beautifully crafted, which faithful Jews tied to their foreheads ("forehead" was symbolical of loyalty to God in their culture) and left arm (to be near the heart). Inside these small leather boxes were four tiny scrolls containing Exodus 13:2–10, Exodus 13:11–17, Deuteronomy 6:4–9, and Deuteronomy 11:13–21. The scribes and Pharisees had made their phylacteries larger than normal (Matthew 23:5) so people could see how "righteous" they were. Likewise, they had enlarged the blue fringes on their clothing (Numbers 15:38–39), which symbolized keeping the commandments of God.

PHYSICAL CREATION
See CREATION.

PHYSICAL DEATH

The separation of the spirit from the physical body (Ecclesiastes 12:7). This death is temporary, since everyone ever born will be resurrected (1 Corinthians 15:22).

As spirits, we will miss our physical bodies during the time from our death to our resurrection (D&C 138:50).

PHYSICAL IMPERFECTIONS

All physical imperfections in our mortal bodies will be healed when we are resurrected. As a result, we will have perfect physical, resurrected bodies (Alma 40:23).

PIONEERS

In a general sense, all who joined the Church and came west during the mid-1880s are called "pioneers."

The original pioneer company which led the westward movement of the Saints to the Salt Lake Valley in 1847 consisted of 143 men, three women, and two children.

PLAN OF EXALTATION
See PLAN OF SALVATION.

PLAN OF HAPPINESS

See also PLAN OF SALVATION. The "great plan of happiness" (Alma 42:8) is one of the scriptural names given to the Father's plan for us. It is designed to enable us to eventually become like Him in every way (D&C 76:95).

PLAN OF REDEMPTION

See also PLAN OF SALVATION. The "plan of redemption" (Alma 12:25) is another name for the plan of salvation (Alma 42:5).

PLAN OF SALVATION

The Father's plan for us (Alma 42:5), designed to enable us to progress to the point of becoming just like Him (D&C 76:95). It consists of many phases, including our premortal life and education as spirit children of the Father (Hebrews 12:9), the creation (Genesis 1, 2), the Fall of Adam and Eve (2 Nephi 2:16–25), earth life (Abraham 3:24–26), physical death (2 Nephi 9:10), the postmortal spirit world, consisting of paradise and prison (Alma 40:11–14), the Second Coming (D&C 88:96–98; 133:46–51), the Millennium (Revelation 20:4; D&C 29:11), the "little season" at the end of the Millennium (D&C 88:111–16), final judgment

(Revelation 20:12), and exaltation for the faithful (D&C 132:19–20).

The Atonement of Jesus Christ is the central focus of the plan. The laws, principles, doctrines, and Priesthood ordinances of the gospel of Jesus Christ enable each individual to use his or her agency to choose the Father's plan or go his or her own way. Missionary work here on earth and in the postmortal spirit world, along with work for the dead, assure that each individual has the full opportunity to hear, understand, accept, or reject the plan before the final judgment.

PLATES OF ETHER
See BOOK OF MORMON PLATES.

PLATES OF MORMON
See BOOK OF MORMON PLATES.

PLATES OF NEPHI
See BOOK OF MORMON PLATES.

PLURAL MARRIAGE
See also MANIFESTO. Plural marriage is the practice of one man having more than one wife. It is often called polygamy, but the technical term is "polygyny," since "polygamy" can mean having more than one wife or more than one husband. Plural marriage was a common practice in biblical times. Among the ancients who had more than one wife were Abraham (Genesis 16:1–3) and Jacob (Genesis 29–30). David is another example, but in his case, he violated the laws of God and

lost his exaltation (D&C 132:39). Yet another example is Solomon, who had seven hundred wives and three hundred concubines (1 Kings 11:1–3). A number of his wives were non-Israelites and led him away from the true God (1 Kings 11:4).

In the Book of Mormon, Lehi and his people were commanded not to engage in the practice of plural marriage (Jacob 2:27). Nevertheless, the Lord told them that if it were necessary for them to practice it, He would command them to do so. He said, "For if I will . . . raise up seed unto me, I will command my people; otherwise they shall hearken unto these things" (Jacob 2:30).

"The law of plural marriage was revealed to the Prophet as early as 1831, but he mentioned it only to a few trusted friends. Under strict commandment from God to obey the law, the Prophet began in 1841 to instruct leading priesthood brethren of the Church concerning plural marriage and their responsibility to live the law. The Prophet Joseph Smith dictated the revelation [D&C 132] to William Clayton in 1843, when it was first written. Nine years passed, however, before the revelation was read in general conference and published.

"On 28–29 August 1852 a special conference was held in the Old Tabernacle on Temple Square in Salt Lake City. On the first day of the conference over one hundred missionaries were called to labor throughout the United States, Australia, India,

China, and the islands of the sea. By holding the conference in August the missionaries were able to get an early start in crossing the plains before the cold weather set in.

"On the second day of the conference, under the direction of President Brigham Young, Orson Pratt made the public announcement that the Church was practicing plural marriage under commandment of God. Speaking of the United States, he declared that 'the constitution gives the privilege to all the inhabitants of this country, of the free exercise of their religious notions, and the freedom of their faith, and the practice of it. Then, if it can be proven to a demonstration, that the Latter-day Saints have actually embraced, as a part and portion of their religion, the doctrine of a plurality of wives, it is constitutional. And should there ever be laws enacted by this government to restrict them from the free exercise of this part of their religion, such laws must be unconstitutional.'

"Brother Pratt then delivered a lengthy discourse from a scriptural standpoint concerning plural marriage. He explained that marriage was ordained of God as the channel for spirits to acquire mortal bodies and that through plural marriage worthy priesthood holders could raise up a numerous righteous posterity unto the Lord. Brigham Young then spoke giving a brief history concerning the revelation on celestial marriage. Thomas Bullock, a clerk in the historian's office, then read the rev-

elation to the congregation for their sustaining vote" (*Church History in the Fulness of Times*, p. 424).

Doctrine and Covenants, section 132, is the revelation from the Lord on celestial marriage as well as on plural marriage. It is helpful to understand, when studying this revelation, that verses 3–33 deal primarily with the law of celestial marriage, and verses 34–66 deal with the law of plural marriage.

Plural marriage was practiced officially by a number of members of the Church until 1890, when the Lord gave a revelation to then President Wilford Woodruff that the practice should be stopped. That revelation is known as Official Declaration—1 (also known as The Manifesto) and is recorded at the end of the Doctrine and Covenants. It was sustained by the members of the Church on October 6, 1890.

Any members of the Church today who choose to enter into plural marriage are excommunicated. They are going contrary to the laws of God as defined in Jacob 2:27, 30, as well as Official Declaration—1.

Elder Bruce R. McConkie taught that plural marriage is not required for exaltation. He said, "Plural marriage is not essential to salvation or exaltation. Nephi and his people were denied the power to have more than one wife and yet they could gain every blessing in eternity that the Lord ever offered to any people" (*MD*, p. 578).

PLURALITY OF GODS

There are three Gods in the God-head, namely, the Father, the Son, and the Holy Ghost (Articles of Faith 1:1). Furthermore, Abraham, Isaac, and Jacob have already become gods (D&C 132:37). The Savior plainly taught that those who faithfully live the gospel can become gods. He said, "Is it not written in your law, I said, Ye are gods?" (John 10:34).

Paul clearly taught the plurality of gods. He said:

1 Corinthians 8:5–6

5 For though there be that are called gods, whether in heaven or in earth, (as there be gods many, and lords many,)

6 But to us there is but one God, the Father, of whom are all things, and we in him; and one Lord Jesus Christ, by whom are all things, and we by him.

The Prophet Joseph Smith tells us that the parentheses in verse 5, above, teach that there are many gods. This reminds us that we can all become gods. He taught that the word "gods" in verse 5 does not refer to idols or, in other words, heathen gods. He said, "Some say I do not interpret the Scripture the same as they do. They say it means the heathen's gods. Paul says there are Gods many and Lords many; and that makes a plurality of Gods, in spite of the whims of all me. . . . You know and I testify that Paul had no allusion to the heathen gods. I have it from God, and get over it if you can. I have a witness of the Holy Ghost, and a testimony that Paul had no allusion to the heathen gods in the text" (*TPJS*, p. 371).

It follows from the above facts that, when those who are worthy from this earth become gods (D&C 132:20), there will be even more gods in the universe. However, even though there are "gods many" (1 Corinthians 8:5), for "us there is but one God, the Father, of whom are all things, and we in him; and one Lord Jesus Christ, by whom are all things, and we by him" (1 Corinthians 8:6).

POLYGAMY

See PLURAL MARRIAGE.

PORNOGRAPHY

Pornography is one of the greatest plagues of the last days. It destroys self-respect and spirituality and causes untold misery. Latter-day prophets have constantly warned against it and continue to do so. We will quote from *True to the Faith* for the words of our living prophets concerning this destructive and addictive tool of the devil:

"Pornography is any material depicting or describing the human body or sexual conduct in a way that arouses sexual feelings. It is distributed through many media, including magazines, books, television, movies, music, and the Internet. It is as harmful to the spirit as tobacco, alcohol, and drugs are to the body. Using pornographic material in any way is a violation of a commandment of God: 'Thou shalt not . . . commit adultery . . . nor do anything like unto it' (D&C 59:6). It can lead to other serious sins. Members of the Church should avoid pornography in any form and should oppose its production, distribution, and use.

"Pornography is tragically addictive. Like other addictions, it leads people to experiment and to seek more powerful stimulations. If you experiment with it and allow yourself to remain caught in its trap, it will destroy you, degrading your mind, heart, and spirit. It will rob you of self-respect and of your sense of the beauties of life. It will tear you down and lead you to evil thoughts and possibly evil actions. It will cause terrible damage to your family relationships.

"Because of the addictive nature of pornography and the harm it can cause to body and spirit, servants of God have repeatedly warned us to shun it. If you are caught in the trap of pornography, stop immediately and seek help. Through repentance, you can receive forgiveness and find hope in the gospel. Go to your bishop or branch president for counsel on how to overcome your problem, and seek healing through the Atonement of Jesus Christ. Ask the Lord to give you the strength to overcome this terrible addiction" (*TF,* pp. 117–18).

POST-EARTH LIFE

See also PARADISE; SPIRIT WORLD.
After we die, we go to the postmortal spirit world (Alma 40:11–14) to await the resurrection. After the final judgment (Revelation 20:12), depending on worthiness, individuals will go to the celestial kingdom (D&C 76:50–53, 70), terrestrial kingdom (D&C 76:71–80), telestial kingdom (D&C 76:81–86), or perdition (D&C 76:30–49).

POSTMORTAL SPIRIT WORLD

See PARADISE.

PRAYER

The Savior gave examples of how to communicate with Heavenly Father through prayer. One such example was the Lord's Prayer (Matthew 6:9–13). Prayers should be addressed to the Father, using appropriate words such as "Our Father in Heaven," "Heavenly Father," "Dear Father," or other appropriate forms of addressing Him. The prayer should be closed in the name of Jesus Christ. It is generally appropriate to close one's eyes to avoid distraction during prayer. Appropriate expressions of thanks for blessings and requests for help for self and others are a common part of many prayers.

If a person is in tune with the Spirit during prayer, he or she may receive inspiration and guidance as to what to say (D&C 46:30; 50:30).

Occasionally some individuals suggest that unless a prayer is at least so long, it is not effective. Caution is advised against such constraints on prayer. A short prayer, for example, came from the Savior on the cross. He prayed, "Father, forgive them; for they know not what they do" (Luke 23:34).

A much longer prayer given by

Jesus is found in John 17. It is called "the great intercessory prayer."

PREDESTINATION

See FOREORDINATION.

PRE-EXISTENCE

See also PREMORTAL LIFE. "Pre-existence" is another term for the premortal life. However, "pre-existence" is being used less and less in Church sermons, gospel lessons, discussions, etc., because it can be confusing to investigators and others who study the teachings of the restored gospel. When they hear that we did things in the pre-existence, they wonder how we could be doing things before we existed. Therefore, terms such as "premortality," "premortal life," and "pre-earth life" are being generally recommended for such teaching.

PREMARITAL SEX

See also CHASTITY, LAW OF. The commandments of God concerning premarital sex are still the same. Any premarital sexual relations are strictly forbidden (Exodus 20:14; Romans 1:29; D&C 59:6). The Church of Jesus Christ of Latter-day Saints teaches strict avoidance of premarital sex as well as complete fidelity in marriage.

PREMORTAL LIFE

See also PRE-EXISTENCE. The phrase "premortal life" refers to our life before we were born into mortality.

The scriptures teach that we lived before we came to earth. For example,

Jeremiah was told, "Before I formed thee in the belly I knew thee; and before thou camest forth out of the womb I sanctified thee, and I ordained thee a prophet unto the nations" (Jeremiah 1:5). In Ecclesiastes, we read that our spirit returns to God when we die: "Then shall the dust return to the earth as it was: and the spirit shall return unto God who gave it" (Ecclesiastes 12:7).

Alma teaches the same basic doctrine to his son, Corianton: "Now, concerning the state of the soul between death and the resurrection—Behold, it has been made known unto me by an angel, that the spirits of all men, as soon as they are departed from this mortal body, yea, the spirits of all men, whether they be good or evil, are taken home to that God who gave them life" (Alma 40:11).

Our premortal existence consisted of two main phases: (1) Our existence as intelligence or intelligences (the correct term has not yet been revealed). (2) Our birth as spirit sons and daughters of heavenly parents, and being reared and taught in our heavenly home.

Intelligence

The most basic part of our being, referred to as either "intelligence" or "intelligences," has existed forever. We came into existence as "spirits" when we were born as "spirit sons and daughters of heavenly parents" (see "Proclamation," paragraph 2).

We know very little about our existence as intelligence or intelligences. One revealed truth teaches: "Intelligence, or the light of truth, was not created or made, neither indeed can be" (D&C 93:29). Furthermore, Joseph Smith taught, "The intelligence of spirits had no beginning, neither will it have an end. . . . Intelligence is eternal and exists upon a self-existent principle" (*HC* 6:311).

Spiritual Birth

The Bible teaches that we are the "offspring of God" (Acts 17:28–29), and that Heavenly Father is "the Father of spirits" (Hebrews 12:9). At some point in eons past, our intelligence was clothed with a spirit body when we were born as spirit children to our heavenly parents. Elder John A. Widtsoe taught, "The eternal ego [*intelligence*] of man was, in some past age of the other world, dim to us, clothed with a spiritual body. That was man's spiritual birth and his entrance into the spiritual world" (Widtsoe, *Evidences and Reconciliations*, 3:74–77).

President Spencer W. Kimball explained our spirit birth as follows: "God is your father. He loves you. He and your mother in heaven value you beyond any measure. They gave your eternal intelligence spirit form, just as your earthly mother and father have given you a mortal body. You are unique. One of a kind, made of the eternal intelligence which gives you claim upon eternal life.

"Let there be no question in your mind about your value as an individual. The whole intent of the gospel plan is to provide an opportunity for each of you to reach your fullest potential, which is eternal progression and the possibility of godhood." (CR [Nov. 1978]).

The First Presidency confirmed this doctrine. They wrote, "Man, as a spirit, was begotten [conceived] and born of heavenly parents, and reared to maturity in the eternal mansions of the Father, prior to coming upon the earth" (The First Presidency, Heber J. Grant and counselors, "The Mormon View of Evolution," *Improvement Era*, September 1925).

All things were created in spirit form during premortality. "And every plant of the field before it was in the earth, and every herb of the field before it grew. For I, the Lord God, created all things, of which I have spoken, spiritually, before they were naturally upon the face of the earth. For I, the Lord God, had not caused it to rain upon the face of the earth. And I, the Lord God, had created all the children of men; and not yet a man to till the ground; for in heaven created I them; and there was not yet flesh upon the earth, neither in the water, neither in the air" (Moses 3:5).

During our premortal life as spirit sons and daughters of God, we were given agency (D&C 29:36), taught the gospel, and allowed and encouraged to grow and progress. The Atonement of Christ worked for us there, even though it had not yet been performed by the Savior. It worked for us there just as it worked for individuals such as Alma, before it was accomplished on earth (Alma 36:11–25). The Bible teaches that the Atonement worked in premortality. Pay special attention to verse 11, where we are taught that the "blood of the Lamb" was working for us in premortality as well as later for the righteous on earth.

Revelation 12:7–11

7 And there was war in heaven: Michael and his angels fought against the dragon; and the dragon fought and his angels,

8 And prevailed not; neither was their place found any more in heaven.

9 And the great dragon was cast out, that old serpent, called the Devil, and Satan, which deceiveth the whole world: he was cast out into the earth, and his angels were cast out with him.

10 And I heard a loud voice saying in heaven, Now is come salvation, and strength, and the kingdom of our God, and the power of his Christ: for the accuser of our brethren is cast down, which accused them before our God day and night.

11 And they overcame him by the blood of the Lamb, and by the word of their testimony; and they loved not their lives unto the death.

Elder Jeffrey R. Holland confirmed that the Atonement worked for us in premortality. He taught, "We could remember that even in the Grand Council of Heaven [in the premortal realm] He loved us and was wonderfully strong, that we triumphed even there by the power of Christ and our faith in the blood of the Lamb" (CR [Oct. 1995]).

The Council in Heaven

After living with our heavenly parents as spirit children, for eons of time, we had progressed to the point that it was time to create an earth for us and give us the opportunity to come to it, through the process of mortal birth. At this point, a grand council was called in heaven, which all of us attended. The plan to create this earth was presented and explained to us and we were given the opportunity to use our agency to accept it or reject it. We were overjoyed at the prospects of coming to earth, and we "shouted for joy," as described in Job, "when the morning stars sang together, and all the sons of God [*spirit sons and daughters of God*] shouted for joy" (Job 38:7).

The Prophet Joseph Smith taught that we all attended this premortal council in heaven and saw the Savior chosen to be our Redeemer. "At the first organization in heaven we were all present, and saw the Savior chosen and appointed and the plan of salvation made, and we sanctioned it [approved it]" (*TPJS*, p. 181).

The Savior Chosen

During the premortal council in heaven, the Savior was chosen to be the Redeemer, and Lucifer rebelled because he desired to be the Redeemer and gain glory for himself. We read:

Moses 4:1–4

1 And I, the Lord God, spake unto Moses, saying: That Satan,

whom thou hast commanded in the name of mine Only Begotten, is the same which was from the beginning, and he came before me, saying—Behold, here am I, send me, I will be thy son, and I will redeem all mankind, that one soul shall not be lost, and surely I will do it; wherefore give me thine honor.

2 But, behold, my Beloved Son, which was my Beloved and Chosen from the beginning, said unto me—Father, thy will be done, and the glory be thine forever.

3 Wherefore, because that Satan rebelled against me, and sought to destroy the agency of man, which I, the Lord God, had given him, and also, that I should give unto him mine own power; by the power of mine Only Begotten, I caused that he should be cast down;

4 And he became Satan, yea, even the devil, the father of all lies, to deceive and to blind men, and to lead them captive at his will, even as many as would not hearken unto my voice.

The War in Heaven

As a result of Lucifer's rebellion, there was a war in heaven. The Bible speaks of this "war in heaven" (Revelation 12:7–9). Since spirits cannot be killed, it was a war of words, philosophies, ideas, false doctrine, true doctrine, peer pressure, and so forth, which is still going on here on earth. It was a war for our souls. President Gordon B. Hinckley described it as a battle for our loyalty. He said, "The book of Revelation speaks briefly of what must have been a terrible conflict for the minds and loyalties of God's children." He then quoted Revelation 12:7–9 (CR [April 2003]).

The Bible Dictionary describes the War in Heaven as follows:

Bible Dictionary

War in Heaven. This term arises out of Revelation 12:7 and refers to the conflict that took place in the premortal existence among the spirit children of God. The war was primarily over how and in what manner the plan of salvation would be administered to the forthcoming human family upon the earth. The issues involved such things as agency, how to gain salvation, and who should be the Redeemer. The war broke out because one-third of the spirits refused to accept the appointment of Jesus Christ as the Savior. Such a refusal was a rebellion against the Father's plan of redemption. It was evident that if given agency, some persons would fall short of complete salvation; Lucifer and his followers wanted salvation to come automatically to all who passed through mortality, without regard to individual preference, agency, or voluntary dedication (see Isaiah 14:12–20; Luke 10:18; Revelation 12:4–13; D&C 29:36–38; Moses 4:1–4). The spirits who thus rebelled and persisted were thrust out of heaven and cast down to the earth without mortal bodies, "and thus came the devil and his angels"

250

·P·

(D&C 29:37; see also Revelation 12:9; Abraham 3:24–28).

The warfare is continued in mortality in the conflict between right and wrong, between the gospel and false principles, etc. The same contestants and the same issues are doing battle, and the same salvation is at stake.

Although one-third of the spirits became devils, the remaining two-thirds were not all equally valiant, there being every degree of devotion to Christ and the Father among them. The most diligent were chosen to be rulers in the kingdom (Abraham 3:22–23). The nature of the conflict, however, is such that there could be no neutrals, then or now (Matthew 12:30; 1 Nephi 14:10; Alma 5:38–40).

First Estate and Second Estate

The terms "first estate" and "second estate" come into play here (Abraham 3:26, 28). "First estate" refers to premortal life. "Second estate" refers to earth life. The one-third of the spirits who became devils did not keep their "first estate." In other words, they did not prove worthy in premortality to come to earth for this final opportunity to progress toward exaltation.

"They who keep their second estate shall have glory added upon their heads for ever and ever" (Abraham 3:26). In other words, those who successfully complete earth life, postmortal spirit world, Millennium, and final judgment will be exalted and become gods.

In summary, our premortal life contained virtually all of the learning and personal growth components of our mortal life, with the big exception that we did not have mortal bodies. Premortality included the teachings of the gospel of Jesus Christ, agency, choice, opposition, the Atonement, opportunities for progression, and so forth until we were prepared to enter mortality (perhaps we could call it the University of Earth) and thus begin the final phase of our education toward exaltation. A major component of this mortal life is the test described in Abraham: "And we will prove them herewith, to see if they will do all things whatsoever the Lord their God shall command them" (Abraham 3:25).

PRESIDENT OF THE AARONIC PRIESTHOOD

The bishop is the president of the Aaronic Priesthood in a ward. "The bishop is the president of the priests quorum, the president of the Aaronic Priesthood, and the presiding high priest in the ward. The bishop also oversees Aaronic Priesthood ordinations and presides over the ward Aaronic Priesthood committee and the bishopric youth committee" (Information on lds.org, August 2007).

On the general Church level, "the Presiding Bishopric is the presidency of the Aaronic Priesthood throughout the Church" (lds.org, Gospel Topics, Bishop).

PRESIDENT OF THE CHURCH

The president of the Church is the senior living Apostle upon the earth.

He is the man who has served as an Apostle longer than any other living man. He is the presiding high priest over the whole earth and the Church and is the president of the "quorum of the Presidency of the Church" (D&C 107:21–22).

PRESIDENT OF THE HIGH PRIESTS QUORUM

The stake president is the president of the high priests quorum, which consists of all of the high priests in the stake. The high priests meet as groups in each ward, led by a high priests group leader.

PRESIDING BISHOP

The presiding bishop of the Church, along with his two counselors, presides over the temporal affairs of the Church, under the direction of the First Presidency. Each member of the presiding bishopric is an ordained bishop. Together they serve as the presidency of the Aaronic Priesthood of the Church. "Temporal affairs of the Church" have typically included "involvement in receiving, distributing, and accounting for member tithes, offerings, and contributions; administration of programs to assist the poor and needy; design, construction, and maintenance of places of worship; and auditing and transferring records of membership" (*EM*, under "Presiding Bishopric").

PRESIDING HIGH PRIEST

See PRESIDENT OF THE CHURCH.

PRESIDING PATRIARCH

See PATRIARCH TO THE CHURCH.

PRIESTCRAFT

Preaching for the purpose of gaining popularity and wealth. Priestcraft is defined in the Book of Mormon, where we are taught that "priestcrafts are that men preach and set themselves up for a light unto the world, that they may get gain and praise of the world; but they seek not the welfare of Zion" (2 Nephi 26:29).

PRIESTESSES

The term "priestesses" is not found in the scriptures. Rather, it is used to describe faithful women who attain exaltation. Elder John Taylor used the term as follows: "You have been ordained kings and queens, and priests and priestesses to your Lord; you have been put in possession of principles that all the kings, potentates, and power upon the earth are entirely ignorant of; they do not understand it; but you have received this from the hands of God" (*JD* 5:189–90).

Bruce R. McConkie taught, "If righteous men have power through the gospel and its crowning ordinance of celestial marriage to become kings and priests to rule in exaltation forever, it follows that the women by their side (without whom they cannot attain exaltation) will be queens and priestesses (Revelation 1:6; 5:10). Exaltation grows out of the eternal union of a man and his wife. Of those whose marriage endures in eternity, the Lord says, 'Then shall they be gods' (D&C 132:20); that is, each of them, the man and the woman, will be a god. As such they will rule over their dominions forever" (*MD*, p. 613).

PRIESTHOOD

See also AARONIC PRIESTHOOD; MELCHIZEDEK PRIESTHOOD. President Joseph F. Smith, the president of the Church from 1901 to 1918, defined the priesthood: "What is the Priesthood? It is nothing more nor less than the power of God delegated to man by which man can act in the earth for the salvation of the human family, in the name of the Father and the Son and the Holy Ghost, and act legitimately; not assuming that authority, nor borrowing it from generations that are dead and gone, but authority that has been given in this day in which we live by ministering angels and spirits from above, direct from the presence of Almighty God. . . . It is the same power and Priesthood that was committed to the disciples of Christ while he was upon the earth, that whatsoever they should bind on earth should be bound in heaven, and that whatsoever they should loose on earth should be loosed in heaven" (Smith, *Gospel Doctrine*, pp. 139–40).

President John Taylor likewise defined the priesthood. He taught, "What is priesthood? . . . it is the government of God, whether on the earth or in the heavens, for it is by that power, agency, or principle that all things are governed on the earth and in the heavens, and by that power that all things are upheld and sustained. It governs all things—it directs all things—it sustains all things—and has to do with all things that God and truth are associated with. It is the power of God delegated to intelligences in the heavens and to men on the earth" (Taylor, *The Gospel Kingdom*, p. 129).

PRIESTHOOD, AARONIC
See AARONIC PRIESTHOOD.

PRIESTHOOD EXECUTIVE COMMITTEE
See PEC.

PRIESTHOOD, LEVITICAL
See LEVITICAL PRIESTHOOD.

PRIESTHOOD, MELCHIZEDEK
See MELCHIZEDEK PRIESTHOOD.

PRIESTHOOD OF AARON
See AARONIC PRIESTHOOD.

PRIESTHOOD OFFICES
See OFFICES IN THE PRIESTHOOD.

PRIESTHOOD ORDINANCES
See ORDINANCES.

PRIESTHOOD QUORUMS
Each priesthood holder in the Church belongs to a quorum. A quorum is a group of priesthood holders presided over by a presidency.

It is a brotherhood of priesthood holders who serve others and work to save souls.

In a normal ward, where there are sufficient members, there is a deacons quorum for Aaronic Priesthood holders ages 12–13, a teachers quorum for Aaronic Priesthood holders ages 14–15, a priests quorum for Aaronic Priesthood holders ages 16–17, and an elders quorum for Melchizedek Priesthood holders who have been ordained to the office of elder. The high priests are part of the stake high priests quorum, presided over by the stake presidency. High priests meet in groups in each ward and are led by a group leader and his two assistants.

The number of members for a full quorum for deacons, teachers, priests, and elders is given in D&C 107:85–89.

PRIMARY
The official organization of the Church for children ages eighteen months through eleven years.

PRIMITIVE CHURCH
As used in the sixth article of faith, the primitive church is the church which Jesus Christ established upon the earth during His mortal ministry.

PRINCE OF DEVILS
Another name for Satan. The Jews accused Jesus of performing His miracles by the power of "the prince of the devils" (Matthew 9:34; 12:24; Mark 3:22).

PRINCE OF PEACE
Another name for Jesus Christ (Isaiah 9:6; 2 Nephi 19:6). The name is also applied to Melchizedek (Alma 13:18) and to Abraham (Abraham 1:2).

PRINCE OF THIS WORLD
Another name for the devil (John 12:31; 14:30 footnote b; 16:11; D&C 127:11).

PRISON, SPIRIT
See PARADISE.

PROBATION
See also DISCIPLINE, CHURCH; DISCIPLINARY COUNCILS. Probation is one possible outcome of a Church disciplinary council. It can be tailored by the bishop or stake president to fit the needs of the member who desires to get his or her life in order with the Lord.

PROBATION, MORTAL
A phrase referring to this mortal life, with the connotation that this life is a test (Abraham 3:25).

PROBATIONARY STATE
A reference to this mortal life (Alma 12:24; 42:10–13).

PROCLAMATIONS OF THE FIRST PRESIDENCY AND QUORUM OF THE TWELVE APOSTLES
Since the restoration of the Church, there have been five official communications from the First Presidency, the

Quorum of the Twelve Apostles, or both, which have been called proclamations. We will quote from the *Encyclopedia of Mormonism* for the first three proclamations, which will be in excerpt form, and for the fourth, which is given in its entirety. Some notes are included for all four, again taken from the *Encyclopedia of Mormonism* under the topic "Proclamations of the First Presidency and the Quorum of the Twelve Apostles." The fifth proclamation is given in its entirety under "Family: A Proclamation to the World, The" in this reference volume. It is commonly referred to as "The Proclamation on the Family" although the title is "The Family: A Proclamation to the World."

Such proclamations are serious and sacred invitations, warnings, teachings, and counsel to members of the Church as well as to the world.

Encyclopedia of Mormonism

In performance of their calling as apostles, prophets, seers, revelators, and spokesmen for The Church of Jesus Christ of Latter-day Saints, the First Presidency and the Quorum of the Twelve Apostles have from time to time issued formal written proclamations, declarations, letters, and various public announcements. These have been addressed sometimes to the members of the Church (as a type of general epistle) and sometimes to the public at large. All such declarations have been solemn and sacred in nature and were issued with the intent to bring forth, build up, and regulate the affairs of the Church as the kingdom of God on the earth.

Subject matter has included instruction on doctrine, faith, and history; warnings of judgments to come; invitations to assist in the work; and statements of Church growth and progress.

Only a few of the many formal declarations have been labeled "Proclamations." Others have been characterized "Official Declarations," "Doctrinal Expositions," or "Epistles." Some have the signature of the First Presidency, some of the First Presidency and the Twelve, and some of the Twelve only. This article considers four documents: (1) Proclamation of the First Presidency on January 15, 1841, at Nauvoo, Illinois; (2) Proclamation of the Twelve Apostles on April 6, 1845, in New York City, and on October 22, 1845, in Liverpool, England; (3) Proclamation of the First Presidency and the Twelve Apostles on October 21, 1865, in Salt Lake City, Utah; and (4) Proclamation from the First Presidency and the Quorum of the Twelve Apostles, April 6, 1980, issued from Fayette, New York.

1. A Proclamation of the First Presidency of the Church to the Saints Scattered Abroad (January 15, 1841, Nauvoo, Illinois)

[This document, signed by Joseph Smith, Sidney Rigdon, and Hyrum Smith, reviews the progress of the Church in spite of hardships and persecution, and speaks at length on the prospects of the settlement of Nauvoo, as the following excerpts illustrate.]

Beloved Brethren: The relationship which we sustain to The Church of Jesus Christ of Latter-day Saints, renders it necessary that we should make known from time to time, the circumstances, situation, and prospects of the Church, and give such instructions as may be necessary for the well being of the Saints, and for the promotion of those objects calculated to further their present and everlasting happiness.

We have to congratulate the Saints on the progress of the great work of the "last days," for not only has it spread through the length and breadth of this vast continent, but on the continent of Europe, and on the islands of the sea, it is spreading in a manner entirely unprecedented in the annals of time. This appears the more pleasing when we consider, that but a short time has elapsed since we were unmercifully driven from the state of Missouri, after suffering cruelties and persecutions in various and horrid forms. . . .

It would be impossible to enumerate all those who, in our time of deep distress, nobly came forward to our relief, and, like the good Samaritan, poured oil into our wounds, and contributed liberally to our necessities, and the citizens of Quincy *en masse*, and the people of Illinois, generally, seemed to emulate each other in this labor of love. . . .

We would likewise make mention of the legislators of this state, who, without respect to parties, without reluctance, freely, openly, boldly, and nobly, have come forth to our assistance, owned us as citizens and friends, and took us by the hand, and extended

to us all the blessings of civil, political, and religious liberty, by granting us, under date of December 16, 1840, one of the most liberal charters, with the most plenary powers ever conferred by a legislative assembly on free citizens, "The City of Nauvoo," the "Nauvoo Legion," and the "University of the City of Nauvoo." . . .

The name of our city (Nauvoo) is of Hebrew origin, and signifies a beautiful situation, or place, carrying with it, also, the idea of rest; and is truly descriptive of the most delightful location. It is situated on the east bank of the Mississippi river, at the head of the Des Moines rapids, in Hancock county, bounded on the east by an extensive prairie of surpassing beauty, and on the north, west, and south, by the Mississippi. . . .

Having been instrumental, in the hands of our heavenly Father, in laying a foundation for the gathering of Zion, we would say, let all those who appreciate the blessings of the Gospel, and realize the importance of obeying the commandments of heaven, who have been blessed with the possession of this world's goods, first prepare for the general gathering; let them dispose of their effects as fast as circumstances will possibly admit, without making too great sacrifices, and remove to our city and county; establish and build up manufactures in the city, purchase and cultivate farms in the county. This will secure our permanent inheritance, and prepare the way for the gathering of the poor. This is agreeable to the order of heaven, and the only principle on which the gathering can be effected. Let the rich, then, and all who can assist in establishing this place, make every preparation to come on without delay, and strengthen our hands, and assist in promoting the happiness of the Saints. . . .

The Temple of the Lord is in process of erection here, where the Saints will come to worship the God of their fathers, according to the order of His house and the power of the Holy Priesthood, and will be so constructed as to enable all the functions of the Priesthood to be duly exercised, and where instructions from the Most High will be received, and from this place go forth to distant lands. Let us then concentrate all our powers, under the provisions of our *magna charta* granted by the Illinois legislature, at the "City of Nauvoo" and surrounding country, and strive to emulate the action of the ancient covenant fathers and Patriarchs, in those things which are of such vast importance to this and every succeeding generation. . . .

The greatest temporal and spiritual blessings which always flow from faithfulness and concerted effort, never attended individual exertion or enterprise. The history of all past ages abundantly attests this fact. In addition to all temporal blessings, there is no other way for the Saints to be saved in these last days [than by the gathering], as the concurrent testimony of all the holy Prophets clearly proves, for it is written—"They shall come from the east, and be gathered from the west; the north shall give up, and the south shall keep not back. The sons of God shall be gathered from far, and His daughters from the ends of the earth."

It is also the concurrent testimony of all the Prophets, that this gathering together of all the Saints, must take place before the Lord comes to "take vengeance upon the ungodly," and to be glorified and admired by all those who obey the Gospel. The fiftieth Psalm, from the first to the fifth verse inclusive, describes the glory and majesty of that event.

The mighty God, and even the Lord hath spoken, and called the earth from the rising of the sun unto the going down thereof. Out of Zion, the perfection of beauty, God hath shined. Our God shall come and shall not keep silence; a fire shall devour before Him, and it shall be very tempestuous round about Him. He shall call to the heavens from above, and to the earth (that He may judge the people). Gather my Saints together unto me; those that have made covenant with me by sacrifice.

We might offer many other quotations from the Scriptures, but believing them to be familiar to the Saints, we forbear.

We would wish the Saints to understand that, when they come here, they must not expect perfection, or that all will be harmony, peace, and love; if they indulge these ideas, they will undoubtedly be deceived, for here there are persons, not only from different states, but from different nations, who, although they feel a great attachment to the cause of truth, have their prejudices of education, and, consequently, it requires some time before these things can be overcome. . . . Therefore, let those who come up to this place be determined to keep the commandments of God, and not be discouraged by those things we have enumerated, and then they will be prospered—the intelligence of heaven will be communicated to them, and they will eventually, see eye to eye, and rejoice in the full fruition of that glory which is reserved for the righteous.

In order to erect the Temple of the Lord, great exertions will be required on the part of the Saints, so that they may build a house which shall be accepted by the Almighty, in which His power and glory shall be manifested. Therefore let those who can freely make a sacrifice of their time, their talents, and their property, for the prosperity of the kingdom, and for the love they have to the cause of truth, bid adieu to their homes and pleasant places of abode, and unite with us in the great work of the last days, and share in the tribulation, that they may ultimately share in the glory and triumph.

We wish it likewise to be distinctly understood, that we claim no privilege but what we feel cheerfully disposed to share with our fellow citizens of every denomination, and every sentiment of religion; and therefore say, that so far from being restricted to our own faith, let all those who desire to locate themselves in this place, or the vicinity, come, and we will hail them as citizens and friends, and shall feel it not only a duty, but a privilege, to reciprocate the kindness we have received from the benevolent and kind-hearted citizens of the state of Illinois.

Joseph Smith,
Sidney Rigdon,
Hyrum Smith,
Presidents of the Church
[HC 4:267–73].

2. Proclamation of the Twelve Apostles of The Church of Jesus Christ of Latter-day Saints (April 6 and October 22, 1845)

[The Proclamation of 1845 was issued by the Twelve only, because at that time there was no First Presidency due to the martyrdom of the Prophet Joseph Smith on June 27, 1844, and a new First Presidency was not organized until December 1847. The Proclamation was apparently made in response to a revelation given January 19, 1841 (D&C 124:1–11). It was first printed in a sixteen-page pamphlet in New York City on April 6, 1845, and again in Liverpool, England, October 22, 1845. It was addressed to the rulers and people of all nations. This document was an announcement that God had spoken from the heavens and had restored the gospel of Jesus Christ to the earth. It spoke of blessings and of punishments to come, issued a warning voice, and invited all who were interested to assist in the building of the kingdom of God on the earth in preparation for the Savior's second coming. On October 3, 1975, President Ezra Taft Benson, president of the Quorum of the Twelve Apostles, spoke of this Proclamation and quoted portions of it in his general conference address (*Ensign* 15 [Oct. 1975]:32–34). Extracts from the 1845 Proclamation follow.]

TO ALL THE KINGS OF THE WORLD, TO THE PRESIDENT OF THE UNITED STATES OF AMERICA; TO THE GOVERNORS OF THE SEVERAL STATES, AND TO THE RULERS AND PEOPLE OF ALL NATIONS.

Greeting.

Know ye that the kingdom of God has come, as has been predicted by ancient prophets, and prayed for in all ages; even that kingdom which shall fill the whole earth, and shall stand for ever. . . .

Therefore we send unto you, with authority from on high, and command you all to repent and humble yourselves as little children before the majesty of the Holy One; and come unto Jesus with a broken heart and a contrite spirit, and be baptized in his name for the remission of sins (that is, be buried in the water, in the likeness of his burial, and rise again to newness of life in the likeness of his resurrection), and you shall receive the gift of the Holy Spirit, through the laying on of the hands of the apostles and elders, of this great and last dispensation of mercy to man.

This Spirit shall bear witness to you of the truth of our testimony, and shall enlighten your minds, and be in you as the spirit of prophecy and revelation; it shall bring things past to your understanding and remembrance, and shall show you things to come. . . .

By the light of this Spirit, received through the ministration of the ordinances—by the power and authority of the Holy Apostleship and Priesthood, you will be enabled to understand, and to be the children of light; and thus be prepared to escape all the things that are coming on the earth, and so stand before the Son of Man.

We testify that the foregoing doctrine is the doctrine or gospel of Jesus Christ in its fulness; and that it is the only true, everlasting, and unchangeable gospel; and the only plan revealed on earth whereby man can be saved. . . .

And we further testify that the Lord has appointed a holy city and temple to be built on this continent, for the Endowment and ordinances pertaining to the priesthood; and for the Gentiles, and the remnant of Israel to resort unto, in order to worship the Lord, and to be taught in his ways and walk in his paths; in short, to finish their preparations for the coming of the Lord. . . .

The Latter-day Saints, since their first organization in the year 1830, have been a poor, persecuted, abused, and afflicted people. They have sacrificed their time and property freely, for the sake of laying the foundation of the kingdom of God, and enlarging its dominion by the ministry of the gospel. They have suffered privation, hunger, imprisonment, and the loss of houses, lands, home, and political rights for their testimony.

And this is not all. Their first founder, Mr. Joseph Smith, whom God raised up as a prophet and apostle, mighty in word and in deed, and his brother Hyrum, who was also a prophet, together with many others, have suffered a cruel martyrdom in the cause of truth, and have sealed their testimony with their blood; and still the work has, as it were, but just begun.

A great, a glorious, and a mighty work is yet to be achieved, in spreading the truth and kingdom among the Gentiles—in restoring, organizing, instructing and establishing the Jews—in gathering, instructing, relieving, civilizing, educating, and administering salvation to the remnant of Israel on this continent—in building Jerusalem in Palestine, and the cities, stakes, temples, and sanctuaries of Zion in America; and in gathering the Gentiles into the same covenant and organization-instructing them in all things for their sanctification and preparation, that the whole Church of the Saints, both Gentile, Jew and Israel, may be prepared as a bride for the coming of the Lord. . . .

Again, we say, by the word of the Lord, to the people as well as to the rulers, your aid and your assistance is required in this great work; and you are hereby invited, in the name of Jesus, to take an active part in it from this day forward.

Open your churches, doors, and hearts for the truth; hear the apostles and elders of the Church of the Saints when they come into your cities and neighbourhoods; read and search the scriptures carefully, and see whether these things are so; read the publications of the Saints, and help to publish them to others; seek for the witness of the Spirit, and come and obey the glorious fulness of the gospel, and help us to build the cities and sanctuaries of our God. . . .

To this city [Zion or New Jerusalem], and to its several branches or stakes, shall the Gentiles seek, as to a standard of light and knowledge; yea, the nations, and their kings and nobles shall say—Come, and let us go up to the Mount Zion, and to the temple of the Lord, where his holy priesthood stand to minister continually before the Lord; and where we may be instructed more fully, and receive the ordinances of remission, and of sanctification, and redemption, and thus be adopted into the family of Israel, and identified in the same covenants of promise. . . .

The city of Zion, with its sanctuary and priesthood, and the glorious fulness of the gospel, will constitute a *standard* which will put an end to jarring creeds and political wranglings, by uniting the republics, states, provinces, territories, nations, tribes, kindred, tongues, people, and sects of North and South America in one great and common bond of brotherhood; while truth and knowledge shall make them free, and love cement their union.

The Lord also shall be their king and their lawgiver; while wars shall cease and peace prevail for a thousand years. . . .

We say, then, in life or in death, in bonds or free, that the great God has spoken in this age.—*And we know it.*

He has given us the holy priesthood and apostleship, and the keys of the kingdom of God, to bring about the restoration of all things as promised by the holy prophets of old.—*And we know it.*

He has revealed the origin and the records of the aboriginal tribes of America, and their future destiny.—*And we know it.*

He has revealed the fulness of the gospel, with its gifts, blessings, and ordinances.—*And we know it.* . . .

He has commanded us to gather together his Saints, on this continent, and build up holy cities and sanctuaries.—*And we know it.*

He has said, that the Gentiles should come into the same gospel and covenant, and be numbered with the house of Israel, and be a blessed people upon this good land for ever, if they would repent and embrace it.—*And we know it.* . . .

He has said, that the time is at hand for the Jews to be gathered to Jerusalem.—*And we know it.*

He has said, that the ten tribes of Israel should also be revealed in the north country, together with their oracles and records, preparatory to their return, and to their union with Judah, no more to be separated.—*And we know it.*

He has said, that when these preparations were made, both in this country and in Jerusalem, and the gospel in all its fulness preached to all nations for a witness and testimony, he will come, and all the Saints with him, to reign on the earth one thousand years.—*And we know it.*

He has said, that he will not come in his glory and destroy the wicked, till these warnings were given, and these preparations were made for his reception.—*And we know it.* . . .

Therefore, again we say to all people, repent, and be baptized in the name of Jesus Christ, for remission of sins, and you shall receive the Holy Spirit, and shall know the truth, and be numbered with the house of Israel. . . . *New York, April 6th,* 1845

TO THE ENGLISH READER.

It will be borne in mind that the foregoing was written in the United States of America, therefore the language, which we have not altered, will be understood as emanating from thence. . . .

W. Woodruff.

Liverpool, October 22nd, 1845 [Liverpool pamphlet, BYU Library, Provo, Utah: see also *MFP* 1:252–66].

3. Proclamation of the First Presidency and the Twelve Apostles (October 21, 1865)

[This document was issued to members of the Church to correct certain theories about the nature of God that had been published by one of the Twelve in official Church literature, without having those statements cleared and verified by the First Presidency and the Twelve.

An apparent major purpose of this Proclamation was to emphasize the established order of the Church, that new doctrine is to be announced only by the First Presidency. A paragraph near the end of the proclamation states:]

It ought to have been known, years ago, by every person in the Church—for ample teachings have been given on the point—that no member of the Church has the right to publish any doctrines, as the doctrines of The Church of Jesus Christ of Latter-day Saints, without first submitting them for examination and approval to the First Presidency and the Twelve. There is but one man upon the earth, at one time, who holds the keys to receive commandments and revelations for the Church, and who has the authority to write doctrines by way of commandment unto the Church. And any man who so far forgets the order instituted by the Lord as to write and publish what may be termed new doctrines, without consulting with the First Presidency of the Church respecting them, places himself in a false position, and exposes himself to the power of darkness by violating his Priesthood (*MFP* 2:239).

[The Proclamation is signed by Brigham Young, Heber C. Kimball, Orson Hyde, John Taylor, Wilford Woodruff, George A. Smith, Amasa M. Lyman, Ezra T. Benson, Charles C. Rich, Lorenzo Snow, Erastus Snow, Franklin D. Richards, and George Q. Cannon (*MFP* 2:235–40).]

4. Proclamation of the First Presidency and the Quorum of the Twelve Apostles of The Church of Jesus Christ of Latter-day Saints (April 6, 1980)

[This document was put forth in commemoration of the 150th anniversary of the organization of the Church. On Sunday, April 6, 1980, a portion of the Sunday morning session of General Conference was broadcast from the newly reconstructed Peter Whitmer, Sr., home in Fayette, New York. President Spencer W. Kimball spoke briefly of the organization of the Church that had occurred on that very spot of ground. He then announced that the Church had a proclamation to declare. President Kimball's concluding words were:]

Now, my brothers and sisters, with the future before us, and sensing deeply the responsibilities and divine mission of the restored Church on this sacred occasion, the First Presidency and the Quorum of the Twelve Apostles declare to the world a proclamation. We have felt it appropriate to issue this statement from here, where the Church began. Accordingly, I shall ask Elder Gordon B. Hinckley of the Quorum of the Twelve Apostles, to speak in my behalf and in behalf of my brethren, to read this proclamation to you and to the world (CR [Apr. 1980]:74).

[Elder Gordon B. Hinckley then read the Proclamation from the Whitmer home in Fayette, New York, which was broadcast by satellite to the Tabernacle in Salt Lake City, and published in the April 12, 1980 Church News, in the May 1980 *Ensign*, and in the April 1980 Conference Report. The full text of the proclamation follows.]

The Church of Jesus Christ of Latter-day Saints was organized 150 years ago today. On this sesquicentennial anniversary we issue to the world a proclamation concerning its progress, its doctrine, its mission, and its message.

On April 6, 1830, a small group assembled in the farmhouse of Peter Whitmer in Fayette Township in the State of New York. Six men participated in the formal organization procedures, with Joseph Smith as their leader. From that modest beginning in a rural area, this work has grown consistently and broadly, as men and women in many lands have embraced the doctrine and entered the waters of baptism. There are now almost four and a half million living members, and the Church is stronger and growing more rapidly than at any time in its history. Congregations of Latter-day Saints are found throughout North, Central, and South America; in the nations of Europe; in Asia; in Africa; in Australia and the islands of the South Pacific; and in other areas of the world. The gospel restored through the instrumentality of Joseph Smith is presently taught in forty-six languages and in eighty-one nations. From that small meeting held in a farmhouse a century and a half ago, the Church has grown until today it includes nearly 12,000 organized congregations.

We testify that this restored gospel was introduced into the world by the marvelous appearance of God the Eternal Father and His Son, the resurrected Lord Jesus Christ. That most glorious manifestation marked the beginning of the fulfillment of the promise of Peter, who prophesied of "the times of restitution of all things, which God hath spoken by the mouth of all his holy prophets since the world began," this in preparation for the coming of the Lord to reign personally upon the earth (Acts 3:21).

We solemnly affirm that The Church of Jesus Christ of Latter-day Saints is in fact a restoration of the Church established by the Son of God, when in mortality he organized his work upon the earth; that it carries his sacred name, even the name of Jesus Christ; that it is built upon a foundation of Apostles and prophets, he being the chief cornerstone; that its priesthood, in both the Aaronic and Melchizedek orders, was restored under the hands of those who held it anciently: John the Baptist, in the case of the Aaronic; and Peter, James, and John in the case of the Melchizedek.

We declare that the Book of Mormon was brought forth by the gift and power of God and that it stands beside the Bible as another witness of Jesus the Christ, the Savior and Redeemer of mankind. Together they testify of his divine sonship.

We give our witness that the doctrines and practices of the Church encompass salvation and exaltation not only for those who are living, but also for the dead, and that in sacred temples built for this purpose a great vicarious work is going forward in behalf of those who have died, so that all men and women of all generations may become the beneficiaries of the saving ordinances of the gospel of the Master. This great, selfless labor is one of the distinguishing features of this restored Church of Jesus Christ.

We affirm the sanctity of the family as a divine creation and declare that God our Eternal Father will hold parents accountable to rear their children in light and truth, teaching them "to pray, and to walk uprightly before the Lord" (D&C 68:28). We teach that the most sacred of all relationships, those family associations of husbands and wives and parents and children, may be continued eternally when marriage is solemnized under the authority of the holy priesthood exercised in temples dedicated for these divinely authorized purposes.

We bear witness that all men and women are sons and daughters of God, each accountable to him; that our lives here on earth are part of an eternal plan; that death is not the end, but rather a transition from this to another sphere of purposeful activity made possible through the Atonement of the Redeemer of the world; and that we shall there have the opportunity of working and growing toward perfection.

We testify that the spirit of prophecy and revelation is among us. "We believe all that God has revealed, all that He does now reveal; and we believe that He will yet reveal many great and important things pertaining to the Kingdom of God" (Articles of Faith 1:9). The heavens are not sealed; God continues to speak to his children through a prophet empowered to declare his word, now as he did anciently.

The mission of the Church today, as it has been from the beginning, is to teach the gospel of Christ to all the world in obedience to the commandment given by the Savior prior to his ascension and repeated in modern revelation: "Go ye into all the world, preach the gospel to every creature, acting in the authority which I have given you, baptizing in the name of the Father, and of the Son, and of the Holy Ghost" (D&C 68:8).

Through the Prophet Joseph Smith the Lord revealed these words of solemn warning: "Hearken ye people from afar; and ye that are upon the islands of the sea, listen together. For verily, the voice of the Lord is unto all men, and there is none to escape; and there is no eye that shall not see, neither ear that shall not hear, neither heart that shall not be penetrated. And the rebellious shall be pierced with much sorrow; for their iniquities shall be spoken upon the housetops, and their secret acts shall be revealed. And the voice of warning shall be unto all people, by the mouths of my disciples, whom I have chosen in these last days" [D&C 1:1–4].

It is our obligation, therefore, to teach faith in the Lord Jesus Christ, to plead with the people of the earth for individual repentance, to administer the sacred ordinances of baptism by immersion for the remission of sins and the laying on of hands for the gift of the Holy Ghost—all of this under the authority of the priesthood of God.

It is our responsibility to espouse and follow an inspired program of instruction and activity, and to build and maintain appropriate facilities for the accomplishment of this, that all who will hear and accept may grow in understanding of doctrine and develop in principles of Christian service to their fellowmen.

As we stand today on the summit of 150 years of progress, we contemplate humbly and gratefully the sacrifices of those who have gone before us, many of whom gave their lives in testimony of this truth. We are thankful for their faith, for their example, for their mighty labors and willing consecrations for this cause

which they considered more precious than life itself. They have passed to us a remarkable heritage. We are resolved to build on that heritage for the blessing and benefit of those who follow, who will constitute ever enlarging numbers of faithful men and women throughout the earth.

This is God's work. It is his kingdom we are building. Anciently the prophet Daniel spoke of it as a stone cut out of the mountain without hands, which was to roll forth to fill the whole earth (see Daniel 2:31–45). We invite the honest in heart everywhere to listen to the teachings of our missionaries who are sent forth as messengers of eternal truth, to study and learn, and to ask God, our Eternal Father, in the name of his Son, the Lord Jesus Christ, "if these things are . . . true. And if ye shall ask with a sincere heart, with real intent, having faith in Christ, he will manifest the truth of it unto you, by the power of the Holy Ghost. And by the power of the Holy Ghost ye may know the truth of all things" (Moroni 10:4–5).

We call upon all men and women to forsake evil and turn to God; to work together to build that brotherhood which must be recognized when we truly come to know that God is our Father and we are his children; and to worship him and his Son, the Lord Jesus Christ, the Savior of mankind. In the authority of the Holy Priesthood in us vested, we bless the seekers of truth wherever they may be and invoke the favor of the Almighty upon all men and nations whose God is the

Lord, in the name of Jesus Christ, amen (CR [Apr. 1980]: 75–77; see also *Ensign,* May 1980, pp.51–53].

5. The Family: A Proclamation to the World, The First Presidency and Council of the Twelve Apostles of The Church of Jesus Christ of Latter-day Saints, given on September 23, 1995

To read the complete text, see "Family: A Proclamation to the World, The" in this reference work.

PROCLAMATION ON THE FAMILY

See FAMILY: A PROCLAMATION TO THE WORLD, THE.

PROLONGING LIFE

Bishops and stake presidents are in possession of counsel from the Church about prolonging life. This counsel is essentially that when competent medical personnel consider dying to be inevitable, death should be looked upon in its true light as an essential part of the Father's plan. Members should not feel obligated to support prolonging the life of a loved one beyond reasonable means. Such decisions are best made in conjunction with fasting and prayer.

PROMISE, HOLY SPIRIT OF

See HOLY GHOST; HOLY SPIRIT OF PROMISE.

PROPHETS

Throughout the earth's history, with some exceptions during times of complete apostasy, the Lord has called prophets to serve as His spokesmen. Examples include Adam, Enoch, Noah, Abraham, Moses, Isaiah, Jeremiah, Ezekiel, Daniel, Lehi, Nephi, Samuel the Lamanite, Mormon, Moroni, Joseph Smith, and each succeeding president of the Church in the dispensation of the fulness of times.

PROPHETS, SEERS, AND REVELATORS

The members of the First Presidency and the members of the Quorum of the Twelve Apostles are sustained by members of the Church as "prophets, seers, and revelators." They speak for the Lord. Their role is summarized in the Doctrine and Covenants. The Savior said, "What I the Lord have spoken, I have spoken, and I excuse not myself; and though the heavens and the earth pass away, my word shall not pass away, but shall all be fulfilled, whether by mine own voice or by the voice of my servants, it is the same" (D&C 1:38).

Seers see the future. They "see" what is coming and warn us of dangers. They see ahead and alert us to opportunities for service. They often see things we do not see. The Prophet Joseph explained the role of seers. We will use **bold** to emphasize what he said about them: "Wherefore, we again say, search the revelations of God; study the prophecies, and rejoice that God grants unto the world **Seers and Prophets**. They are **they who** saw the mysteries of godliness; **they saw** the flood before it came; **they saw** angels ascending and descending upon a ladder that reached from earth to heaven; **they saw** the stone cut out of the mountain, which filled the whole earth; **they saw** the Son of God come from the regions of bliss and dwell with men on earth; **they saw** the deliverer come out of Zion, and turn away ungodliness from Jacob; **they saw** the glory of the Lord when he showed the transfiguration of the earth on the mount; **they saw** every mountain laid low and every valley exalted when the Lord was taking vengeance upon the wicked; **they saw** truth spring out of the earth, and righteousness look down from heaven in the last days, before the Lord came the second time to gather his elect; **they saw** the end of wickedness on earth, and the Sabbath of creation crowned with peace; **they saw** the end of the glorious thousand years, when Satan was loosed for a little season; **they saw** the day of judgment when all men received according to their works, and **they saw** the heaven and the earth flee away to make room for the city of God, when the righteous receive an inheritance in eternity" (*TPJS*, pp. 12–13).

PROPITIATION

As used in the scriptures, "propitiation" means "atonement" and refers to the Atonement of Christ (Romans 3:25; 1 John 2:2; 4:10).

PROXIES

See PROXY; PROXY ORDINANCES.

PROXY

A term which means "standing in for someone else." For example, "proxy baptisms" is a phrase which refers to being baptized for the dead.

PROXY ORDINANCES

See also BAPTISM FOR THE DEAD; DEAD, BAPTISM FOR; PROXY. The Church of Jesus Christ of Latter-day Saints believes in performing ordinances of salvation for the dead (D&C 128:15) in temples. Paul spoke of this type of proxy ordinance work for the dead when he asked, "Else what shall they do which are baptized for the dead, if the dead rise not at all? why are they then baptized for the dead?" (1 Corinthians 15:29).

Since the Savior initiated preaching to those who had died and gone to the postmortal spirit world without having the benefits of His gospel (1 Peter 3:18–20; D&C 138), it follows that those who accept the gospel in the spirit world need the ordinances of salvation. Such ordinances are called "proxy ordinances" since they are done by mortals for those who have died. Such work for the dead includes baptisms, washings and anointings, ordination to the priesthood for deceased brethren, sealings (marriages), and sealing families together.

Even though ordinance work is done for the dead by the living, it is not binding on them. They have their agency to accept or reject proxy work done for them.

PSEUDEPIGRAPHA

The word "Pseudepigrapha" comes from Greek and means "false writings" or "writings falsely attributed to a prominent or well-known person." Pseudepigrapha, then, refers basically to a group of early writings not included in the Bible.

·Q–R·

QUEENS

See PRIESTESSES.

QUORUM OF THE TWELVE APOSTLES

See APOSTLES, THE TWELVE.

QUORUMS

See PRIESTHOOD QUORUMS.

RABBI

A term which means "Master" (John 1:38). It was a term of respect and honor in Jewish culture (Matthew 23:7). Jesus was frequently referred to as "Rabbi" (John 1:38, 49; 3:2, 26; 6:25).

RABBONI

See also RABBI. "Rabboni" meant "Master" (John 20:16) or "Teacher" (John 20:16 footnote a). It was a term of high regard in Jewish culture. Mary Magdalene referred to the Savior as "Rabboni" when He appeared to her at the garden tomb (John 20:16).

RAPHAEL

We do not know who this angel is. The only clue we have is that Joseph Smith referred to him along with many other angels who restored keys from previous dispensations. The Prophet said, "And the voice of Michael, the archangel; the voice of Gabriel, and of Raphael, and of divers angels, from Michael or Adam down to the present time, all declaring their dispensation, their rights, their keys, their honors, their majesty and glory, and the power of their priesthood; giving line upon line, precept upon precept; here a little, and there a little; giving us consolation by holding forth that which is to come, confirming our hope!" (D&C 128:21).

REBAPTISM

When a member of the Church has been excommunicated, he or she can only return to membership by being rebaptized. In such cases, the individual's membership record shows the date of the original baptism, rather than the date of rebaptism. The sins that led to excommunication are washed away through sincere repentance and the rebaptism. Thus, the Lord's comforting words, "I, the Lord, remember them no more" (D&C 58:42) are in effect. Also, with the original baptismal date on the records, the questions will not come up about a more recent date of baptism because of information on the membership record.

Some rebaptisms are necessary in the case of lost membership records or where records of the baptism were not filled out in the first place.

REBAPTISMS

Starting in Nauvoo and continuing until 1897, many members of the Church were rebaptized, often as a means of rededicating themselves to God. "Rebaptism served as a ritual of recommitment but was not viewed as essential to salvation. Members often sought rebaptism when called to assist in colonization or to participate in one of the united orders. On some occasions, the Saints were rebaptized as they prepared for marriage or entrance into the temple. Early members also rebaptized some of the sick among them as an act of healing. Because of misuse by some Church members, all such practices of rebaptism were discontinued in 1897" (*EM*, under "Rebaptism").

"Oftentimes Latter-day Saints had been rebaptized in conjunction with important milestones, such as marriage or entering the United Order or sometimes for improvement of health. These rebaptisms were recorded on Church membership records. The First Presidency grew concerned that some members were substituting rebaptism for true repentance. In 1893, stake presidents were instructed not to require rebaptism of Saints wishing to attend the dedication of the Salt Lake Temple, and in 1897 the practice of rebaptism was discontinued altogether" (*Church History in the Fulness of Times*, p. 448).

RECOMMENDS

Members of the Church who desire to enter temples must obtain a "temple recommend" from a member of their bishopric and also a member of their stake presidency. A number of questions designed to evaluate the member's worthiness to enter the temple are asked at both interviews. Upon entering a temple, the member is required to show the recommend at the recommend desk near the front entry.

A recommend must be renewed every two years.

RECORDER, TEMPLE

Each temple has a temple "recorder" who serves on the Temple Executive Council, consisting of the temple president, his two counselors, the temple matron, and the recorder. Among other duties, the recorder is responsible to see that all ordinance work is properly recorded.

Joseph Smith gave instructions regarding "recorders" (D&C 127:6; 128:2–4).

REDEEMER

See also JESUS CHRIST. "Redeemer" is another name for Jesus Christ (Job 19:25; Isaiah 44:6; 1 Nephi 10:14; D&C 34:1), with the connotation that He "redeems" us unconditionally from physical death, and from our sins if we repent and live according to His gospel.

REDEMPTION OF THE DEAD

See PROXY ORDINANCES.

REFINER'S FIRE

The imagery of the refiner's fire is found in Malachi 3:3 and repeated in 3 Nephi 24:3 as well as D&C 128:24. The imagery comes from the process of refining precious metal as used in ancient times. An example of the process is found in the refining of gold. The gold ore is placed in a crucible, and a fire is used to heat the ore until it becomes molten. At that point, the gold, which is heavier than the rock in which it is imbedded, settles to the bottom of the pot and the imperfections and molten rock rise to the top, where they are scraped off or ladled off. As more and more ore is added and heated by the fire, more and more gold is produced. Finally, pure gold is all that remains. All the impurities have been refined out by fire.

The symbolism of the refiner's fire applies to all of us. When we are going through hard times, it is said that we are going through the refiner's fire. In other words, the Lord is allow-ing troubles and difficulties to come upon us, even when we are doing our best to do His will, in order to develop desirable character traits within us.

REGIONAL REPRESENTATIVES

The first Regional Representatives were called in 1967. They were part-time lay officers of the Church and were called by the First Presidency. Their principal responsibility was to train stake leaders. They did not have line authority but served under the general direction of the Quorum of the Twelve Apostles and received specific directions from their respective Area Presidencies. They reported directly to their Area Presidencies, and presided at stake conferences when assigned to do so.

In the Saturday morning session of the 1997 April general conference, President Gordon B. Hinckley announced the calling of Area Authority Seventies (later, the title was shortened to Area Seventy). The calling of Area Authority Seventies is described as follows: "Whereas other officers of the church, who belong not unto the Twelve, neither to the Seventy, are not under the responsibility to travel among all nations, but are to travel as their circumstances shall allow, notwithstanding they may hold as high and responsible offices in the church" (D&C 107:98).

With the calling of Area Authority Seventies, the Regional Representatives were released.

REINCARNATION

The idea that people live, die, and come back as another person to live another life, repeated any number of times. The idea that people are reincarnated is a false doctrine. The Bible teaches that we only die once (Hebrews 9:27).

RELIEF SOCIETY

The Relief Society is the adult women's organization of The Church of Jesus Christ of Latter-day Saints, serving women from ages eighteen and up. It is the largest women's organization in the world. It was organized on March 17, 1842, by the Prophet Joseph Smith in Nauvoo, Illinois. Emma Smith was selected as its first president.

On April 28, 1842, Joseph Smith addressed the women of the new Relief Society organization and gave them instruction and counsel. Among other things, he said, "I now turn the key in your behalf in the name of the Lord, and this Society shall rejoice, and knowledge and intelligence shall flow down from this time henceforth; this is the beginning of better days to the poor and needy, who shall be made to rejoice and pour forth blessings on your heads" (*HC* 4:606–7).

Over 165 years have passed since the organization of the Relief Society. Members of this women's organization of the Church now number over five and a half million in 170 countries. Immeasurable good has been done and continues to be done through countless acts of service and kindness by these sisters throughout the world today.

RELIGIOUS EDUCATION

See CHURCH EDUCATIONAL SYSTEM.

REMISSION OF SINS

See also FORGIVENESS. "Remission of sins" is a scriptural phrase for "forgiveness of sins" (Matthew 26:28; Mark 1:4; Luke 3:3; 3 Nephi 1:23; Moroni 8:25–26; D&C 13:1; Articles of Faith 1:4).

REPENTANCE

See FORGIVENESS; REMISSION OF SINS.

REPLENISH

The Lord commanded Adam and Eve to "multiply and replenish the earth" (Genesis 1:28). Many people think "replenish" means "refill." Such is not the case. "Replenish" means "fill" (see Genesis 1:28 footnote c).

REPLENISH THE EARTH

See REPLENISH.

REST OF THE LORD

This phrase means "heaven," in other words, the celestial kingdom (Moroni 7:3).

The word "rest," as used in D&C 84:24, means "exaltation."

RESTITUTION OF ALL THINGS

A phrase which means "the restoration of the full gospel of Jesus Christ." It refers to the restoration through the Prophet Joseph Smith. Peter used this phrase when he was responding to those who were amazed at the healing of the lame man (Acts 3:1–11). He invited them to repent and taught them about Jesus Christ, "Whom the heaven must receive until the times of restitution of all things, which God hath spoken by the mouth of all his holy prophets since the world began" (Acts 3:21).

RESTORATION, THE

The latter-day restoration of the full gospel and church of Jesus Christ through the Prophet Joseph Smith. This restoration was prophesied in the Bible (Daniel 2:35, 44–45; Ezekiel 37:15–19; Malachi 4:5–6; Acts 3:19–21; Ephesians 1:10).

This restoration of the true church of Jesus Christ began with Joseph Smith's first vision in the spring of 1820 (JS—H 1:1–5; 20) and continued with the coming forth of the Book of Mormon (JS—H 1:27–54). The Aaronic Priesthood was restored by John the Baptist on May 15, 1829 (D&C 13), and shortly thereafter, Peter, James, and John restored the Melchizedek Priesthood (D&C 27:12).

On April 6, 1830, the Church was officially organized (D&C 20, 21), and over the next several years, various heavenly messengers restored the rest of the priesthood keys needed for a full restoration of the Savior's true church (D&C 128:21; 110:11–16). Thus it had the same priesthood, doctrines, and ordinances, and the same "organization that existed in the Primitive Church, namely, apostles, prophets, pastors, teachers, Evangelists, and so forth" (Articles of Faith 1:6). All of the keys of the priesthood which had been given to man on earth from Adam's time onward were thus restored.

RESTORATION OF ALL THINGS

See RESTORATION, THE.

RESTORATION OF BLESSINGS

When a member who has received the higher ordinances of the temple is excommunicated, those ordinances are lost along with all other blessings and privileges of membership in the Lord's Church. If the member is a male, his Melchizedek Priesthood is likewise gone. Thus, when such an individual returns to the Church through rebaptism, these blessings need to be restored. After a waiting period of at least a year from the time of rebaptism, and after worthiness interviews with the bishop and stake president, arrangements are made for the "restoration of blessings." The ordinance is performed by a priesthood leader who is authorized by the First Presidency. Rather than being "re-endowed," "re-ordained," "re-sealed," etc., the person has hands laid upon his or her head by the authorized priesthood leader and he "restores" the appropriate previous blessings.

Once these blessings have been

restored by this ordinance, the individual's membership record uses the original dates of the ordinances. This is a significant reminder that, upon sincere and complete repentance of sins, "I the Lord, remember them no more" (D&C 58:42).

RESTORATION OF THE GOSPEL

See RESTORATION, THE.

RESTORED CHURCH

See RESTORATION, THE.

RESURRECTED BEINGS

See also IMMORTAL BODY. Resurrected beings are "resurrected personages, having bodies of flesh and bones" (D&C 129:1). When Jesus appeared to the disciples after His resurrection, He explained His resurrected body to them, saying, "Behold my hands and my feet, that it is I myself: handle me, and see; for a spirit hath not flesh and bones, as ye see me have" (Luke 24:39).

Amulek taught that the resurrection is the reuniting of the spirit and the body. He said, "The spirit and the body shall be reunited again in its perfect form; both limb and joint shall be restored to its proper frame" (Alma 11:43).

RESURRECTED BODIES

See also IMMORTAL BODY; RESURRECTED BEINGS. The resurrection reunites the spirit and body permanently. Resurrected bodies are perfect (Alma 11:43; 40:23).

However, the scriptures teach that there will be some differences in resurrected bodies, depending on which degree of glory an individual goes to. The Lord explained this fact in the Doctrine and Covenants. We will quote relevant verses and add notes in brackets within the verses:

D&C 88:28–32

28 They who are of a celestial spirit [*those who lived worthy of celestial glory*] shall receive the same body which was a natural body; even ye shall receive your bodies, and your glory shall be that glory by which your bodies are quickened [*resurrected*].

29 Ye who are quickened by a portion of the celestial glory shall then receive of the same, even a fulness [*of the celestial glory and blessings and privileges*].

30 And they who are quickened by a portion of the terrestrial glory [*those who are resurrected into terrestrial glory*] shall then receive of the same [*the terrestrial kingdom*], even a fulness [*will receive a terrestrial body*]. [*Note that it does not say a "natural body" or "your bodies" as was the case for celestials in verse 28, above. In other words, a terrestrial body differs from a celestial body.*]

31 And also they who are quickened by a portion of the telestial glory shall then receive of the same [*the telestial kingdom*], even a fulness [*all the blessings and privileges, along with the limitations of telestial*

glory and telestial bodies].

32 And they who remain [*sons of perdition*] shall also be quickened [*resurrected*]; nevertheless, they shall return again to their own place [*outer darkness*], to enjoy that which they are willing to receive, because they were not willing to enjoy that which they might have received.

Paul taught this same doctrine as follows:

1 Corinthians 15:39–42

39 All flesh is not the same flesh: but there is one kind of flesh of men, another flesh of beasts, another of fishes, and another of birds.

40 There are also celestial bodies, and bodies terrestrial: but the glory of the celestial is one, and the glory of the terrestrial is another.

41 There is one glory of the sun, and another glory of the moon, and another glory of the stars: for one star differeth from another star in glory.

42 So also is the resurrection of the dead.

Furthermore, Joseph Fielding Smith also taught this doctrine. He said, "In the resurrection there will be different kinds of bodies. . . . The body a man receives [in the resurrection] will determine his place hereafter. . . . There will be several classes of resurrected bodies; some celestial, some terrestrial, some telestial, and some sons of perdition. Each of these classes will differ from the others by prominent and marked distinctions; . . . celestial bodies . . . will shine like the sun as our Savior's does, . . . terrestrial bodies will not shine like the sun, but they will be more glorious than the bodies of those who receive the telestial glory. . . . In both of these kingdoms [terrestrial and telestial] there will be changes in the bodies and limitations. They will not have the power of increase, neither the power or nature to live as husbands and wives, for this will be denied them and they cannot increase. Those who receive the exaltation in the celestial kingdom will have the 'continuation of the seeds forever' (D&C 132:19). They will live in the family relationship. In the terrestrial and in the telestial kingdom there will be no marriage. Those who enter there will remain 'separately and singly' (D&C 132:15–32) forever" (*DS* 2:286–88).

RESURRECTION

See also RESURRECTED BEINGS; RESURRECTED BODIES. All people will be resurrected, regardless of whether they were righteous or wicked (1 Corinthians 15:22). Resurrection is the permanent reuniting of the body and the spirit (Alma 11:43). We will be happy to get our physical body back at this time (D&C 138:50).

Resurrection is a priesthood ordinance. We do not yet have the keys to this ordinance. Brigham Young taught:

"It is supposed by this people that we have all the ordinances in our possession for life and salvation, and exaltation, and that we are administering these ordinances. This is not the case. We are in possession of all the ordinances that can be administered in the flesh; but there are other ordinances and administrations that must be administered beyond this world. I know you would ask what they are. I will mention one. We have not, neither can we receive here, the ordinance and the keys of the resurrection. They will be given to those who have passed off this stage of action and have received their bodies again, as many have already done and many more will. They will be ordained, by those who hold the keys of the resurrection, to go forth and resurrect the Saints just as we receive the ordinance of baptism, then the keys of authority to baptize others for the remission of their sins. This is one of the ordinances we cannot receive here, and there are many more." (*Discourses of Brigham Young*, pp. 397–98.)

"Then angels will come and begin to resurrect the dead, and the Savior will also raise the dead, and they [the worthy men who were dead] will receive the keys of the resurrection, and will begin to assist in that work." (*Discourses of Brigham Young*, p. 115.)

"Some person holding the keys of the resurrection, having previously passed through that ordeal, will be delegated to resurrect our bodies, and our spirits will be there and prepared to enter into their bodies." (*Discourses*

of Brigham Young, p. 373.)

President Spencer W. Kimball also taught that resurrection is a priesthood ordinance. He said:

"Today you or I could not stand here and call to life a dead person. But, the day will come when I can take my wife by the hand and raise her out of the grave in the resurrection. The day will come when you can bring each of your family who has preceded you in death back into a resurrected being, to live forever" (President Spencer W. Kimball, Manchester England Area Conference, June 21, 1976).

REVELATION

See also INSPIRATION. Revelation is communication from God (D&C 8:2–3). Generally speaking, revelation is more direct and powerful than inspiration. When a person sees a vision, hears a voice, sees an angel, etc., there is no question as to whether or not God is communicating with him or her. Joseph Smith received many such revelations, which are included in the Doctrine and Covenants and elsewhere.

REVELATOR

Another name for the Apostle John. He is often referred to as John the Revelator because of his vision, recorded in the Bible as the book of Revelation, in which many future events were revealed.

REVELATORS

See PROPHETS, SEERS, AND REVELATORS.

REVERENCE

Reverence is much more than merely being quiet. It is a deep, inner respect for that which is sacred. Reverence invites meditation and contemplation of life's meaning and the purposes of God for His children. Indeed, it invites communication with God.

The scriptures speak of reverence in conjunction with worship of God (Leviticus 19:30). Likewise, the scriptures speak of reverence for those in authority, including parents (Hebrews 12:9) as well as for the laws of the land (D&C 134:7).

RIGHT HAND

See HAND, THE RIGHT.

ROBE

See also ROBES OF RIGHTEOUSNESS. In biblical symbolism, "robe" is symbolic of royalty and status. It is also symbolic of acceptance by God, as in 2 Nephi 4:33 where Nephi says, "O Lord, wilt thou encircle me around in the robe of thy righteousness! O Lord, wilt thou make a way for mine escape before mine enemies!" See also Isaiah 61:10. In Revelation 7:9, white robes are given to those who live in the presence of God (celestial glory). The "best robe" for the prodigal son (Luke 15:22) would be symbolic of potential for highest status, in other words, exaltation.

ROBES OF RIGHTEOUSNESS

See also ROBE; ROBES, WHITE. The phrase "robes of righteousness," as used in the scriptures, means exaltation (D&C 29:12; 109:76; 2 Nephi 9:14).

ROBES, WHITE

In the vision given to John, recorded in the Book of Revelation, he saw "a great multitude, which no man could number, of all nations, and kindreds, and people, and tongues, stood before the throne, and before the Lamb, clothed with white robes, and palms in their hands" (Revelation 7:9). The "white robes" here are symbolic of exaltation (see also Revelation 6:11; 7:13–14).

ROCK

"Rock" is often used symbolically in the scriptures to mean the Savior and building upon His gospel (Psalm 18:31; Matthew 7:24–25; 1 Corinthians 10:4).

ROCK OF AGES

See also ROCK. Although it is not found in the scriptures, this phrase refers to the Savior.

ROCK OF HEAVEN

Another name for the Savior (Moses 7:53).

ROCK OF OFFENCE

Another name for the Savior (Isaiah 8:14; Romans 9:33; 1 Peter 2:8), carrying the connotation that the wicked are offended by Christ and His gospel, as well as by the righteous who seek to follow Christ.

· S ·

SABBATH DAY

See also LORD'S DAY. Our modern prophets have given counsel about how to observe the Sabbath Day:

"The Sabbath is the Lord's day, set apart each week for rest and worship. In Old Testament times, God's covenant people observed the Sabbath on the seventh day of the week because God rested on the seventh day when He had created the earth. The Lord emphasized the importance of Sabbath observance in the Ten Commandments:

" 'Remember the sabbath day, to keep it holy.

" 'Six days shalt thou labour, and do all thy work:

" 'But the seventh day is the sabbath of the Lord thy God: in it thou shalt not do any work, thou, nor thy son, nor thy daughter, thy manservant, nor thy maidservant, nor thy cattle, nor thy stranger that is within thy gates:

" 'For in six days the Lord made heaven and earth, the sea, and all that in them is, and rested the seventh day: wherefore the Lord blessed the sabbath day, and hallowed it' (Exodus 20:8–11).

"After the Resurrection of Jesus Christ, which occurred on the first day of the week, the Lord's disciples began observing the Sabbath on the first day of the week, Sunday (see Acts 20:7).

"In the latter days, the Lord has commanded us to continue observing the Sabbath. He has promised that if we obey this commandment, we will receive 'the fulness of the earth' (see D&C 59:16–20).

"Because the Sabbath is a holy day, it should be reserved for worthy and holy activities. Abstaining from work and recreation is not enough. In fact, if we merely lounge about doing nothing on the Sabbath, we fail to keep the day holy. In a revelation given to Joseph Smith in 1831, the Lord commanded: 'That thou mayest more fully keep thyself unspotted from the world, thou shalt go to the house of prayer and offer up thy sacraments upon my holy day; for verily this is a day appointed unto you to rest from your labors, and to pay thy devotions unto the Most High' (D&C 59:9–10). In harmony with this revelation, we attend sacrament meeting each week. Other Sabbath-day activities may include praying, meditating, studying the scriptures and the teachings of latter-day prophets, writing letters to family members and friends, reading wholesome material, visiting the sick and distressed, and attending other Church meetings" (*TF*, pp. 145–47).

SABAOTH

"Sabaoth" is defined by the Lord as "the creator of the first day, the beginning and the end" (D&C 95:7).

SACKCLOTH

A coarse, usually dark fabric (Revelation 6:12) made from the hair of camels or goats or both. It was used in biblical times for making sacks and bags. When people were in mourning in ancient times, they wore clothing made from sackcloth to symbolize their distress and sorrow (Genesis 37:34; Jeremiah 4:8; Esther 4:3). It was also worn as a symbol of humility (2 Kings 19:1; Matthew 11:21; Helaman 11:19).

SACKCLOTH AND ASHES

See also SACKCLOTH. In ancient times, during times of mourning, it was customary to dress in sackcloth and spread ashes upon one's self (Esther 4:3).

SACRAMENT

See also LAST SUPPER; SACRAMENT MEETING. In The Church of Jesus Christ of Latter-day Saints, the word "sacrament" is used almost exclusively to mean the ordinance of partaking of bread and water as symbols of the Savior's atoning sacrifice for all mankind (Matthew 26:26–28).

The sacrament is administered weekly in sacrament meetings throughout the Church. In partaking of the sacrament, worthy members of the Church both make covenants and renew their covenants of baptism. "When you partake of the sacrament, you witness to God that your remembrance of His Son will extend beyond the short time of that sacred ordinance. You promise to remember Him always. You witness that you are willing to take upon yourself the name of Jesus Christ and that you will keep His commandments. In partaking of the sacrament and making these commitments, you renew your baptismal covenant (see Mosiah 18:8–10; D&C 20:37)" (*TF*, p. 148).

The sacrament prayers which the priests read as they bless the sacrament must be given exactly word for word. The reason for this is that they are a covenant between the Lord and the members who are going to partake of it. The same applies to the baptismal prayer, the endowment, the covenant made during temple marriage, and in sealing families together in the temple.

The sacrament prayers were given by the Lord in a revelation to the Prophet Joseph Smith. They are:

D&C 20:77, 79

77 O God, the Eternal Father, we ask thee in the name of thy Son, Jesus Christ, to bless and sanctify this bread to the souls of all those who partake of it, that they may eat in remembrance of the body of thy Son, and witness unto thee, O God, the Eternal Father, that they are willing to take upon them the name of thy Son, and always remember him and keep his commandments which he has given them; that they may always have his Spirit to be with them. Amen.

79 O God, the Eternal Father, we ask thee in the name of thy Son, Jesus Christ, to bless and sanctify

this wine to the souls of all those who drink of it, that they may do it in remembrance of the blood of thy Son, which was shed for them; that they may witness unto thee, O God, the Eternal Father, that they do always remember him, that they may have his Spirit to be with them. Amen.

A careful reading of the sacrament prayers reveals that we make the following covenants with the Lord in partaking of the sacred emblems of the sacrament:

1. We remember the body of the Savior which He gave for us and the blood which He shed for us during the Atonement.

2. We take upon us His name, which includes standing "as witnesses of God at all times and in all things, and in all places" (Mosiah 18:9).

3. We covenant to always remember Him.

4. We covenant to keep His commandments.

In return for making and keeping the covenants involved in the sacrament, the Lord promises members that they will "always have his Spirit to be with them." This is a priceless blessing. Since a major role of the Holy Ghost is to guide and direct us in all things necessary to enter exaltation (John 14:26; 15:26; 16:13), if we have His Spirit with us con-

stantly, we will attain exaltation.

In the early days of the Church in this dispensation, bread and wine were used in administering the sacrament. However, in a revelation given to Joseph Smith in August 1830, the Lord said, "It mattereth not what ye shall eat or what ye shall drink when ye partake of the sacrament, if it so be that ye do it with an eye single to my glory—remembering unto the Father my body which was laid down for you, and my blood which was shed for the remission of your sins" (D&C 27:2). Water is now used in place of wine for that portion of the sacrament.

SACRAMENT MEETING

See also SACRAMENT. Sacrament meeting is a weekly meeting held on Sunday by the congregations of the Church in most parts of the world, as part of a three-hour meeting block. The most important part of this meeting is the opportunity for worthy members to partake of the sacrament. In addition to the sacrament of bread and water, the meeting consists of an opening and closing prayer, the singing of hymns, talks, testimonies (on fast Sunday), and special musical numbers.

Members are commanded by the Lord to attend weekly sacrament meetings (D&C 59:9), and those not of our faith are welcome to attend.

SACRED GROVE

See also FIRST VISION. The Sacred Grove is the name of the grove of trees near the Joseph Smith Sr. home near Palmyra, New York, where fourteen-year-old Joseph Smith went to pray about which church to join. In response to his humble prayer in that spring of 1820, the Father and Son appeared to him (JS—H 1:5–20).

The Sacred Grove is now part of a visitors' center operated by the Church which hosts large numbers of visitors annually.

SACRIFICES, ANIMAL

See ANIMAL SACRIFICE.

SACRIFICES, HUMAN

Human sacrifices are the ultimate blasphemy created by Satan in mockery of the sacrifice of the Son of God.

SACRIFICIAL LAMB

See also LAMB; LAMB OF GOD; PASCHAL LAMB; PASSOVER. Sacrificial lambs were used according to the law of Moses in ancient Israel to symbolize the sacrifice of the "Lamb of God" (John 1:29; 1 Nephi 10:10; D&C 88:106).

SADDUCEES

See also PHARISEES. An influential group or sect among the Jews who wielded much influence in government and daily life at the time of the Savior's mortal ministry. The Sadducees, who did not believe in angels, spirits, or the resurrection (BD, under "Sadducees"), were normally at odds with the Pharisees, who did. However, they joined forces against Jesus (Matthew 16:1). After the Savior's crucifixion, resurrection, and ascension to heaven, the Sadducees continued to oppose the ministry of the Apostles because they, too, taught the resurrection of the dead (Acts 4:1–3).

SAINT, SAINTS

The Church of Jesus Christ of Latter-day Saints does not believe in the idea of having patron saints. Neither does it believe in canonizing the names of past martyrs or famous Christians, or in praying to such.

The word "saints," as used in the full name of the Church, simply refers to members of the Church.

The term "saints" comes from the Greek "hagios" and means "holy ones," "set apart," or "separate." It was used by Paul to refer to members of the Church in his day (Phil. 1:1).

SALT LAKE TEMPLE

Construction on the Salt Lake Temple of The Church of Jesus Christ of Latter-day Saints began on February 14, 1853. The massive structure was dedicated forty years later, on April 6, 1893, by President Wilford Woodruff. It is one of the most famous architectural features of Salt Lake City, Utah.

Sacred ordinances of salvation for the living and the dead are performed in the temple, including marriages for eternity and baptisms for the dead. Because of the sacred nature of the ordinances performed within its walls, only worthy members of the Church are allowed to enter it.

SALT LAKE TEMPLE ARCHITECTURAL SYMBOLISM

The Salt Lake Temple is unique among the many temples constructed by the Church, because of the architectural symbolism included in its design. A few of these symbolism features include:

1. Angel Moroni: Symbolizes the restoration of the gospel and continued revelation from heaven to man on earth.

2. The Three East Towers: Symbolize the Melchizedek Priesthood. They are six feet taller (210 feet) than the west towers (204 feet), symbolizing that the Melchizedek priesthood presides over the Church in spiritual matters and all other concerns. They also represent the President of the Church and his two counselors and also represent the stake president and his two counselors, on a local level.

3. The Three West Towers: Represent the Aaronic Priesthood, working under the direction of the Melchizedek Priesthood. They also represent the Presiding Bishopric of the Church and the bishop and his two counselors at the local level.

4. The Twelve Little Towers on Each of the Six Main Towers: Represent the Twelve Apostles, who support the First Presidency and all the work of the Church. These sets of twelve towers represent the high council at the local level, as they support the stake presidency.

5. The Four Corner Main Towers: Represent the four corners of the earth, symbolizing that missionary work must take the gospel to the whole world.

6. Cloud Stones near the Top of the East Center Tower, with Rays of Light Piercing Through: Represent the gospel being taken to the four corners of the earth and the gospel light piercing through superstition and spiritual darkness.

7. The Big Dipper on the West Center Tower: Represents that those who are lost may look to the priesthood for guidance and thus find their way back to God.

8. The Dedicatory Inscription, "Holiness to the Lord," on the East Center Tower: Represents the reality of the establishment of God's kingdom on earth with the temple as His personal sanctuary where heaven and earth are joined and where man on earth can commune with God in heaven and God can commune with man on earth.

9. The All-Seeing Eye (set in the window below the dedicatory inscription on the east center tower): Symbolizes that God can always see you and knows when you need His help. It also represents that God can see all the good deeds and evil deeds of man.

10. The Clasped Hand (next window down from the all-seeing eye, east center tower): Represents the hand of fellowship of one member to another within the gospel.

11. Star Stones (around the top of the temple): Represent the heavens and the fact that man on earth must keep his eyes toward heaven and God's help to him.

12. Sun Stones, Moon Stones, Earth Stones (in descending order on various facades of the temple): Symbolize the various kingdoms of glory in the next life. Earth stones (near ground level) represent telestial glory. Moon stones represent terrestrial glory. Sun stones represent celestial glory. They are to be read from the ground up, symbolizing that man on earth must look heavenward. They also represent the various stages of the earth's progress, eventually ending up as a celestial planet.

(Source: Article entitled "Exterior Symbolism of the Salt Lake Temple: Reflecting the Faith That Called the Place into Being," by Richard G. Oman, *BYU Studies*, Vol. 36, Number 4, 1996–97. This article uses notes from Truman O. Angell, who was the architect for the Salt Lake Temple).

SALVATION

The term "salvation," as used in the scriptures, almost always means "exaltation" (2 Timothy 2:10; Mosiah 3:17; Alma 34:15; D&C 6:13). However, it can also refer to freedom from death, which is a gift to all through the Atonement of Christ. It can also, depending on context, mean salvation in the terrestrial or telestial kingdom (D&C 76:86–88).

SALVATION BY GRACE
See GRACE.

SALVATION FOR THE DEAD
See PROXY ORDINANCES.

SALVATION OF CHILDREN

All children who die before the age of eight go to heaven. Joseph Smith was given a vision in which he "beheld that all children who die before they arrive at the years of accountability are saved in the celestial kingdom of heaven" (D&C 137:10).

Furthermore, President Joseph F. Smith taught that all such children will receive exaltation, which means that they will attain the highest degree of glory in the celestial kingdom. He said, "Such children are in the bosom of the Father. They will inherit their glory and their exaltation, and they will not be deprived of the blessings that belong to them" (Smith, *Gospel Doctrine*, p. 453).

This brings up the question of how they can be exalted, since they were not married on earth. The answer is simple. In the postmortal spirit world or during the Millennium, they will choose a mate and, during the Millennium, mortals will be married by proxy for them in a temple. Thus, they will go on to their exaltation.

SALVATION OF THE DEAD
See PROXY ORDINANCES.

SAME GENDER ATTRACTION

President Gordon B. Hinckley stated the position of the Church on this subject. He said, "We believe that marriage between a man and a woman is ordained of God. We believe that marriage may be eternal through exercise of the power of the everlasting priesthood in the house of the Lord.

"People inquire about our position on those who consider themselves so-called gays and lesbians. My response is that we love them as sons and daughters of God. They may have certain inclinations which are powerful and which may be difficult to control. Most people have inclinations of one kind or another at various times. If they do not act upon these inclinations, then they can go forward as do all other members of the Church. If they violate the law of chastity and the moral standards of the Church, then they are subject to the discipline of the Church, just as others are.

"We want to help these people, to strengthen them, to assist them with their problems and to help them with their difficulties. But we cannot stand idle if they indulge in immoral activity, if they try to uphold and defend and live in a so-called same-sex marriage situation. To permit such would be to make light of the very serious and sacred foundation of God-sanctioned marriage and its very purpose, the rearing of families" (CR [Oct. 1998]).

In public communications on this sensitive issue, the Church generally uses the term "same gender attraction," rather than "same sex attraction" or other common terms and phrases, in order to differentiate between having feelings for the same sex as opposed to acting out on those feelings. The Lord's law of chastity applies to all people. Thus, regardless of gender attraction, reserving sexual activity for marriage applies to all of God's children. All who keep God's laws regarding the powers of procreation, whether single or married, as well as the other laws and commandments of the gospel, can gain salvation and exaltation. On the other hand, all who break the laws of God, including the law of chastity, must repent in order to be forgiven. Justifying sexual transgression, regardless of reasons, does not change God's laws.

In 2007, the Church published a pamphlet entitled "God Loveth His Children" which addresses the issues of same gender attraction. It can be obtained from local bishops and stake presidents or from Church headquarters by calling 1–800–453–3860.

An interview with Elder Dallin H. Oaks of the Twelve Apostles, and Elder Lance B. Wickman, of the Seventy (which, in 2007, was accessible on the Church website, lds.org, under "News and Events," then "Newsroom," then "Public Issues," then "Same Gender Attraction") addresses many issues regarding same gender attraction and provides understanding of the principles and doctrines upon which the Church's stand is based, on this sensitive and often difficult matter. The complete text of this interview is included here:

Same-Gender Attraction: An Interview with Elder Dallin H. Oaks of the Twelve, and Elder Lance B. Wickman, of the Seventy (available on lds.org, 2007)

The continuing public debate over same-gender marriage has prompted many questions from the news media, the general public and Church members in relation to the position of The Church of Jesus Christ of Latter-day Saints on the marriage issue specifically and on homosexuality in general.

The following interview was conducted with Elder Dallin H. Oaks, a member of the Quorum of the Twelve Apostles of the Church, and Elder Lance B. Wickman, a member of the Seventy. These senior Church leaders responded to questions from two members of the Church's Public Affairs staff. The transcript of the interview appears below in order to help clarify the Church's stand on these important, complex and sensitive issues.

PUBLIC AFFAIRS: At the outset, can you explain why this whole issue of homosexuality and same-gender marriage is important to the Church?

ELDER OAKS: This is much bigger than just a question of whether or not society should be more tolerant of the homosexual lifestyle. Over past years we have seen unrelenting pressure from advocates of that lifestyle to accept as normal what is not normal, and to characterize those who disagree as narrow-minded, bigoted and unreasonable. Such advocates are quick to demand freedom of speech and thought for themselves, but equally quick to criticize those with a different view and, if possible, to silence them by applying labels like "homophobic." In at least one country where homosexual activists have won major concessions, we have even seen a church pastor threatened with prison for preaching from the pulpit that homosexual behavior is sinful. Given these trends, The Church of Jesus Christ of Latter-day Saints must take a stand on doctrine and principle. This is more than a social issue—ultimately it may be a test of our most basic religious freedoms to teach what we know our Father in Heaven wants us to teach.

PUBLIC AFFAIRS: Let's say my 17-year-old son comes to talk to me and, after a great deal of difficulty trying to get it out, tells me that he believes that he's attracted to men—that he has no interest and never has had any interest in girls. He believes he's probably gay. He says that he's tried to suppress these feelings. He's remained celibate, but he realizes that his feelings are going to be devastating to the family because we've always talked about his Church mission, about his temple marriage and all those kinds of things. He just feels he can't live what he thinks is a lie any longer, and so he comes in this very upset and depressed manner. What do I tell him as a parent?

ELDER OAKS: You're my son. You will always be my son, and I'll always be there to help you.

The distinction between feelings or inclinations on the one hand, and behavior on the other hand, is very clear. It's no sin to have inclinations that if yielded to would produce behavior that would be a transgression. The sin is in yielding to temptation. Temptation is not unique. Even the Savior was tempted.

The New Testament affirms that God has given us commandments that are difficult to keep. It is in 1 Corinthians chapter 10, verse 13: "There hath no temptation taken you but such as is common to man: but God is faithful, who will not suffer you to be tempted above that ye are able; but will with the temptation also make a way to escape, that ye may be able to bear it."

I think it's important for you to understand that homosexuality, which you've spoken of, is not a noun that describes a condition. It's an adjective that describes feelings or behavior. I encourage you, as you struggle with these challenges, not to think of yourself as a "something" or "another," except that you're a member of The Church of Jesus Christ of Latter-day Saints and you're my son, and that you're struggling with challenges.

Everyone has some challenges they have to struggle with. You've described a particular kind of challenge that is very vexing. It is common in our society and it has also become politicized. But it's only one of a host of challenges men and women have to struggle with, and I just encourage you to seek the help of the Savior to resist temptation and to refrain from behavior that would cause you to have to repent or to have your Church membership called into question.

PUBLIC AFFAIRS: If somebody has a very powerful heterosexual drive, there is the opportunity for marriage. If a young man thinks he's gay, what we're really saying to him is that there is simply no other way to go but to be celibate for the rest of his life if he doesn't feel any attraction to women?

ELDER OAKS: That is exactly the same thing we say to the many members who don't have the opportunity to marry. We expect celibacy of any person that is not married.

ELDER WICKMAN: We live in a society which is so saturated with sexuality that it perhaps is more troublesome now, because of that fact, for a person to look beyond their gender orientation to other aspects of who they are. I think I would say to your son or anyone that was so afflicted to strive to expand your horizons beyond simply gender orientation. Find fulfillment in the many other facets of your character and your personality and your nature that extend beyond that. There's no denial that one's gender orientation is certainly a core characteristic of any person, but it's not the only one.

What's more, merely having inclinations does not disqualify one for any aspect of Church participation or membership, except possibly marriage as has already been talked about. But even that, in the fullness of life as we understand it through the doctrines of the restored gospel, eventually can become possible.

In this life, such things as service in the Church, including missionary service, all of this is available to anyone who is true to covenants and commandments.

PUBLIC AFFAIRS: So you are saying that homosexual feelings are controllable?

ELDER OAKS: Yes, homosexual feelings are controllable. Perhaps there is an inclination or susceptibility to such feelings that is a reality for some and not a reality for others. But out of such susceptibilities come feelings, and feelings are controllable. If we cater to the feelings, they increase the power of the temptation. If we yield to the temptation, we have committed sinful behavior. That pattern is the same for a person that covets someone else's property and has a strong temptation to steal. It's the same for a person that develops a taste for alcohol. It's the same for a person that is born with a "short fuse," as we would say of a susceptibility to anger. If they let that susceptibility remain uncontrolled, it becomes a feeling of anger, and a feeling of anger can yield to behavior that is sinful and illegal.

We're not talking about a unique challenge here. We're talking about a common condition of mortality. We don't understand exactly the "why," or the extent to which there are inclinations or susceptibilities and so on. But what we do know is that feelings can be controlled and behavior can be controlled. The line of sin is between the feelings and the behavior. The line of prudence is between the susceptibility and the feelings. We need to lay hold on the feelings and try to control them to keep us from getting into a circumstance that leads to sinful behavior.

ELDER WICKMAN: One of the great sophistries of our age, I think, is that merely because one has an inclination to do something, that therefore acting in accordance with that inclination is inevitable. That's contrary to our very nature as the Lord has revealed to us. We do have the power to control our behavior.

PUBLIC AFFAIRS: If we were to look back at someone who had a "short fuse," and we were to look at their parents who might have had a short fuse, some might identify a genetic influence in that.

ELDER OAKS: No, we do not accept the fact that conditions that prevent people from attaining their eternal destiny were born into them without any ability to control. That is contrary to the plan of salvation, and it is contrary to the justice and mercy of God. It's contrary to the whole teaching of the Gospel of Jesus Christ, which expresses the truth that by or through the power and mercy of Jesus Christ we will have the strength to do all things. That includes resisting temptation. That includes dealing with things that we're born with, including disfigurements, or mental or physical incapacities. None of these stand in the way of our attaining our eternal destiny. The same may be said of a susceptibility or inclination to one behavior or another which if yielded to would prevent us from achieving our eternal destiny.

PUBLIC AFFAIRS: You're saying the Church doesn't necessarily have a position on "nurture or nature."

ELDER OAKS: That's where our doctrine comes into play. The Church does not have a position on the causes of any of these susceptibilities or inclinations, including those related to same-gender attraction. Those are scientific questions—whether nature or nurture—those are things the Church doesn't have a position on.

ELDER WICKMAN: Whether it is nature or nurture really begs the important question, and a preoccupation with nature or nurture can, it seems to me, lead someone astray from the principles that Elder Oaks has been describing here. Why somebody has a same-gender attraction . . . who can say? But what matters is the fact that we know we can control how we behave, and it is behavior which is important.

PUBLIC AFFAIRS: Is therapy of any kind a legitimate course of action if we're talking about controlling behavior? If a young man says, "Look, I really want these feelings to go away . . . I would do anything for these feelings to go away," is it legitimate to look at clinical therapy of some sort that would address those issues?

ELDER WICKMAN: Well, it may be appropriate for that person to seek therapy. Certainly the Church

doesn't counsel against that kind of therapy. But from the standpoint of a parent counseling a person, or a Church leader counseling a person, or a person looking at his or her same-gender attraction from the standpoint of "What can I do about it here that's in keeping with gospel teachings?" the clinical side of it is not what matters most. What matters most is recognition that "I have my own will. I have my own agency. I have the power within myself to control what I do."

Now, that's not to say it's not appropriate for somebody with that affliction to seek appropriate clinical help to examine whether in his or her case there's something that can be done about it. This is an issue that those in psychiatry, in the psychology professions have debated. Case studies I believe have shown that in some cases there has been progress made in helping someone to change that orientation; in other cases not. From the Church's standpoint, from our standpoint of concern for people, that's not where we place our principal focus. It's on these other matters.

ELDER OAKS: Amen to that. Let me just add one more thought. The Church rarely takes a position on which treatment techniques are appropriate, for medical doctors or for psychiatrists or psychologists and so on.

The second point is that there are abusive practices that have been used in connection with various mental attitudes or feelings. Over-medication in respect to depression is an example that comes to mind. The aversive therapies that have been used in connection with same-sex attraction have contained some serious abuses that have been recognized over time within the professions. While we have no position about what the medical doctors do (except in very, very rare cases—abortion would be such an example), we are conscious that there are abuses and we don't accept responsibility for those abuses. Even though they are addressed at helping people we would like to see helped, we can't endorse every kind of technique that's been used.

PUBLIC AFFAIRS: Is heterosexual marriage ever an option for those with homosexual feelings?

ELDER OAKS: We are sometimes asked about whether marriage is a remedy for these feelings that we have been talking about. President Hinckley, faced with the fact that apparently some had believed it to be a remedy, and perhaps that some Church leaders had even counseled marriage as the remedy for these feelings, made this statement: "Marriage should not be viewed as a therapeutic step to solve problems such as homosexual inclinations or practices." To me that means that we are not going to stand still to put at risk daughters of God who would enter into such marriages under false pretenses or under a cloud unknown to them. Persons who have this kind of challenge that they cannot control could not enter marriage in good faith.

On the other hand, persons who have cleansed themselves of any trans-gression and who have shown their ability to deal with these feelings or inclinations and put them in the background, and feel a great attraction for a daughter of God and therefore desire to enter marriage and have children and enjoy the blessings of eternity—that's a situation when marriage would be appropriate.

President Hinckley said that marriage is not a therapeutic step to solve problems.

ELDER WICKMAN: One question that might be asked by somebody who is struggling with same-gender attraction is, "Is this something I'm stuck with forever? What bearing does this have on eternal life? If I can somehow make it through this life, when I appear on the other side, what will I be like?"

Gratefully, the answer is that same-gender attraction did not exist in the pre-earth life and neither will it exist in the next life. It is a circumstance that for whatever reason or reasons seems to apply right now in mortality, in this nano-second of our eternal existence.

The good news for somebody who is struggling with same-gender attraction is this: 1) It is that "I'm not stuck with it forever." It's just now. Admittedly, for each one of us, it's hard to look beyond the "now" sometimes. But nonetheless, if you see mortality as now, it's only during this season. 2) If I can keep myself worthy here, if I can be true to gospel commandments, if I can keep covenants that I have made, the blessings of exaltation and eternal life that

Heavenly Father holds out to all of His children apply to me. Every blessing—including eternal marriage—is and will be mine in due course.

ELDER OAKS: Let me just add a thought to that. There is no fullness of joy in the next life without a family unit, including a husband, a wife, and posterity. Further, men are that they might have joy. In the eternal perspective, same-gender activity will only bring sorrow and grief and the loss of eternal opportunities.

PUBLIC AFFAIRS: A little earlier, Elder Oaks, you talked about the same standard of morality for heterosexuals and homosexuals. How would you address someone who said to you, "I understand it's the same standard, but aren't we asking a little more of someone who has same-gender attraction?" Obviously there are heterosexual people who won't get married, but would you accept that they at least have hope that "tomorrow I could meet the person of my dreams." There's always the hope that that could happen at any point in their life. Someone with same-gender attraction wouldn't necessarily have that same hope.

ELDER OAKS: There are differences, of course, but the contrast is not unique. There are people with physical disabilities that prevent them from having any hope—in some cases any actual hope and in other cases any practical hope—of marriage. The circumstance of being currently unable to marry, while tragic, is not unique.

It is sometimes said that God could not discriminate against individuals in this circumstance. But life is full of physical infirmities that some might see as discriminations—total paralysis or serious mental impairment being two that are relevant to marriage. If we believe in God and believe in His mercy and His justice, it won't do to say that these are discriminations because God wouldn't discriminate. We are in no condition to judge what discrimination is. We rest on our faith in God and our utmost assurance of His mercy and His love for all of His children.

ELDER WICKMAN: There's really no question that there is an anguish associated with the inability to marry in this life. We feel for someone that has that anguish. I feel for somebody that has that anguish. But it's not limited to someone who has same-gender attraction.

We live in a very self-absorbed age. I guess it's naturally human to think about my own problems as somehow greater than someone else's. I think when any one of us begins to think that way, it might be well be to look beyond ourselves. Who am I to say that I am more handicapped, or suffering more, than someone else?

I happen to have a handicapped daughter. She's a beautiful girl. She'll be 27 next week. Her name is Courtney. Courtney will never marry in this life, yet she looks wistfully upon those who do. She will stand at the window of my office which overlooks the Salt Lake Temple and look at the brides and their new husbands as they're having their pictures taken. She's at once captivated by it and saddened because Courtney understands that will not be her experience here. Courtney didn't ask for the circumstances into which she was born in this life, any more than somebody with same-gender attraction did. So there are lots of kinds of anguish people can have, even associated with just this matter of marriage. What we look forward to, and the great promise of the gospel, is that whatever our inclinations are here, whatever our shortcomings are here, whatever the hindrances to our enjoying a fullness of joy here, we have the Lord's assurance for every one of us that those in due course will be removed. We just need to remain faithful.

PUBLIC AFFAIRS: Elder Wickman, when you referred earlier to missionary service, you held that out as a possibility for someone who felt same-gender attraction but didn't act on it. President Hinckley has said that if people are faithful, they can essentially go forward as anyone else in the Church and have full fellowship. What does that really mean? Does it mean missionary service? Does it mean that someone can go to the temple, at least for those sacraments that don't involve marriage? Does it really mean that someone with same-gender attraction so long as they're faithful, has every opportunity to participate, to be called to service, to do all those kinds of things that anyone else can?

ELDER WICKMAN: I think the short answer to that is yes! I'd look to Elder Oaks to elaborate on that.

ELDER OAKS: President Hinckley has helped us on that subject with a clear statement that answers all questions of that nature. He said, "We love them (referring to people who have same-sex attractions) as sons and daughters of God. They may have certain inclinations which are powerful and which may be difficult to control. If they do not act upon these inclinations, then they can go forward as do all other members of the Church."

To me that means that a person with these inclinations, where they're kept under control, or, if yielded to are appropriately repented of, is eligible to do anything in the Church that can be done by any member of the Church who is single. Occasionally, there's an office, like the office of bishop, where a person must be married. But that's rather the exception in the Church. Every teaching position, every missionary position can be held by single people. We welcome to that kind of service people who are struggling with any kind of temptation when the struggle is a good struggle and they are living so as to be appropriate teachers, or missionaries, or whatever the calling may be.

ELDER WICKMAN: Isn't it really the significance of the Atonement in a person's life? Doesn't the Atonement really begin to mean something to a person when he or she is trying to face down the challenges of living, whether they be temptations or limitations? The willingness to turn to the Savior, the opportunity of going to sacrament service on a Sunday, and really participating in the ordinance of the sacrament . . . listening to the prayers, partaking of those sacred emblems. Those are opportunities that really help us to come within the ambit of the Savior's Atonement. Viewed that way, then any opportunity to serve in the Church is a blessing. As has been mentioned, there is a relatively tiny handful of callings within the Church that require marriage.

ELDER OAKS: There is another point to add here, and this comes from a recent statement of the First Presidency, which is a wonderful description of our attitude in this matter: "We of The Church of Jesus Christ of Latter-day Saints reach out with understanding and respect for individuals who are attracted to those of the same gender. We realize there may be great loneliness in their lives, but there must also be recognition of what is right before the Lord."

PUBLIC AFFAIRS: What would you say to those members in society, members of the Church, who may look at same-gender attraction as different than other temptations, than any other struggle that people face? First of all, do you think it's a fair assessment that some people have that feeling? What would you say to them?

ELDER OAKS: I think it is an accurate statement to say that some

people consider feelings of same-gender attraction to be the defining fact of their existence. There are also people who consider the defining fact of their existence that they are from Texas or that they were in the United States Marines. Or they are red-headed, or they are the best basketball player that ever played for such-and-such a high school. People can adopt a characteristic as the defining example of their existence and often those characteristics are physical.

We have the agency to choose which characteristics will define us; those choices are not thrust upon us.

The ultimate defining fact for all of us is that we are children of heavenly parents, born on this earth for a purpose, and born with a divine destiny. Whenever any of those other notions, whatever they may be, gets in the way of that ultimate defining fact, then it is destructive and it leads us down the wrong path.

PUBLIC AFFAIRS: Both of you have mentioned the issue of compassion and this feeling about needing to be compassionate. Let's fast-forward the scenario that we used earlier, and assume it's a couple of years later. My conversations with my son, all our efforts to love our son and keep him in the Church have failed to address what he sees as the central issue—that he can't help his feelings. He's now told us that he's moving out of the home. He plans to live with a gay friend. He's adamant about it. What should be the proper response of a Latter-day Saint parent in that situation?

ELDER OAKS: It seems to me that a Latter-day Saint parent has a responsibility in love and gentleness to affirm the teaching of the Lord through His prophets that the course of action he is about to embark upon is sinful. While affirming our continued love for him, and affirming that the family continues to have its arms open to him, I think it would be well to review with him something like the following, which is a statement of the First Presidency in 1991: "The Lord's law of moral conduct is abstinence outside of lawful marriage and fidelity within marriage. Sexual relations are proper only between husband and wife, appropriately expressed within the bonds of marriage. Any other sexual conduct, including fornication, adultery, and homosexual and lesbian behavior is sinful. Those who persist in such practices or influence others to do so are subject to Church discipline."

My first responsibility as a father is to make sure that he understands that, and then to say to him, "My son, if you choose to deliberately engage in this kind of behavior, you're still my son. The Atonement of Jesus Christ is powerful enough to reach out and cleanse you if you are repentant and give up your sinful behavior, but I urge you not to embark on that path because repentance is not easy. You're embarking on a course of action that will weaken you in your ability to repent. It will cloud your perceptions

of what is important in life. Finally, it may drag you down so far that you can't come back. Don't go that way. But if you choose to go that way, we will always try to help you and get you back on the path of growth.

ELDER WICKMAN: One way to read the Book of Mormon is as a book of encounters between fathers and sons. Some of those encounters were very positive and reinforcing on the part of the father of a son. Some were occasions where a father had to tell his son or his sons that the path that they were following was incorrect before the Lord. With all, it needs to be done in the spirit of love and welcoming that, as Elder Oaks mentioned, "You're always my son." There's an old maxim which is really true for every parent and that is, "You haven't failed until you quit trying." I think that means both in terms of taking appropriate opportunities to teach one's children the right way, but at all times making sure they know that over all things you'll love them.

PUBLIC AFFAIRS: At what point does showing that love cross the line into inadvertently endorsing behavior? If the son says, "Well, if you love me, can I bring my partner to our home to visit? Can we come for holidays?" How do you balance that against, for example, concern for other children in the home?

ELDER OAKS: That's a decision that needs to be made individually by the person responsible, calling upon the Lord for inspiration. I can imagine that in most circumstances the parents would say, "Please don't do that. Don't put us into that position." Surely if there are children in the home who would be influenced by this example, the answer would likely be that. There would also be other factors that would make that the likely answer.

I can also imagine some circumstances in which it might be possible to say, "Yes, come, but don't expect to stay overnight. Don't expect to be a lengthy house guest. Don't expect us to take you out and introduce you to our friends, or to deal with you in a public situation that would imply our approval of your 'partnership.' "

There are so many different circumstances, it's impossible to give one answer that fits all.

ELDER WICKMAN: It's hard to imagine a more difficult circumstance for a parent to face than that one. It is a case by case determination. The only thing that I would add to what Elder Oaks has just said is that I think it's important as a parent to avoid a potential trap arising out of one's anguish over this situation.

I refer to a shift from defending the Lord's way to defending the errant child's lifestyle, both with him and with others. It really is true the Lord's way is to love the sinner while condemning the sin. That is to say we continue to open our homes and our hearts and our arms to our children, but that need not be with approval of their lifestyle. Neither does it mean we need to be constantly telling them that

their lifestyle is inappropriate. An even bigger error is now to become defensive of the child, because that neither helps the child nor helps the parent. That course of action, which experience teaches, is almost certainly to lead both away from the Lord's way.

ELDER OAKS: The First Presidency made a wonderful statement on this subject in a letter in 1991. Speaking of individuals and families that were struggling with this kind of problem, they said, "We encourage Church leaders and members to reach out with love and understanding to those struggling with these issues." Surely if we are counseled as a body of Church membership to reach out with love and understanding to those "struggling with these issues," that obligation rests with particular intensity on parents who have children struggling with these issues . . . even children who are engaged in sinful behavior associated with these issues.

PUBLIC AFFAIRS: Is rejection of a child to some degree the natural reaction of some parents whenever their children fall short of expectations? Is it sometimes easier to "close the window" on an issue than deal with it?

ELDER OAKS: We surely encourage parents not to blame themselves and we encourage Church members not to blame parents in this circumstance. We should remember that none of us is perfect and none of us has children whose behavior is entirely in accord with exactly what we would have them do in all circumstances.

We feel great compassion for parents whose love and protective instincts for their challenged children have moved them to some positions that are adversary to the Church. I hope the Lord will be merciful to parents whose love for their children has caused them to get into such traps.

PUBLIC AFFAIRS: Let's fast-forward again. My son has now stopped coming to church altogether. There seems no prospect of him returning. Now he tells me he's planning on going to Canada where same-gender marriage is allowed. He insists that he agrees that loving marriage relationships are important. He's not promiscuous; he has one relationship. He and his partner intend to have that relationship for the rest of their lives. He cannot understand that a lifetime commitment can't be accepted by the Church when society seems to be moving in that way. Again, if I am a Latter-day Saint father, what would I be expected to tell him?

ELDER WICKMAN: For openers, marriage is neither a matter of politics, nor is it a matter of social policy. Marriage is defined by the Lord Himself. It's the one institution that is ceremoniously performed by priesthood authority in the temple [and] transcends this world. It is of such profound importance . . . such a core doctrine of the Gospel of Jesus Christ, of the very purpose of the creation of this earth. One hardly can get past the first page of Genesis without seeing that very clearly. It is not an institution to be tampered with by mankind, and certainly not to be tampered with by those who are doing so simply for their own purposes. There is no such thing in the Lord's eyes as something called same-gender marriage. Homosexual behavior is and will always remain before the Lord an abominable sin. Calling it something else by virtue of some political definition does not change that reality.

ELDER OAKS: Another way to say that same thing is that the Parliament in Canada and the Congress in Washington do not have the authority to revoke the commandments of God, or to modify or amend them in any way.

PUBLIC AFFAIRS: On some gay web sites there are those who argue that homosexual behavior is not specifically prohibited in the Bible, particularly in the New Testament. Some argue that Jesus Christ's compassion and love for humanity embraces this kind of relationship. What is the Church's teaching about that?

ELDER WICKMAN: For one thing, those who assert that need to read their Bible more carefully. But beyond that, it is comparing apples and oranges to refer to the love that the Savior expressed for all mankind, for every person, for every man and woman and child, with the doctrine related to marriage.

In fact, the Savior did make a declaration about marriage, albeit in a somewhat different context. Jesus said that "For this cause shall a man leave his father and mother and cleave unto his wife and they twain shall be one flesh. What God has joined together let no man put asunder."

We usually think of that expression in the context of two people, a man and a woman, being married and the inappropriateness of someone trying to separate them. I think it may have a broader meaning in a doctrinal sense. Marriage of a man and a woman is clear in Biblical teaching in the Old Testament as well as in the New [Testament] teaching. Anyone who seeks to put that notion asunder is likewise running counter to what Jesus Himself said. It's important to keep in mind the difference between Jesus' love and His definition of doctrine, and the definition of doctrine that has come from apostles and prophets of the Lord Jesus Christ, both anciently and in modern times.

PUBLIC AFFAIRS: What of those who might say, "Okay. Latter-day Saints are entitled to believe whatever they like. If you don't believe in same-gender marriages, then it's fine for you. But why try to regulate the behavior of other people who have nothing to do with your faith, especially when some nations in Europe have legally sanctioned that kind of marriage? Why not just say, "We don't agree with it doctrinally for our own people" and leave it at that. Why fight to get a Constitutional amendment [in the United States], for example?"

ELDER WICKMAN: We're not trying to regulate people, but this notion that "what happens in your house doesn't affect what happens in my house" on the subject of the institution of marriage may be the ultimate sophistry of those advocating same-gender marriage.

Some people promote the idea that there can be two marriages, co-existing side by side, one heterosexual and one homosexual, without any adverse consequences. The hard reality is that, as an institution, marriage like all other institutions can only have one definition without changing the very character of the institution. Hence there can be no coexistence of two marriages. Either there is marriage as it is now defined and as defined by the Lord, or there is what could thus be described as genderless marriage. The latter is abhorrent to God, who, as we've been discussing, Himself described what marriage is—between a man and a woman.

A redefinition of that institution, therefore, redefines it for everyone—not just those who are seeking to have a so-called same gender marriage. It also ignores the definition that the Lord Himself has given.

ELDER OAKS: There's another point that can be made on this. Let's not forget that for thousands of years the institution of marriage has been between a man and a woman. Until quite recently, in a limited number of countries, there has been no such thing as a marriage between persons of the same gender. Suddenly we are faced with the claim that thousands of years of human experience should be set aside because we should not discriminate in relation to the institution of marriage. When that claim is made, the burden of proving that this step will not undo the wisdom and stability of millennia of experience lies on those who would make the change. Yet the question is asked and the matter is put forward as if those who believe in marriage between a man and a woman have the burden of proving that it should not be extended to some other set of conditions.

PUBLIC AFFAIRS: There are those who would say that that might have applied better in the 1950s or earlier than in the 21st century. If you look at several nations in Europe, for example, traditional marriage is so rapidly on the decline that it is no longer the norm. If marriage is evolving, ought we to resist those kind of social changes?

ELDER OAKS: That argument impresses me as something akin to the fact that if we agree that the patient is sick and getting sicker, we should therefore approve a coup de grace. The coup de grace which ends the patient's life altogether is quite equivalent to the drastic modification in the institution of marriage that would be brought on by same-gender marriage.

PUBLIC AFFAIRS: You talked about the harm that could come on society by redefining marriage. What would you say to those people who declare: "I know gay people who are in long-term committed relationships. They're great people. They love each other. What harm is it going to do my

marriage as a heterosexual to allow them that same 'rite?' "

ELDER WICKMAN: Let me say again what I said a moment ago. I believe that that argument is true sophistry, because marriage is a unified institution. Marriage means a committed, legally sanctioned relationship between a man and a woman. That's what it means. That's what it means in the revelations. That's what it means in the secular law. You cannot have that marriage coexisting institutionally with something else called same-gender marriage. It simply is a definitional impossibility. At such point as you now, as an institution, begin to recognize a legally-sanctioned relationship, a committed relationship between two people of the same gender, you have now redefined the institution to being one of genderless marriage.

As we've mentioned in answer to other questions, [genderless marriage] is contrary to God's law, to revealed Word. Scripture, ancient and modern, could not be clearer on the definition that the Lord and His agents have given to marriage down through the dispensations.

But it has a profound effect in a very secular way on everybody else. What happens in somebody's house down the street does in very deed have an effect on what happens in my house and how it's treated. To suggest that in the face of these millennia of history and the revelations of God and the whole human pattern they have the right to redefine the whole institution for everyone is presumptuous in the extreme and terribly wrong-headed.

ELDER OAKS: Another point to be made about this is made in a question. If a couple who are cohabiting, happy, and committed to one another want to have their relationship called a marriage, why do they want that? Considering what they say they have, why do they want to add to it the legal status of marriage that has been honored and experienced for thousands of years? What is it that is desired by those who advocate same-gender marriage? If that could be articulated on some basis other than discrimination, which is not a very good argument, it would be easier to answer the question that you have asked, and I think it would reveal the soundness of what we've already heard.

There are certain indicia of marriage—certain legal and social consequences and certain legitimacy—which if given to some relationship other than marriage between a man and a woman tend to degrade if not destroy the institution that's been honored over so many thousands of years.

In addition, if people want to legalize a particular relationship, we need to be careful if that kind of relationship has been disapproved for millennia. Suddenly there's a call to legalize it so they can feel better about themselves. That argument proves a little too much. Suppose a person is making a living in some illegal behavior, but feels uneasy about it. (He may be a professional thief or he may be selling a service that is illegal, or whatever it may be.) Do we go out and legalize his behavior because he's being discriminated against in his occupational choices or because he doesn't feel well about what he's doing and he wants a "feel good" example, or he wants his behavior legitimized in the eyes of society or his family? I think the answer is that we do not legalize behavior for those reasons unless they are very persuasive reasons brought forward to make a change in the current situation.

PUBLIC AFFAIRS: Would you extend the same argument against same-gender marriage to civil unions or some kind of benefits short of marriage?

ELDER WICKMAN: One way to think of marriage is as a bundle of rights associated with what it means for two people to be married. What the First Presidency has done is express its support of marriage and for that bundle of rights belonging to a man and a woman. The First Presidency hasn't expressed itself concerning any specific right. It really doesn't matter what you call it. If you have some legally sanctioned relationship with the bundle of legal rights traditionally belonging to marriage and governing authority has slapped a label on it, whether it is civil union or domestic partnership or whatever label it's given, it is nonetheless tantamount to marriage. That is something to which our doctrine simply requires us to speak out and say, "That is not right. That's not appropriate."

As far as something less than that—as far as relationships that give to some pairs in our society some right but not all of those associated with marriage—as to that, as far as I know, the First Presidency hasn't expressed itself. There are numbers of different types of partnerships or pairings that may exist in society that aren't same-gender sexual relationships that provide for some right that we have no objection to. All that said . . . there may be on occasion some specific rights that we would be concerned about being granted to those in a same-gender relationship. Adoption is one that comes to mind, simply because that is a right which has been historically, doctrinally associated so closely with marriage and family. I cite the example of adoption simply because it has to do with the bearing and the rearing of children. Our teachings, even as expressed most recently in a very complete doctrinal sense in the Family Proclamation by living apostles and prophets, is that children deserve to be reared in a home with a father and a mother.

PUBLIC AFFAIRS: On the issue of a Constitutional amendment prohibiting same-gender marriage, there are some Latter-day Saints who are opposed to same-gender marriage, but who are not in favor of addressing this through a Constitutional amendment. Why did the Church feel that it had to step in that direction?

ELDER OAKS: Law has at least two roles: one is to define and regulate the limits of acceptable behavior. The other is to teach principles for individuals to make individual choices. The law declares unacceptable some things that are simply not enforceable, and there's no prosecutor who tries to enforce them. We refer to that as the teaching function of the law. The time has come in our society when I see great wisdom and purpose in a United States Constitutional amendment declaring that marriage is between a man and a woman. There is nothing in that proposed amendment that requires a criminal prosecution or that directs the attorneys general to go out and round people up, but it declares a principle and it also creates a defensive barrier against those who would alter that traditional definition of marriage.

There are people who oppose a federal Constitutional amendment because they think that the law of family should be made by the states. I can see a legitimate argument there. I think it's mistaken, however, because the federal government, through the decisions of life-tenured federal judges, has already taken over that area. This Constitutional amendment is a defensive measure against those who would ignore the will of the states appropriately expressed and require, as a matter of federal law, the recognition of same-gender marriages—or the invalidation of state laws that require that marriage be between a man and a woman. In summary, the First Presidency has come out for an amendment (which may or may not be adopted) in support of the teaching function of the law. Such an amendment would be a very important expression of public policy, which would feed into or should feed into the decisions of judges across the length and breadth of the land.

ELDER WICKMAN: Let me just add to that, if I may. It's not the Church that has made the issue of marriage a matter of federal law. Those who are vigorously advocating for something called same-gender marriage have essentially put that potato on the fork. They're the ones who have created a situation whereby the law of the land, one way or the other, is going to address this issue of marriage. This is not a situation where the Church has elected to take the matter into the legal arena or into the political arena. It's already there.

The fact of the matter is that the best way to assure that a definition of marriage as it now stands continues is to put it into the foundational legal document of the United States. That is in the Constitution. That's where the battle has taken it. Ultimately that's where the battle is going to be decided. It's going to be decided as a matter of federal law one way or the other. Consequently it is not a battleground on such an issue that we Latter-day Saints have chosen, but it has been established and we have little choice but to express our views concerning it, which is really all that the Church has done.

Decisions even for members of the Church as to what they do with respect to this issue must of course rest with each one in their capacity as citizens.

PUBLIC AFFAIRS: The emphasis that has been placed in this conversation on traditional marriage between a man and a woman has been consistent throughout. Do you see any irony in the fact that the Church is so publicly outspoken on this issue, when in the minds of so many people in the United States and around the world the Church is known for once supporting a very untraditional marriage arrangement—that is, polygamy?

ELDER OAKS: I see irony in that if one views it without the belief that we affirm in divine revelation. The 19th century Mormons, including some of my ancestors, were not eager to practice plural marriage. They followed the example of Brigham Young, who expressed his profound negative feelings when he first had this principle revealed to him. The Mormons of the 19th century who practiced plural marriage, male and female, did so because they felt it was a duty put upon them by God.

When that duty was lifted, they were directed to conform to the law of the land, which forbad polygamy and which had been held constitutional. When they were told to refrain from plural marriage, there were probably some who were unhappy, but I think the majority were greatly relieved and glad to get back into the mainstream of western civilization, which had been marriage between a man and a woman. In short, if you start with the assumption of continuing revelation, on which this Church is founded, then you can understand that there is no irony in this. But if you don't start with that assumption, you see a profound irony.

PUBLIC AFFAIRS: What about various types of support groups for those with same-gender affliction?

ELDER WICKMAN: I think we neither encourage nor discourage them, but much would depend on the nature of those groups. We certainly discourage people getting involved with any group or organization that foster living a homosexual lifestyle.

Ultimately, the wisest course for anybody who's afflicted with same-gender attraction is to strive to extend one's horizon beyond just one's sexual orientation, one's gender orientation, and to try to see the whole person. If I'm one that's afflicted with same-gender attraction, I should strive to see myself in a much broader context . . . seeing myself as a child of God with whatever my talents may be, whether intellect, or music, or athletics, or somebody that has a compassion to help people, to see myself in a larger setting and thus to see my life in that setting.

The more a person can look beyond gender orientation, the happier and more fulfilling life is likely to be. The worst possible thing for any of us—no matter what our temptations, no matter what our mortal inclinations may be—is to become fixated with them, to dwell on them. When

we do that, not only do we deny the other things that comprise us, but experience teaches that there will be an increased likelihood that eventually we will simply succumb to the inclination.

ELDER OAKS: The principle that Elder Wickman has talked about, in a nutshell, is that if you are trying to live with and maintain ascendancy over same-gender attractions, the best way to do that is to have groups that define their members in terms other than same-gender attractions.

PUBLIC AFFAIRS: If you had to describe this enormously complex question in a couple of basic principles, what would that be?

ELDER OAKS: God loves all of His children. He has provided a plan for His children to enjoy the choicest blessings that He has to offer in eternity. Those choicest blessings are associated with marriage between a man and a woman by appropriate priesthood authority to bring together a family unit for creation and happiness in this life and in the life to come.

We urge persons with same-gender attractions to control those and to refrain from acting upon them, which is a sin, just as we urge persons with heterosexual attractions to refrain from acting upon them until they have the opportunity for a marriage recognized by God as well as by the law of the land. That is the way to happiness and eternal life. God has given us no commandment that He will not give us the strength and power to observe. That is the Plan of salvation for His children, and it is our duty to proclaim that plan, to teach its truth, and to praise God for the mission of His Son Jesus Christ. It is Christ's atonement that makes it possible for us to be forgiven of our sins and His resurrection that gives us the assurance of immortality and the life to come. It is that life to come that orients our views in mortality and reinforces our determination to live the laws of God so that we can qualify for His blessings in immortality.

PUBLIC AFFAIRS: Thank you.

SAME SEX ATTRACTION

See SAME GENDER ATTRACTION.

SAME SEX MARRIAGE

See SAME GENDER ATTRACTION.

SANCTIFICATION

A scriptural term which usually means "exaltation" (1 Corinthians 1:30; D&C 20:31).

SANHEDRIN

The Sanhedrin was the highest governing body among the Jews at the time of the Savior's mortal mission. It was their senate and "supreme court" in both civil and religious matters (see BD, under "Sanhedrin").

SATAN

See also LUCIFER. The name Satan means "the slanderer" (BD, under "Satan"). "Satan" is one of the many names given to the devil in the scrip-

tures (Example: Revelation 12:7–9). "Perdition" is another one of his names (D&C 76:26). "Perdition" means "complete loss, utter ruin" (Webster's 1980 New World Dictionary).

SAVIOR

Spelled "Saviour" in the Bible (Isaiah 43:11; Luke 2:11; John 4:42) and "Savior" in the Book of Mormon (1 Nephi 10:4; 2 Nephi 6:18; Mormon 8:6), the Doctrine and Covenants (D&C 19:41; 66:1; 133:25), and the Pearl of Great Price (Moses 1:6; JS—H 1:34). "Savior" is one of the names given to Jesus Christ, the Son of God, with the connotation that He "saves" all from physical death (1 Corinthians 15:22) and saves us from our sins if we repent and live the gospel (2 Nephi 9:21).

SCATTERING OF ISRAEL

See also GATHERING OF ISRAEL. The scattering of Israel, because of wickedness, was warned of and prophesied by the Lord's prophets (Leviticus 26:33; Deuteronomy 28:64; Jeremiah 9:16). In scattering Israel, the Lord placed the blood of Israel, in other words, Abraham's descendants through Jacob (Israel), throughout all nations. The Lord told Abraham that his descendants are to be the means of bringing the gospel to the whole world and blessing all nations (Abraham 2:9–11). Thus, through the scattering, and now the gathering of Israel, all nations in the world are being blessed.

SCHOOL OF THE PROPHETS

The school of the prophets is mentioned five times in the Doctrine and Covenants (D&C 88:127, 136, 137; 90:7; 95:10). It was organized in Kirtland, Ohio, early in 1833, according to the commandment given by the Lord in D&C 88:118–19, for the purpose of instructing early leaders of the church in doctrine and scripture as well as some secular topics such as grammar. The first session of the school met January 23, 1833, and the school ended in April 1833. Joseph Smith presided and Orson Hyde was the main teacher (*EM*, under "Schools of the Prophets").

The School of the Prophets was usually held in a room above Newel K. Whitney's store in Kirtland. During the session of the school held on February 27, 1833, the revelation now known as the Word of Wisdom (D&C 89) was given.

SCRIBES

The scribes in New Testament times were influential teachers and interpreters of the law of Moses among the Jews. They were usually Pharisees (BD, under "Scribes") and were often seen with the Pharisees confronting the Savior as He taught (Matthew 12:38; 15:1–2; 21:15; Luke 15:2; John 8:3).

SCRIPTURE

The Lord defined "scripture" as "whatsoever they shall speak when moved upon by the Holy Ghost shall be scripture, shall be the will of the Lord, shall be the mind of the Lord, shall be the word of the Lord, shall be the voice of the Lord, and the power of God unto salvation" (D&C 68:4).

Elder Harold B. Lee explained verse 4, above, as follows: "It is not to be thought that every word spoken by the General Authorities is inspired, or that they are moved upon by the Holy Ghost in everything they read and write. Now you keep that in mind. I don't care what his position is, if he writes something or speaks something that goes beyond anything that you can find in the standard church works, unless that one be the prophet, seer, and revelator—please note that one exception—you may immediately say, 'Well, that is his own idea.' And if he says something that contradicts what is found in the standard church works [the Bible, Book of Mormon, Doctrine and Covenants, Pearl of Great Price] (I think that is why we call them 'standard'—it is the standard measure of all that men teach), you may know by that same token that it is false, regardless of the position of the man who says it" ("The Place of the Living Prophet, Seer, and Revelator" [address delivered to seminary and institute of religion faculty, July 8, 1964], p. 14. Quoted in the *Doctrine and Covenants Student Manual*, Rel. 324–25, used by the Institutes of Religion of the Church, 1981, p. 144).

SEALED IN FOREHEAD

See SYMBOLISM IN THE SCRIPTURES.

SEALED PLATES
See BOOK OF MORMON PLATES.

SEALING

The Savior told His Apostles, "And I will give unto thee the keys of the kingdom of heaven: and whatsoever thou shalt bind on earth shall be bound in heaven: and whatsoever thou shalt loose on earth shall be loosed in heaven" (Matthew 16:19).

This sealing power is found today in The Church of Jesus Christ of Latter-day Saints, where worthy priesthood holders serving in the temples have authority to "seal" couples and families together for eternity. Those who live worthy of their sealing will live in their own family units forever (D&C 132:19–20).

SEALING POWER

Malachi prophesied that Elijah would come to earth in the last days and restore the power to seal families together for eternity (Malachi 4:5–6). He came to the Kirtland Temple on April 3, 1836, and restored this power to Joseph Smith and Oliver Cowdery, saying:

D&C 110:14–16

14 Behold, the time has fully come, which was spoken of by the mouth of Malachi—testifying that he [Elijah] should be sent, before the great and dreadful day of the Lord come—

15 To turn the hearts of the fathers to the children, and the children to the fathers, lest the whole earth be smitten with a curse—

16 Therefore, the keys of this dispensation are committed into your hands; and by this ye may know that the great and dreadful day of the Lord is near, even at the doors.

SEALINGS FOR THE DEAD

A phrase used often by members of the Church in reference to temple work for the dead in which deceased couples and families are sealed together for eternity.

SEALINGS FOR THE LIVING

Couples who were previously married by civil authorities "until death do you part," in other words, for time only, and who belong to The Church of Jesus Christ of Latter-day Saints, can go to a Church temple and be "sealed" together for eternity. These ordinances are called "sealings for the living."

SECOND COMFORTER
See FIRST COMFORTER.

SECOND COMING OF CHRIST

See also SIGNS OF THE TIMES; MILLENNIUM. There are many prophecies about the Second Coming of Jesus Christ. It is a much-anticipated event among those who believe in the Bible. As members of the Church, with both ancient and modern scripture, as well as with the words and teachings of our modern prophets, seers, and revelators, we are in a position to know even more about this major event in the plan of salvation. We will first take a brief look at some "comings" of the Savior in the last days, near the time of His coming but which are not *the* Second Coming. We will list them, not necessarily in sequence:

Major Appearances of the Savior Before the Second Coming

1. To those in the New Jerusalem in America (3 Nephi 21:23–25; D&C 45:66–67).

2. To the Jews in Jerusalem (D&C 45:48; 51–53; Zechariah 12:10; 14:2–5).

3. To those assembled at Adam-ondi-Ahman (Daniel 7:9–10, 13–14; D&C 116).

Bruce R. McConkie gave some details about the meeting at Adam-ondi-Ahman. He said: "We now come to the least known and least understood thing connected with the second coming. . . . It is a doctrine that has scarcely dawned on most of the Latter-Day Saints themselves; . . . Before the Lord Jesus descends openly . . . there is to be a secret appearance to selected members of His Church. He will come in private to his prophet and to the apostles then living . . . and further, all the faithful members of the church then living and all the faithful saints of all the ages past will be present . . . and it will take place in Davies County, Missouri, at a place called Adam-Ondi-Ahman. . . . The grand summation of the whole matter comes

in these words: 'and also with all those whom my Father hath given me out of the world' (D&C 27:14). The sacrament is to be administered . . . this, of course, will be a part of the Grand Council at Adam-Ondi-Ahman" (McConkie, *The Millennial Messiah*, pp. 578–79 and 587).

The Actual Second Coming

The scriptures describe a number of details in conjunction with the actual Second Coming of the Lord. We will list a number of them here:

1. The wicked will be destroyed by the glory of the coming Savior.

D&C 19:5

19 For a desolating scourge shall go forth among the inhabitants of the earth, and shall continue to be poured out from time to time, if they repent not, until the earth is empty, and the inhabitants thereof are consumed away and utterly destroyed by the brightness of my coming.

2 Nephi 12:10, 19, 21

10 O ye wicked ones, enter into the rock, and hide thee in the dust, for the fear of the Lord and the glory of his majesty shall smite thee.

19 And they shall go into the holes of the rocks, and into the caves of the earth, for the fear of the Lord shall come upon them and the glory of his majesty shall smite them, when he ariseth to shake terribly the earth.

21 To go into the clefts of the rocks, and into the tops of the

ragged rocks, for the fear of the Lord shall come upon them and the majesty of his glory shall smite them, when he ariseth to shake terribly the earth.

2. The Savior will appear in the sky, coming from the east.

JS—Matthew 1:26

26 For as the light of the morning cometh out of the east, and shineth even unto the west, and covereth the whole earth, so shall also the coming of the Son of Man be.

3. The Savior will be wearing red, symbolizing the blood of the unrepentant wicked who now must answer to the law of justice. They refused the law of mercy offered through the Atonement. Whether or not the Savior's clothing is literally red or symbolically is red, the imagery is the same. The color represents the blood of the wicked who are destroyed at His coming.

D&C 133:46–51

46 And it shall be said: Who is this that cometh down from God in heaven with dyed garments [*with dyed clothing*]; yea, from the regions which are not known, clothed in his glorious apparel, traveling in the greatness of his strength?

47 And he shall say: I am he who spake in righteousness, mighty to save.

48 And the Lord shall be red in his apparel [*clothing*], and his garments like him that treadeth in the wine–vat [*like one who has been treading grapes in the wine tub*].

49 And so great shall be the glory of his presence that the sun shall hide his face in shame, and the moon shall withhold its light, and the stars shall be hurled from their places.

50 And his voice shall be heard: I have trodden the wine–press alone, and have brought judgment upon all people; and none were with me [*Jesus had to do the Atonement alone*];

51 And I have trampled them [*the wicked*] in my fury, and I did tread upon them in mine anger, and their blood have I sprinkled upon my garments [*clothing*], and stained all my raiment [*clothing*]; for this was the day of vengeance [*the law of justice is being satisfied*] which was in my heart [*which is part of the plan of salvation, which the Savior is carrying out for the Father, along with the law of mercy*].

4. The faithful Saints will be literally taken up to meet Him.

D&C 88:96

96 And the saints that are upon the earth, who are alive, shall be quickened and be caught up to meet him.

5. The dead, who have died since the resurrection of Christ, and who are worthy of celestial glory will be resurrected.

D&C 88:97

97 And they who have slept in their graves shall come forth, for their graves shall be opened; and they also shall be caught up to meet

him in the midst of the pillar of heaven—

6. The continents will be moved back together and the earth will be restored to a condition such as in the Garden of Eden (Articles of Faith 1:10, footnote f). In other words, it will receive its "paradisiacal glory" in preparation for the Millennium.

D&C 133:23–24

23 He shall command the great deep, and it shall be driven back into the north countries, and the islands shall become one land;

24 And the land of Jerusalem and the land of Zion shall be turned back into their own place, and the earth shall be like as it was in the days before it was divided.

7. The hosts of heaven plus the righteous who have just been resurrected and the righteous mortals who have just been caught up to meet Him, will descend to the earth with the Savior when He comes.

D&C 88:96-98

96 And the saints that are upon the earth, who are alive, shall be quickened and be caught up to meet him.

97 And they who have slept in their graves shall come forth, for their graves shall be opened; and they also shall be caught up to meet him in the midst of the pillar of heaven—

98 They are Christ's, the first fruits, they who shall descend with him first, and they who are on the earth and in their graves, who are first caught up to meet him; and all this by the voice of the sounding of the trump of the angel of God.

8. Not everyone will be caught off guard, as with "a thief in the night." The righteous will be ready and will know that His coming is getting close. However, the wicked will be caught off guard.

D&C 106:4–5

4 And again, verily I say unto you, the coming of the Lord draweth nigh, and it overtaketh the world as a thief in the night—

5 Therefore, gird up your loins, that you may be the children of light, and that day shall not overtake you as a thief.

9. The wicked will wish they could die and somehow avoid facing the Savior at this time.

Revelation 6:16–17

16 And said to the mountains and rocks, Fall on us, and hide us from the face of him that sitteth on the throne, and from the wrath of the Lamb:

17 For the great day of his wrath is come; and who shall be able to stand?

10. The scriptures inform us that no one will tell us the exact time of His coming.

Matthew 24:36

36 But of that day and hour knoweth no man, no, not the angels of heaven, but my Father only.

Mark 13:32

32 But of that day and that hour knoweth no man, no, not the angels which are in heaven, neither the Son, but the Father.

D&C 49:7

7 I, the Lord God, have spoken it; but the hour and the day no man knoweth, neither the angels in heaven, nor shall they know until he comes.

11. Worldly conditions will not improve between now and the Second Coming.

D&C 84:97

97 And plagues shall go forth, and they shall not be taken from the earth until I have completed my work, which shall be cut short in righteousness—

D&C 97:23

23 The Lord's scourge shall pass over by night and by day, and the report thereof shall vex all people; yea, it shall not be stayed until the Lord come;

The Savior's Second Coming will usher in the Millennium. The Savior said, "For I will reveal myself from heaven with power and great glory, with all the hosts thereof, and dwell in righteousness with men on earth a thousand years, and the wicked shall not stand" (D&C 29:11).

Malachi describes the wicked lifestyles that will cause people to be burned:

Malachi 3:2–5

2 But who may abide the day of his coming? and who shall stand when he appeareth? for he is like a refiner's fire, and like fullers' soap:

3 And he shall sit as a refiner and purifier of silver: and he shall purify the sons of Levi, and purge them as gold and silver, that they may offer unto the LORD an offering in righteousness.

4 Then shall the offering of Judah and Jerusalem be pleasant unto the Lord, as in the days of old, and as in former years.

5 And I will come near to you to judgment; and I will be a swift witness against the sorcerers, and against the adulterers, and against false swearers, and against those that oppress the hireling in his wages, the widow, and the fatherless, and that turn aside the stranger from his right, and fear not me, saith the Lord of hosts.

We learn from D&C 76:103 and Revelation 22:15 that the people Malachi described above are basically those who are living a telestial lifestyle. We also learn from modern revelation that those living a terrestrial or celestial lifestyle at the time of the Savior's coming will not be destroyed. Joseph Fielding Smith taught that such people will survive the Second Coming and will continue living on earth during the Millennium. He said, "There will be millions of people, Catholics, Protestants, agnostics, Mohammedans, people of all classes and all beliefs, still permitted to remain upon the face of the earth, but they will be those who have lived clean lives, those who have been free from wickedness and corruption. All who belong, by virtue of their good lives, to [at least] the terrestrial order, . . . will remain upon the face of the earth during the millennium" (*DS* 1:86–87).

SECOND DEATH

Depending on context, "second death" can refer to (1) Sons of perdition (D&C 76:37). (2) Those who go to the telestial kingdom (D&C 63:17; 76:103; Helaman 14:18–19; Revelation 21:8). (3) Any who come under the law of justice rather than the law of mercy (Alma 12:32). (4) Any who do not attain the celestial kingdom (Revelation 20:6). (5) The condition of being out of the direct presence of God. Such was the case with Adam and Eve after they were cast out of the Garden of Eden (D&C 29:41).

SECOND ESTATE

See also FIRST ESTATE. "Second estate" is a reference to mortality. "Keep their second estate" (Abraham 3:26) is a phrase referring to those who live worthy in this life to receive exaltation. This would also apply to little children who die before the age of accountability (D&C 137:10) as well as to individuals who accept and live the gospel when it is preached to them in the postmortal spirit world (D&C 138:31–34, 58–59).

SECRET COMBINATIONS

See GADIANTON ROBBERS.

SEED OF ABRAHAM

See ABRAHAM, SEED OF.

SEED OF CHRIST

Those who follow Christ and live His gospel are His "seed." They are described symbolically as His "sons and his daughters" (Mosiah 5:7).

Isaiah spoke symbolically of His "seed" (Isaiah 53:10) and Abinadi, in the Book of Mormon, explained what Isaiah meant:

Mosiah 15:1–13

10   And now I say unto you, who shall declare his generation? Behold, I say unto you, that when his soul has been made an offering for sin he shall see his seed. And now what say ye? And who shall be his seed?

11   Behold I say unto you, that whosoever has heard the words of the prophets, yea, all the holy prophets who have prophesied concerning the coming of the Lord—I say unto you, that all those who have hearkened unto their words, and believed that the Lord would redeem his people, and have looked forward to that day for a remission of their sins, I say unto you, that these are his seed, or they are the heirs of the kingdom of God.

12   For these are they whose sins he has borne; these are they for whom he has died, to redeem them from their transgressions. And now, are they not his seed?

13   Yea, and are not the prophets, every one that has opened his mouth to prophesy, that has not

fallen into transgression, I mean all the holy prophets ever since the world began? I say unto you that they are his seed.

SEERS

See PROPHETS, SEERS, AND REVELATORS.

SEMINARIES

See CHURCH EDUCATIONAL SYSTEM.

SENSUAL, SENSUALITY

These terms are used in reference to the lusts of the flesh, and generally carry the connotation of sexual immorality (Jude 1:18-19; D&C 20:20; 29:35; Moses 5:13; 6:49).

SEPTUAGINT

A translation of the Old Testament into Greek, made several centuries BC.

SEPULCHER

Another name for tombs or graves.

SERMON ON THE MOUNT

See also BEATITUDES. The Sermon on the Mount was given in Galilee at the beginning of the second year of the Savior's mortal ministry. It is recorded in Matthew, chapters 5–7. It was repeated by the Savior in America, with some significant changes, as recorded in 3 Nephi 12–14.

Many Christians consider the Sermon on the Mount to contain a series of desirable ethical behaviors, and indeed it does. But they are much more than this. As explained in 3 Nephi as well as in the JST (the Joseph Smith Translation of the Bible), the righteous behaviors stressed here by the Master are among those which enable baptized members of the Church to obtain celestial glory and exaltation. You may wish to make a cross reference in the heading to Matthew, chapter 5, in your Bible, which sends you to 3 Nephi 12:1–2, wherein we are told that the sermon which follows in 3 Nephi (basically, the Sermon on the Mount as given to the Nephites) is addressed to baptized members of the Church, and is a series of instructions for continuing after baptism to the point of qualifying for celestial glory.

SEVENTY

Since 1986, "Seventy" is a Melchizedek Priesthood office used only for General Authorities called to serve in one of the quorums of the Seventy. They serve under the direction of the First Presidency and the Quorum of the Twelve Apostles.

This calling of Seventy is described by the Lord in the Doctrine and Covenants:

D&C 107:25, 34, 93–97

25 The Seventy are also called to preach the gospel, and to be especial witnesses unto the Gentiles and in all the world—thus differing from other officers in the church in the duties of their calling.

34 The Seventy are to act in the name of the Lord, under the direc-

tion of the Twelve or the traveling high council, in building up the church and regulating all the affairs of the same in all nations, first unto the Gentiles and then to the Jews;

93 And it is according to the vision showing the order of the Seventy, that they should have seven presidents to preside over them, chosen out of the number of the seventy;

94 And the seventh president of these presidents is to preside over the six;

95 And these seven presidents are to choose other seventy besides the first seventy to whom they belong, and are to preside over them;

96 And also other seventy, until seven times seventy, if the labor in the vineyard of necessity requires it.

97 And these seventy are to be traveling ministers, unto the Gentiles first and also unto the Jews.

SHEOL

The Prophet Joseph Smith used this word as he pled with the Lord while in Liberty Jail (D&C 121:4). It is a Hebrew word for hell.

SHILOH

Another name for Christ (JST, Genesis 50:24).

SICK, BLESSING THE

See ADMINISTERING TO THE SICK.

SIGN OF THE DOVE

Joseph Smith explained the sign of the dove as follows: "The sign of the dove was instituted before the creation of the world, a witness for the Holy Ghost, and the devil cannot come in the sign of a dove. The Holy Ghost is a personage, and is in the form of a personage. It does not confine itself to the *form* of the dove, but in *sign* of the dove. The Holy Ghost cannot be transformed into a dove; but the sign of a dove was given to John to signify the truth of the deed, as the dove is an emblem or token of truth and innocence" (*TPJS* pp. 275–76).

SIGNS OF THE TIMES

Signs of the times are prophecies which have been given throughout the ages by the Lord. They will be fulfilled in the last days, signaling that the Second Coming of Jesus Christ is getting close.

The Second Coming of Christ is mentioned over 1,500 times in the Old Testament and some 300 times in the New Testament. It is a much-anticipated event in our day. The signs of the times are designed to strengthen testimonies and provide encouragement and confidence in the hearts of believers in a day when many no longer even believe in God. Every one of these prophecies will be fulfilled.

Unfortunately, whether intentional or not, many who teach and discuss the signs of the times seem to end up causing fear and panic in the hearts and minds of their listeners. Let's see what the Savior says about this. In Joseph Smith—Matthew, chapter 1, the Master answers questions asked by His disciples concerning the times which will precede the second coming. As His disciples listened intently, it appears that fear and concern entered their hearts. In response, Jesus counseled them not to be troubled by the signs of the times. He said:

JS—Matthew 1:23

23 Behold, I speak these things unto you for the elect's sake; and you also shall hear of wars, and rumors of wars; see that ye be not troubled, for all I have told you must come to pass; but the end is not yet.

The Savior went on to emphasize the value of preparation as well as the fact that the signs of the times are designed to strengthen people's testimonies. He taught:

JS—Matthew 1:35, 37, 39

35 Although, the days will come, that heaven and earth shall pass away; yet my words shall not pass away, but all shall be fulfilled.

37 And whoso treasureth up my word, shall not be deceived, for the Son of Man shall come, and he shall send his angels before him with the great sound of a trumpet, and they shall gather together the remainder of his elect from the four winds, from one end of heaven to the other.

39 So likewise, mine elect, when they shall see all these things, they shall know that he is near, even at the doors;

The scriptures clearly state that no one knows the time of the Savior's coming (Matthew 24:36; Mark 13:32; D&C 49:7). In spite of such scriptures as these, some people still insist on trying to pin down the timing of the Second Coming. For instance, some have been heard to say that even though we can't know the day and hour, we can know the month and year. Some make elaborate calculations, based on personal interpretation of scriptures combined with the statements of prophets to narrow down the timing. When others refuse to accept their calculations as being inspired, they respond by saying that those who are truly in tune with the Spirit will gain a witness that what they claim is true. Still others claim that our prophets and Apostles today do indeed know the exact day and hour, but have been instructed not to tell us.

Elder M. Russell Ballard, of the Quorum of the Twelve, spoke to a BYU devotional audience in the Marriott Center about the last days and signs of the times, on March 12, 1996. He said (**bold** added for emphasis), "I am called as one of the apostles to be a special witness of Christ in these exciting, trying times, and **I do not know when He is going to come again**. As far as I know, none of my brethren in the Council of the Twelve or even in the First Presidency knows. And I would humbly suggest to you, my young brothers and sisters, that **if we do not know, then nobody knows**, no matter how compelling their arguments or how reasonable their calculations."

While there are many more signs of the times, we will list a brief summary of thirty-seven of them here:

37 Signs of the Times

1. Discovery of America, establishment of USA (1 Nephi 22:7; 3 Nephi 21:4).

2. Coming forth of the Book of Mormon (Ezekiel 37:16–19).

3. Restoration of the Priesthood (Malachi 4:4–6).

4. Restoration of the true Church (Acts 3:19–21).

5. The Church will grow to fill the whole earth (Daniel 2:35, 44–45).

6. Scattered Israel will be gathered. (1 Nephi 10:14).

7. Lost Ten Tribes return (D&C 133:26–34).

8. Times of the Gentiles fulfilled (D&C 45:25).

9. Jews return to Jerusalem (D&C 133:13).

10. Jews accept the true gospel (2 Nephi 30:7).

11. Elijah comes (Malachi 4:5–6).

12. Christ will come to His temple (Malachi 3:1).

13. Genealogical research increases dramatically (Malachi 4:6).

14. Sun darkened and moon becomes as blood (Matthew 24:29; Revelation 6:12; Joel 2:28–32; President Hinckley, Saturday morning conference, Oct. 2001).

15. Diseases, plagues, pestilences to sweep the earth (D&C 45:31; Joseph Smith—Matthew 1:29).

16. Knowledge, science, etc., to increase dramatically (Daniel 12:4).

17. Wars and rumors of wars (D&C 45:26; JS—M 1:23).

18. Famines, tornadoes, earthquakes, natural disasters to abound (D&C 45:26, etc.).

19. Strikes, anarchy, violence to increase (McConkie, *Mormon Doctrine*, p. 726).

20. Sexual immorality, homosexuality, etc., abounds (2 Timothy 3:3, 6).

21. The Spirit to stop working with the wicked (D&C 63:32).

22. Peace taken from the earth (D&C 1:35).

23. Jerusalem to be a "cup of trembling" to people around it (Zechariah 12:2).

24. False churches, false prophets abound (Revelation 13:13–14, etc.).

25. People refuse to believe the signs of the times (2 Peter 3:3–4).

26. Signs and wonders on earth and in the heavens (D&C 45:40).

27. Lamanites to blossom as the rose (D&C 49:24).

28. New Jerusalem to be built (Moses 7:63–64).

29. Many temples to be built (President Benson, Elder McConkie,

April Conference, 1980).

30. Temple to be built in Jerusalem (*TPJS*, p. 286).

31. Battle of Armageddon (Zechariah 12).

32. Meeting at Adam-ondi-Ahman (Daniel 7:9–14).

33. Two prophets killed in Jerusalem (Revelation 11).

34. Mount of Olives divides in two (Zechariah 14:4).

35. Righteous are taken up (D&C 88:96).

36. Wicked are burned (Malachi 4:1; 2 Nephi 12:10, 19, 21; D&C 5:19).

37. Everyone sees Christ coming (Revelation 1:7).

SIN AGAINST THE HOLY GHOST

See also PERDITION, SONS OF. Joseph Smith taught what it means to sin against the Holy Ghost. He said, "All sins shall be forgiven, except the sin against the Holy Ghost; for Jesus will save all except the sons of perdition. What must a man do to commit the unpardonable sin? He must receive the Holy Ghost, have the heavens opened unto him, and know God, and then sin against Him. After a man has sinned against the Holy Ghost, there is no repentance for him. He has got to say that the sun does not shine while he sees it; he has got to deny Jesus Christ when the heavens have been opened

unto him, and to deny the plan of salvation with his eyes open to the truth of it; and from that time he begins to be an enemy. This is the case with many apostates of The Church of Jesus Christ of Latter-day Saints" (*TPJS*, p. 358).

Furthermore, the Prophet said, "Those who sin against the Holy Ghost cannot be forgiven in this world or in the world to come; they shall die the second death. Those who commit the unpardonable sin are doomed to Gnolom—to dwell in hell, worlds without end. As they concoct scenes of bloodshed in this world, so they shall rise to that resurrection which is as the lake of fire and brimstone" (*TPJS*, p. 361).

In the Doctrine and Covenants, the Lord revealed additional details about what it takes to sin against the Holy Ghost, in other words, to become a son of perdition. He said:

D&C 76:30–35

30 And we saw a vision of the sufferings of those with whom he made war and overcame, for thus came the voice of the Lord unto us:

31 Thus saith the Lord concerning all those who know my power, and have been made partakers thereof, and suffered themselves through the power of the devil to be overcome, and to deny the truth and defy my power—

32 They are they who are the sons of perdition, of whom I say that it had been better for them never to have been born;

33 For they are vessels of wrath, doomed to suffer the wrath of God, with the devil and his angels in eternity;

34 Concerning whom I have said there is no forgiveness in this world nor in the world to come—

35 Having denied the Holy Spirit after having received it, and having denied the Only Begotten Son of the Father, having crucified him unto themselves and put him to an open shame.

For notes and explanations of the above verses, see Perdition, Sons of, in this reference work.

SMALL PLATES OF NEPHI
See BOOK OF MORMON PLATES.

SON AHMAN
Another name for Jesus Christ (D&C 95:17).

SON OF MAN
See also MAN OF HOLINESS. Son of Man is another name for Jesus Christ. Another name for Heavenly Father is Man of Holiness (Moses 6:57). Therefore, Son of Man of Holiness is another name for the Savior. It is sometimes shortened to "Son of man" in the scriptures (Matthew 16:27).

SON OF THE MORNING
A phrase used in the scriptures in reference to Lucifer (Isaiah 14:12; 2 Nephi 24:12; D&C 76:26, 27).

SONG, NEW
"New song" is a scriptural phrase which means that something can now be celebrated that could not be celebrated before. For example, the "new song" mentioned in D&C 84:98 is sung, beginning with verse 99. And what is being celebrated that could not be celebrated before? Answer: the Millennium (see verses 99–102).

SONS OF BELIAL
Another name for wicked people (Judges 19:22; 1 Kings 21:10).

SONS OF GOD
The righteous (Genesis 6:2; D&C 34:3).

SONS OF PERDITION
See PERDITION, SONS OF.

SPEAKING IN TONGUES
See GIFTS OF THE SPIRIT.

SPIRIT PRISON
See PARADISE.

SPIRIT WORLD
See also PARADISE. The postmortal spirit world is upon this earth. Joseph Smith taught: "Enveloped in flaming fire, they are not far from us, and know and understand our thoughts, feelings, and motions, and are often pained therewith" (*TPJS*, p. 326).

Brigham Young explained: "When you lay down this tabernacle, where are you going? Into the spiritual world. Are you going into Abraham's bosom? No, not anywhere nigh there [*Abraham has already been resurrected (D&C 133:55) and become a god (D&C 132:37)*] but into the spirit world. Where is the spirit world? It is right here" (DBY, p. 376).

SPIRITS

We are the spirit children of our Heavenly Father (Hebrews 12:9; Acts 17:28–29; "Proclamation," paragraph 2). We were born as spirits in premortality. Our spirit bodies are composed of spirit matter (D&C 131:7–8) and look much like physical bodies (Ether 3:6–9, 16). When we die, our spirit leaves our mortal body and goes either to paradise or spirit prison (Alma 40:11–13).

All things were created in spirit form before they were created physically (Moses 3:5).

SPIRITS IN PRISON

See also PARADISE. The spirit world has two main divisions, paradise and prison (Alma 40:11–14). Little children who die before age eight and the faithful, baptized members of the Church go to paradise (see information under "Paradise" in this book). The wicked, along with all who have not yet accepted and lived the gospel faithfully go to spirit prison. Another name for "prison" might well be "spirit world mission field" since the gospel is preached there "to those who had died in their sins, without a knowledge of the truth, or in transgression,

having rejected the prophets" (D&C 138:32).

Through the missionary work set up by the Savior while His body was in the tomb (1 Peter 3:18–20), the gospel will be preached in spirit prison. Those who accept the gospel there, who did not have their full opportunity to do so here on earth (D&C 76:74), can receive baptism and other ordinances of salvation by proxy, and thus eventually progress to exaltation on final judgment day. Of the dead who do this, President Joseph F. Smith taught:

D&C 138:58–59

58 The dead who repent will be redeemed, through obedience to the ordinances of the house of God,

59 And after they have paid the penalty of their transgressions, and are washed clean, shall receive a reward according to their works, for they are heirs of salvation.

SPIRITUAL CREATION

See also CREATION. All things were created in spirit form before they were created physically. The Lord said:

Moses 3:5–9

5 And every plant of the field before it was in the earth, and every herb of the field before it grew. For I, the Lord God, created all things, of which I have spoken, spiritually, before they were naturally upon the face of the earth. For I, the Lord God, had not caused it to rain upon the face of the earth. And I, the Lord God, had created all the children of men; and not yet a man

to till the ground; for in heaven created I them; and there was not yet flesh upon the earth, neither in the water, neither in the air;

6 But I, the Lord God, spake, and there went up a mist from the earth, and watered the whole face of the ground.

7 And I, the Lord God, formed man from the dust of the ground, and breathed into his nostrils the breath of life; and man became a living soul, the first flesh upon the earth, the first man also; nevertheless, all things were before created; but spiritually were they created and made according to my word.

8 And I, the Lord God, planted a garden eastward in Eden, and there I put the man whom I had formed.

9 And out of the ground made I, the Lord God, to grow every tree, naturally, that is pleasant to the sight of man; and man could behold it. And it became also a living soul. For it was spiritual in the day that I created it; for it remaineth in the sphere in which I, God, created it, yea, even all things which I prepared for the use of man; and man saw that it was good for food. And I, the Lord God, planted the tree of life also in the midst of the garden, and also the tree of knowledge of good and evil.

SPIRITUAL DEATH

See also SECOND DEATH. "Spiritual death is the condition of one who is spiritually cut off, temporarily or permanently, from the presence of God. LDS scriptures speak of two spiritual deaths, and the concept manifests itself in many ways.

"The first type of spiritual death is the actual separation from God that automatically comes upon all born into mortality as a consequence of the Fall of Adam. All mortals will be redeemed from this death, as well as from physical death, through Christ's Atonement and resurrection (1 Corinthians 15:21–23; 2 Nephi 9:10–15; Helaman 14:15–19; D&C 29:41), to be brought back into God's presence to stand before him.

"The second spiritual death will be finalized on the day of judgment for those who have not repented (Revelation 2:11; 20:6–15; Alma 12:16–36). It is the result of a lifetime of choices. For those who ultimately lose the inclination or ability to repent, or commit unpardonable sin, it becomes perdition (2 Peter 3:7; Alma 34:35; 40:25–26) or 'banishment from the presence of God and from his light and truth forever' (Doctrines of Salvation 2:216–30). This does not extinguish the spirit of man, however, for it is eternal (see Alma 12:18; 42:9). The Savior's Atonement gives all mankind the opportunity to avoid the second spiritual death and gain immortality and eternal life.

"The spiritually 'dead' may be grouped into several types and categories. For example, Satan and the spirits who joined him during the war in heaven are eternally spiritually dead (D&C 29:36–39; 76:25–29). They are sons of perdition (see 2

Nephi 9:8–9). Mortals who sin 'unto death' (D&C 64:7) by denying the Son after the Father has revealed him will join 'the only ones on whom the second death shall have any power' (D&C 76:30–38). In yet another sense, all people on earth over the age of accountability are to a certain extent spiritually dead, depending on their present state of repentance and their degree of sensitivity to the Light of Christ and to the Holy Ghost" (*EM*, under "Spiritual Death").

SPIRITUAL GIFTS

See GIFTS OF THE SPIRIT.

STAKE, STAKES

In The Church of Jesus Christ of Latter-day Saints, a stake (D&C 107:74) is an ecclesiastical unit composed of several wards. A ward is a local unit, generally consisting of about 250 to 500 members and presided over by a bishop. A stake is presided over by a stake president. The stake president has two counselors and together they form the stake presidency.

STAKE PATRIARCHS

See PATRIARCHS, STAKE.

STAKE PRESIDENT, STAKE PRESIDENCY

See STAKE, STAKES.

STANDARD WORKS

See HOLY SCRIPTURES.

STAR, THE MORNING

There are two definitions of "morning star" in the scriptures: (1) The very best, in other words, exaltation (Revelation 2:28). (2) Another name for Jesus Christ (Revelation 22:16).

STEWARDSHIP

A word that generally means property, goods, responsibilities, and so forth, as used in the Bible (Luke 16:2–4). However, as used in the Doctrine and Covenants, it is used primarily in conjunction with the Law of Consecration and refers to property deeded to individual members of the Church who were living the Law of Consecration (D&C 72:5).

STICK OF EPHRAIM

A scriptural term which refers to the Book of Mormon (Ezekiel 37:16; D&C 27:5).

STICK OF JOSEPH

See also STICK OF EPHRAIM. The Stick of Joseph refers to the Book of Mormon (Ezekiel 37:19).

STICK OF JUDAH

A scriptural term which refers to the Bible (Ezekiel 37:19).

STILLBORN CHILDREN

Righteous parents can look forward to raising their stillborn children during the Millennium. We will quote three sources on this:

Encyclopedia of Mormonism

Although temple ordinances are not performed for stillborn children, no loss of eternal blessings or family unity is implied. The family may record the name of a stillborn child on the family group record followed by the word *stillborn* in parentheses (*EM*, under "Stillborn").

Church Handbook of Instructions

Temple ordinances are not performed for stillborn children, but no loss of eternal blessings or family unity is implied. The family may record the name of a stillborn child on the family group record followed by the word *stillborn* in parentheses (Church Handbook of Instructions, 1998, p. 76).

Bruce R. McConkie

The spirit enters the body at the time of quickening, months prior to the actual normal birth. The value and comfort attending a knowledge of this eternal truth is seen in connection with stillborn children. Since the spirit entered the body before birth, stillborn children will be resurrected and righteous parents shall enjoy their association in immortal glory (McConkie, *Doctrinal New Testament Commentary*, pp. 84–85).

STORAGE, FOOD

The Church teaches members to be prepared by having food storage, as well as some financial reserves, for future emergency needs.

Rumors seem to flourish on this topic. Some say that the Brethren are no longer teaching food storage because it is too late. Some indicate that we should have at least two years supply on hand. Some combine isolated statements by individual General Authorities into emails and circulate them over the Internet in a sort of panic or "doomsday" mode. The Lord does not communicate with His people via rumors and the like. We do well to stay close to the Brethren for advice and information on all matters, including food storage.

In 2007, the Brethren published and distributed a pamphlet about family home storage and one about family finances. In the one on food storage, entitled "Family Home Storage," the First Presidency said, "We encourage Church members worldwide to prepare for adversity in life by having a basic supply of food and water and some money in savings. We ask that you be wise as you store food and water and build your savings. Do not go to extremes; it is not prudent, for example, to go into debt to establish your food storage all at once. . . . We realize that some of you may not have financial resources or space for such storage. Some of you may be prohibited by law from storing large amounts of food. We encourage you to store as much as circumstances allow" ("Family Home Storage," p. 2).

Regarding how much food storage to have, the Brethren encourage to first "build a one week supply of food. Then you can gradually increase your supply until it is sufficient for three months . . . where permitted, gradually complete your one-year supply with food that will last a long time and that you can use to stay alive, such as wheat, white rice, and beans" ("Family Home Storage," p. 3).

STOREHOUSES, BISHOPS'
See BISHOPS' STOREHOUSE.

STRAIGHT AND NARROW PATH
See STRAIT AND NARROW PATH.

STRAIT
A term which has at least three meanings in the scriptures: (1) To be in trouble or in a difficult dilemma (1 Chronicles 21:13). (2) Not enough room, too confined (2 Kings 6:1). (3) Narrow (Matthew 7:13–14).

STRAIT AND NARROW PATH
See also STRAIT; STRAIT GATE. Among other possible definitions of this phrase, it can, in effect, mean "the narrow and narrowing way" (Jacob 6:11). In other words, as a person determines to join the Church and live the gospel, his or her options in life are "narrowed" down considerably. And then as determination to do even better at being faithful increases, the individual makes righteous choices which make the path even "narrower."

STRAIT GATE
A phrase which is used to mean the "narrow gate." In context, it means that there is only one way to heaven and that is through Christ and His gospel (Matthew 7:13–14). Baptism by immersion by those who have the authority to perform it is also the "strait gate" (D&C 22:2).

STRONG DRINK
As used in the Word of Wisdom (D&C 89:7), "strong drink" means alcoholic beverages.

SUCCESSION IN THE PRESIDENCY
When the president of the Church dies, succession is automatic. A quote from an Institute of Religion student manual confirms this. "Succession in the prophetic office is automatic and proceeds according to apostolic seniority in the Quorum of the Twelve. . . . The leadership change is automatic and instantaneous. A special revelation is not necessary" (Teachings of the Living Prophets, p. 32).

The Lord has already put things in place by His choice of who has now been an Apostle the longest. When President Harold B. Lee died, Spencer W. Kimball, his successor, explained the process of succession as follows: "Full provision has been made by our Lord for changes. Today there are fourteen apostles holding the keys in suspension, the twelve and the two counselors to the President, to be brought into use if and when circumstances allow, all ordained to leadership in their turn as they move forward in seniority.

"There have been some eighty apostles so endowed since Joseph Smith, though only eleven have occupied the place of the President of the Church, death having intervened; and since the death of his servants is in the power and control of the Lord, he permits to come to the first place only the one who is destined to take that leadership. Death and life become the controlling factors. Each new apostle in turn is chosen by the Lord and revealed to the then living prophet who ordains him.

"The matter of seniority is basic in the first quorums of the Church. All the apostles understand this perfectly, and all well-trained members of the Church are conversant with this perfect succession program" (CR [Oct. 1972]:29; or *Ensign*, Jan. 1973, p. 34).

Bruce R. McConkie likewise explained this process: "Now, this is the pattern; this is the system. Succession in the presidency happens in an orderly and systematized way, because the Lord has conferred upon the members of the Council of the Twelve all of the keys and powers and authorities that have ever been held in any dispensation or any age of the past. Every key is given to each apostle who is set apart a member of the Council of the Twelve. But because keys are the right of presidency, they lie dormant, as it were, in each man unless and until he becomes the senior apostle and is thus in a position of presidency to direct the labors and the work of all others. Therefore succession occurs, as it were, automatically.

"As the last heartbeat of President Lee ceased, the mantle of leadership passed to President Kimball, whose next heartbeat was that of the living oracle and presiding authority of God on earth. From that moment the Church continued under the direction of President Kimball.

"It was not required, nor was it requisite or needed, that the Lord give any revelation, that any special direction be given. The law was already ordained and established. God does not look down each morning and say, 'The sun shall rise.' He has already established the law, he has set the sun in the firmament, and the sun operates in harmony with established law in its rising. And so it was with the transfer of leadership from President Lee to President Kimball.

"When the President of the Church passes on, the First Presidency is disorganized, and the mantle of leadership—the reins of presidency—go to the senior man left and to the Council of the Twelve as a body; in effect the Council of the Twelve then becomes the First Presidency of the Church and so continues unless and until a formal reorganization takes place" (McConkie, in Speeches of the Year, pp. 19–20, 25).

SUICIDE

In the 1989 General Handbook of Instructions, which is given to bishops and stake presidents to help them in their duties, Church leaders instructed, "A person who takes his own life may not be responsible for his acts. Only God can judge such a matter. A person who has considered suicide seriously or has attempted suicide should be counseled by his bishop and may be encouraged to seek professional help."

If a member of the Church does commit suicide, a normal funeral is conducted. And if he or she was endowed, the body should be dressed in temple clothing in preparation for burial, the same as with any other deceased endowed member.

SUN

Symbolically, the sun represents the celestial glory (1 Corinthians 15:40–41; D&C 76:96).

SUNDAY

Before the Savior's crucifixion and resurrection, the Sabbath was the "seventh" day of the week, in other words, Saturday (Exodus 20:10). However, after His resurrection, the Sabbath was changed to "the first day of the week," in other words, Sunday (Acts 20:7).

SUNDAY SCHOOL

The Sunday School organization in wards and branches of the Church is given the responsibility of teaching the gospel on Sundays during the meeting block, to those from age twelve through adults.

The first Sunday School of the Church was organized by Richard Balliantyne, with permission of his bishop, in Salt Lake City, Utah, during the winter of 1849. Fifty children from age eight to fourteen attended.

SUPPER OF THE GREAT GOD

This phrase comes from Revelation 19:17. In that context, it refers to the final wars and battles leading up to the Second Coming. The "supper" is provided by the carcasses of the wicked for the carrion birds that are invited.

SUSTAINING CHURCH OFFICERS

Early in the restoration of The Church of Jesus Christ of Latter-day Saints, the Lord instructed that church leaders and officers be sustained. In the revelation, it is called "common consent" (D&C 26:2).

SYMBOLISM IN THE SCRIPTURES

Symbolism is infinitely deep. In other words, through the use of symbolism in the scriptures, the temple endowment, the sacrament, and so forth, the Holy Ghost can teach one lesson one time, another lesson at a later time, and yet additional lessons to the person who is spiritually in tune each time through that particular passage of scripture or ordinance.

The scriptures make much use of symbolism. We will present some of these common symbols here:

Scriptural Symbolism

Colors

white: purity; righteousness; exaltation (example: Revelation 3:4–5).

black: evil; famine; darkness (example: Revelation 6:5–6).

red: sins; bloodshed (example: Revelation 6:4; D&C 133:51).

blue: heaven; godliness; remembering and keeping God's commandments (example: Numbers 15:37–40).

green: life; nature (example: Revelation 8:7).

amber: sun; light; divine glory (example: D&C 110:2; Revelation 1:15; Ezekiel 1:4, 27; 8:2).

scarlet: royalty (example: Daniel 5:29; Matthew 27:28–29).

silver: of worth, but less than gold (example: Isaiah 48:10; 1 Nephi 20:10. The phrase "but not with silver" is deleted in 1 Nephi, perhaps implying that we are not being refined to be "second best," i.e., silver, rather to be gold, which is the best, exaltation).

gold: the best; exaltation (example: Revelation 4:4).

Body Parts

eye: perception; light and knowledge.

head: governing

ears: obedience; hearing

mouth: speaking

hair: modesty; covering

members: offices and callings

heart: the inner person; courage

hands: action; acting

right hand: covenant hand; making covenants

bowels: center of emotion; whole being

loins: posterity; preparing for action ("gird up your loins")

liver: center of feeling

reins: kidneys; center of desires, thoughts

arm: power

foot: mobility; foundation

toe: associated with cleansing rites (example: Leviticus 14:17)

nose: anger (example: 2 Samuel 22:16; Job 4:9)

tongue: speaking

blood: life of the body

knee: humility; submission

shoulder: strength; effort

forehead: total dedication, loyalty (example: loyalty to God, Revelation 14:1; loyalty to wickedness, Revelation 13:16)

Numbers

one: unity; God

three: God; Godhead. A word repeated three times means superlative, "most" or "best" (example: Isaiah 6:3)

four: mankind; earth (see Smith's Bible Dictionary, 1972, p. 456); (example: Revelation 7:1, four angels over four parts of the earth)

seven: completeness; perfection. (example: when man lets God help, it leads to perfection [4 + 3 = 7])

ten: numerical perfection (example: Ten Commandments; tithing); well-organized (example: Satan is well-organized, Revelation 13:1).

twelve: divine government; God's organization (example: JST, Revelation 5:6)

40 days: literally 40 days; sometimes means "a long time" as in 1 Samuel 17:16.

forever: endless; can sometimes be a specific period or age, not endless (see BYU Religious Studies Center Newsletter, Vol. 8, No. 3, May 1994)

Other Symbolism

horse: victory; power to conquer (example: Revelation 19:11; Jeremiah 8:16)

donkey: peace; submission (example: Christ came in peace at the Triumphal Entry, symbolized by riding on a donkey Matthew 21:5)

palms: joy; triumph, victory (example: John 12:13; Revelation 7:9)

wings: power to move, act, etc. (example: Revelation 4:8; D&C 77:4)

crown: power; dominion; exaltation (example: Revelation 2:10; 4:4)

robes: royalty; kings, queens; exaltation (example: Revelation 6:11; 7:14; 2 Nephi 9:14; D&C 109:76; 3 Nephi 11:8)

SYNAGOGUES
Buildings used for worship in Jewish culture (Matthew 4:23).

·T·

TABERNACLE
See MORMON TABERNACLE.

TABERNACLE CHOIR
See MORMON TABERNACLE CHOIR.

TABERNACLE, EARTHLY, MORTAL
Another term for mortal or physical body (Moroni 9:6; Mosiah 3:5).

TABERNACLE ORGAN
The famous Tabernacle Organ in the Tabernacle on Temple Square, in Salt Lake City, Utah, was commissioned by Brigham Young and built at his request under the direction of Joseph Harris Ridges (1827–1914). It was installed in the tabernacle in 1867, and has been rebuilt a number of times. The center large pipes are the originals and their mellow tones are still heard today.

TARES
Weeds that look very similar to wheat while in the growing stage (Matthew 13:24–30). The Lord gave additional insights to the parable of

the wheat and the tares in our day (D&C 86).

TATTOOS

Modern prophets have counseled against getting tattooed. "Latter-day prophets strongly discourage the tattooing of the body. Those who disregard this counsel show a lack of respect for themselves and for God. The Apostle Paul taught of the significance of our bodies and the danger of purposefully defiling them: 'Know ye not that ye are the temple of God, and that the Spirit of God dwelleth in you? If any man defile the temple of God, him shall God destroy; for the temple of God is holy, which temple ye are' (1 Corinthians 3:16–17). If you have a tattoo, you wear a constant reminder of a mistake you have made. You might consider having it removed" (*TF*, p. 167).

TELESTIAL

See DEGREES OF GLORY; THREE DEGREES OF GLORY.

TELESTIAL BEINGS

See THREE DEGREES OF GLORY.

TEMPLE

Temples are holy buildings where sacred ordinances of salvation are performed for the living and the dead. Normal church meetings are not held in the temples of the Church.

The members of the public are invited to open houses after a temple is completed, but once it is dedicated to the Lord, only worthy members with current temple recommends are allowed to enter it and participate in ordinances such as baptisms for the dead, washings and anointings, eternal marriages, and sealing couples and families together forever.

TEMPLE GARMENTS

See GARMENTS.

TEMPLE MARRIAGE

See CELESTIAL MARRIAGE.

TEMPLE ORDINANCES

See TEMPLE.

TEMPLE RECOMMEND

See RECOMMENDS.

TEMPLE SQUARE

A block in Salt Lake City, Utah, which encompasses the Salt Lake Temple, the Tabernacle, the Assembly Hall, and Museums and visitors' centers. It is one of the most highly visited tourist attractions in the West.

TEN TRIBES, LOST

See LOST TEN TRIBES.

TEN TRIBES OF ISRAEL

See LOST TEN TRIBES.

TERRESTRIAL

See THREE DEGREES OF GLORY.

TERRESTRIAL GLORY

See THREE DEGREES OF GLORY.

TERRESTRIAL KINGDOM

See THREE DEGREES OF GLORY.

TESTAMENT OF CHRIST, ANOTHER

The subtitle of the Book of Mormon. It is a solemn reminder that the Book of Mormon is another witness to the divinity of Jesus Christ. On average, the Savior is mentioned one way or another every 1.7 verses in the Book of Mormon.

TESTIMONY OF JESUS CHRIST

See LIVING CHRIST, THE

TESTIMONY OF THE APOSTLES

See LIVING CHRIST, THE

THREE DEGREES OF GLORY

See also DEGREES OF GLORY. The three degrees of glory are, from the lowest to the highest, the telestial kingdom, the terrestrial kingdom, and the celestial kingdom. Paul spoke of these three different kingdoms of glory to which people can be assigned on Judgment Day (1 Corinthians 15:39–42).

The Lord has revealed much more detail about these kingdoms of glory in our day, especially in D&C 76. We will provide some verses from section 76 describing each of these degrees of glory, adding some notes and commentary as we go:

Telestial Glory
(D&C 76:81–89, 98–106, 109–12)

We will use **bold** for emphasis.

81 And again, **we saw the glory of the telestial**, which glory is that of the lesser, even **as the glory of the stars differs from that of the glory of the moon** in the firmament [*there is much difference between the glory of telestials and the glory of terrestrials*].

82 These are **they who received not the gospel of Christ**, neither the testimony of Jesus. [*These are people who willfully rejected Christ and His full gospel, after being given a fair opportunity to accept it.*]

83 These are **they who deny not the Holy Spirit** [*they did not deny the Holy Ghost; therefore, they are not sons of perdition*].

84 These are **they who are thrust down to hell**. [*These people will be turned over to Satan to suffer for their own sins, because they were not willing to repent and allow Christ's Atonement to pay for their sins. See verse 106, also D&C 19:15–19.*]

85 These are **they who shall not be redeemed from the devil until the last resurrection**, until the Lord, even Christ the Lamb, shall have finished his work. [*In D&C 88:100–101, we are taught that those who receive telestial glory must wait until the end of the Millennium (the thousand years of peace) to be resurrected. Combining this reference with verse 85, above, we learn that telestials will be turned over to Satan to suffer for their sins, during the time that the Millennium is going on upon the earth. They will not be redeemed from the devil until they are resurrected into telestial bodies.*]

86 These are **they who receive not of his fulness in the eternal**

world [*they will not gain the blessings of celestial glory and exaltation*], **but of the Holy Spirit through the ministration of the terrestrial** [*the Holy Ghost can have influence in the telestial kingdom; also, those in the terrestrial kingdom can visit those in the telestial kingdom*];

87 And **the terrestrial through the ministration of the celestial**.

88 **And also the telestial receive it** [*the limited blessings for them as mentioned in verse 86, above*] **of** [*through*] **the administering of angels who are appointed to minister for them**, or who are appointed to be ministering spirits for them; for **they** [*those who go to telestial glory*] **shall be heirs of salvation** [*will receive a degree of salvation, not celestial, rather, telestial, which is still so wonderful we cannot imagine it—see verse 89, next; also, they*].

89 And **thus we saw**, in the heavenly vision, the glory of **the telestial**, which surpasses all understanding [*which is far more glorious and beautiful that any of us can imagine*];

99 For **these are they who are of Paul, and of Apollos, and of Cephas**.

100 **These are they who say they are some of one and some of another**—some **of Christ** and some of **John**, and some of **Moses**, and some of **Elias**, and some of **Esaias** [*an ancient prophet who lived in the days of Abraham—see Bible Dictionary, under "Esaias," and D&C 84:11–3*], and some of **Isaiah**, and some of **Enoch**; [*Paul was, of course,*

a member of the Church. *If you check Acts 18:24 and 19:1 & 5, you will see that Apollos and Cephas likewise were faithful followers of Christ. So were the other prophets mentioned in verse 100. So, what is the message here? Throughout the world's history, there have been various sects and religions who have claimed to believe the Bible, in which the words of Christ and the prophets are taught. Yet, their creeds and teachings vary greatly. Also, there have been a number of members of the true Church who have broken away and set up their own false churches, based on the teachings of past prophets, rejecting the teachings of the living prophets. (See also Articles of Faith, by James E. Talmage, 1981, p. 369.)*]

101 But **received not the gospel, neither the testimony of Jesus, neither the prophets, neither the everlasting covenant.** [*These are the wicked, who rejected the Savior and His prophets, and who refused to enter into the covenants of the gospel, required of those who desire exaltation. They refused to repent, when the principles of righteousness were explained to them, and foolishly or blatantly continued in their wicked ways.*]

102 Last of all, these all are they who will not be gathered with the saints, to be caught up unto the church of the Firstborn, and received into the cloud.

103 **These are they who are liars, and sorcerers, and adulterers, and whoremongers, and whosoever loves and makes a lie.**

104 These are **they** who **suffer the wrath of God on earth.**

105 These are **they** who **suffer the vengeance of eternal fire** [*they will be turned over to Satan to be punished for their own sins, since they refused to repent—see verse 106, next; also verses 84–84 and D&C 19:15–17*].

106 These are **they** who **are cast down to hell and suffer the wrath of Almighty God**, until the fulness of times [*until the end of the Millennium—see verse 85*], when Christ shall have subdued all enemies under his feet, and shall have perfected his work;

109 But behold, and lo, **we saw the glory and the inhabitants of the telestial world**, that **they were as innumerable as the stars in the firmament of heaven, or as the sand upon the seashore**;

110 And heard the voice of the Lord saying: **These all shall bow the knee, and every tongue shall confess to him** who sits upon the throne forever and ever;

111 For **they shall be judged according to their works**, and every man shall receive according to his own works, his own dominion, in the mansions which are prepared;

112 And **they shall be servants of the Most High; but where God and Christ dwell they cannot come, worlds without end**.

Terrestrial Glory
(D&C 76:71–80, 87, 91, 97)

71 And again, **we saw the terrestrial world**, and behold and lo, **these are they** who are of the terrestrial, **whose glory differs from that of the church of the Firstborn** [*celestial glory, specifically, exaltation—see verses 54 and 67*] who have received the fulness of the Father [*who have received exaltation*], **even as that of the moon differs from the sun** in the firmament. [*In other words, the terrestrial kingdom is as different in glory from the celestial kingdom as the moon is different from the sun.*]

72 Behold, these are **they who died without law**; [*Elder Melvin J. Ballard explained this as follows: "Now, I wish to say to you that those who died without law, meaning the pagan nations, for lack of faithfulness, for lack of devotion, in the former life, are obtaining all that they are entitled to. I don't mean to say that all of them will be barred from entrance into the highest glory. Any one of them who repents and complies with the conditions might also obtain celestial glory, but the great bulk of them will only obtain terrestrial glory" (in Hinckley,* Sermons of Melvin J. Ballard, *p. 251. Quoted in the* Doctrine and Covenants Student Manual, *1981, p. 164.)*]

73 And also they who are **the spirits of men kept in prison** [*in spirit prison*], **whom the Son visited** [*see 1 Peter 3:18–2; 4:6, D&C 138*], and preached the gospel unto them, that they might be judged according to men in the flesh [*so that they can be judged by the same standards as people on earth who have the gospel*];

74 **Who received not the testimony of Jesus in the flesh, but**

afterwards received it. [*In short, this appears to mean those who had a valid opportunity to "receive" the gospel (to incorporate the gospel into their lives) during mortality, but who intentionally chose not to, and then "afterwards received it" (in the spirit world).*]

75 These are they who are **honorable men of the earth, who were blinded by the craftiness of men**. [*These are good and honorable people, who are honest, keep the law of chastity, keep their word, help others, and live respectable, clean lives. Yet, among other things, it appears that they do not want to be tied down by church obligations, time-consuming meetings, and so forth. Joseph Fielding Smith spoke of this category of people. He said: "Into the terrestrial kingdom will go all those who are honorable and who have lived clean virtuous lives, but who would not receive the Gospel, but in the spirit world repented and accepted it as far as it can be given unto them. Many of these have been blinded by tradition and the love of the world, and have not been able to see the beauties of the Gospel" (Church History and Modern Revelation, 1:287–88)*].

76 These are they who receive of his glory [*they get some glory*], but not of his fullness [*but not full glory like celestials*].

77 These are they who receive of the presence of the Son [*Jesus will visit them*], but not of the fulness of the Father.

78 Wherefore, they are bodies terrestrial, and not bodies celestial

[*their resurrected bodies are terrestrial, not celestial*], and differ in glory as the moon differs from the sun.

79 These are **they who are not valiant in the testimony of Jesus**; wherefore, they obtain not the crown over the kingdom of our God. [*"Crown" is symbolic of exaltation, of ruling and reigning as gods. Those who have a testimony but intentionally do not live according to it, fall into this category. They still fulfill the other qualifications for terrestrial glory, such as being honorable and keeping the law of chastity, but they are not valiant and faithful in living the gospel, keeping their covenants, fulfilling their church obligations, and so forth.*]

80 And now **this is the end of the vision which we saw of the terrestrial**, that the Lord commanded us to write while we were yet in the Spirit.

Celestial Glory
(D&C 76:50-70, 92-96)

Those who go to the celestial kingdom are faithful, baptized members of the Church who have the gift of the Holy Ghost, who strive to keep the commandments and thus qualify to be "washed and cleansed from all their sins" (verse 52). Little children who die before the age of accountability will be in the highest degree of glory in the celestial kingdom, in other words, in exaltation (D&C 137:10).

50 And again we bear record— for **we saw** and heard, and this is the testimony of the gospel of

Christ concerning **them who shall come forth in the resurrection of the just** [*"resurrection of the just" is another term for those who gain celestial glory*]—

51 **They are they who received the testimony of Jesus** [*"Received" is an active verb, meaning one that denotes action. The action here is that of receiving the gospel into one's life and living in conformity to its commandments and covenants*], and **believed on his name** [*"Belief" in this context is much more than mere acknowledging. It includes actively living the gospel, and believing that it will lead to salvation, because of the Atonement of Christ*] and **were baptized** after the manner of his burial, being buried in the water in his name, and this according to the commandment which he has given—

52 That by **keeping the commandments** they might be **washed and cleansed from all their sins**, and **receive the Holy Spirit** by the laying on of the hands [*were confirmed members of the Church*] of him who is ordained and sealed unto this power;

53 And who **overcome by faith** [*in other words, overcome the sins and temptations of the world through faith in the Lord Jesus Christ*], and **are sealed by the Holy Spirit of Promise** [*the Holy Ghost is the "Holy Spirit of Promise"*], which the Father sheds forth upon all those who are just and true.

54 They are they who are **the church of the Firstborn.**

55 **They are they into whose hands the Father has given all things** [*in other words, they have been given exaltation*]—

56 They are they who are **priests and kings**, who have received of his fulness, and of his glory; [*Faithful women in the Church are also included in the context of verse 56, above. Bruce R. McConkie taught: "If righteous men have power through the gospel and its crowning ordinance of celestial marriage to become kings and priests to rule in exaltation forever, it follows that the women by their side (without whom they cannot attain exaltation) will be* **queens and priestesses** *(Revelation 1:6; 5:10). Exaltation grows out of the eternal union of a man and his wife. Of those whose marriage endures in eternity, the Lord says, "Then shall they be gods" (D&C 132:20); that is, each of them, the man and the woman, will be a god. As such they will rule over their dominions forever (MD, p. 613)*].

57 And are **priests of the Most High, after the order of Melchizedek**, which was after **the order of Enoch**, which was after **the order of the Only Begotten Son.**

58 Wherefore, as it is written, **they are gods**, even the **sons of God** [*meaning that they have done all things necessary to become "heirs" of God, in other words, gods*]—

59 Wherefore, **all things are theirs**, whether life or death, or things present, or things to come, all are theirs and **they are Christ's,**

and Christ is God's.

60 And **they shall overcome all things**.

61 Wherefore, let no man glory in man [*don't build your life upon the philosophies and false wisdom of man*], but rather let him glory in God, who shall subdue all enemies under his feet [*those who remain loyal to God are guaranteed to overcome all obstacles to exaltation*].

62 **These shall dwell in the presence of God and his Christ forever** and ever.

63 **These are they whom he shall bring with him, when he shall come in the clouds of heaven to reign on the earth** [*during the Millennium*] over his people.

64 These are they who shall have part in **the first resurrection**.

65 These are they who shall come forth in **the resurrection of the just**. [*The terms, "first resurrection" and "resurrection of the just" both refer to those who will be in the celestial kingdom. Another term for this is "the morning of the first resurrection."*]

66 These are they who are come unto **Mount Zion** [*in other words, they will dwell with Christ in New Jerusalem—see D&C 84:2*], and unto **the city of the living God** [*in this context, this means celestial kingdom—see Revelation 21, heading and verse 2*], **the heavenly place, the holiest of all** [*celestial glory*].

67 These are they who have come to an **innumerable** company of angels ["*innumerable" people will attain exaltation*], to **the general assembly** and **church of Enoch, and of the First-**

born [*scriptural terms for "exaltation"*].

68 **These are they whose names are written in heaven** [*in the "Book of Life"—see Revelation 3:5*], where God and Christ are the judge of all.

69 **These are** they who are **just men** [*people who were exact in living the gospel*] **made perfect** [*a process*] through Jesus the mediator of the new covenant, who wrought out this perfect atonement through the shedding of his own blood.

70 **These are they whose bodies are celestial** [*they will have celestial resurrected bodies*], whose glory is that of the sun, even the glory of God, the highest of all, whose glory the sun of the firmament is written of as being typical.

92 And thus we saw **the glory of the celestial**, which **excels in all things**—where God, even the Father, reigns upon his throne forever and ever;

93 Before whose throne all things bow in humble reverence, and give him glory forever and ever.

94 They who dwell in his presence are the church of the Firstborn; and **they see as they are seen, and know as they are known** [*in other words, they are gods and have the same powers that God has*], having received of his fulness and of his grace;

95 And **he makes them equal in power, and in might, and in dominion**.

96 And the glory of the celestial is one, even as the glory of the sun is one.

THREE NEPHITES

Three of the Savior's Nephite disciples or Apostles were translated and are still alive (3 Nephi 28:7). They will continue to serve here on earth until the Second Coming of Christ, when they will die and be resurrected. For additional details as to what "translation" means, you may wish to read all of 3 Nephi 28.

THREE WITNESSES

See BOOK OF MORMON WITNESSES.

TIMES OF THE GENTILES

See FIRST TO BE LAST; FULNESS OF THE GENTILES.

TITHING

Tithing means "ten percent." Thus, tithing is ten percent of a person's annual income (D&C 119:4). Faithful members of The Church of Jesus Christ of Latter-day Saints pay tithing.

In the reference above (D&C 119:4), the word "interest" is used instead of "income." President Spencer W. Kimball defined "interest" as "income" (October 1980 General Conference). The term "interest" was commonly used in the early days of the Church to mean "income," as evidenced in D&C 124:89.

It is quite common for members of the Church to attempt to get General Authorities of the Church to give a more detailed description of how they should calculate their tithing. However, they leave it up to the individual and simply define tithing as ten percent of annual income.

TONGUES

Another word for languages (Genesis 10:31; Acts 2:4).

TONGUES, GIFT OF

See GIFTS OF THE SPIRIT.

TONGUES, INTERPRETATION OF

See GIFTS OF THE SPIRIT.

TRANSFIGURATION

Being enabled by the Holy Ghost to physically be in the direct presence of God without being destroyed by His glory (Moses 1:11). Transfiguration is a temporary state, lasting only as long as the occasion requires it.

TRANSLATED BEINGS

See also THREE NEPHITES. John the Apostle was translated (D&C 7:3) as were the Three Nephites (3 Nephi 28). Being translated is not the same as dying and being resurrected. Rather, changes are made in such individuals' mortal bodies such that they are not subject to the normal frailties of mortality. They continue living over the years until their earthly mission is ended. Mormon gives some details about translation in 3 Nephi 28.

Moses and Elijah were translated (see Mount of Transfiguration in this reference book) in order to minister to the Savior when he took Peter, James, and John up on the Mount of Transfiguration (Matthew 17:1–9). Moses and Elijah were resurrected at the time of the Savior's resurrection (D&C 133:54–55).

TRINITY
See GODHEAD.

TWELVE APOSTLES
See APOSTLE; APOSTLES, THE TWELVE.

TWELVE, SYMBOLISM OF
See SYMBOLISM IN THE SCRIPTURES.

·U·

UNCHASTITY
See CHASTITY, LAW OF.

UNITED ORDER
See CONSECRATION.

UNPARDONABLE SIN
See SIN AGAINST THE HOLY GHOST.

URIM AND THUMMIM
An instrument provided by the Lord to prophets whereby they may receive revelation and be assisted in translating languages (Exodus 28:30; Leviticus 8:8; Numbers 27:21: Deuteronomy 33:8; 1 Samuel 28:6; Ezra 2:63; Nehemiah 7:65; JS—H 1:35).

"Urim and Thummim" is a Hebrew term that means "Lights and Perfections" (BD, under "Urim and Thummim").

Abraham had a Urim and Thummim (Abraham 3:1) with which he learned about the planets and stars and was taught much about astron-omy and the plan of salvation (Abraham 3:2–28).

Joseph Smith was given the Urim and Thummim which was formerly used by the brother of Jared (BD, under "Urim and Thummim).

It was by the power of the Urim and Thummim that Joseph Smith was enabled to translate the Book of Mormon plates (D&C 10:1).

"The place where God resides is a great Urim and Thummim" (D&C 130:8). Furthermore, "This earth, in its sanctified and immortal state, will be made like unto crystal and will be a Urim and Thummim to the inhabitants who dwell thereon, whereby all things pertaining to an inferior kingdom, or all kingdoms of a lower order, will be manifest to those who dwell on it; and this earth will be Christ's" (D&C 130:9).

Those who attain the celestial kingdom will be given a white stone which will serve them as a Urim and Thummim (D&C 130:11).

·V·

VICARIOUS

See also PROXY; PROXY ORDI-NANCES. The term "vicarious" means "proxy," in other words, "to stand in for someone else." Thus, we often use the phrase "vicarious ordinances" for the dead.

VICARIOUS ORDINANCES

See VICARIOUS.

VIRGIN BIRTH

As prophesied by Isaiah, Jesus Christ was born to a virgin named Mary (Isaiah 7:14). Nephi was shown "a virgin, most beautiful and fair above all other virgins" and then was told, "Behold, the virgin whom thou seest is the mother of the Son of God, after the manner of the flesh" (1 Nephi 11:15, 18).

·W·

WAR IN HEAVEN

See PREMORTAL LIFE, WAR IN HEAVEN.

WARD

A congregation of about 250 to 500 members of the Church presided over by a bishop. Several wards make a stake.

WASHINGS AND ANOINTINGS

Washings and anointings are associated with what we call "initiatory" ordinances in temples.

When the Lord commanded the Saints to build the Kirtland Temple, Joseph Smith taught, "The main object was to build unto the Lord a house whereby He could reveal unto His people the ordinances of His house and the glories of His kingdom, and teach the people the way of salvation; for there are certain ordinances and principles that, when they are taught and practiced, must be done in a place or house built for that purpose. . . . It is for the same purpose that God gathers together His people in the last days, to build unto the Lord a house to prepare them for the ordinances and endowments, washings and anointings, etc." (*TPJS*, p. 308).

"Ritual anointings were a prominent part of religious rites in the biblical world. Recipients of the anointing included temple officiants (Exodus 28:41), prophets (1 Kings 19:16), and kings (1 Samuel 16:3; 1 Kings 1:39). In addition, sacral objects associated with the Israelite sanctuary were anointed (Exodus 30:22–29). Of equal importance in the religion of the Israelites were ablutions or ceremonial washings (Exodus 29:4–7). To ensure religious purity, Mosaic law required that designated individuals receive a ritual washing, sometimes in preparation for entering the temple (Exodus 30:17–21; Leviticus 14:7–8; 15:5–27).

"The washings and anointings of the biblical period have a parallel today in The Church of Jesus Christ of Latter-day Saints. In response to a commandment to gather the Saints and to build a house "to prepare them for the ordinances and endowments, washings, and anointings" (TPJS, p. 308), these ordinances were introduced in the Kirtland Temple on January 21, 1836 (HC 2:379–83). In many respects similar in purpose to ancient Israelite practice and to the washing of feet by Jesus among his disciples, these modern LDS rites are performed only in temples set apart and dedicated for sacred purposes (D&C 124:37-38; HC 6:318–19).

"Many symbolic meanings of washings and anointings are traceable in the scriptures. Ritual washings (Hebrews 9:10: D&C 124:37) symbolize the cleansing of the soul from sins and iniuities. They signify the washing away of the pollutions of the Lord's people (Isaiah 4:4). Psalm 51:2 expresses the human longing and divine promise:

'Wash me thoroughly from mine iniquity, and cleanse me from my sin' (cf. Psalm 73:13; Isaiah 1:16).

"The anointing of a person or object with sacred ointment represents sanctification (Leviticus 8:10–12) and consecration (Exodus 28:41), so that both become 'most holy' (Exodus 30:29) unto the Lord. In this manner, profane persons and things are sanctified in similitude of the messiah (Hebrew 'anointed one'), who is Christ (Greek 'anointed one') (EM, under "Washings and Anointings").

WATCHMEN

Symbolic of prophets. Watchmen literally were sentries set on towers or on the walls of cities to watch out for danger and warn the residents of the city as needed (Isaiah 62:6; D&C 101:45).

Prophets are, symbolically, our "watchmen on the tower." They receive revelation from God and warn us of dangers in society that can damage us spiritually.

WENTWORTH LETTER
See ARTICLES OF FAITH.

WHITE HORSE PROPHECY

President Joseph F. Smith spoke of the White Horse Prophecy. He said:

"The ridiculous story about the 'red horse,' and 'the black horse,' and 'the white horse,' and a lot of trash that has been circulated about, and printed, and sent around as a great revelation given by the Prophet

Joseph Smith, is a matter that was gotten up, I understand, some ten years after the death of the Prophet Joseph Smith, by two of our brethren, who put together some broken sentences from the Prophet that they may have heard him utter from time to time, and formulated this so-called revelation out of it, and it was never spoken by the Prophet in the manner in which they have put it forth. It is simply false; that is all there is to it.

"Now, these stories of revelations that are being circulated around are of no consequence, except for rumor and silly talk by persons that have no authority. The fact of the matter is simply here and this. No man can enter into God's rest unless he will absorb the truth insofar that all error, all falsehood, all misunderstanding and misstatements, he will be able to sift thoroughly and dissolve, and know that it is error and not truth. When you know God's truth, when you enter into God's rest, you will not be hunting after revelations from Tom, Dick, and Harry all over the world. You will not be following the will of the wisps of the vagaries of men and their own ideas. When you know the truth, you will abide in the truth, and the truth will make you free, and it is only the truth that will free you from the errors of men, and from the falsehood and misrepresentations of the evil one, who lies in wait to deceive and to mislead the people of God from the paths of righteousness and truth" (CR [Oct. 1918]: 58).

WHITE STONE
See URIM AND THUMMIM.

WHOREDOMS
A scriptural term for sexual immorality (2 Nephi 9:36; Jacob 3:5). The most common use of "whoredom" in the scriptures is to symbolize apostasy and breaking covenants made with the Lord (Numbers 14:33).

WITNESSES, BOOK OF MORMON
See BOOK OF MORMON WITNESSES.

WIVES, PLURAL
See PLURAL MARRIAGE.

WORD OF WISDOM
See also ALCOHOL; COFFEE; TEA; TOBACCO. The Word of Wisdom is the Lord's law of health (D&C 89) given to His Saints in the last days. It is a law of spiritual well-being as well (D&C 89:18–21).

The Word of Wisdom forbids the use of tea, coffee, alcohol, and tobacco, and specifically recommends the use of a number of healthy foods. It is a revelation from the Lord and was given through the Prophet Joseph Smith in Kirtland, Ohio, on February 27, 1833. Brigham Young gave the background for this revelation as follows: "I think I am as well acquainted with the circumstances which led to the giving of the Word of Wisdom as any man in the Church, although I was not present at the time to witness them. The first school of the prophets was held in a small room situated over the Prophet Joseph's kitchen, in a house which belonged to Bishop Whitney. . . . The brethren came to that place for hundreds of miles to attend school in a little room probably no larger than eleven by fourteen. When they assembled together in this room after breakfast, the first they did was to light their pipes and, while smoking, talk about the great things of the kingdom and spit all over the room, and as soon as the pipe was out of their mouths a large chew of tobacco would then be taken. Often when the Prophet entered the room to give the school instructions he would find himself in a cloud of tobacco smoke. This, and the complaints of his wife at having to clean so filthy a floor, made the Prophet think upon the matter, and he inquired of the Lord relating to the conduct of the Elders in using tobacco, and the revelation known as the Word of Wisdom was the result of his inquiry. You know what it is and can read it at your leisure" (*JD* 12:158).

We will give each verse of section 89 and add notes and commentary as we go along. There are many important aspects to this revelation. For instance, as you study it you would do well to note that there are more "do's" than "don'ts" contained in it. Also, pay careful attention to the fact that it is not a system of vegetarianism. We will do more with this when we get to verses 12–13.

As you will see, in verse 2, the Word of Wisdom was not a commandment when it was first given. However, in a general conference of the Church, held on September 9, 1851, President Brigham Young presented it to the members as a commandment. Still, many did not comply, perhaps not considering it to be as serious and important as other commandments. Finally, in the 1930s, under the direction of President Heber J. Grant, the Word of Wisdom became a temple recommend item and thus began to be "locked in" as a vital part of being a faithful Saint. It has now become a commandment in the full sense of the word, just in time to protect us from "evils and designs which do and will exist in the hearts of conspiring men" (verse 4), such as the rampant drug culture, drunken driving, sexual immorality which often goes with smoking and drinking, and so forth.

The first three verses were written by the Prophet Joseph Smith as an introduction to the revelation.

D&C 89

1 **A WORD OF WISDOM, for the benefit of the council of high priests** [*the school of the prophets*], assembled in Kirtland, **and the church**, and also the Saints in Zion [*the members at that time in Jackson County, Missouri*]—

2 To be **sent greeting; not by commandment or constraint** [*see background notes for this section, in this book, for when it became a*

commandment], but by revelation and the word of wisdom, **showing forth the order and will of God in the temporal salvation of all saints in the last days—**

3 Given for **a principle with promise** [*explained in verses 18– 21*], **adapted to the capacity of the weak and the weakest of all saints** [*in other words, there is ulti- mately no excuse for not living the Word of Wisdom*], who are or can be called saints. [*Even though the Word of Wisdom serves us as a law of health, some wonder why we are required to abstain completely from the harmful substances included in the Word of Wisdom, rather than being allowed to use them with moderation. The Lord gives the reason next, in verse 4. Perhaps you have noticed that, in many cases, the forbidden substances in the Word of Wisdom serve as "gateway drugs" to more harmful substances.*]

4 Behold, verily, thus saith the Lord unto you: **In consequence of evils and designs which do and will exist in the hearts of conspir- ing men in the last days, I have warned you, and forewarn you,** by giving unto you this word of wisdom by revelation—

5 That **inasmuch as any man drinketh wine or strong drink among you, behold it is not good,** neither meet [*necessary; wise*] in the sight of your Father, only [*except*] in assembling yourselves together to offer up your sacraments before him [*in other words, except for use with*

the sacrament; as you know, we no longer use wine, rather water—com- pare with D&C 27:2*].

6 And, behold, **this should be wine, yea, pure wine of the grape of the vine, of your own make.**

7 And, again, **strong drinks are not for the belly,** but for the wash- ing of your bodies.

8 And again, **tobacco is not for the body, neither for the belly, and is not good for man,** but is an herb for bruises and all sick cattle, to be used with judgment and skill.

9 And again, **hot drinks** are not for the body or belly. [*The Prophet Joseph Smith explained that the term "hot drinks" means tea and coffee. He said: "I under- stand that some of the people are excusing themselves in using tea and coffee, because the Lord only said 'hot drinks' in the revelation of the Word of Wisdom. Tea and coffee are what the Lord meant when he said 'hot drinks' " (in Widtsoe, Word of Wisdom, pp. 85–86).*]

10 And again, verily I say unto you, **all wholesome herbs** [*a word meaning "vegetables and plants" in Joseph Smith's day*] God hath ordained for the constitution, nature, and use of man—

11 **Every herb in the season thereof,** and **every fruit in the season thereof**; all these to be used with prudence and thanksgiving.

12 Yea, **flesh also of beasts and of the fowls of the air,** I, the Lord, have ordained [*authorized*] for the use of man with thanksgiving; **nev- ertheless they are to be used spar-**

ingly [*"sparingly" seems to be the key word, here*]; [*"The Word of Wisdom is not a system of vegetarianism. Clearly, meat is permitted [see D&C 42:18]"* (*Widtsoe*, Evidences and Reconciliations, *3:156–57. Quoted in the* Doctrine and Covenants Student Manual, *1981, p. 210).*

13 And **it is pleasing unto me that they should not be used, only in times of winter, or of cold, or famine.** [*There were groups in the Kirtland area who advocated not eating meat. One of these was the Shaking Quakers, all of whom avoided eating pork as a matter of religion, and many of whom likewise made abstinence from all meat a matter of religious belief. See heading to section 49). With this in mind, we might read verse 13, above as follows: And it is pleasing unto me that they [the flesh of beasts and . . . fowls—verse 12] should not be used only in times of winter, or cold, or famine, like Ann Lee and the Shaking Quakers teach. Rather, they are to be used sparingly."*]

14 **All grain is ordained for the use of man and of beasts, to be the staff of life**, not only **for man** but **for the beasts of the field** [*domestic animals*], and **the fowls of heaven**, and **all wild animals** that run or creep on the earth;

15 And **these** [*perhaps meaning the wild animals mentioned in verse 14, above—we don't know for sure*] **hath God made for the use of man only in times of famine and excess of hunger.**

16 **All grain is good for the food of man**; as **also the fruit**

of the vine; that which yieldeth fruit, **whether in the ground** [*such as potatoes, radishes, carrots, and so forth*] **or above the ground—**

17 Nevertheless, wheat for man, and **corn for the ox**, and **oats for the horse**, and **rye for the fowls and for swine, and for all beasts of the field** [*domestic animals*], and **barley for all useful animals**, and for mild drinks, as also other grain.

[*In verse 3, above, we were told that the Word of Wisdom is "a principle with promise." The promised blessings are given in verses 18–21, next. This is an important part of the Word of Wisdom that, unfortunately, is often left out of discussions and conversations about it.*]

18 **And all saints who remember to keep and do these sayings, walking in obedience to the commandments** [*an additional stipulation for receiving these blessings*], **shall receive health in their navel and marrow to their bones** [*a Biblical phrase meaning "the support and blessings of the Lord," as was the case with Daniel and his three companions—see Daniel 1:6–20, also see Proverbs 3:7–10*];

19 **And shall find wisdom and great treasures of knowledge, even hidden treasures** [*meaning, among other things, will have better knowledge and stronger testimonies of the gospel*];

20 **And shall run and not be weary, and shall walk and not faint** [*they will be strengthened by the Lord and will not be stopped in*

pursuing the path to exaltation].

21 **And I, the Lord, give unto them a promise, that the destroying angel shall pass by them, as the children of Israel, and not slay them**. Amen.

[*President J. Reuben Clark Jr. spoke of these promises as follows (**bold** added for emphasis): "This does not say and this does not mean, that to keep the Word of Wisdom is to insure us against death, for death is, in the eternal plan, co-equal with birth. This is the eternal decree (1 Corinthians 15:22; 2 Nephi 9:6). But it does mean that the destroying angel, he who comes to punish the unrighteous for their sins, as he in olden time afflicted the corrupt Egyptians in their wickedness (Exodus 12:23, 29), shall pass by the Saints, 'who are walking in obedience to the commandments,' and who 'remember to keep and do these sayings.' **These promises do mean that all those who qualify themselves to enjoy them will be permitted so to live out their lives that they may gain the full experiences and get the full knowledge which they need in order to progress to the highest exaltation in eternity**, all these will live until their work is finished and God calls them back to their eternal home, as a reward" (CR [Oct. 1940]: 17–18).*]

Concerning other harmful substances and the laws of health, the following counsel was given by the Church in 2004: "Anything harmful that people purposefully take into their bodies is not in harmony with

the Word of Wisdom" (*TF*, p. 186).

WORKS, STANDARD

The standard works of the Church are the Bible, the Book of Mormon, the Doctrine and Covenants, and the Pearl of Great Price.

WORTHINESS

"Worthy" means being qualified to participate in ordinances, receive answers to prayer, represent the Lord, and so forth. Some people are too hard on themselves. They think that "worthy" means "perfect." Elder Marvin J. Ashton, of the Quorum of the Twelve Apostles, summarized the subject of worthiness as follows: "It occurs to me that there are probably hundreds or even thousands who do not understand what worthiness is. Worthiness is a process, and perfection is an eternal trek. We can be worthy to enjoy certain privileges without being perfect.

"I am also convinced of the fact that the speed with which we head along the straight and narrow path isn't as important as the direction in which we are traveling. That direction, if it is leading toward eternal goals, is the all-important factor" (Ashton, *Ensign*, p. 21).

WRATH

Another word for "anger" (2 Samuel 11:20; Luke 4:28).

WRATH OF GOD

See INDIGNATION, RIGHTEOUS.

·Y–Z·

YEARS OF ACCOUNTABILITY

The scriptures define this as eight years of age (D&C 68:25, 27).

YOUNG MEN

See also AUXILIARY ORGANIZATIONS OF THE CHURCH; MUTUAL IMPROVEMENT ASSOCIATION. Young Men is the official organization of the Church for male members of the Church ages 12–17.

YOUNG WOMEN

See also AUXILIARY ORGANIZATIONS OF THE CHURCH; MUTUAL IMPROVEMENT ASSOCIATION. Young Women is the official organization of the Church for young women ages 12–17.

ZION

"Zion" is used so many different ways in the scriptures that it can be somewhat confusing. We will quote from the Bible Dictionary for clarification: "The word *Zion* is used repeatedly in all the standard works of the Church, and is defined in latter-day revelation as 'the pure in heart' (D&C 97:21). Other usages of Zion have to do with a geographical location. For example, Enoch built a city that was called Zion (Moses 7:18–19); Solomon built his temple on Mount Zion (1 Kings 8:1; cf. 2 Samuel 5:6–

7); and Jackson County, Missouri, is called Zion in many of the revelations in the D&C, such as 58:49–50; 62:4; 63:48; 72:13; 84:76; 104:47. The city of New Jerusalem, to be built in Jackson County, Missouri, is to be called Zion (D&C 45:66–67). The revelations also speak of "the cause of Zion" (D&C 6:6; 11:6). In a wider sense all of North and South America are Zion (*HC* 6:318–19). For further references see 1 Chronicles 11:5; Psalms 2:6; 99:2; 102:16; Isaiah 1:27; 2:3; 4:3–5; 33:20; 52:1–8; 59:20; Jeremiah 3:14; 31:6; Joel 2:1–32; Amos 6:1; Obadiah 1:17, 21; Hebrews 12:22–24; Revelation 14:1–5; and many others. (In the New Testament, *Zion* is spelled *Sion*.)" (BD, under "Zion").

ZION, LAND OF

See ZION.

ZION'S CAMP

Zion's Camp was the name of a small army of Saints who were commanded by the Lord (D&C 103) to travel the thousand miles from Kirtland, Ohio, to Jackson County, Missouri, to help the members of the Church there who had been driven out by mobs (D&C 103:30–34).

"An advance party of 20 left Kirtland on May 1, 1834, to prepare the first camp at New Portage, near present-day Akron, Ohio, and the main group of about 85 joined them on May 6. When Joseph and Hyrum's contingents rendezvoused at the Allred settlement, east of Paris, Monroe County, Missouri, there were approximately 200 men, 11 women, and 7 children. Included in these figures were the 20 men, women, and children comprising Hyrum's company from the Pontiac, Michigan, area.

"The marchers were well armed, carrying muskets, pistols, swords, and knives, and they attempted to prevent the Missourians from knowing of the expedition. But Jackson County residents learned of their coming and burned down virtually all the remaining Mormon buildings. Lacking in military training, the members of Zion's Camp conducted military exercises and sham battles along the way of the 900-mile journey. They were organized into groups of ten and fifty, with a captain over each. After the rendezvous at the Salt River on June 8, Lyman Wight, a veteran of the War of 1812, was elected general of the camp, and William Cherry, a British dragoon for twenty years, was made drill master.

"Contrary to the attempted military discipline, the men sometimes quarreled among themselves. On June 3, as the group approached the Mississippi, Joseph warned them that in consequence of their misconduct a scourge would strike the camp. His words proved prophetic when, at the conclusion of their journey on June 23

at Rush Creek in Clay County, Missouri, cholera struck the camp. Some sixty-eight men were afflicted, and thirteen of them and one woman died of the disease. Earlier at Fishing River a band of about 300 armed Missourians threatened to invade the camp, but a fierce hailstorm drove them off and prevented a conflict.

"In the meantime, negotiations were conducted between the Zion's Camp leaders, Missouri State officials, and the citizens of Jackson County. Joseph Smith learned that, contrary to expectations, Governor Dunklin would not provide troops to escort the Mormons into Jackson County, fearing a civil war if he did. The two sides exchanged proposals for buying out each other's property in Jackson County, but these efforts broke down.

"On June 22, 1834, while still at Fishing River, the Prophet received a revelation that rebuked some members of the Church for not sufficiently supporting Zion's Camp, but accepted the sacrifice of the camp members. They were not to fight but to wait for the Lord to redeem Zion (D&C 105). The experience had been intended to test their faith. The revelation directed the Saints to build goodwill in the area in preparation for the time when Zion would be recovered by legal rather than military means. Since there was little more to be done to help the displaced Jackson County Saints, the remaining Zion's Camp supplies were distributed to the refugees, and the camp disbanded on June 30, 1834. Most of the troops soon returned to Ohio.

"Zion's Camp failed to achieve its ostensible purpose of protecting the Jackson County Saints. In retrospect, however, Brigham Young and other participants felt that they learned valuable lessons. In subsequent migrations, the Mormons used the organizational experience gained in Zion's Camp. Most importantly, they had answered the Lord's call (D&C 103). Nine of the first twelve apostles and all of the first Quorum of Seventy (seven presidents and sixty-three members) were later called from the ranks of Camp members" (*EM*, under "Zion's Camp).

SOURCES

Anderson, Richard L. *Investigating the Book of Mormon Witnesses*. Salt Lake: Deseret Book, 1981.

Ashton, Marvin J. "On Being Worthy," *Ensign*, May 1989.

Cannon, George Q. *Gospel Truth: Discourses and Writings of George Q. Cannon*. Salt Lake City: Deseret Book, 1987.

Church History in the Fulness of Times. Institute of Religion manual. Salt Lake City: The Church of Jesus Christ of Latter-day Saints, 1989.

Conferene Reports of The Church of Jesus Christ of Latter-day Saints. Salt Lake City: The Church of Jesus Christ of Latter-day Saints, 1898 to present.

Cook, Lyndon W. *Revelations of Joseph Smith*. Salt Lake City: Deseret Book, 1985.

Encyclopedia of Mormonism. Edited by Daniel H. Ludlow. 5 vols. New York: Macmillan, 1992.

Faust, James E. First Presidency Message, "Enriching Your Marriage," *Ensign*, April 2007.

The First Presidency. *All Is Safely Gathered In: Family Finances* [pamphlet]. Salt Lake City: Intellectual Reserve, 2007.

The First Presidency and Quorm of the Twelve Apostles of The Church of Jesus Christ of Latter-day Saints. "The Family: A Proclamation to the World," September 23, 1995.

First Presidency Message, *Improvement Era*, August 1916.

Guide to the Scriptures. Online; available from www.lds.org.

Jenson, Andrew. *Historical Record*. Dec. 1888.

Journal of Discourses. 26 vols. London: Latter-day Saints' Book Depot, 1854–86.

Lee, Harold B. "The Way to Eternal Life," *Ensign*, Nov. 1971.

The Life and Teachings of Jesus and His Apostles. New Testament Student Manual, Rel. 211–12. Salt Lake City: The Church of Jesus Christ of Latter-day Saints, 1978.

McConkie, Bruce R. *Doctrinal New Testament Commentary*. 3 vols. Salt Lake City: Bookcraft, 1965–73.

———. *Mormon Doctrine*. Salt Lake City: Bookcraft, 1975.

———. *The Mortal Messiah*. Salt Lake City: Deseret Book, 1981.

———. "Succession in the Presidency," in Speeches of the Year, 1974. Quoted in *Teachings of the Living Prophets Student Manual Religion 333*. Salt Lake: Church Educational System, 1982.

Messages of the First Presidency. Compiled by James R. Clark. 6 vols. Salt Lake City: Bookcraft, 1965–75.

Petersen, Mark E. *The Great Prologue*. Salt Lake City: Deseret Book, 1975.

Pratt, Parley P. *Key to the Science of Theology/A Voice of Warning.* Salt Lake City: Deseret Book, 1965.

Reed, R. *The Gospel as Taught by Calvin.* Grand Rapids, Michigan: Baker Book House, 1979.

———. *History of The Church of Jesus Christ of Latter-day Saints.* Edited by B. H. Roberts. 2d ed. rev., 7 vols. Salt Lake City: The Church of Jesus Christ of Latter-day Saints, 1932–51.

———. *Lectures on Faith.* Salt Lake City: Deseret Book, 1985.

———. *Teachings of the Prophet Joseph Smith.* Selected by Joseph Fielding Smith. Salt Lake City: Deseret Book, 1976.

Smith, Joseph F. *Gospel Doctrine: Selections from the Sermons and Writings of Joseph F. Smith.* Salt Lake City: Deseret Book, 1977.

Smith, Joseph Fielding. *Church History and Modern Revelation.* Salt Lake: The Council of the Twelve Apostles. Salt Lake City: Deseret Book, 1946.

———. *Doctrines of Salvation.* Compiled by Bruce R. McConkie, 3 vols. Salt Lake City: Bookcraft, 1954–1956.

———. *Essentials in Church History.* 19th ed. Salt Lake City: Deseret Book, 1964.

———. *The Signs of the Times.* Salt Lake: Deseret Book, 1970.

Smith, Lucy Mack. *History of Joseph Smith by His Mother.* Salt Lake City: Stevents & Wallis, Inc., 1945.

———. *History of Joseph Smith by His Mother, Lucy Mack Smith.* Salt Lake City: Bookcraft, 1958.

Talmage, James E. *Articles of Faith.* Salt Lake City: Deseret Book, 1984.

———. *Jesus the Christ.* Salt Lake City: Deseret Book, 1962.

Taylor, John. *The Gospel Kingdom. Selections of Writings and Discourses of John Taylor, Third President of The Church of Jesus Christ of Latter-day Saints.* Salt Lake City: Bookcraft, 1943.

———. *The Gospel Kingdom. Selections of Writings and Discourses of John Taylor, Third President of The Church of Jesus Christ of Latter-day Saints.* Selected by G. Homer Durham. Salt Lake City: Bookcraft, 1987.

Teachings of the Presidents of the Church—Brigham Young. Salt Lake City: The Church of Jesus Christ of Latter-day Saints, 1997.

True to the Faith—A Gospel Reference. Salt Lake City: Intellectual Reserve, 2004.

Widtsoe, John A. *Evidences and Reconciliations*, Vol. 3. Salt Lake City: Bookcraft, 1960.

———. *The Word of Wisdom: A Modern Interpretation.* Salt Lake: Deseret Book.

Young, Brigham. *Discourses of Brigham Young.* Compiled by John A. Widtsoe. Salt Lake: Deseret Book, 1977.

ABOUT THE AUTHOR

David J. Ridges taught for the Church Educational System for thirty-five years and is in his twenty-fifth year of teaching at BYU Campus Education Week. He taught adult religion classes and Know Your Religion classes for BYU Continuing Education for many years. He has served as a curriculum writer for the Sunday School as well as for the seminaries and institutes of religion of the Church.

He has served in many callings in the Church, including Gospel Doctrine teacher, bishop, stake president, and patriarch. He and Sister Ridges served a full-time eighteen month mission, training senior CES missionaries and helping coordinate their assignments throughout the world.

Brother Ridges and his wife, Janette, are the parents of six sons and daughters and make their home in Springville, Utah.